Commercial Aspects of Trusts and Fiduciary Obligations

Edited by
Ewan McKendrick

CLARENDON PRESS · OXFORD
THE NORTON ROSE M5 GROUP
1992

Oxford University Press, Walton Street, Oxford OX2 6DP
Oxford New York Toronto
Delhi Bombay Calcutta Madras Karachi
Petaling Jaya Singapore Hong Kong Tokyo
Nairobi Dar es Salaam Cape Town
Melbourne Auckland
and associated companies in
Berlin Ibadan

Oxford is a trade mark of Oxford University Press

Published in the United States
by Oxford University Press, New York

British Library Cataloguing in Publication Data
Data available

Library of Congress Cataloging in Publication Data
Commercial aspects of trusts and fiduciary obligations / edited by
Ewan McKendrick.
"The Norton Rose M5 Group."
Includes index.
1. Trusts and trustees—Great Britain. 2. Commercial law—Great
Britain. 3. Trusts and trustees. 4. Commercial law.
I. McKendrick, Ewan. II. Norton Rose M5 Group.
KD1480.C66 1992 346.4105'9—dc20 [344.10659] 92–15521
ISBN 0–19–825765–1

Typeset by Pentacor PLC, High Wycombe, Bucks
Printed in Great Britain by
Bookcraft Ltd.
Midsomer Norton, Avon

PREFACE

The origins of this book lie in the first Oxford Law Colloquium held in St. John's College, Oxford on 12–13 September 1991, organized by the Faculty of Law of the University of Oxford and The Norton Rose M5 Group, a national association of seven major independent law firms. This, it is hoped, will be the first of many such conferences run on a biennial basis.

The Oxford Law Colloquium arose out of the mutual desire of academics and practitioners to promote a conference in the nature of a high-level workshop in which distinguished speakers would present the structure and conceptual framework of a chosen subject and identify policy issues and trends in legal thinking. The subject chosen for each conference will permit the exploration of fundamental concepts, principles, policies, and trends in particular fields of law of mutual interest and importance. Academic and practical issues will be brought together in the exposition and detailed discussion of the chosen subject and in case studies to be discussed in specialist groups. The Colloquium is intended, *inter alia*, to (i) stimulate a high level of debate by an exchange of views and information among experts; (ii) concentrate on fundamental concepts, policies, and trends rather than the minutiae of English law; (iii) adopt an international and comparative approach to the subject, with particular emphasis on European developments; (iv) blend academic and practitioner knowledge and skills; and (v) provide an opportunity to influence legal policy.

The first subject, Commercial Aspects of Trusts and Fiduciary Obligations, was chosen because of its considerable theoretical and practical importance. As Goodhart and Jones pointed out in 1980 '[f]rom time to time equitable doctrine has infiltrated into English commercial law' ((1980) 43 MLR 489). During the 1980s and early 1990s this infiltration has increased considerably and this is demonstrated in all the chapters of the book as the authors discuss the impact of the law of trusts and the law of fiduciaries upon such diverse subjects as insolvency law, company law, and conflicts of law and the complex relationship between statutory regulation and equitable rules of fiduciary obligation. The contributions to this volume, based on the papers presented at the Colloquium, demonstrate the need for us to think more carefully about the relationship between equity and commercial law and about the way in which we classify legal subjects so that, at the various points of intersection, the law can be developed in a coherent and rational manner.

The contributors to this volume are drawn from both the practising and the academic world and bring their own specialist knowledge to bear on their chosen subjects. Those from the practising world are all from The Norton Rose M5 Group and, while many of the contributors from the academic world are from the Law Faculty of the University of Oxford, we were very pleased that Professor Paul Finn of the Australian National University, Professor Klaus Hopt of the Institut fur Internationales Recht, University of Munich, and Professor Jeffrey Schoenblum of Vanderbilt University were all able to accept our invitation to participate in this venture. Their contributions add an important international and comparative dimension to this volume.

I would like to express my gratitude to the contributors for complying with the very tight deadlines which were laid down for them. Sir Peter Millett and Sir Peter Gibson kindly agreed to chair the colloquium sessions and their introductory remarks are reproduced immediately after this Preface.

Finally, I would like to thank Professor Goode, Professor Birks, and Professor Prentice of the University of Oxford and the partners and staff of The Norton Rose M5 Group for their hard work in the organization of the Colloquium and in the preparation of the manuscripts for publication

EWAN McKENDRICK

St Anne's College, Oxford
March 1992

CONTENTS

LIST OF CONTRIBUTORS

HAMISH ANDERSON, Partner; Bond Pearce; 1991/2 President of the Insolvency Lawyers' Association.

JACK BEATSON, Law Commissioner for England and Wales; Fellow of Merton College, Oxford.

Professor PETER BIRKS, Regius Professor of Civil Law in the University of Oxford and Fellow of All Souls College, Oxford.

PAUL L. DAVIES, Reader in the Law of the Enterprise, University of Oxford, and Fellow of Balliol College, Oxford.

Professor PAUL FINN, Professor of Law, Australian National University.

Professor ROY GOODE, Norton Rose Professor of English Law in the University of Oxford and Fellow of St John's College, Oxford.

PETER GRAHAM, Partner, Norton Rose.

Professor KLAUS J. HOPT, Director of the Institute of International Law, University of Munich, Germany.

Professor D. D. PRENTICE, Allen & Overy Professor of Corporate Law, University of Oxford and Fellow of Pembroke College.

Professor JEFFREY SCHOENBLUM, Professor of Law, Vanderbilt University, USA.

HARRY WIGGIN, Partner, Burges Salmon, Solicitors, Bristol.

Table of Cases

Belgium

Canada

England and Wales

Germany

New Zealand

Scotland

United States

Table of Statutes

United States

ABBREVIATIONS

ALJ	*Australian Law Journal*
Brit. Yearbook Int. Law	*British Yearbook of International Law*
Brooklyn J. Int. Law	*Brooklyn Journal of International Law*
Bus. Lawyer	*Business Lawyer*
Calif. LR	*California Law Review*
CLJ	*Cambridge Law Journal*
CMLR	*Common Market Law Review*
Colum. LR	*Columbia Law Review*
Cornell ILJ	*Cornell International Law Journal*
Cornell LR	*Cornell Law Review*
Cornell LQ	*Cornell Law Quarterly*
Duke LJ	*Duke Law Journal*
Ga. J. Int. Law	*Georgia Journal of International Law*
Geo. Was. LR	*George Washington Law Review*
Harv. LR	*Harvard Law Review*
ICLQ	*International and Comparative Law Quarterly*
ILJ	*Industrial Law Journal*
JBL	*Journal of Business Law*
JZ	*Juristen-Zeitung*
Law Soc. Gaz.	*Law Society Gazette*
LMCLQ	*Lloyd's Maritime and Commercial Law Quarterly*
Loyola LR	*Loyola Law Review*
LQR	*Law Quarterly Review*
Melb. ULR	*Melbourne University Law Review*
Mich. LR	*Michigan Law Review*
MLR	*Modern Law Review*
NYULR	*New York University Law Review*
NZLJ	*New Zealand Law Journal*
Ohio St. LJ	*Ohio State Law Journal*
OJLS	*Oxford Journal of Legal Studies*
Osg. HLJ	*Osgoode Hall Law Journal*
Sask. LR	*Saskatchewan Law Review*
U. Chi. LR	*University of Chicago Law Review*
UNSW Law Journal	*University of New South Wales Law Journal*
U. Pa. LR	*University of Pennsylvania Law Review*
Valparaiso ULR	*Valparaiso University Law Review*
Wake Forest LR	*Wake Forest Law Review*

ZHR	*Zeitschrift für das gesamte Handelsrecht und Wirtschaftsrecht*
ZVglRWiss	*Zeitschrift*

INTRODUCTION

Sir Peter Gibson

A legal historian surveying the work of the English courts in the last few decades will have noted the marked decline in cases to do with formal trusts in family settlements or wills and yet the continued and indeed increasing frequency of cases involving trusts in other forms or other equitable obligations, often in a commercial context, and in particular involving the fiduciary obligations of those in whom trust or confidence is reposed, and the consequences of any breaches of those obligations. The presence of such traditional equity elements in the thinking of those conducting litigation may be one of the several reasons why at least since the mid-1980s the workload of the Chancery Division has been growing at a rate of over 10 per cent per annum compound. But it would be wrong to measure the importance of equity in the modern world by reference to a Division of the English High Court, as it is apparent from the reported cases that throughout the common law world the doctrines of equity continue, as the editors of *Snell's Equity* (29th edn., p. v.) put it, to show great vitality. The theme of the Colloquium was chosen in recognition of the continuing practical importance of equity in the law today.

It is at first blush surprising that the principles still governing the conduct of fiduciaries, even those involved in commerce, should be those devised in a now distant age when the Court of Chancery was concerned to impose high standards of prudent and conscientious behaviour on a trustee of a family settlement. That such principles are still relevant reflects the timeless acceptability of the principles, which are often mirrored in other jurisdictions owing nothing to the common law tradition, and more practically it reflects the considerable breadth of those principles. As Lord Upjohn pointed out in *Phipps* v. *Boardman* ([1967] 2 A.C. 46, 123), 'rules of equity have to be applied to such a great diversity of circumstances that they can only be stated in the most general terms and applied with particular attention to the exact circumstances of a case'. One sees equity at its elastic pragmatic best—or worst—in the way that it deals with fiduciaries, because what the fiduciary is obliged to do or not to do will vary according to the particular type of fiduciary and the particular circumstances in question. The judge, frankly, enjoys the flexibility thereby afforded, anxious to do what he sees as justice in the case before him. For the practitioner, concerned to advise on and manage the conflicts of interest that so frequently arise, the uncertainty thereby engendered produces difficulties. Those difficulties may be compounded when the legislature intervenes in an area where the common law obligations otherwise obtain but omits to spell out the intended effect of that intervention on those obligations.

Six papers were presented on the first day of the Colloquium. The first, by Paul Finn (Chapter 1), contains a masterly survey of fiduciary law throughout the common law world as that law affects commercial dealings today, with particular attention directed to the role of fiduciary law in regulating the multi-functional business enterprise and the large professional partnership. The second and third chapters focus on an area of law of current topicality for English practitioners. The enactment of the Financial Services Act 1986, followed by the promulgation of tomes of regulations pursuant to that Act and coupled with the reorganization of the structures of the financial markets, allowing conflicts of interests to arise in situations where they had previously been prohibited, has caused anxieties as to the relationship between the common law fiduciary duties and the duties imposed by the regulations. The reality of those anxieties was recognized by the Government in referring to the Law Commission, and by the Law Commission in undertaking, the current project in this field. Peter Graham in Chapter 2 looks at the history of the statutory regulation of the financial services industry and the recognition of Chinese Walls in the regulatory scheme. Jack Beatson in Chapter 3 discusses the approaches which the courts may adopt when faced with conflicts between regulatory rules made in the public law sphere and fiduciary obligations under the general law.

Chapters 4–6 address the topic of directors' duties, which continue to pose problems of substantial practical difficulty as the right balance between the accountability of directors and their freedom of action is sought by the legislature and the courts in the changed circumstances of recent years. The corporate world has seen take-over boom and bust, management buy-outs, the widespread use of nominee directors, privatization of companies with monopoly or near-monopoly positions, international frauds on an unprecedented scale, and a deep recession with investors and creditors suffering severe losses and looking for targets to sue. There have been significant statutory changes, with, for example, greater emphasis placed on imposing sanctions on misbehaving directors, such as through disqualification and wrongful trading orders, and in addition members of a company have been given greater scope to complain of unfairly prejudicial conduct by the company. All this has focused attention on how directors ought to behave in relation to shareholders and creditors.

Dan Prentice in Chapter 4 discusses the general principle that directors owe fiduciary duties only to the company and not directly to shareholders and creditors and considers the judicial and statutory developments which affect the application of that principle. Next Paul Davies explores the question of the enforceability by individual shareholders of fiduciary duties owed by directors to the company. Finally, Klaus Hopt (Chapter 6) provides us with a view from the Continent of directors' duties to shareholders and creditors, thereby enabling a useful comparison to be made between the civil law and common law approaches.

INTRODUCTION

Sir Peter Millett

When I introduced the speakers at the second session of the Oxford Law Colloquium held at St John's College, Oxford, I suggested that the time had come to cease to use the expressions 'constructive trust' and 'constructive trustee' in relation to the recovery of misapplied assets. There are, indeed, powerful arguments for dispensing with the concepts themselves as having no relevance in this context. As Professor Birks demonstrates in Chapter 8, the accessory is not a trustee and his personal liability is not dependent on the existence of any trust; while I have argued elsewhere that the trust which is operating where a restitutionary claim has a proprietary base is a resulting and not a constructive trust. But I was concerned only to make a semantic point: the use of the language of constructive trust has become such a fertile source of confusion that it would be better if it were abandoned. Sometimes it is the necessary foundation for a proprietary claim, sometimes for a purely personal claim.

The use of the phrase 'constructive trustee' is even more confusing. The accessory, charged with 'knowing assistance' in the misdirection of the plaintiff's money, is held to be 'liable to account as constructive trustee'. As Professor Birks points out, the last three words add nothing. But they are worse than superfluous, they are misleading. The accessory is not a trustee, and he may never have received the trust property in any sense, ministerially or otherwise. I have argued elsewhere that the words mean that he is liable to account 'as if he was a constructive trustee (which, strictly speaking he is not)'. The danger is that he may be thought to mean that he is liable to account 'as a constructive trustee because he is one'.

It would help to reduce confusion if in future we were to abandon these phrases in relation to the recovery of the misapplied assets, and distinguish instead between personal and proprietary claims. The phrase 'constructive trust' would not, of course, disappear from our vocabulary. There is still a need for it, for example, in relation to proprietary claims in respect of what are now commonly called 'deemed agency gains'.

I
Statutory Regulation of Financial Services and General Fiduciary Obligations

1

FIDUCIARY LAW AND THE MODERN COMMERCIAL WORLD

Paul Finn

There are five major issues of moment in contemporary fiduciary law. Four are of potential relevance to the concerns of this volume. The first, and seemingly perennial question, is that fundamental one: who is a fiduciary— what is a fiduciary relationship?[1] The second is the manner in which and the extent to which fiduciary principles should be applied to commercial relationships and dealings—an issue which in one direction is calling into question the extent to which fiduciary obligations should be allowed to supplement those bargained for in negotiated commercial contracts,[2] and in another, the use that can or should properly be made of fiduciary notions to achieve what is, in effect, a duty of good faith and fair dealing in contract formation, performance, and enforcement.[3] The third, and in some ways the most intractable, is the proper role to be given fiduciary law in regulating the modern, multi-function business enterprise and the large professional partnership: this is the arena in which the issues of client-conflict, of secrecy and disclosure, of the efficacy of 'Chinese Walls and cones of silence' and the like, vex and threaten.[4] The fourth is the product of the recent revitalization of the jurisdiction to award damages for breach of fiduciary duty[5] and presages the development of what is, in effect, a surrogate tort of negligence. The final issue, which I merely mention, though it is not of immediate

---

[1] The writer has written on this matter at some length in T. G. Youdan (ed.), *Equity, Fiduciaries and Trusts* (The Carswell Co., Toronto, 1989). ch. 1. The later decision of the Supreme Court of Canada in *Lac Minerals Ltd.* v. *International Corona Resources Ltd.* (1989) 61 DLR (4th) 14 has done little to clarify the question.

[2] See e.g. *E. Pfeiffer Weinkellerei-Weineinkauf GmbH & Co.* v. *Arbuthnot Factors Ltd.* [1988] 1 WLR 151; *Noranda Australia Ltd.* v. *Lachlan Resources N.L.* (1988) 14 NSWLR 1.

[3] This is less of an issue in Britain than in other common law countries given the relative disfavour shown in Britain to the imposition of duties of good faith and fair dealing on contracting parties: see P. D. Finn, 'The Fiduciary Principle', in Youdan (ed.), supra, n. 1; see also *Energy Law '90*, 111–13 (P.D. Finn), cf. 147–9 (P. D. Rouse), International Bar Assoc., Graham & Trotman Ltd., London, 1990).

[4] There has been a plethora of recent case law on these issues involving, in particular, the large law firm: see e.g. *Re a firm of Solicitors* [1992] 1 All ER 353; *MacDonald Estate* v. *Martin* [1991] 1 WWR 705 (S.C. of Can.); *National Mutual Holding Pty. Ltd.* v. *Sentry Corp.* (1989) 87 A.L.R. 539.

[5] See W. M. C. Gummow, 'Compensation for Breach of Fiduciary Duty', in Youdan (ed.), supra, n. 1.

interest, is the role fiduciary law should have in regulating the actions and conduct of the officers and agencies of government.[6]

Each of the first four of these could be a chapter in itself. Though referring to all, it is my intention to concentrate primarily on the third—fiduciary law and the multi-function business and the professional firm. My comments will be confined to the general principles of the common law and this, often, from an international perspective. The two succeeding chapters will consider how, if at all, statute has disfigured or transformed the common law landscape in this country.

1. A Fiduciary—A Fiduciary Relationship?

The answer to this, the most fundamental question, continues to elude us.[7] The question itself presupposes that we have a developed conception of the purpose and burden of fiduciary law. Yet these are matters on which there is widespread disagreement throughout the common law world. The present Chief Justice of the High Court of Australia has justly observed that 'the fiduciary relationship is a concept in search of a principle'.[8] Confusion here has had a number of causes: the use of the 'fiduciary' to fill hiatuses in available doctrines—hence, for example, the modern propensity to manufacture a fiduciary relationship between the directors of a marginally solvent company and corporate creditors;[9] the dilution of fiduciary obligations to exact what is in essence a duty of good faith and fair dealing;[10] the colourable findings of fiduciary relationships to gain access to equitable, but particularly profit-based, remedies;[11] uncertainty as to what precisely are fiduciary duties and whether they encompass in some measure the law of undue influence,[12] breach of confidence,[13] and, in relation to professional advisers, a negligence-like duty of care;[14] etc. When this has been acknowledged, it should equally

---

[6] The principal areas in which this has been seen so far in Britain are in the regulation of local government authorities and enforcing secrecy on civil servants.

[7] See generally Finn, 'The Fiduciary Principle', supra, n. 3; see also R. Flannigan, 'Fiduciary Obligation in the Supreme Court' (1990) 54 *Sask. LR* 45.

[8] Sir Anthony Mason, 'Themes and Prospects', in P. D. Finn (ed.), *Essays in Equity* (Law Book Co., Sydney, 1985), 246.

[9] The subject of Ch. 4.

[10] A prevalent phenomenon in Canadian, New Zealand, and United States jurisprudence in particular: see Finn, 'The Fiduciary Principle', supra, n. 3; see also *Pacific Industrial Corp. S.A. v. Bank of New Zealand* [1991] 1 NZLR 368; *Plaza Fibreglass Manufacturing Ltd. v. Cardinal Insurance Co.* (1990) 68 DLR (4th) 586.

[11] An excellent UK example is *English v. Dedham Vale Properties Ltd.* [1978] 1 WLR 93; cf. the judgment of Deane, J. in *Hospital Products Ltd. v. U.S. Surgical Corp.* (1984) 55 A.L.R. 417.

[12] See e.g. *National Westminster Bank plc v. Morgan* [1985] AC 686; and cf the treatment of *Tate v. Williamson* (1866) LR 2 Ch. App. 54 in *Bank of Credit and Commerce v. Aboody* [1990] 1 QB 923.

[13] Cf *Lac Minerals Ltd. v. International Corona Resources Ltd.* (1989) 61 DLR (4th) 14.

[14] The subject of some controversy in Canadian and New Zealand law in relation to the liability of particularly solicitors for non-disclosure: but for the Canadian reaction, see the comments of Southin, J. in *Giradet v. Crease & Co.* (1987) 11 BCLR (2d) 361, at 362; and see Finn, 'The Fiduciary Principle', supra, n. 3, 25–6, 28–30.

be said that, for somewhat different reasons, the laws of Britain and Australia hold most closely to the old orthodoxies.[15]

For reasons of space, but also because the matter has been dealt with elsewhere,[16] I will simply note without elaboration my own understanding of (i) when, in our respective systems, a person can properly be said to be a fiduciary; and (ii) what is the obligation imposed in consequence of a fiduciary finding.

At best, all one can give is a description of a fiduciary—and one which, if it expresses the fiduciary idea, is no more precise than a description of the tort of negligence. It is as follows:

> A person will be a fiduciary in his relationship with another when and in so far as[17] that other is entitled to expect[18] that he will act in that other's interests or (as in a partnership) in their joint interests, to the exclusion of his own several interest.

Put crudely, the central idea is service of another's interests. And the consequential obligation a fiduciary finding attracts is itself one designed essentially to procure loyalty in service. It can be cast compendiously in the following terms:

> A fiduciary
> (*a*) cannot misuse his position, or knowledge or opportunity resulting from it, to his own or to a third party's possible advantage; or
> (*b*) cannot, in any matter falling within the scope of his service, have a personal interest or an inconsistent engagement with a third party— unless this is freely and informedly consented to by the beneficiary or is authorized by law.[19]

Two themes, it should be noted, are embodied in this: one, concerned with misuse of position, aims to preclude the fiduciary from using his position to advantage interests other than his beneficiary's; the second, concerned with conflicts of interest or of duty, aims to preclude the fiduciary from being swayed in his service by considerations of personal or third-party interest.

The one general comment I would make both of the description given and of the rather severe obligation that fiduciary law imposes, is that our preparedness to discriminate amongst the host of 'service relationships' to be found in contemporary society and to designate some only as fiduciary (for

[15] In Australia, though the traditional line was held by the High Court in *Hospital Products Ltd.* v. *U.S. Surgical Corp.* (1984) 55 A.L.R. 417, the pressure for more 'creative' uses was blunted both by the evolution of unconscionability-based doctrines and by the scope for invention given Australian courts by the Trade Practices Act, 1974, s. 52.

[16] See Finn, 'The Fiduciary Principle', supra, n. 3.

[17] Relationships commonly are fiduciary in part, non-fiduciary in part.

[18] That entitlement may arise from what one party undertakes or appears to undertake—cf. *Croce* v. *Kurnit* 565 F. Supp. 884 (1982)—for the other; from what actually is agreed between the parties; or, for reasons of public policy, from legal prescription.

[19] The above is an adaptation of the formulation of Deane J. in *Chan* v. *Zacharia* (1983) 53 A.L.R. 417, at 435—the most comprehensive formulation to be found in modern Anglo-Australian law.

Paul Finn

example, solicitor or financial adviser and client) is informed in some measure by considerations of public policy aimed at preserving the integrity and utility of these relationships, given the expectation that the community is considered to have of behaviour in them, and given the purposes they serve in society. This, as will later be seen, is likely to have quite some bearing on how the courts are prepared to apply fiduciary duties to multi-function business enterprises and large professional partnerships.

For the purposes of this chapter, one particular matter arising from the description of a fiduciary warrants brief examination. It relates to the possible fiduciary status of the information provider or adviser.

1.1. 'THE ADVISER/INFORMATION PROVIDER'[20]

Here I will merely make a number of general observations and then illustrate the problem, first through the banker–customer relationship and secondly through the difficulties which can arise where a person dealing with another's agent relies upon that agent for information, explanation, or guidance.

1. While one can find readily enough judicial assertions that at least particular types of advisers are fiduciary,[21] it is clear that so diverse are the circumstances in which, and the reasons for which, information, opinion, and advice are exchanged in commercial and business dealings, that no instructive generalization can be made other than that 'the mere giving of advice does not convert a business relationship . . . into a fiduciary relationship'.[22]

2. The expectations that can be had of an information provider/adviser may vary widely. These, for the most part, will be unrelated to any consideration of loyal service: they will demand no more than honesty, frank disclosure, care and skill, or accuracy; and if they attract consequential legal responsibilities at all, these will ensue from doctrines in tort, contract, or equity which are quite unrelated to fiduciary law.[23]

3. The expectation required to found a fiduciary finding requires a 'crossing of the line'[24] from that merely of honesty, care, and skill and the like. It requires a factual matrix which can justify both the entitlement to expect that the adviser is acting, and the consequential obligation that he must act, in the other's interest in the giving of advice, information, etc.

4. That expectation will be found, ordinarily as of course, where the function the adviser represents himself as performing, and for which he is consulted, is that of counselling an advised party as to how his interests will or might best be served in a matter which our society considers to be of

---

[20] The following draws upon Finn 'The Fiduciary Principle', supra, n. 3. 49 ff.

[21] See e.g. *Daly* v. *Sydney Stock Exchange Ltd.* (1986) 160 CLR 371.

[22] *Warren* v. *Percy Wilson Mortgage and Finance Corp.* 472 NE 2d 364, at 367 (1984); and see the division of opinion in *Burns* v. *Kelly Peters & Associates Ltd.* (1987) 16 BCLR (2d) 1.

[23] See e.g. *Cornish* v. *Midland Bank plc* [1985] 3 All ER 513; *Merrill, Lynch, Pierce, Furner & Smith Inc.* 377 NW 2d 605 (1985).

[24] *Lloyds Bank* v. *Bundy* [1975] QB 326, at 342 *per* Sachs, LJ

importance to the advised's personal or financial well-being,[25] and in which the adviser would be expected both to be disinterested (save for his remuneration if any) and to be free of adverse responsibilities. Thus the fiduciary status of the lawyer, the stockbroker, and the accountant, at least when acting in an advisory, and not merely in a ministerial, capacity.

5. That expectation, ordinarily, should not be found where in the circumstances the *adviser* is reasonably entitled to expect that (*a*) the other party, because of his position, knowledge, etc. will make his own evaluation of the matter including the information or advice given and will in consequence exercise an independent judgment in his own interests in the subject of decision;[26] or (*b*) the other is assuming the responsibility for how his own interests are to be served in the matter, howsoever incompetent in this he may in fact be.[27] The first of these is often invoked, particularly in United States decisions, when dismissing the suggestion of fiduciary responsibilities arising from information exchanges between business persons in a business dealing.[28] The latter provides the apparent rationale in the United States for denying a broker's fiduciary responsibility to an investor operating a non-discretionary account,[29] and, in the United Kingdom, for a like denial when a bank manager simply provides explanatory information about the nature and effect of a transaction.[30]

6. The problematic case for fiduciary law relates to the person who proffers advice or information but who has, and who is expected to have, a manifest personal interest, or else an adverse agency role for another, in the matter. To illustrate this brief reference will be made to dealings between banker and customer/guarantor and dealings with another's known agent.

1.2. BANKS[31]

It clearly is possible for a bank, because of the manner in which it conducts itself either in its financial[32] dealings with a customer or borrower, or in its dealings with a customer's guarantor, to find itself in a fiduciary relationship.[33] The matter of difficulty lies in ascertaining when, realistically, it

[25] We have not as yet, for example, taken the view that the advisory services given by travel agents, interior design consultants, consulting engineers, architects, etc. are of this variety.

[26] See e.g. *James* v. *Australia and New Zealand Banking Group Ltd.* (1986) 64 A.L.R. 347, at 366–8.

[27] Incompetence will bear on the issue of whether a dealing between the parties is unconscionable in the circumstances: see in England *National Westminster Bank plc* v. *Morgan* [1985] AC 686; in Australia, the somewhat different rule in *Commercial Bank of Australia* v. *Amadio* (1983) 151 CLR 447.

[28] See e.g. *Umbaugh Pole Building Co. Inc.* v. *Scott* 390 NE 2d 320 (1979).

[29] See e.g. *Horn* v. *Ray E. Friedman & Co.* 776 F. 2d 7773 (1985).

[30] Cf *Cornish* v. *Midland Bank plc* [1985] 3 All ER 513.

[31] K. Curtis, 'The Fiduciary Controversy: Injection of Fiduciary Principles into the Bank-Depositor and Bank-Borrower Relationship'(1987) 20 *Loyola LR* 795.

[32] Excluded from consideration here is the situation in which a bank is providing discrete advisory services to a customer, etc.

[33] Or one of undue influence if, as seems to be the case in England, these are not properly to be called 'fiduciary': see *National Westminster Bank plc* v. *Morgan* [1985] AC 686—a decision

could be said that this is so given the bank's known self-interest in the dealing,[34] and that a fiduciary responsibility would require the bank to act in the other party's interests. The situation must be uncommon where fiduciary altruism as opposed merely to fair dealing could be expected from an obviously interested party: English courts, for example, have acknowledged that banks 'are not charitable institutions'.[35] I would suggest that it should be most unlikely to be found beyond the following three circumstances which are themselves very distinctive. (1) Where the course of the relationship can found the expectation, not only that advice will be given but that, where necessary, it will be given adversely to the bank's interests.[36] (2) Where the bank has created the expectation that it is advising or will advise in the customer's interest in a matter because its own interest therein is represented to be formal, nominal, or technical—the basis, perhaps, for the influential United States decision, *Stewart* v. *Phoenix National Bank*.[37] And (3) where the bank, though expected to act in its own interest in the actual dealing *inter se*, has created the expectation that it will otherwise advise in the customer's interests, for example, on the wisdom of an investment proposal in respect of which a loan application is made. The Canadian decision, *Haywood* v. *Bank of Nova Scotia*,[38] and the recent Australian Federal Court decision of *Smith* v. *Commonwealth Bank of Australia*[39] reflect this eventuality.

The above three situations suggest at least environments in which a fiduciary entitlement could feasibly arise. Reason is there in each case to found an expectation that the bank's interest will not be an operative consideration in the advice expected or given. But without such reason, it is difficult to see how a fiduciary rather than a good faith and fair dealing or reasonable care and skill expectation could exist in the face of the bank's own manifest interest in the dealing. Not surprisingly, in some number of recent New Zealand and Canadian cases where a fiduciary duty has been imposed on banks in contexts other than the three mentioned, the substance of the duty has nothing whatever to do with loyalty but everything to do with fair dealing.[40]

1.3 ANOTHER'S AGENT

It is by no means uncommon for the adviser of one party to a dealing to find himself being relied upon by the other party for assistance or advice going beyond a mere explanation of the purport and effect of the dealing. There is which, lamentably, confuses both the law relating to undue influence and that relating to unconscionable dealing.

[34] Cf *Stenberg* v. *Northwestern Nat. Bank of Rochester* 238 NW 2d 218, 219 (1976).

[35] *National Westminster Bank plc* v. *Morgan* [1983] 3 All ER 85, at 91 per Dunn, LJ.

[36] If *Lloyds Bank Ltd.* v. *Bundy* [1975] QB 326 had anything fiduciary in it as Sachs, LJ suggested, it could only have been sustained on the above basis.

[37] 64 P. 2d 101 (1937).

[38] (1984) 45 OR (2d) 542.

[39] F.C. of A., 11 Mar. 1991, Von Doussa, J.; aff'd. (1991) 102 A. L. R. 453.

[40] See e.g. *Pacific Industrial Corp. S.A.* v. *Bank of New Zealand* [1991] 1 NZLR 368; for a similar example in the insurance context see *Plaza Fibreglass Manufacturing Ltd.* v. *Cardinal*

authority enough, especially from Canada, to demonstrate the vulnerability of such an adviser to claims in negligence, particularly for non-disclosure of information relevant to the dealing.[41] And as in the case of the bank, it clearly is possible, because of the manner in which he conducts himself[42] in his relationship with the third party, for the adviser to be held that party's fiduciary.[43] The one obvious instance where this commonly occurs is where the adviser, notwithstanding the adverse representation, invites or appears to invite, accepts or appears to accept[44] the third party's reliance upon him as that party's adviser in the proposed dealing—the classic case of dual representation. But beyond this, the circumstances must be distinctive indeed in which a fiduciary, rather than a mere 'neighbourhood' relationship, could realistically be found *at least where the adviser is known by the third party to be representing the interests of the other party in the proposed dealing.*[45] That knowledge would stand as an obvious and, in most instances, an insuperable impediment to any credible assertion by the third party that he was entitled to relax his self-interested vigilance or independent judgment in favour of the adviser's protection or judgment because he was justified in believing that the adviser was acting in his interests in the matter.

2. Commercial Contracts

That contractual and fiduciary relationships may co-exist between the same parties has never been doubted. Indeed, the existence of a basic contractual relationship has in many situations provided a foundation for the erection of a fiduciary relationship.[46]

This acknowledged—and there is voluminous case law to support it—it is equally the case that courts in many jurisdictions have demonstrated some reticence in subjecting parties to commercial agreements negotiated at arms' length, to fiduciary duties (save in clear[47] (or traditional[48]) cases) and this notwithstanding that 'commercial transactions [do not as such] stand outside

Insurance Co. (1990) 68 DLR (4th) 586; and see also *Standard Investments Ltd.* v. *Canadian Imperial Bank of Commerce* (1985) 22 DLR (4th) 410.

[41] This case law has built up on the authority of the influential decision of the British Columbia Court of Appeal in *Tracy* v. *Atkins* (1980) 105 DLR (3d) 632; see e.g. *Klingspon* v. *Ramsay* [1985] 5 WWR 411; *Gerlock v Safety Mart Foods Ltd.* (1982) 42 BCLR 137.

[42] Cf *Jacques* v. *Seabrook* [1982] 4 WWR 167—a doubtful case in its reasoning.

[43] See *Croce* v. *Kurnit* 565 F. Supp. 884 (1982); *Cohen* v. *Goodfriend* 665 F. Supp. 152, at 159 (1987).

[44] Cf *Croce* v. *Kurnit*, supra.

[45] This should be emphasized because the third party (*a*) may be unaware of any representation of an adverse interest; (*b*) while knowing that the adviser has some connection with that adverse interest (i) may be known by the adviser to have misconceived the adviser's role in relation to that interest; or (ii) may, none the less, believe or be led to believe that the adviser has been made available or has assumed to act as adviser for the third party: cf. *Croce* v. *Kurnit*, supra.

[46] *Hospital Products Ltd.* v. *U.S. Surgical Corp.* (1984) 55 A.L.R. 417, at 454 per Mason, J.

[47] E.g. where a contract itself creates a trust: cf. *Barclays Bank Ltd.* v *Quistclose Investments Ltd.* [1970] AC 567; *Stephens Travel Service International Pty. Ltd.* v. *Qantas Airways Ltd.* (1988) 13 NSWLR 331.

[48] E.g. commercial agency agreements.

the fiduciary regime'.[49] That reticence flows in some measure from an acceptance (i) that, at least in contracts of this type, the parties themselves, first and foremost, are to be the authors of their respective rights and obligations, and (ii) that fiduciary duties should, in consequence, only be imposed upon them when, and to the extent that, this is necessary and appropriate to give effect to the expectations they could properly entertain in consequence of their contract given the business setting in which it occurs.[50] Here all I can do is illustrate this briefly and with little explanation, in a number of distinct contexts, before noting one apparently exceptional case.

2.1. COMMERCIAL CONTRACTORS AS FIDUCIARIES

Because of the capacity we characterfztically attribute to commercial parties to conserve their own interests, and because of our preparedness to assign the risk to them if they do not,[51] the scope allowed to a commercial contractor to raise a fiduciary relationship *dehors* the contract for reasons of trust and confidence reposed, ascendancy and dependence, etc.,[52] is limited indeed. In consequence the fiduciary question is ordinarily one of whether a commercial contract itself, given its formal incidents and the setting in which it occurs, does or does not create a fiduciary relationship.[53] An appraisal (i) of the manner in which, and the apparent purpose for which, rights, powers, duties, and discretions are allocated by the contract; (ii) of the contract's particular commercial or business setting; and (iii) of the self-serving actions lawfully open to a party both under, and notwithstanding the contract[54] will, as a rule, indicate decisively whether the role and reason of a party in the contract (or in a discrete part of it)[55] can properly be said to be to serve his own interests, the parties' joint interests, or the interests of the other party. In the Californian decision, *Rickel* v. *Schwinn Bicycle Co.*,[56] for example, consideration of a distributorship agreement led to the finding that there was nothing fiduciary in it, the Court concluding its purpose to be to promote the

---

[49] *Hospital Products Ltd.* v. *U.S. Surgical Corp.*, supra, 456 *per* Mason J. This theme has been canvassed by Mr Justice Kennedy in 'Equity in a Commercial Context', in P. D. Finn (ed.). *Equity and Commercial Relationships* (Law Book Co., Sydney, 1987) 13 ff.; see also J. R. F. Lehane, 'Fiduciaries in a Commercial Context', in Finn (ed.), *Essays in Equity*, above, n. 8, and the observations of Sopinka J. in *Lac Minerals Ltd.* v. *International Corona Resources Ltd.* (1989) 61 DLR (4th) 14, at 60–1.

[50] For an example of such a usage of 'expectations' see the judgment of Priestley, JA in *Walker* v. *Corboy* (1990) 19 NSWLR 382, at 385–6.

[51] Themes implicit in much Anglo-Australian law, but often made explicit in US decisions.

[52] Fiduciary relationships can, often do, arise as a result of the factual phenomena of trust, etc. present in the actual relationship of parties: see Finn, 'The Fiduciary Principle', supra n. 3, 41 ff.

[53] This question is explored at some length in P. D. Finn, 'Contract and the Fiduciary Principle'(1989) 12 *UNSW Law Journal* 76.

[54] See e.g. *Rickel* v. *Schwinn Bicycle Co.* 192 Cal. Rptr. 732 (1983).

[55] Relationships, clearly, can be fiduciary in part, non-fiduciary in part: see *Hospital Products Ltd.* v. *U.S. Surgical Corp.* (1984) 55 A.L.R. 417, at 455.

[56] 192 Cal. Rptr. 732 (1983).

'non-mutual profit' of the parties and noting in this the right each had to make a range of decisions adverse to the other's interests.[57]

Three comments should be made of this process of relationship character-ization. First, it excludes as of course from any question of fiduciary responsibility, those contractual powers and rights which a party has to protect or to further its own interests—drastic though the effect of their exercise might be on the other party's interests (e.g. a franchisor's discretionary power to terminate the franchise).[58]

Secondly, relatively little difficulty has been encountered where the fiduciary issue has been no more than whether the purpose of a contractual relationship is to serve both parties' several interests or the interests of one alone. Agency contracts, for example, we characterize as fiduciary as of course. Loans, sales, and mortgage contracts, not so—unless specific and atypical provisions in the contract contrive a contrary conclusion (usually in relation to a discrete part of the relationship).[59] Unlike with agencies, we do not perceive the structure and design of loans, sales, etc. as warranting either party being entitled to expect that the relationship exists other than to serve each party equally and severally.

Thirdly, the most significant difficulties experienced in recent times in a number of common law countries have arisen when the characterization issue has been whether the contractual relationship or powers in it, exists for the parties' joint rather than for their several interests. This has been particularly so in what may be described as 'co-operative contractual arrangements': non-partnership joint ventures, distributorships, franchises, licensing agree-ments, and the like. An initial problem lies, often, in identifying the true nature of the relationship itself. What in name is a joint venture may in fact be a partnership,[60] a distributorship in fact a true agency—and thus both may be fiduciary. This said, both distributorships and franchises exist as a rule to serve the 'non-mutual profit' of each party and should not be found fiduciary save in exceptional circumstances.[61] The great preponderance of

---

[57] Similar emphases can be found, e.g. in *Jirna Ltd.* v. *Mister Donut of Canada Ltd.* (1971) 22 DLR (3d) 639; affi'd. (1973) 40 DLR (3d) 303; *Hospital Products Ltd.* v. *U.S. Surgical Corp.*, supra, Gibbs, CJ.

[58] The exercise of such rights and powers can raise fair dealing questions in an acute form: see *Dunfee* v. *Baskin-Robbins Inc.* 720 P. 2d 1148 (1988); and see D. A. De Mott, 'Beyond Metaphor: An Analysis of Fiduciary Obligation'(1988) *Duke LJ* 879.

[59] E.g. a *Quistclose* trust in a loan; a reservation of title clause in a sales agreement: but cf. *E. Pfeiffer Weinkellerei-Weineinkauf GmbH & Co.* v. *Arbuthnot Factors Ltd.* [1988] 1 WLR 151; or a mortgagee's power to control disbursements under a mortgage contract: see e.g. *Gabrish* v. *Malvern Federal Savings & Loan Assoc.* 517 A. 2d 547 (1986).

[60] See e.g. *Canny Gabriel Jackson Advertising Pty. Ltd.* v. *Volume Sales (Finance) Ltd.* (1974) 131 CLR 321; *United Dominion Corp. Ltd.* v. *Brian Pty. Ltd.* (1985) 157 CLR 1; and cf. *Reynes-Retana* v. *PTX Food Corp.* 709 SW 2d 695 (1986).

[61] That is (i) where a particular provision of the agreement on its proper construction is designed to be exercised by one party either in the parties' joint interest or in the interest of the other alone; (ii) if a 'trusteeship' is created of an asset in the relationship: cf. the dissenting judgment of Mason J. in *Hospital Products Ltd.* v. *U.S. Surgical Corp.* (1984) 55 ALR 417; or (iii)

recent authority accords with this view.[62] The non-partnership joint venture is more problematic. Though ordinarily structured for the several profit of each participant, its management provisions may well attract fiduciary incidents[63] and, because of the relationships it may create to property, to confidential information, or to the 'area of interest', it may be fiduciary for other reasons.[64]

The final comment that should be made here is that, with fiduciary law being ordinarily an alien presence in commercial contracts, it is in this context in particular in some number of Commonwealth countries that the debate is now being waged as to whether or not courts should commit themselves to a doctrine of good faith in contract performance and enforcement along lines similar to that to be found in the United States in the Uniform Commercial Code, §1-203 and §2–103(1)(b) and the Restatement of Contracts, Second, §205.[65] Britain, for the moment, remains outside this debate.[66]

2.2 SUPPLEMENTING CONTRACTUAL OBLIGATIONS WITH FIDUCIARY ONES

There is now a significant body of Australian[67] and United States[68] authority affirming that the contractual obligations of negotiated commercial contracts will in any event only be supplemented by fiduciary ones to the extent that

controversially, if the contract is such that one party is required to surrender all independence to the other party.

[62] For recent US decisions see *C. Peppas Co. Inc.* v. *E. & J. Gallo Wines* 610 F. Supp. 662 (1985); *W.K.T. Distributing Co.* v. *Sharp Electronics Corp.* 746 F. 2d 1333 (1984); *Rickel* v. *Schwinn Bicycle Co.* 192 Cal. Rptr. 732 (1983); *St Joseph Equipment* v. *Massey-Ferguson Inc.* 546 F. Supp. 1245, (1982); *Power Motive Corp.* v. *Mannesmann Demag Corp.* 617 F. Supp. 1048 (1985); *Chmieleski* v. *City Products Corp.* 660 SW 2d 275 (1983); in Canada, *Jirna Ltd.* v. *Mister Donut of Canada Ltd.* (1971) 22 DLR (3d) 639; in Australia, *Hospital Products Ltd.* v. *U.S. Surgical Corp.*, supra.

[63] In the case of an 'operator' they invariably will on agency grounds; but cf. the difficult decision of *Molchan* v. *Omega Oil & Gas Ltd.* (1988) 47 DLR (4th) 481.

[64] Joint ventures have been considered at some length by the writer in 'Good Faith, Unconscionability and Fiduciary Duties' in *Energy Law '90*, above, n. 3, 103 ff.; see also P. J. Keeley, 'Commentary from the USA.', ibid. 154 ff.

[65] See e.g. H. K. Lücke, 'Good Faith and Contractual Performance', in P.D. Finn (ed.), *Essays on Contract*, (Law Book Co., Sydney, 1987); recent NZ case law, for its part, is prone to findings of 'fiduciary duties of good faith and fair dealing': see e.g. *Attorney-General* v. *Offshore Mining Ltd.*, C. of A. of NZ, 28 Apr. 1988; *Pacific Industrial Corp. S.A.* v. *Bank of New Zealand* [1991] 1 NZLR 368; there is now a reasonably extensive Canadian writing on this question: see e.g. B. J. Reiter, 'Good Faith in Contracts'(1983) 17 *Valparaiso ULR* 705; and see e.g. *McKinlay Motors Ltd.* v. *Honda Canada Inc.*, Newf. SC, 22 Nov. 1990.

[66] See e.g. *Interfoto Picture Library Ltd.* v. *Stiletto Visual Programmes Ltd.* [1988] 1 All ER 348, at 352; *Banque Keyser Ullman S.A.* v. *Skandia (U.K.) Insurance Co. Ltd.* [1989] 3 WLR 25, at 80.

[67] See *Hospital Products Ltd.* v. *U.S. Surgical Corp.* (1984) 55 A.L.R. 417 at 455; *Australian Oil & Gas Corp. Ltd.* v. *Bridge Oil Ltd.*, C of A of NSW, 12 Apr. 1989; *Noranda Australia Ltd.* v. *Lachlan Resources N.L.* (1988) 14 NSWLR 1.

[68] See e.g. *Deauville Corp.* v. *Federated Department Stores Inc.* 756 F. 2d 1183, at 1194 (1985); *Frankfurt Oil Co.* v. *Snakard* 279 F. 2d 436, at 443 (1960).

these are 'consistent with and conform to the terms of the contract itself'.[69] Even where such a contract expressly manifests a fiduciary intent, the courts have demonstrated an unpreparedness to give the duty of loyalty any greater effect than is necessary to effectuate the contract according to its terms. In *Noranda Australia Ltd.* v. *Lachlan Resources N.L.*[70]—a resources joint venture case—for example, though the contract itself expressly declared that the 'relationship of the parties shall be fiduciary in nature', it was held that this would not qualify those contractual provisions which, according to their terms as contractual provisions, allowed the parties to pursue 'recognisable and distinct interests of their own'.[71]

2.3 Commercial Agencies and Monetary Receipts

The proper characterization—trust or not—to be given to the monetary receipts of an agent (whether arising by way of advances from a principal[72] or as receipts on account of a principal[73]) can be distinctly problematic if the agency contract itself does not address expressly the manner in which those receipts are to be held or accounted for by the agent.[74] And commonly the contract is silent. Though we have some number of guides, 'tests', etc. which can structure the characterization question (for example, the proceeds of sale of a principal's property are prima facie trust property in the agent's hands),[75] the two obviously significant influences upon judicial findings in this area are the rival ones (*a*) of the inconvenience to the ordinary conduct of the agent's business that a trust finding might occasion;[76] and (*b*) of the access a trust finding could give a principal to those receipts or their proceeds in the event either of the agent's bankruptcy,[77] or of their misuse.[78] Distinctively, when the receipt occurs in a commercial relationship, and especially when there are on-going dealings between the parties, the former (the 'inconvenience') consideration has assumed primacy in practice. While it cannot be correct to say, though some courts have come close to it,[79] that trusts have no place in commercial agencies, it is none the less clearly the case

---

[69] *Hospital Products Ltd.* v. *U.S. Surgical Corp.*, supra, at 455 Mason, J.

[70] (1988) 14 NSWLR 1.

[71] Ibid., 14.

[72] See e.g. *Bank of Novia Scotia* v. *Societe General (Canada)* (1988) 58 Alta. LR (2d) 193; *Neste Oy* v. *Lloyds Bank plc* [1983] 2 Lloyd's Rep. 658.

[73] See e.g. *Southern Cross Commodities Pty. Ltd.* v. *Ewing* (1986) 6 ACLC 647; *Westpac Banking Corp. Ltd.* v. *Savin* [1985] 2 NZLR 41.

[74] This subject is discussed in P. D. Finn, *Fiduciary Obligations* (Law Book Co., Sydney, 1977), 101 ff.; see also *Stephens Travel Service International Ltd.* v. *Qantas Airways Ltd.* (1988) 13 NSWLR 331.

[75] See e.g. *Palette Shoes Pty. Ltd.* v. *Krohn* (1937) 58 CLR 1, at 30.

[76] See e.g. the comments of Bramwell, LJ in *New Zealand & Australian Land Co.* v. *Watson* (1881) 7 QBD 374, at 382.

[77] See e.g. *Westpac Banking Corp.* v. *Savin* [1985] 2 NZLR 41.

[78] Cf *Rankin* v. *Naftalis* 557 SW 2d 940, at 944 (1977).

[79] See e.g. the observations of Bingham, J. in *Neste Oy* v. *Lloyds Bank plc* [1983] 2 Lloyd's Rep. 658, at 665.

that the courts will readily infer that 'the expectations of persons engaged in business with [such] agents . . . , and [of] such agents themselves, would not extend to anything other than a creditor–debtor relationship existing between them'.[80] If the issue of principle is whether the imposition of a trust is necessary and appropriate to effectuate the relationship between the parties that is envisaged by their contract, the business character of the contract and of the parties, and its commercial setting and purpose will as a rule influence decisively the trust question if the contract itself is silent or equivocal on the matter.[81]

2.4. The Exception: Contractual Negotiations

Here I wish merely to draw attention to three matters. First, and as starkly illustrated in the decision of the Supreme Court of Canada in *Lac Minerals Ltd.* v. *International Corona Resources Ltd.*,[82] it is now well accepted that confidential information disclosed in and for the purposes of contract negotiations will be protected from misuse or misappropriation by the recipient of the information.[83] For secrecy law to be brought into play, though, the information recipient must know or have reason to know that the information itself is confidential and that restriction is being placed upon its use or disclosure. For this reason prudence dictates that an express secrecy agreement be concluded for the purposes of negotiations if 'proprietary' information is to be disclosed.

Secondly, where parties are negotiating for a relationship which will itself be fiduciary—usually a partnership or a joint venture—it has now been accepted in both Commonwealth and United States jurisdictions that fiduciary duties can arise in advance of a binding agreement being reached and for the purpose of protecting the opportunity, the subject of the negotiations, from the pre-emptive strike of one of the parties. But given the staging that occurs in the 'courtship period', it is a matter of controversy as to when such duties will so arise. If the formal question asked by the courts is whether, notwithstanding the absence of a concluded agreement, a relation-ship of 'mutual trust and confidence' has developed,[84] their preparedness to make an affirmative finding for the purpose of protecting an opportunity would seem to be influenced by

    (*a*) the extent to which the opportunity is specific to one of the parties;[85]

---

[80] *Walker* v. *Corboy* (1990) 19 NSWLR 382.

[81] But for a borderline case see *Westpac Banking Corp.* v. *Savin* [1985] 2 NZLR 41.

[82] (1989) 61 DLR (4th) 14.

[83] E.g. *Mechanical & General Inventions Co. Ltd.* v. *Austin* [1935] AC 346; *Seager* v. *Copydex Ltd.* [1967] 1 WLR 923; *Talbot* v. *General Television Corp. Pty. Ltd.* [1980] VR 224; *A.B. Consolidated Ltd.* v. *Europe Strength Food Co. Pty. Ltd.* [1978] 2 NZLR 515.

[84] This, as many US fiduciary decisions emphasize, is not simply the 'trust' that businessmen may have in each other: see e.g. *Everston* v. *Cannon* 411 NW 2d 612 (1987).

[85] Cf *Fraser Edmiston Pty. Ltd.* v. *AGT (Queensland) Pty. Ltd.* [1988] 2 Qd. R. 1.

(*b*) the degree to which the subject-matter of the proposed relationship has been particularized;[86] and

(*c*) the point that has been reached in negotiation—especially in the parties' delineation of their proposed relationship.[87]

Given that parties, necessarily, are to be expected to consult self-interest both in negotiating and in committing themselves to an agreement, the best that can be said generally here is that the guiding factor in judicial decision is likely to be whether the nature and course of negotiations has reasonably created such expectation of common purpose in relation to the opportunity in question as would make one party's appropriation of it unfair and unjust.

Thirdly, a live issue in many common law jurisdictions is as to when duties of information disclosure can or should arise in the course of contract negotiations to correct known or probable misconceptions or to eliminate information disparities.[88] While this question is not, intrinsically, a fiduciary one,[89] I merely note that the High Court of Australia has held that where parties are negotiating for a relationship which will itself be fiduciary, a fiduciary-based duty of disclosure can arise prior to formal agreement being reached.[90] This acknowledged, it is none the less unlikely that fiduciary law will be allowed to be invoked in commercial negotiations so as to relieve one party of the obligation to exercise due diligence in the protection of its own interests.[91]

3. The Multi-Function Business and the Large Professional Partnership

Many important rules which have an impact on modern business structures and dealings are emissaries of the past. And our problem lies in their appropriate adaptation to contemporary circumstances. The forms of relationship, the manner of dealing, presupposed in a variety of enduring rules and doctrines of present relevance, possess a remarkable simplicity. To overgeneralize somewhat, our conception of the agent, for example, has been informed by that of the natural person acting personally for another in a single, limited, and discrete transaction. Likewise the adviser has been perceived very much as the individual professional acting on the basis of information which, if not in his own head, was none the less readily accessible

---

[86] Cf *Marr* v. *Arabco Traders Ltd.* [1987] 1 NZBLC 102, 372.

[87] Cf *United Dominions Corp. Ltd.* v. *Brian Pty. Ltd.* (1985) 60 A.L.R. 741; *Lac Minerals Ltd.* v. *International Corona Resources Ltd.* (1989) 61 DLR (4th) 14; *Amalgamated Television Services Pty. Ltd.* v. *Television Corp.* Ltd. [1969] 2 NSWR. 257.

[88] This issue has been considered by the writer in 'The Fiduciary Principle', supra, n. 3, at 16 ff; and in 'Good Faith and Nondisclosure', in P. D. Finn (ed.), *Essays on Torts* (Law Book Co., Sydney, 1989).

[89] Though fiduciary notions have been abused in some number of particularly US jurisdictions to author a duty of disclosure.

[90] *United Dominion Corp. Ltd.* v. *Brian Pty. Ltd.* (1985) 60 A.L.R. 741.

[91] Much US case law on non-disclosure emphasizes this obligation: see e.g. *Denison State Bank* v. *Madiera* 640 P. 2d 1235, at 1243 (1982); see also *Day* v. *Mead* [1987] 2 NZLR 443.

to him. Similarly the rules of fiduciary law have drawn their inspiration and vitality from relatively simple relationships and dealings[92] in which the relevant actors were natural persons usually known to each other and in which the business or professional function of the person subject to fiduciary duties was of a known and limited character and was geographically confined. The world presupposed in all of this is no longer our world. The small, single-purpose agency and the sole practitioner may still be with us. But so also now are the multi-function and geographically dispersed business enterprise providing disparate client services, and the large professional firm with regional, national, and international offices. To be added to this are the capacities we now possess to acquire, store, and retrieve information on scales which even in recent times were beyond our contemplation.

Our rules on agency, advice-giving, fiduciaries, and the like doubtless address important values and needs in human relationships and dealings. But how should they evolve properly to meet the business and professional circumstances in which we now find ourselves? This question is most problematic for fiduciary law though not necessarily for reasons internal to itself. Its odyssey from the early nineteenth century (its formative period) to today gives some reason for pause on this score. The advent *en masse* of the limited liability company with its various sizes and hues produced the first major disruption in fiduciary law's measured progress and it called into question its simple conceptions and its adaptive capacity. Pragmatism more so than principle ordained by whom and to whom fiduciary duties were owed in the internal arrangements of companies—with the resultant exclusion of the director–shareholder relationship from the fiduciary regime[93] now appearing the more anomalous as we flirt with a fiduciary relationship between directors of marginally solvent companies and corporate creditors. Equally, if fiduciary duties could work tolerably well in regulating dealings between a director and his company—though even here fine, often unconvincing, distinctions had to be drawn[94]—they have proved unequal to the task of determining when and why a director should be accountable to his company for pursuing a profit-making opportunity on his own account. As a result, we seem to be in the process of evolving a 'line of business' test which artificially sterilizes a sphere of activity from the private concerns of directors.[95] The areas of uncertainty or of contrivance can be multiplied— the limits fiduciary law sets to legitimate defensive tactics in take-overs; the countenancing of directorships of competing companies; etc. The message in all of this, though, is a simple one. If the courts regularly enough reiterate the uncompromising standards fiduciary law imposes in the corporate context,

---

[92] The strict settlement stands as an obvious exception to this.

[93] Except in exceptional circumstances: see e.g. *Coleman v. Myers* [1977] 2 NZLR 225.

[94] See e.g. *Burland v. Earle* [1902] AC 83, *P. & O. Steam Navigation Co. Ltd v. Johnson* (1937–38) 60 CLR 189.

[95] For a discussion see R. P. Austin, 'Fiduciary Accountability for Business Opportunities' in Finn (ed.), *Equity and Commercial Relationships*, above, n. 49.

they have none the less tempered significantly, or else artificially contrived, the scope they have been prepared to give those standards—apparently so as to accommodate and balance the often conflicting demands and interests of companies, of those implicated in a company's affairs, and, I venture to suggest, of public interests.

Companies forced at least the recognition that fiduciary dogma is not an altogether immutable thing—even if the metamorphoses that companies compelled are not always explicitly acknowledged or susceptible to a principled justification. That a metamorphosis occurred is, though, the matter of note as we now grapple with the impact to be given fiduciary law on modern business structures and practices. And the contemporary problem here is not with the bare question of whether particular business or firm–client relationships are fiduciary: orthodox principles, ordinarily, can resolve that issue. It is with the regulatory effect a fiduciary finding is to have on the actions and practices of a business both within and beyond the particular relationship in question. Impulses from two separate sources—one essentially factual, the other essentially legal—have exaggerated the fiduciary problem.

The factual matters are themselves products of the multi-function business and large firm phenomenon. I simply note three of the more significant. First, size and diversification have magnified client proliferation with the point commonly being reached where service enterprises, wittingly or unwittingly, are servicing simultaneously or serially clients who themselves have potentially adverse or conflicting interests. Secondly, diversification coupled with electronic data storage has made enterprises significant repositories of information both about clients and of relevance to client services. As will be seen, the law as it now stands imposes conflicting obligations on such bodies in respect of the uses they are or are not to make of information in their hands—and this, primarily, to protect clients' interests. Thirdly, administrative arrangements and work practices can either induce or inhibit both the *de facto* fragmentation of enterprises into their various service functions and the isolation of personnel on function lines.

More troubling, though, than even the factual matters noted, are a number of currently, if uncritically, accepted legal propositions which compound the fiduciary problem. I note the more important of these.

1. A company is one person in law no matter how many and dispersed its various departments and branches.[96] Conversely, related companies, though administratively integrated, are separate legal persons.[97]

2. Unless a partnership relationship is terminated *ad hoc* for the particular matter, a person who engages the services of a partner engages the services of

[96] See e.g. *Harrods Ltd.* v. *Lemon* [1931] 2 KB 157; *Comeau* v. *Canada Permanent Trust Co.* (1980) 27 NBR (2d) 126; *Standard Investments Ltd.* v. *Canadian Imperial Bank of Commerce* (1985) 22 DLR (4th) 410.

[97] See e.g. *Bank of Tokyo Ltd.* v. *Karoon* [1987] AC 45; and see also 'Commercial Law' Note(1991) 65 Aust. LJ 352.

the partnership and not merely of the person who actually renders the service.[98]

3. Client information imparted to, or acquired by, a company or firm in confidence for a particular purpose, cannot, without lawful authority or excuse, be used for any other purpose without the client's consent.

4. A person engaged to provide advice is obliged to 'put at his client's disposal not only his skill but also his knowledge, so far as is relevant; and if he is unwilling to reveal his knowledge to his client, he should not act for him. What he cannot do is to act for the client and at the same time withhold from him any relevant knowledge that he has.'[99]

5. A person in a fiduciary position can only act lawfully in a way which otherwise would constitute a breach of fiduciary duty, if he has the informed consent of his client to his so acting. Furthermore, in the words of Lord Thankerton:

[w]hen a party, holding a fiduciary relationship, commits a breach of his duty by non-disclosure of material facts, which his constituent is entitled to know in connection with the transaction, he cannot be heard to maintain that disclosure would not have altered the decision to proceed with the transaction, because the constituent's action would be solely determined by some other factor, such as the valuation by the other party of the property proposed to be mortgaged. Once the court has determined that the non-disclosed facts were material, speculation as to what course the constituent, on disclosure, would have taken is not relevant.[100]

Each of these propositions, if applied strictly, is capable of producing quite anomalous results.

Fiduciary law, as is well known, is intolerant of undisclosed conflicts of interest or of duty. Yet one or more of four types of conflict are a constant hazard for most large enterprises rendering 'fiduciary' services, and are an endemic problem for some. It is in relation to these four types of conflict that the appropriate adaptation question arises most sharply. Before considering each individually, the four should be noted briefly.

1. *Same-matter conflicts*, i.e. where two parts of a company or two members of a firm act in the same matter for separate parties having adverse interests in that matter. Though the factual problem which arises here commonly results from conflicts between and disparities in information possessed in the separate representations, the legal issue centres first and foremost on the nature of the obligation of loyalty owed to each of the separate clients.

2. *Former-client conflict*, i.e. where a firm or company, having acted for a client in a particular matter, subsequently acts against that client in the same or in a related matter. Much the most commonly litigated instance of this

---

[98] *McNaughton* v. *Tauranga County Council* (No.2) (1987) 12 NZTPA 429; *Davey* v. *Wooley, Hames, Dale & Dingwall* (1983) 133 DLR (3d) 649; *D. & J. Constructions Pty. Ltd.* v. *Head* (1987) 9 NSWLR 118, at 122–3.

[99] *Spector* v. *Ageda* [1973] Ch. 30, at 48 *per* Megarry, J.

[100] *Brickenden* v. *London Loan & Savings Co.* [1934] 3 DLR 465, at 469.

relates to law firms—bodies not of immediate concern to the purposes of this volume. The critical issue in this type of conflict is the protection of the former client from the possibility of information abuse.

3. *Separate-matter conflicts*, i.e. where a company or firm, having dealt with a client in one matter, obtains information which is relevant to another matter in which it later acts for another client. Here the issues are hydra-headed and can range from secrecy protection through guarding against defective advice to fraud prevention.

4. *'Fair-dealing' conflicts*, i.e. where a company or firm, which both itself trades in, and acts in an agency capacity for the purchase or sale of, a particular commodity, discharges its agency function in a particular matter by itself buying from or selling to its client-principal. Given fiduciary law's inveterate objection to self-dealing, the issue here—if it is to be an issue at all —is whether the self-dealing rule has been applied too uncritically to agents who act in a purely ministerial fashion in effecting the purchase or sale instructions of a principal.[101]

It needs to be acknowledged that reported case law in Commonwealth jurisdictions on the first three of the above conflicts relates primarily—but by no means exclusively—to legal advisers. That a lawyer is the defendant, especially where the matter in question can affect the administration of justice, does undoubtedly have a significant effect upon the courts' application of fiduciary rules to conflicts involving lawyers. This, as will be seen, can be particularly so in cases of former client conflict. It equally needs to be emphasized, however, that *for the purposes of the fiduciary rules* themselves lawyers do not attract any different or additional responsibilities to those applied to fiduciaries generally.[102] For this reason lawyer–client cases will be used in the following analysis though reference will be made, where appropriate, to the possible effect the status of the defendant might or does have on the manner of application of fiduciary rules.

3.1. SAME-MATTER CONFLICTS

These are in the very heartland of fiduciary law, though English law in contrast with some Commonwealth jurisdictions (particularly Canada and New Zealand) has been slow to appreciate the full significance of this. The agent or adviser acting for two parties with adverse interests in the same matter not only owes each party those common law duties of care, skill, and the like appropriate to the function assumed, he also owes each a duty of loyalty. We are only now beginning to appreciate how much the latter can overshadow the former in importance.

[101] Cf *R. H. Deacon & Co. Ltd.* v. *Varga* (1972) 30 DLR (3d) 653; affd. (1973) 41 DLR (3d) 767; *Glennie* v. *McDougall & Cowans Holdings Ltd.* [1935] 2 DLR 561 at 579—though neither is a self-dealing case, the decision in the former and observations in the latter allow for the fiduciary relationship in agencies to be manipulated by the precise function undertaken.

[102] English case law has on occasion used the 'Officer of the court' notion to enhance lawyer–client obligations: see e.g. *Re a Firm of Solicitors* [1992] 1 All ER 353.

Loyalty's effect is twofold. First, if the fiduciary is being remunerated by either or both of the parties, the 'conflict of duty interest' theme in the fiduciary's obligation requires him to disclose to each client that he is being remunerated by the other.[103] Secondly, much more importantly, until each client agrees to the contrary, or unless there is a legally acknowledged custom to the contrary,[104] each client is entitled to, and is entitled to assume that he has, the undivided loyalty of the fiduciary he has engaged. The rule here is simple and inexorable: 'Fully informed consent apart, an agent cannot lawfully place himself in a position in which he owes a duty to another which is inconsistent with his duty to his principal.'[105]

The law's object here is twofold: (*a*) to preserve the expectation the client is entitled to have that it is his interests alone that the fiduciary is safeguarding; and (*b*) to preclude the fiduciary from putting himself in a position 'where he may be required to choose between conflicting duties, or be led to an attempt to reconcile conflicting interests'.[106] Fully informed consent alone can produce compliance with this rule. But the disclosure this can entail to secure such a consent is the critical matter.

It now is clear, though the contrary is commonly assumed, that the disclosure is *not* limited simply to the fact of the double employment as such.[107] The purpose of the disclosure is to appraise each client in turn as to the extent to which the fiduciary's exertions on his behalf will or may be qualified or compromised, so that each client in turn can then determine whether, in view of the adverse and possibly qualified representation, he should permit the fiduciary to continue to act in the matter. This can require, in effect, a projection into the future to anticipate possible future conflicts. But the disclosure requirement does not end at this point even if, at this stage, both clients agree to the dual representation (whether or not qualified for one or other of them for some purposes). Given this body of law's intent to ensure that the fiduciary will in fact continue to act in the several interests of each client within the scope of their respective engagements, it further requires that if an actual conflict later arises within the scope of the double engagement[108] all material facts bearing on that conflict must then be disclosed. Though such a conflict can arise in many ways, it is commonly occasioned by the acquisition in one relationship of confidential client

---

[103] See e.g. *Fullwood* v. *Hurley* [1928] 1 KB 498, at 502.

[104] Cf *Jones* v. *Canavan* [1972] 2 NSWLR 236.

[105] *North and South Trust Co.* v. *Berkeley* [1971] 1 WLR 470, at 484–5.

[106] *Anderson* v. *Eaton* 293 P. 788, at 790 (1930).

[107] See e.g. *Farrington* v. *Rowe, McBride & Partners* [1985] 1 NZLR 83, *Mid-Northern Fertilizers Ltd.* v. *Connel, Lamb, Gerard & Co.*, HC of NZ, 18 Sept. 1986, Thorp, J.—an influential but still unreported decision; *In re Kamp* 194 A. 2d 236, at 240; see also 'Developments: Conflict of Interest in the Legal Profession'(1981) 94 Harv. LR 1244, at 1303 et seq; *Haywood* v. *Roadknight* [1927] VLR 512.

[108] It should here be noted that a qualified retainer may exclude from the scope of the engagement a matter which would give rise to an actual conflict but for that qualified representation.

information which, if made available to the other party, could possibly affect that other's consent to the fiduciary's continuing either to act in the matter or to act in the manner proposed.[109] Here is the well-known no-win situation. If the fiduciary discloses that information he will be liable to one party for breach of confidence; if he does not, he will be liable to the other for breach of fiduciary duty.[110] It needs to be emphasized that this latter liability is for breach of fiduciary duty arising from non-disclosure[111] notwithstanding that the same default may coincidentally give rise also to possible liability in negligence.[112]

Three comments should here be made of fiduciary law's significance and effects in this arena.

1. Though it allows a fiduciary, through disclosure and consent, to immunize himself from liability, the law will not compel him to make a disclosure to one party thereby breaching his duty to the other.[113]

2. At least in the case of the fiduciary-adviser, the effect of the disclosure requirement falls little short of making any breach of his duties as an adviser itself a breach of fiduciary duty. New Zealand and Canadian case law emphatically illustrate this.[114]

3. While English law has been slow to develop the potential of *Nocton* v. *Ashburton's*[115] imprimatur on damages claims for loss resulting from breach of fiduciary duty,[116] the contrary is very much the case in other Commonwealth countries. Two clear reasons for this, at least in this context, are, first, that fiduciary law throws the onus on the adviser of proving that a full disclosure has been made; and secondly, if the views of Lord Thankerton on the consequences of non-disclosure (quoted earlier) are given full effect, that damages may be recoverable on a fiduciary basis where, for reasons of

---

[109] See e.g. *Day* v. *Mead* [1987] 2 NZLR 443; *Standard Investments Ltd.* v *Canadian Imperial Bank of Commerce* (1985) 22 DLR (4th) 410; *Moody* v. *Cox & Hatt* [1917] 2 Ch. 71; though they are not same-matter conflicts, see also the Canadian decisions of *Jacks* v. *Davis* (1982) 141 DLR (3d) 355; affirming [1980] 6 WWR 11 and *Canson Enterprises Ltd.* v. *Boughton & Co.* (1992) 85 D. L. R. (4th) 129.

[110] See e.g. *Moody* v. *Cox & Hatt*, above.

[111] See *Brickenden* v. *London Loan & Savings Co.* [1934] 3 DLR 465 (J.C. of P.C.); *Day* v. *Mead* above; *Farrington* v. *Rowe, McBride & Partners* [1985] 1 NZLR83.

[112] It is the negligence liability that seems to be assumed in such English cases as *North & South Trust Co.* v. *Berkeley* [1971] 1 WLR 470 and *Neushul* v. *Mellish & Harkavy* (1966) 111 Sol. Jo. 399. On dual liability see *Mid-Northern Fertilizers Ltd.* v. *Connel, Lamb, Gerard & Co.*, HC of NZ, 18 Sept. 1986, Thorp, J.; see also *Caliguire* v. *De Lucia* (1983) 25 Man. R. (2d) 98; *How* v. *Carman* [1931] SASR 413.

[113] See *North & South Trust Co.* v. *Berkeley* [1971] 1 WLR 470.

[114] See e.g. *Day* v. *Mead* [1987] 2 NZLR 443; *Farrington* v. *Rowe, McBride & Partners* [1985] 1 NZLR 83; *Mid-Northern Fertilisers Ltd.* v. *Connel, Lamb, Gerard & Co.*, supra; *Brickenden* v. *London Loan & Savings Co.* [1934] 3 DLR 465; *Standard Investments Ltd* v. *Canadian Imperial Bank of Commerce* (1985) 22 DLR (4th) 410; see also 'Good Faith and Nondisclosure,' in Finn (ed.), *Essays on Torts*, above, n. 88, 169–70.

[115] [1914] AC 932.

[116] On which see the Hon. Mr Justice Gummow, 'Compensation for Breach of Fiduciary Duty', in Youdan (ed.), *Equity, Fiduciaries and Trusts*, above, n. 1.

causation, etc., they may not be so recoverable in a negligence action.[117]

Translating all of this to the multi-function business and the large partnership, one finds that size itself brings new hazards. Most obviously, a business may itself be unaware that it is, in fact, acting for adverse interests in the same matter.[118] But if this be thought to be a mitigating factor,[119] the courts for their part have seen ignorance to be a vice not a virtue, with liability in some form well-nigh inevitable.[120] This does, none the less, throw up the appropriate adaptation issue in an acute form. If an enterprise is, in fact, able to achieve a *de facto* segregation, the one from the other, of the representatives involved in the separate representations—be this through 'Chinese Walls', physical/geographic separation, etc.—could it not be said that even without informed consent the spirit of fiduciary law's rule has been satisfied: separate representation, in fact, has been secured for each client even if the segregated parts may well have to deal with each other in an adversarial way?

Whatever virtue segregation may be found to have in the context of other types of conflict, it is highly improbable, I would suggest, that it will be held to be an effective alternative to full disclosure here and for three reasons. First, the legal vice in these conflicts is not the possibility of information use and abuse as such. It is the compromising of a fiduciary's duty of loyalty. Whatever efficacy 'Walls' etc. might have as information protection devices, segregation is not a loyalty-engendering contrivance:[121] it simply does not address the vice that inheres in concurrent adverse representation. A client is entitled to assume that the business or firm he has engaged as a fiduciary is representing his interests alone in the matter in question—an assumption that the business or firm should not be allowed to falsify in its own business interests by its own unilateral action. There is, I would suggest, an important public policy consideration which is operative here. If public confidence is to be maintained in the integrity of businesses rendering 'fiduciary services', such businesses must act openly with a client public whose reliance they invite.[122]

---

[117] For a dramatic, but in the writer's view questionable, illustration, see *Mid-Northern Fertilisers Ltd.* v. *Connel, Lamb, Gerard & Co.*, HC of NZ, 18 Sept. 1986, Thorp, J. For a more detailed consideration see 'Good Faith and Nondisclosure', in Finn (ed.), *Essays on Torts*, above, n. 88, 166 ff. The principles governing damages awards are a matter of real contention in Canadian law: see e.g. *Canson Enterprises Ltd.* v. *Boughton & Co.* (1992) 85 D. L. R. (4th) 129.

[118] See e.g. *Harrods Ltd.* v. *Lemon* [1931] 2 KB 157; *Comeau* v. *Canada Permanent Trust Co.* (1980) 27 NBR (2d) 126; *Standard Investments Ltd.* v. *Canadian Imperial Bank of Commerce* (1985) 22 DLR (4th) 410.

[119] i.e. because the enterprise, being unaware of the dual representation, cannot (through its agents in each engagement) be said to be in any position to be tempted to favour the interests of one or other of the clients.

[120] See the three cases cited in n. 118 above.

[121] A matter often acknowledged in US literature particularly in the law firm disqualification context: see e.g. 'The Chinese Wall Defense to Law Firm Disqualification' (1980) 128 U.Penn. LR 677; 'Developments: Conflicts of Interest in the Legal Profession'(1981) 94 Harv LR 1244.

[122] Cf the 'shingle theory' adopted by the S.E.C. in the US: see N. S. Poser, 'Conflicts of Interest within Securities Firms,' (1990) 16 Brooklyn J. Int. L. 111, at 116–17.

Secondly, and technically, segregation does not counter the legal consequences of engaging a company or firm: in either case it, and not merely its
separate agents or departments, assumes legal responsibility to the client for
the service provided. Thirdly, segregation does not overcome the potentially
compromising impact of a company's or firm's own institutional interest in
retaining both clients and of carrying the matter to its completion.[123]

In the end, then, I am suggesting that we are unlikely to see any significant
attempt here on the part of the courts to adapt the burden of fiduciary law so
as to alleviate in any way the problems that size and diversification can create
for businesses. The requirement of disclosure and consent will, I venture,
reign supreme. In consequence the law will make a practical necessity of the
development of client information systems designed to reveal possible client
conflicts.

3.2. FORMER-CLIENT CONFLICTS

It is commonplace for a firm or business to acquire confidential information
in one client relationship which is or could be relevant to a service rendered in
another. The legal issues this phenomenon can raise are considered generally
in Section 3.3. Within that phenomenon, though, is quite a distinctive class
of case which, for legal and practical purposes, has attracted a special
attention in its own right. It is where a fiduciary (usually advisory) service is
rendered to client A, and then the same firm or business undertakes to render
an adverse fiduciary service to client B in the same or in a significantly related
matter. The paradigm case—now evidenced in a burgeoning case law in
Commonwealth countries—is that of the law firm, and particularly of the
now inelegantly described 'mega-firm',[124] assuming so to act. Though not
simply a problem for law firms,[125] its present close association in the law with
the practice of law (a subject not of particular relevance to this volume)
warrants only a brief sketch of the issues inherent in this type of conflict.

The practical context in which such a conflict is ordinarily raised is in
proceedings by the first client to restrain the fiduciary's continuing to act in
the second-client relationship because of an apprehended misuse of first-
client information. At the heart of the matter is the question of what steps the
law should take, what steps a firm or business should be obliged to take, to
protect the confidences of the first client. But the matter is not seen simply in
orthodox breach of confidence terms, because it is coloured by the fiduciary
character of the first-client relationship in virtue of which the information
was obtained.[126] Issues of public interest and public policy which bear on the

---

[123] For an unusual business consultancy context in which the efficacy of 'Walls' was doubted,
see *McNaughton* v. *Tauranga County Council (No. 2)* (1987) 12 NZ.T.P.A. 429.

[124] See e.g. *MacDonald Estate* v. *Martin* [1991] 1 WWR 705, at 725 (S.C. of Can.).

[125] It is potentially one for any agency providing particularly advisory fiduciary services.

[126] So much is this so in contemporary Australian law that the issue of possible misuse in the
second-client relationship is tested on 'conflict of duty and interest' grounds: see e.g. *National
Mutual Holdings Pty. Ltd.* v. *Sentry Corp.* (1989) 87 A.L.R. 589; *Mallesons Stephen Jaques* v.
KPMG Peat Marwick, 19 Oct. 1990, SC of WA, Ipp J.

importance to be attributed to maintaining public confidence in the integrity of the particular type of first-client relationship in question, have a heavy impact on the protective stance to be taken. In the context of law firms, for example, the twin needs of creating a lawyer–client environment in which uninhibited communication can be fostered by assured information security, and of maintaining public confidence in the legal system itself, have been made paramount to the interest of 'second clients' in being able to engage the lawyer of their choice. The general inference to be drawn from this—and it is one of importance to other professions and businesses—is that public policy is likely to have a variable impact on the treatment given this type of conflict on an industry by industry basis. What holds for a law firm might not hold (at least to the same extent or with the same severity) for accountants.

Public policy apart, there are three issues of legal principle which attend this type of conflict. Not all have been addressed adequately in the case law, and each has produced inconsistent responses. Here I will simply note these issues and will consider only one in any detail—because of its relevance to large firms and to the role, if any, to be given Chinese Walls in 'former-client' cases. The issues can be put briefly.

1. If the first-client relationship is one in which confidential information is characteriztically imparted, and is one in which, given the nature of the particular matter in question, it is likely in fact to have been imparted, to what extent should the first client be obliged to identify and particularize that information in proceedings to restrain the fiduciary's acting in the second-client relationship? Consistent with the protective policy underlying confidentiality, should the court, in effect, presume that confidences have been given?[127]

2. If the fiduciary is a partnership—and particularly a large partnership—is the confidential information obtained (or presumed to have been obtained) in the first relationship to be imputed to all members of the firm, and if so, rebuttably or irrebuttably? This is a matter of some moment if different partners are involved in the two relationships.[128]

3. By what standard should an apprehended misuse be judged? Here there can be found a spectrum of possibilities. The prevailing trend in the law firm cases favours a test based on what a reasonable man, informed of the facts, would apprehend in the circumstances.[129]

[127] Cf *Mills* v. *Day Dawn Block Gold, Mining Co. Ltd.* (1881) 1 QLJR 62; *T.C. & Theatre Corp.* v. *Warner Bros. Pictures* 113 F. Supp. 265 (1953).

[128] This question sharply divided the Supreme Court of Canada in *MacDonald Estate* v. *Martin* [1991] 1 WWR 705; see also *Mallesons Stephen Jaques* v. *KPMG Peat Marwick*, supra. Imputation is generally accepted in US law-firm cases but there is considerable controversy as to whether or not this presumption should be rebuttable: see e.g. F. W. Hammersmith, 'In Defense of a Double Standard, Etc'(1986) *20 Journal of Law Reform* 245; 'The Chinese Wall Defense to Law-Firm Disqualification' (1980) 128 U.Penn. LR 677.

[129] See e.g. *In re a Firm of Solicitors* [1992] 1 All ER 353; *MacDonald Estate* v. *Martin*, supra; see also *Mallesons Stephen Jaques* v. *KPMG Peat Marwick*, 19 Oct. 1990, SC cf WA, Ipp, J.; *National Mutual Holdings Pty. Ltd.* v. *Sentry Corp.* (1989) 87 A.L.R. 539; cf. *D. & J. Constructions Pty. Ltd.* v. *Head* (1987) 9 NSWLR 118.

The second of these—imputation—warrants comment. Anglo-Australian law, for the most part, has not addressed this issue directly, the courts ordinarily treating the possibility of communication of client information between partners in terms of record-keeping practices,[130] probable contact or discussion between partners, adventitious exchanges, etc. None the less there is a basic question of principle here arising out of the legal consequences to be attributed to a client's engaging a firm. The orthodoxy is that, special agreement apart, a person who engages the services of a partner engages the services of the partnership and not merely of the person who actually renders the service. The client's disclosure is to the partnership and the consequential duty of secrecy is owed by the partnership. Furthermore, as indicated later in this chapter, it is probably the case that each partner has a prima-facie right of access to information in the hands of the firm.[131] If this suggests that, as a matter of principle, the knowledge of one partner should be assumed to be the knowledge of all, that conclusion is one a bare majority of the Supreme Court of Canada was unprepared to draw in the recent decision, *Macdonald Estate* v. *Martin*,[132] primarily for the reasons (*a*) that it involves 'an assumption which is unrealistic in the era of the mega-firm',[133] and (*b*) that it would have a 'transfer' effect as partners changed firms or as firms amalgamated.[134] But whether or not imputation is to be accepted as the correct principle of law—and the Supreme Court in lieu of it adopted a rebuttable inference of 'shared confidences' —the vital question remains when, if at all, it should be allowed to a partnership to show that those rendering the second-client service have been and will continue to be effectively insulated from the first-client information *and* should be permitted to act in the second relationship. Both the Supreme Court and the English Court of Appeal[135] have not gone so far as to say that in no circumstances will the use of Walls be capable of having this effect and to that extent can be taken as holding that any imputation (or possibility of shared confidences) principle is rebuttable. None the less, in the law firm context, they have signalled that Walls will be viewed with little sympathy (save in truly exceptional cases).[136] That lack of sympathy, if reflecting an evident scepticism about the efficacy of Walls themselves, seems also to be informed in some measure by the public policy implications of allowing a Wall defence to law firms, even if the Wall itself could be shown to be effective. But by not totally discountenancing Walls in 'former-client' cases, they have left open a

---

[130] Cf *Fruehauf Finance Corp. Pty. Ltd.* v. *Feez Ruthning*, [1991] 1 Qd. R. 558.

[131] A right which is ordinarily curtailed for practical purposes by internal procedures.

[132] [1991] 1 WWR 705.

[133] Ibid., 725.

[134] But on amalgamation see *National Mutual Holdings Pty. Ltd.* v. *Sentry Corp.* (1989) 87 A.L.R. 539.

[135] In *Re a Firm of Solicitors* [1992] 1 All ER 353.

[136] A similar lack of sympathy is evident in contemporary Australian and NZ case law: see *Mallesons Stephen Jaques* v. *KPMG Peat Marwick*, SC of WA, 19 Oct. 1990, Ipp J.; *D. & J. Constructions Pty. Ltd.* v. *Head* (1987) 9 NSWLR 118; and see the NZ cases referred to in M. Dean and C. Finlayson, 'Conflicts of Interest' [1990] NZ Law Jo. 43.

corridor of opportunity for their use (and possibly more readily countenanced use) in other industries.

3.3. SEPARATE-MATTER CONFLICTS

Of all types of conflict these are potentially the most problematic, particularly for the diversified enterprise. They are a by-product of the law of secrecy. And they are conflicts in which the hazard of liability is compounded by uncertainty or artificiality in the law. Their factual context is simple enough. A service enterprise (E) acquires confidential information from or about a client (A) in the course of a dealing with A. E later deals with another client (B) in a matter quite distinct from the dealing with A, but in which that information is of relevance either to E or to B. And the problem? When, if at all, can E use that information for its own or B's benefit? When can A complain of its use or disclosure? When can B complain if it is not disclosed to B? Simply to aid exposition I will divide this type of conflict into two classes: the first where E assumes a fiduciary or advisory responsibility to B in the later dealing (e.g. as agent, adviser, or trustee); the second where E acts as a principal in that dealing (e.g. as a lender or as a creditor obtaining a guarantee).

3.3.1. *Acting as a Fiduciary or Adviser*

The simple example of the issue is that of a financial services business which, having acquired confidential information from one client (whether adverse or not), assumes to advise another client in a matter in which that information is material. The one legal proposition at least which is clear here is that, in the absence of the consent of the first client, any unauthorized use or disclosure of the information[137] by the adviser will be actionable[138] and will expose the adviser to the full range of equitable remedy—as it could also the second client if it knows or has reason to know that the information is being misused for its benefit. As in the case of 'former-client' conflicts the temptation to make such a misuse may prove to be irresistible or simply unavoidable. But equally, and quite fortuitously, the adviser may act in a way in its dealings with the second client which creates the appearance that the information has been misused, though such has not in fact occurred. Whatever may be found to be the desirable policy choice to be made legislatively (for example, in insider trading legislation), it is probable that, in so far as the former client is concerned, it will only be able to restrain the adviser where a misuse of its information is feared, or when, in the circumstances, there are reasonable grounds for that apprehension. It is, I suggest, unlikely that the courts here will be prepared to take as protective a stance for the first client as they now are taking in 'former-client' cases (itself a recent development in Common-

---

[137] Cf *American Medicorp Inc.* v. *Continental Illinois National Bank and Trust Co. of Chicago* 475 F. Supp. 5 (1977).

[138] Unless it falls within one of secrecy law's narrow exceptions—an unlikely contingency in most cases in this context.

wealth jurisdictions)—at least where the first-client relationship is not a fiduciary one, for example, banker–customer.

Doubtless the large practical and social concern relates to misuse and to the steps that should appropriately be taken, both by businesses themselves and through legislative and other prescriptions and proscriptions, to reassure the public of the integrity of our commercial institutions. Surprisingly, though, the significant and existing *legal* problem arises where the adviser respects its secrecy obligation. Here the great matters of contention are the potential liabilities to the second client that can flow from non-use or non-disclosure of relevant first-client confidential information. Though attention here will be given to this dimension of 'separate-matter' conflicts', some of the matters to be considered are also of significance to misuse.

As Anglo-Australian law now stands (the position may well be different in Canada and in the United States),[139] non-use and non-disclosure are not here seen as involving any question of fiduciary law:[140] liability, if it arises, is perceived—correctly in my view—to flow simply from some dereliction of duty as agent, trustee, adviser, etc. In consequence exposure will only be to a possible liability for loss in negligence, breach of contract, etc.

A simple, but often unacceptable, response occasionally made to the question of second-client liability, is that the business's possession of another's confidential information is in a sense adventitious, and as it is duty-bound not to reveal it, it should advise the second client on the basis of information it possesses *other than* that of the former client.[141] But this obviously will be objectionable where the confidential information falsifies the information it otherwise possesses. As the United States decision *Black* v. *Shearson, Hammill & Co.*[142] illustrates, to allow an adviser so to advise can be to allow it to perpetrate a fraud upon the second client.

Fraud liability, then, is one hazard. The *Spector* v. *Ageda*, negligence liability is another: an adviser cannot justify a failure to make relevant information available to a client because that information is subject to a duty of secrecy to a third party. And for trustees there is a third: if they have funds invested in a company, and then learn in confidence from it or from a third party that it is destined for insolvency, it may well be the case that if the shares are not sold and later become valueless, they will be liable to the beneficiaries for that loss[143]—save where a sale would be illegal under insider trading legislation.[144]

---

[139] See e.g. *Jacks* v. *Davis* (1982) 141 DLR (3d) 355; *Canson Enterprises Ltd.* v. *Boughton & Co.* (1992) 85 D. L. R. (4th) 129, and see Poser, 'Conflicts of Interest within Securities Firms,' above n. 122, esp. at 116 ff.

[140] We have not as yet, in this 'second-client' context, brought duties of confidence into the fiduciary regime as to make the conflict merely of a duty of secrecy owed one party and a fiduciary duty the other, a 'conflict of duties' for the purposes of fiduciary law.

[141] Cf *Kabwand Pty. Ltd.* v. *National Australia Bank Ltd.* (1989) ATPR 40–950.

[142] 72 Cal. Rptr. 157 (1968).

[143] See generally Jacobs, *Law of Trusts in Australia*, 5th edn. (Butterworths, Sydney, 1986), ss. 2201 ff..

[144] Cf *Investors Management Co. Inc.* (1970–1) C.C.H Fed. Sec. LR 80, 514 at 80, 522 (US).

These possibilities might be difficult enough when applied to the sole practitioner and the small business. Applied to large and particularly to diversified, geographically dispersed businesses, they pose formidable problems, primarily because of information disaggregation. Though such a business might in fact be possessed of relevant but confidential information, because of the activities of one of its departments or branches, another department or branch may, and may reasonably, remain or be kept ignorant of that information notwithstanding its relevance to a matter in hand in that department: the loans department may know, the trusts or investment advice department may not.

The two, necessarily related, defensive lines being taken today by businesses are aimed (whether openly acknowledged or not) at securing an adaptation of the law to meet the circumstances in which businesses now find themselves. The one, through devices such as 'Chinese Walls', aims to contrive a state of ignorance of relevant confidential information in the person or persons who actually render the second-client service on the business's behalf. The other is to challenge the apparently unlimited character of the *Spector* v. *Ageda* obligation of advisers.

Among the virtues attributed to diversified service enterprises and partnerships is their capacity to aggregate information, skill, and experience better to render more efficient and effective client services. And if commerce, governments, and the economy have been the beneficiaries of that capacity, it is, none the less, built upon a fissure which, if opened, has the capacity, at least in law, to falsify the claim made. That fissure is the law of secrecy.

Little attention has been given in our respective jurisprudences outside the public sector to the impact of secrecy obligations owed to third parties on the internal operations of bodies subject to such obligations.[145] The issues raised here can, for the most part, only be considered in the light of general principle.[146] Their importance, though, warrants a brief excursus into secrecy law.

3.3.1.1 Secrecy and the Internal Operations of a Business: An Excursus. Our concern is *not* with the confidential information created by or for a business or partnership, but with such information supplied by, or acquired about, a third party in the course of rendering a service to that party. The following propositions would, as a matter of principle, seem to be applicable to the use and handling of that information by the business-recipient. They are, in the main, analogues of those that hold in the public sector.

---

[145] On the public sector see e.g. R. *v Birmingham City District Council, ex parte 0.* [1983] 1 AC 578; *Slater* v. *Bisset* (1986) 69 ACTR 25; *Molomby* v. *Whitehead* (1985) 63 A.L.R. 282; *Bennets* v. *Board of Fire Commissioners of NSW* (1967) 87 W.N. (N.S.W.) (Pt.1) 307; *Smith Kline & French Laboratories (Australia) Ltd.* v. *Secretary, Dept. of Community Services and Health* (1990) 89 A.L.R. 87; aff'd. (1991) 99 A.L.R. 679; *Smith Kline & French Laboratories Ltd.* v. *Attorney-General* [1989] 1 NZLR 385; *Re Smith Kline & French Laboratories Ltd.* [1989] 2 WLR 397.

[146] United States authority is of virtually no assistance in the matter given secrecy law's different course in that country.

1. Confidential information obtained in and for the purpose of rendering a particular client-service can lawfully be used only for the purposes of that service unless the client consents to the contrary. The primary difficulty involved in this lies in determining what of the information so acquired will be subjected to secrecy's protection—a difficulty acknowledged in the influential judgment of the Court of Appeal in *Tournier* v. *National Provincial and Union Bank of England*.[147] That information can vary from merely the identity of the information supplier to some or all of the substance of what is supplied.

2. In so far as the supplier is concerned it must be taken as authorizing the dissemination within the recipient institution of the information supplied (*a*) to the extent necessary to perform the service for which the information is supplied; and (*b*) to the extent required by the ordinary record keeping procedures utilized by the business engaged.[148]

3. In so far as the officers and employees of that enterprise are concerned, their rights of access to, and rights to authorize the dissemination of, client information so protected would seem to be governed by the following principles:

(*a*) the directors/principals of the business have a prima-facie right of access to the information but have no right to use it, or to authorize its dissemination within the business, beyond what is necessary to render the service;

(*b*) employee access to the information is governed by the 'need to know' principle, but that principle itself can only allow access which is consistent with the duty of secrecy—in other words the 'need to know' principle does not authorize access, or justify access being given, simply because it would facilitate an employee's performance of a service to a third party in which that information is relevant or material.

It would be an affectation of innocence to suggest that the above propositions are honoured in the internal operations of businesses and partnerships. But if they reflect the probable effect of the legal obligation of the business-recipient, not only is its capacity freely to disseminate information within the business seriously compromised, it is, in effect, obliged to segregate—to 'wall' if you like—client information for functional purposes. Secrecy law simply undercuts in some measure the lawful capacity for information aggregation in ways that make that information generally accessible. It involves within itself a walling requirement. To this extent at least the argument for Chinese Walls accords with at least one dimension of a service-business's legal obligations.

To return now to our main theme, the problem for business is that its client responsibilities have two dimensions, not merely one. Secrecy law—

---

[147] [1924] 1 KB 461.
[148] On this last see *Slater* v. *Bissett* (1986) 69 ACTR 25.

and its inherent 'walling' requirement—delineates a business's responsibility to an information supplier. But then there is its responsibility to third-party clients. It is that responsibility which creates the Gordian knot. The argument for Chinese Walls and for a qualification to the *Spector* v. *Ageda* obligation seeks to cut the knot one way—by giving primacy to a prior secrecy obligation over any later third-party responsibility. This particular resolution can have potentially unattractive consequences for third parties. And it is not the only possible approach. An alternative solution—to alter the protection given by secrecy law—may have some justifications in social utility in some circumstances. But it could have direct consequences both for the supply of information to business and for the preparedness to utilize business services. Then there is the Glass–Steagall type of solution: the legally required segregation of functions. While unacceptable to business, and probably damaging to the effective operations of some industries, it does highlight the primary cause of the legal problem under consideration: that a variety of services are being performed by emanations of the one legal person (or partnership). The *Glass–Steagall* solution does, however, point up the path to the possible resolution of the *legal* difficulties involved in 'separate-matter' conflicts and that is in the need to reappraise our jurisprudence on the consequences of legal personality.

In the same way that we increasingly are being forced to acknowledge the artificiality of treating related companies as separate legal persons for all purposes,[149] so also may it not be the case that it can be similarly artificial to treat the company—and especially the large and diversified company—as a single, monolithic legal person for all purposes and in all circumstances? If it has, and can convincingly demonstrate that it has, segregated and insulated one of its service activities (in a way that is reasonable to render that service), could it not reasonably be said that its potential liabilities in and for the rendering of that service should prima facie be determined as if the department rendering that segregated service was a separate legal person? The burden of this is, of course, to exclude conflicting duties in fact incurred by the company in other departments, from operative effect upon the segregated department when rendering its services. And it would allow for segregation to contrive the limits of the *Spector* v. *Ageda* obligation.[150]

This is not the place to explore in detail the burden of the above suggestion. I would merely note that there is, of course, a number of suppositions in it, not the least of which is that effective segregation through 'Chinese Walls' etc. (*a*) can actually be achieved—a possibility seriously doubted by some commentators[151] and viewed sceptically in Commonwealth judicial decisions (admittedly in 'same matter' and 'former client' conflict cases);[152] and (*b*) is, in fact, commercially desirable. I would also note that

---

[149] See e.g. (1991) 65 Aust. LJ 352.
[150] Cf the majority judgment *MacDonald Estate* v. *Martin* [1991] 1 WWR 705.
[151] See e.g. Poser, 'Conflicts of Interest within Securities Firms', above, n. 122.
[152] *D. & J. Constructions Pty. Ltd.* v. *Head*, (1987) 9 NSWLR 118; *McNaughton* v. *Tauranga*

the suggestion does not presuppose an absence of managerial oversight of a segregated department.[153]

For the present, though, what is likely to be the effect of segregation (assuming its practical efficacy is accepted by a court) on a business's potential liability for loss to a client relying for advice, etc. on the segregated area when adverse information is otherwise possessed by the business? Here I merely advance a number of necessarily speculative propositions.

1. If those managerially responsible for the oversight of the insulated area's operations know or have reason to know that that area is acting upon false or inaccurate information, the business itself must be quite vulnerable to allegations of fraud.

2. If merely those who receive the adverse information have reasonable grounds for believing that other and insulated parts of the business might be acting or advising in ways which they would not if possessed of that information, then the law of negligence looms as a possible basis of liability to third parties relying on those other areas.

3. Beyond the above, the issue would seem to become one of possible liability in negligence (or breach of contract) on the basis that, though the insulated area acted reasonably given the information available to it, the business itself possessed information which, if known to that area, would have rendered its actions negligent. For the adviser, this is the *Spector* v. *Ageda* issue. The size of a business may be such, its offices so geographically dispersed, or its functions so disparate, that it would be unreasonable to say that its fortuitous possession of relevant information in one place or in one activity should render it liable for services rendered in another place or activity, given that even without 'segregation' that information could not reasonably be expected to be accessible to the insulated area. One need merely consider the problems such a potential liability would raise for banks with numerous branches. But even where size itself may not be a potential protection, segregation may be found to be so at least where the segregated area deals with its clients on the explicit basis that that area can and will only act on such information possessed by the business as is lawfully accessible to that area. The object in dealing on such a basis is to deny a client any reasonable expectation that the business it has engaged would use or disclose for that client's benefit any information which was subject to a secrecy obligation to another client.[154]

County Council (No.2) (1987) 12 NZTPA 429; see the minority judgment in *MacDonald Estate* v. *Martin* [1991] 1 WWR 705; see also Dean and Finlayson, 'Conflicts of Interest', above, n. 136. But cf. *Slade* v. *Shearson, Hammil & Co. Inc.* 517 F. 2d 398 (1974).

[153] Indeed its absence would in principle carry possible personal liabilities for senior management itself, liabilities which for practical purposes are unlikely to be enforced short of liquidation of the company. It is relevant here to note that such oversight remains necessary if the segregated department itself is not to be made an unwitting instrument of fraud or deception—even though oversight itself operates as some qualification on effective segregation.

[154] Cf *Kabwand Pty. Ltd.* v. *National Australia Bank Ltd.* (1989) 11 ATPR 40–950; this qualified form of retainer is now commonly employed by large firms in Australia.

3.3.2. Acting as a Principal

Here I merely note three matters both because of their possible practical significance and because they appear to provide anomalous exceptions to the ordinary rules governing commercial secrecy. In one of these an information recipient, though subject to a duty of secrecy to a client, may none the less be entitled to use (though not disclose)[155] information about that client in determining the manner of its dealing with a third party. In the other two, it may be positively required to disclose such information to a third party with whom it is dealing. All three situations commonly arise in banking contexts.

The use case, which I simply note without further comment, is exemplified in the controversial holding in the United States decision, *Washington Steel Corp.* v. *T. W. Corp.*[156]

In making loans, unless it is to take imprudent risks with the funds on deposit with the bank, the commercial loan department must be free to make full use of the information available to it. If, for example, a competitor of a borrower seeks a loan for a purpose which the loan department knows, from information in its files supplied by that borrower, is preordained to failure, it should hardly be permitted, let alone required, to ignore that information, finance a foolhardy venture, and write off a bad loan. Thus, we hold only that the use within that loan department of information received from one borrower, in evaluating a loan to another borrower, does not, without more, state a cause of action against the bank.

The two disclosure cases are products (*a*) of the 'special circumstances' doctrine in the law of suretyship;[157] and (*b*) of the onus thrown upon the superior party to a dealing affected by the law of undue influence/unconscionable dealing.[158] Either of these can affect a bank when taking a third-party guarantee of the debts of one of its own customers. In both, while insisting that the bank make disclosures which will or can reveal confidential customer information, the courts have given little attention to the question whether compliance with that disclosure requirement will or can itself precipitate an actionable breach of confidence.[159] The implicit assumption is that it would not. In both cases the duty of disclosure is usually premissed in part on a failure of the third party (who invariably is obtaining a derivative benefit from the dealing, e.g. the continuation of a line of finance because of the guarantee) to act openly towards the person to whom the consequential disclosure is required. It is, in my view, highly improbable that courts in either England or Australia will allow the action for breach of confidence any place in these two contexts.

---

[155] *Kabwand Pty. Ltd.* v. *National Australia Bank Ltd.*, above, *American Medicorp Inc.* v. *Continental Illinois National Bank and Trust Co. of Chicago* 475 F. Supp. 5 (1977).

[156] 602 F. 2d 594, at 604 (1979).

[157] Cf *Goodwin* v. *National Bank of Australasia Ltd.* (1968) 117 CLR 173.

[158] *National Westminster Bank plc* v. *Morgan* [1985] AC 686; *Commercial Bank of Australia* v. *Amadio* (1983) 151 CLR 447.

[159] But cf. *Westpac Banking Corp.* v. *Robinson* (1990) ASC 56–002.

3.4. FAIR-DEALING CONFLICTS

The long-standing orthodoxy is that a person in a fiduciary position cannot buy from or sell to his beneficiary any property falling within the ambit of the fiduciary service he has undertaken[160] unless

(*a*) full value is given[161] after the beneficiary gives a fully informed and independent[162] consent to the sale or purchase; or

(*b*) the fiduciary relationship itself is constituted on terms which gives the fiduciary the right to sell or to buy.[163]

I do not intend here to rehearse in any detail the nature and incidents of the various rules and subrules which inform this prohibition. These are reasonably well-known. My concern is merely with one matter of relevance to this work.

A positively voluminous case law spanning several centuries and involving the dealings of agents, brokers, solicitors, trustees, managers, and others has, I suggest, produced a somewhat uncritical view of how the law might be applied in some instances. Fiduciary law's concern in such dealings is twofold: (i) to guard against the fiduciary's possible misuse of superior knowledge, information, or judgment which, because of the nature and circumstances of the relationship, should be used only for the benefit of the beneficiary; and (ii) to preclude the fiduciary function performed being possibly influenced by a conflict of duty and interest.

It is commonly enough assumed that once a person assumes a function that characteriztically attracts fiduciary responsibilities, those responsibilities will, as of course, have general effect upon the manner in which that person can and should discharge that function. The misconception in this was pointedly noted by Fletcher Moulton, LJ in *Re Coomber*.[164] And as Frankfurter, J. observed in *S.E.C.* v. *Cheney Corp.*,[165] '[t]o say a man is a fiduciary only begins the analysis'. The reason I advert to this is to ask the question whether we have too readily assumed the applicability of the 'fair-dealing' rule in all circumstances to the dealings of agents, trustees, etc. without first asking whether they are relevantly fiduciaries.

Simply to crystallize the issue let me begin by quoting observations of the Privy Council in an Australian appeal,[166] on whether an agent, without advising at all in the matter and having been instructed (*inter alia*) to raise a loan of £12,000 at 5 per cent, could itself be the lender:

The rule of law as to an agent not acting as a principal really rests on the consideration of a conflicting interest in the person of the agent, but in a contract such as this was, to

---

[160] Dealings outside that service are unaffected by fiduciary law: see *McPherson* v. *Watt* (1877) 3 App. Cas. 254, at 270–1.

[161] Except where an undervalue is deliberately agreed.

[162] If the circumstances attract undue influence principles.

[163] Cf *Hordern* v. *Hordern* [1910] AC 465.

[164] [1911] 1 Ch. 723, at 728–9.

[165] 318 US 80, at 85 (1942).

[166] *Dalgety & Co. Ltd.* v. *Gray* (1919) 26 CLR 249, at 256.

get a mortgage on specified terms, there could be no conflicting interest, and their Lordships can see no reason whatever why the defendants should not have advanced the £12,000 themselves, assuming that there was no special stipulation to the contrary.

Is this unexceptionable and does it also hold for a broker in receipt of explicit instructions to purchase or sell in like conditions?

The question throws this back to the first matter considered in this chapter: who is a fiduciary, what is a fiduciary relationship? As a convenient form of shorthand we regularly describe certain types of functionary as fiduciaries because of who they are: agents, directors, trustees, etc.[167] This usage is, ordinarily, harmless enough. None the less, it conceals the true nature of the fiduciary question. Put simply (and slightly inaccurately)[168] a person becomes a fiduciary, not because of his status, but because of what he assumes or is taken as having assumed to do in a particular relationship. To the extent, and only to the extent, that in that role the beneficiary is entitled to expect he will act in the beneficiary's interests, will he be that beneficiary's fiduciary. Importantly this can mean that the role of an agent, a trustee, etc. may only be fiduciary in part (if at all),[169] in the particular circumstances of a given relationship. In consequence, actions taken in the relationship which, in the circumstances of a different relationship, might offend fiduciary principles, are inoffensive because they fall outside the scope of the fiduciary part of the relationship. Perhaps the most obvious instance where, in a relationship otherwise fiduciary, a particular matter is to be taken as falling outside the fiduciary regime, is, in my opinion, where the beneficiary assumes personal responsibility for the protection of his own interests to the exclusion of the fiduciary. The difficult question, though, lies in determining when this can properly be said to be so—especially in relation to agents who characteriztically perform advisory/negotiating functions in the type of agency they discharge.

The 'fair-dealing' rule is commonly expressed in terms which prohibit a purchase or sale by an agent even where the price is set by the principal.[170] As a generalization this may be a fair representation of how the rule ordinarily applies. But consider the following three examples:

(1) An estate agent is engaged to sell his principal's house, the principal specifying the sale price.

(2) An agent is instructed to sell shares in a traded company at a designated price in circumstances where advice has been sought or received on the sale, or else could be expected (where appropriate)

---

[167] One of the more explicit examples of this is to be found in the Restatement (Second) of Agency, s. 13.

[168] See Finn, 'The Fiduciary Principle', supra, n. 3, 54.

[169] Cf *Sinnett* v. *Darby* (1886) 13 VLR 97; see also *Gould* v. *O'Carroll* (1963) 81 W.N. (Pt. 1) (N.S.W.) 170; and *Holder* v. *Holder* [1968] Ch. 353.

[170] See e.g. 3 Am. Jur. 2d, 'Agency' § 236; 3 CJS, 'Agency' § 284–5.

because of past dealings or because of the particular circumstances in which the agent is engaged.[171]

(3) An agent is instructed to sell shares in a traded company at a designated price in circumstances where advice is not sought, received, or expected.

Save in truly exceptional circumstances, the agent in example 1 would be a fiduciary for the purposes of the 'fair-dealing' rule because of the advisory and negotiating role expected of such an agent, as also because of the necessarily speculative nature of prices so set. Likewise in example 2, the 'reliance factor' stemming from the advisory function would attract a fiduciary responsibility in the sale.[172] But what of example 3? The agent–client relationship in the effecting of the sale here is not, in my opinion, a fiduciary one. The agent's function is purely ministerial, the client assuming responsibility to the exclusion of the agent as to how the client's interests are best to be served. The agent is not being expected to put at his client's disposal such knowledge, information, or judgment as the agent may have about the wisdom etc. of the sale: it is not a 'reliance relationship'.[173] Nor can it be said that a purchase by the agent would 'result in any realistic way in a conflict of duty and interest'.[174] Whether one says, as I would, that the agent was not relevantly a fiduciary,[175] or, alternatively, that the 'fair-dealing' rule should not be applied 'in a case where the reasons behind the rule do not exist',[176] the purchase should be unimpeachable. In suggesting this conclusion, I am of course positing a quite distinctive (though common) form of agency.[177] But then we do need to remind ourselves as we generalize about the incidence of fiduciary duties that '[t]here is no class of case in which one ought more carefully to bear in mind the facts of the case . . . than cases which relate to fiduciary and confidential relations and the action of the Court with regard to them'.[178]

The view I have put makes the application of the 'fair-dealing' rule, ultimately, an instance-specific one, albeit one in which the exceptional case proposed is unlikely to be the operative one save in quite distinctive circumstances. The exceptional case may, however, provide some sort of comfort to brokers in particular, at least in some of their client dealings.

---

[171] Cf *Thompson* v. *Meade* (1891) 7 TLR 698.

[172] In this it is important to note that in *Thompson* v. *Meade*, supra, a prior exchange occurred between broker and client in which the broker indicated the price at which the client subsequently asked him to purchase.

[173] Cf *R. H. Deacon & Co.* v. *Varga* (1973) 41 DLR (3rd) 767.

[174] Cf *Jones* v. *Canavan* [1972] 2 NSWLR 236, at 245 per Jacobs, JA.

[175] Cf *R. H. Deacon & Co.* v. *Varga*, above.

[176] *Holder* v. *Holder* [1968] Ch. 353, at 392 per Harman, LJ; see also the view of Jacobs, J. in *Gould* v. *O'Carroll* (1963) 81 W.N. (Pt. 1) (N.S.W.) 170.

[177] The fact of an external market which itself sets prices can be a factor of some importance in this as well: see *Jones* v. *Canavan* [1972] 2 NSWLR 236.

[178] In *Re Coomber: Coomber* v. *Coomber* [1911] 1 Ch. 723, at 729 per Fletcher Moulton, LJ.

4. Damages

Nocton v. *Ashburton*[179] was a portentous decision. Yet its message was lost for more than half a century. Whatever the unfortunate ravages that the earlier fraud case, *Derry* v. *Peek*,[180] inflicted on equity jurisprudence, *Nocton* at least kept intact the jurisdiction to award compensation (or damages) for breach of fiduciary duty. For understandable reasons, attention on remedy in the fiduciary context tended to focus on the powerful profit-stripping remedies that could be unleashed against a delinquent fiduciary;[181] the damages remedy languished apparently unnoticed and unwanted. But no longer.[182] In Australia,[183] New Zealand,[184] and Canada[185] it has been embraced by the courts with the fervour of fresh converts. In England in contrast, the response remains muted[186] outside the now well-accepted case of breach of confidence actions.[187] As far as England is concerned a particularly potent, fiduciary-based, surrogate 'tort' awaits in the wings— and it is one having the advantages of those presumptions, reversals in the onus of proof, etc. that fiduciary law confers. My purpose here is to make the point that any consideration of fiduciary law's possible impact in commerce must take this dimension of it into account.

The remedy itself has been well discussed elsewhere relatively recently.[188] Here I would simply note that

  (*a*) it is used regularly to compensate for economic loss—but not only for economic loss: it has, for example, been used to compensate for nervous shock and injury to a plaintiff's feelings;[189]

  (*b*) it apparently admits of awards of exemplary damages;[190]

---

[179] [1914] AC 932.

[180] (1889) 14 App. Cas. 337.

[181] For a treatment see the Hon. Mr Justice J. B. Kearney, 'Accounting for a Fiduciary's Gains in Commercial Contexts', in Finn (ed.), *Equity and Commercial Relationships*, above, n. 49.

[182] For two scholarly examinations see The Hon. Mr Justice Gummow, 'Compensation for Breach of Fiduciary Duty', in Youdan (ed.). *Equity, Fiduciaries and Trusts*, above, n. 1; and I. E. Davidson, 'The Equitable Remedy of Compensation'(1982) 13 Melb. U.L.Rev. 349.

[183] See e.g. *Hill* v. *Rose* [1990] VR 129; *Fraser Edmiston Pty. Ltd.* v. *AGT (Qld) Pty. Ltd.* [1988] 2 Qd. R. 1; *Catt* v. *Marac Australia Ltd.* (1986) 9 NSWLR 639; *Markwell Bros. Pty. Ltd.* v. *CPN Diesels Queensland Ltd.* [1983] 2 Qd. R. 508.

[184] See e.g. *McKaskell* v. *Benseman* [1989] 3 NZLR 75; *Day* v. *Mead* [1987] 2 NZLR 443; and see also *Aquaculture Corp.* v. *New Zealand Green Mussel Co. Ltd.* [1990] 3 NZLR 299.

[185] The case law is voluminous. See e.g. *Canson Enterprises Ltd.* v. *Boughton & Co.* (1992) 85 D. L. R. (4th) 129; *Guerin* v. *R.* [1984] 2 SCR. 335.

[186] The jurisdiction was for example, assumed in *O'Sullivan* v. *Management Agency Ltd.* [1985] 1 QB 428.

[187] E.g. *Dowson & Mason Ltd.* v. *Potter* [1986] 2 All ER 418.

[188] See the Hon. Mr Justice Gummow, 'Compensation for Breach of Fiduciary Duty', supra, n. 182.

[189] See e.g. *McKaskell* v. *Benseman*, [1989] 3 NZLRR 75; *Szarfer* v. *Chodos* (1986) 27 DLR (4th) 388—an extraordinary case; *Frame* v. *Wilson* [1987] 2 SCR. 99, at 151 per Wilson J. (diss.).

[190] See e.g. *McKaskell* v. *Benseman*, supra; *Aquaculture Corp.* v. *New Zealand Green Mussel Co. Ltd.* [1990] 3 NZLR 299; *Guertin* v. *Royal Bank* (1983) 43 OR (2d) 363, at 377–8.

(*c*) if, as is commonly assumed, a tort analogue is the most appropriate one to be adopted in assessing damages,[191] to what extent are causation, foreseeability and remoteness,[192] 'contributory negligence',[193] and duties to mitigate loss[194] to be of relevance? and,

(*d*) to revert to earlier parts of this chapter, this remedy in Commonwealth jurisdictions is progressively displacing negligence-based ones in 'same-matter' conflicts and in conflict of duty and interest cases.[195]

We have here a remedy of some significance. All it lacks after years of neglect is a developed jurisprudence to explain its proper workings!

5. Conclusion

My task, as I have understood it, has been to give an overview (necessarily lightly sketched) of fiduciary law's possible parts and places in commerce generally. If there is much that is merely descriptive in what I have said, there is much to describe. But now, to introduce a note of scepticism, it is appropriate to make at least these additional observations. First, while not wishing to deprecate this body of law's intent to impose standards of acceptable conduct on those falling within its domain, one can seriously question its general ability to realize that intent beyond cases of fiduciary relationships arising out of commercial contracts.[196] The thing it abhors is the secret, the undisclosed, the covert personal interest, conflicting duty, etc. But it is the covertness of the very phenomenon it attacks—when coupled with the often formidable difficulty involved in its detection—that mars its utility as a viable and effective regulatory instrument on its own. We have, for example, known for decades the legal wrong involved in insider trading. This body of law has been impotent in the face of that particular challenge. If we seriously are committed to the maintenance of certain standards in particular fields of commerce, we must, perforce, consider other ways.

Secondly, one vital role we have attributed historically to fiduciary law is that of helping to maintain public confidence in persons and institutions rendering client services to which we attribute particular social importance. Necessarily it could only do this through the example of individual cases. Again one can only wonder, given the scale of business operations, the impersonal quality of many types of fiduciary relationship, and the obvious

---

[191] *Nocton* itself suggested a deceit analogue: and see e.g. *Burns* v. *Kelly Peters & Associates Ltd.* (1987) 16 BCLR (2d) 1.

[192] See e.g. *Brickenden* v. *London Loan & Savings Co.* [1934] 3 DLR 465; *Mid-Northern Fertilisers Ltd.* v. *Connel, Lamb, Gerard & Co.*, HC of NZ, 18 Sept. 1986, Thorp, J.; *Canson Enterprises Ltd.* v. *Boughton & Co.* (1992) 85 D. L. R. (4th) 129.

[193] See e.g. *Day* v. *Mead* [1987] 2 NZLR 443.

[194] See e.g. *Burke* v. *Cory* (1959) 19 DLR (2d) 252; *Laskin* v. *Bache & Co. Inc.* [1972] 1 OR 465.

[195] The cases referred to in the footnotes to this Section amply attest to this.

[196] Where there is a realistic prospect of the parties themselves policing the proper performance of roles in their relationship.

temptations to dereliction of formal duty, whether individual example (even when accompanied by punitive sanctions)[197] can assuage distrust where trust is necessary. The United Kingdom does not seem to have experienced the same level of public revelation of commercial impropriety as is to be found in Australia. But from Australian experience a salutary lesson on this theme is to be learned.

Thirdly, there are the standards of fiduciary law themselves. These, in my view, are quite defensible—provided their purposes are understood and they are applied with sensitivity. I would merely note in this, for example, that Canadian invocation of 'the fiduciary' can on occasion be quite breath-taking.[198] What, however, can be objectionable are some effects of the interaction of these standards with other rules of law: the consequences we attribute as of course to corporate personality; the uncertain rules on the imputation of knowledge in partnerships; the *Spector* v. *Ageda* adviser's obligation; etc. Furthermore, the perceived severity of the standards may well itself reflect upon the gulf between what is demanded of a business when a fiduciary, and what is otherwise allowed to it in English law when it is not. Though conscious that I here trespass upon sensitive ground,[199] I do wonder whether 'the fiduciary' would be perceived as such an anomaly in its exacting standards if English law had committed itself more enthusiastically to obligations of good faith and fair dealings: obligations which are common-place in civil and United States law and which are receiving more explicit recognition in Commonwealth countries. Good faith, though, is another story.

[197] E.g. the various litigations etc. arising out of the Guinness take-over.

[198] Cf the dissenting judgment of Wilson J. in *Frame* v. *Wilson* [1987] 2 SCR. 99; and note the remonstrance of Southin J. in *Giradet* v. *Crease & Co.* (1987) 11 BCLR (2d) 316, at 362.

[199] But cf. the Hon. Mr Justice Steyn, 'The Role of Good Faith and Fair Dealing in Contract Law: A Hair-Shirt Philosophy?', 1991 Royal Bank of Scotland Law Lecture, 16 May 1991.

2

THE STATUTORY REGULATION OF FINANCIAL SERVICES IN THE UNITED KINGDOM AND THE DEVELOPMENT OF CHINESE WALLS IN MANAGING CONFLICTS OF INTEREST

Peter Graham

This chapter has two objectives. The first is to take a brief look at the history of statutory regulation of the financial services industry in the UK. The second is to review the development of Chinese Walls as an accepted means of regulating conflicts of interest within the context of the statutory regulation of financial services.

1. A Brief History of Statutory Regulation of Financial Services in the UK

The issue of securities to the public has been regulated since 1900 by the Companies Acts, but, with certain limited exceptions,[1] dealing in securities was not regulated by statute until 1939. In that year the first Prevention of Fraud (Investments) Act was passed, partly in response to an outbreak of fraudulent share pushing in the early 1930s and partly in response to the growth of the unit trust movement. That Act was amended by the Companies Act 1947[2] and consolidated in the Prevention of Fraud (Investments) Act 1958 (PFIA).

This legislation made it an offence for someone to carry on the business of dealing in securities without being licensed, under an annual licence, by the Board of Trade. This licence was normally both easy to obtain and to renew. Certain categories of person were exempted from the need to be licensed. These included members of the London Stock Exchange, members of an association of dealers in securities, managers and trustees of an authorized

---

[1] Statutes were passed in the 17th and 18th cent. to regulate brokers and jobbers but they either lapsed or were not rigorously enforced.

[2] ss. 117 and 118 of the Companies Act 1947.

unit trust, statutory corporations, industrial and provident societies, building societies, and persons granted exempted dealer status by the Board of Trade.

Licensed dealers (but technically not exempted dealers or others specifically exempted under the PFIA) were required to comply with Conduct of Business Rules[3] made by the Board of Trade under powers conferred by the PFIA.

The legislation had a number of other objectives. It provided for the Board of Trade to regulate authorized unit trusts. It regulated the distribution of circulars relating to 'investments' (a wider expression than 'securities') and it introduced the offence of fraudulently inducing persons to buy or sell investments or participate in certain other transactions relating to investments.

The Conduct of Business Rules were first made in .1960 and were substantially revised in 1983. The 1983 Rules[4] for the first time introduced regulations relating to the holding of client money and client investments, the activity of investment management, the disclosure of a material interest in a transaction to be entered into on behalf of a client, and the making of dealer's recommendations. Of particular interest is the way in which the Rules addressed conflicts of interest. There are three Rules worthy of note in this context.

First, Rule 8 contained the first reference in UK legislation to Chinese Walls, a subject which is addressed in more detail in the second part of this chapter. What Rule 8 said was that a licensed dealer was absolved from notifying a client of a material interest which the dealer had (or was deemed to have) in a transaction to be effected with or for the client where the part of the business dealing with the client was divided by a Chinese Wall from the part of the business in which the interest arose, provided that it was reasonable to assume that no individual who was involved on behalf of the dealer, directly or indirectly, was aware of the interest in question. The definition of a Chinese Wall which is set out in these Rules is addressed later in the second part of this chapter.

Secondly, a dealer was prohibited (by Rule 14) from effecting on behalf of a client with whom the dealer had entered into an investment management contract (whether discretionary or not) a transaction which related to investments in which the licensed dealer acted as principal or as agent for a person connected with the dealer. This prohibition did not apply in certain circumstances, for example where the client had given his express written agreement to the dealer effecting that particular transaction in that particular capacity or where the client acquiesced in the transaction with full knowledge of the circumstances. Rule 14(4) went on to state that nothing in Rule 14 was to be taken as 'affecting any rule of law prohibiting a person in a fiduciary position from profiting therefrom or enabling any contract made by him to be

---

[3] The Licensed Dealers (Conduct of Business) Rules 1960.
[4] The Licensed Dealers (Conduct of Business) Rules 1983.

avoided as it applies to the relation between a licensed dealer and a managed account client'. In other words where a fiduciary relationship subsisted between a licensed dealer and his managed account client, the existing common law rules affecting fiduciaries would not be affected by this rule.

Thirdly, the Rules (Rule 27) introduced the concept of 'good market practice' by providing that 'to the extent that there exist generally accepted standards as to what constitutes good market practice in respect of any matters not expressly covered by these rules, a licensed dealer shall comply with such standards and for the purposes of this "rule 'market" includes the whole or any part of the activity regulated by or under the Act'.

Even before the 1983 Rules were published a number of financial scandals had persuaded the Government that a more fundamental review of the law was needed. In 1980, insider dealing by individuals became a criminal offence.[5] In July 1981 Professor L. C. B. Gower was commissioned by the Secretary of State for Trade to undertake a review to advise on the need for new legislation to regulate investor protection. In January 1982 his discussion document entitled *Review of Investor Protection* was published. This surveyed the statutory and non-statutory regulation relating to all kinds of investments and concluded that the law was 'complicated, uncertain and irrational' and that a new statutory framework incorporating a balance between Government regulation and self-regulation was needed.

This discussion document was followed by a more detailed report, Part I of which was published in January 1984.[6] The report recommended that a new Investor Protection Act, relying where possible on self-regulation, should replace the PFIA and that the new Act should make it a criminal offence to carry on any type of investment business unless registered. The principal philosophy underlying these proposals was that the degree of regulation should be no greater than was necessary to protect reasonable people from being made fools of. This was followed in swift succession by a Government White Paper in January 1985[7] and in due course by the Financial Services Act 1986 (FSA), an Act which has revolutionised the regulation of the financial services industry in the UK.

The FSA resulted in the creation of the Securities and Investments Board (SIB) and five self-regulatory organizations (SROs). Two of these SROs have now merged to form The Securities and Futures Authority (SFA). The other three are IMRO, LAUTRO, and FIMBRA.[8] In addition certain recognised professional bodies (RPBs), such as the Law Society and the three Institutes of Chartered Accountants, regulate investment business carried on by their

---

[5] Part V of the Companies Act 1980. These provisions are now contained in the Company Securities (Insider Dealing) Act 1985.

[6] Review of Investor Protection—Cmnd. 9125. Part II was published in 1985.

[7] Financial Services in the United Kingdom—Cmnd. 9432.

[8] IMRO stands for Investment Management Regulatory Organization Limited; LAUTRO stands for Life Assurance and Unit Trust Regulatory Organization; and FIMBRA stands for Financial Intermediaries, Managers and Brokers Regulatory Association.

members. Authorization to carry on investment business may be obtained through membership of an SRO or certification by an RPB or by direct authorization by the SIB itself.

The original structure of the regulatory framework comprised the FSA itself, the rules of the SIB and the rules of the SROs and RPBs which had to provide protection 'at least equivalent' to that provided by the rules of the SIB. The SIB, to which most of the functions of the Government under the Act were delegated by statutory instrument,[9] was given extensive rule-making powers relating to conduct of business, financial resources, the handling of clients' money, cold calling, the creation of cooling-off periods for investors, and, to back up and give credibility to the new regime of investor protection, the creation of a compensation fund. In addition the SIB was given wide powers to investigate the conduct of investment business in the UK and to enforce the provisions of the FSA. In particular it was empowered to seek injunctions against persons flouting or likely to flout the FSA and also to seek restitution orders. The FSA also contained important provisions regulating the issue of investment advertisements and the promotion and authorization of collective investment schemes.

The reported actions brought by the SIB since the FSA was brought into force illustrate the practical application of its enforcement powers. In 1989 the SIB, on an ex-parte application, sought and obtained a mareva injunction against Pantell SA, a Swiss company, in order to freeze its assets here. Pantell SA had been sending advertisements from addresses outside the UK to individuals in the UK contrary to section 57 of the FSA and it was arguable that they had also been unlawfully carrying on investment business in the UK by offering its services to persons in the UK.[10] More recently[11] the High Court has gone so far as to hold that a solicitor who is knowingly concerned in his client's unlawful financial services transactions can be ordered to repay sums paid to the client by investors so as to restore them to the position they were in before the transactions were entered into. The question of whether the solicitors had knowingly been concerned in a contravention of the FSA by Pantell SA has yet to be decided but it is clear that, in this context, a solicitor will not be shielded by professional privilege.

In another case the SIB obtained an injunction pursuant to section 61 of the FSA preventing a Belgian company in liquidation and the officer winding it up under Belgian law from conducting investment business in the UK.[12] The SIB has also used the powers under section 72 of the FSA to petition for the winding up of an authorized investment business where the company concerned is unable to meet its debts or it is just and equitable to wind it up.

Another feature of the scheme of investor protection was the right to claim damages under section 62 of the FSA for loss caused by a breach of rules

---

[9] SI 1987 No. 942.
[10] *SIB* v. *Pantell S.A. and Another* [1990] 1 Ch. 426.
[11] *SIB* v. *Pantell S.A. and Others* (No. 2) [1991] 3 WLR 857.
[12] *SIB* v. *Vandersteen Associates NV* [1991] BCLC 206.

made by the SIB, an SRO, or an RPB. However, as yet there appear to be no reported cases of actions brought under section 62.

Was the FSA, together with the rules which it spawned, designed to be a comprehensive code of law in relation to investment business? Those involved in trying to understand and comply with the new regulations might be forgiven for believing so and for assuming that the new regulations had subsumed the common law duties affecting investment businesses. In so far as this issue was addressed by the Government's White Paper, however, it seems that the Government intended the new legislation to create an additional layer of protection which would exist side by side with the fiduciary duties imposed by the law of agency. It was therefore not surprising (although it was perhaps unhelpful) that the FSA itself made no overt general reference to the relationship between rules made under it and parallel or overlapping duties arising under the common law. As a result the legislation did not attempt to reconcile conflicts arising between common law duties and duties created by statutory regulation.

The rulebooks of the SIB and the SROs became over-complicated and a fundamental review was initiated by the SIB. This led to a number of changes being made to the FSA in the Companies Act 1989. These are set out in Part VIII (sections 192 to 206) of the Companies Act 1989. The most significant of these changes were as follows:

1. The SIB was empowered to issue statements of principle with respect to the conduct and financial standing expected of persons authorized to carry on investment business. Non-compliance with a statement of principle would constitute grounds for the taking of disciplinary action but would not of itself give rise to an action for damages by third parties.

2. The SIB was empowered to issue conduct of business rules which would be binding on authorized persons regulated by SROs and not only firms directly authorized by the SIB. These rules would not, however, bind members of an RPB.

3. The rules of the SROs and RPBs would only have to afford 'adequate protection' (as opposed to 'equivalent protection') for investors when looked at together with the principles and conduct of business rules laid down by the SIB.

4. The right to sue for damages under section 62 of the FSA was, subject to certain limited exceptions, restricted to private investors.[13]

Interestingly, section 204 of the Companies Act 1989 required the SIB, the SROs, and the RPBs to take account when framing their rules and codes of practice (and in the case of the SIB the statement of principles) of the consequential costs of compliance. It was a sign that the Government recognised that the pendulum of investor protection had swung too far in favour of the investor and that the costs of compliance had become excessive.

---

[13] See SI 1991 No. 489 which defines 'private investor' and also specifies the circumstances in which action may be brought by a person other than a private investor.

The new framework is not yet fully in place. The SIB published the Statement of Principles in April 1990 and these are now in force. The Core Conduct of Business Rules were published on 30 January 1991 and will be brought into force as regards members of an SRO at the same time as the SRO brings its so-called 'third-tier' rules into force.

The Principles enunciated by the SIB are ten in number. Briefly, these cover a firm's duty to observe high standards of integrity (Principle 1), to act with due skill, care, and diligence (Principle 2), to observe high standards of market conduct (Principle 3), to make enquiries as to its customers' circumstances and investment objectives (Principle 4), to provide comprehensible and timely information to customers (Principle 5), to avoid or manage conflicts of interest (Principle 6), to safeguard a customer's assets which it controls or for which it is responsible (Principle 7), to maintain adequate financial resources (Principle 8), to maintain a proper internal organization including well-defined compliance procedures (Principle 9), and to deal with its regulator in an open and co-operative manner (Principle 10).

The Core Conduct of Business Rules go into considerably more detail on the conduct of investment business. They are designed to flesh out the Principles without descending into the level of detail of the original rulebook and they represent a welcome advance.

As regards their relationship with common law duties there are two rules of particular interest. The first is Rule 15, which prohibits a firm from excluding, in any written communication or agreement, any duty or liability which it has under the FSA or under the regulatory system or, unless it is reasonable to do so, any duty to act with skill, care, and diligence which is owed to a *private* customer in connection with the provision of investment services or any liability for breach of such duty. This effectively extends the Unfair Contract Terms Act 1977, which in certain respects does not apply to contracts relating to the creation or transfer of securities or any right or interest in securities, although it does apply to investment advisory contracts and investment managements contracts. It is worth noting that there is no prohibition in the Core Rules against excluding or varying *fiduciary* duties (except in so far as a particular fiduciary duty may include a duty to act with skill, care and diligence).

The second rule of interest is Rule 36 concerning Chinese Walls, which is considered in the second part of this chapter.

The rulebooks of the SROs are currently being revised to take account of the new framework. The 'third-tier' rules are expected to come into force in late 1991 or during 1992[14] whereupon all participants in this industry, regulator and regulated alike, may be expected to breathe a collective sigh of relief.

[14] The IMRO Rules came into force on 30 November 1991. The SFA Rules mostly came into force on 1 April 1992. The FIMBRA Rules are due to be published in October 1992 and to come into force in December 1992.

Finally, mention should also be made of the draft Investment Services Directive which was originally tabled by the European Commission in January 1989. Certain of the proposals contained in the present draft have become contentious within the European Community and there is little sign at present of agreement being reached on the principal outstanding issues. If the draft Directive is in due course adopted it may, depending on its final form, require some modifications to be made to the new FSA framework.

2. 'Chinese Walls'

Turning now to the subject of Chinese Walls, it is necessary to acknowledge that the concept of a Chinese Wall was originally developed in the United States of America in the 1960s as a defence to an action for fraudulent trading in securities using confidential price-sensitive information.[15]

Chinese Walls are private rules internal to an organization which are designed to manage conflicts of interest or duty. They are to be distinguished from so-called 'firewalls' which are legal rules imposed by legislation or regulations in order to protect the solvency of a regulated business.[16]

Chinese Walls made their first appearance in the UK in the Companies Bill 1973, which never became law owing to the fall of Edward Heath's Government in 1974. Clause 12 of that Bill provided for insider dealing in securities to be prohibited. In particular it proposed to make it an offence for a company to deal in securities at a time when any director or employee of that company was precluded by law from dealing in them. Clause 14(3) of the Bill introduced an exception where

(a) the decision to enter into the transaction was taken on its behalf by a person other than the director or employee

(b) arrangements were then in existence for securing that the information was not communicated to that person and that no advice with respect to the transaction was given to him by a person in possession of the information and

(c) the information was not in fact so communicated and advice was not in fact so given.

Clause 14(3)(b) in effect defined a Chinese Wall although the expression 'Chinese Wall' did not itself make an appearance until the Licensed Dealers (Conduct of Business) Rules 1983. Rule 2 thereof defined a Chinese Wall as 'an established arrangement whereby information known to persons involved in one part of a business is not available (directly or indirectly) to those involved in another part of the business and it is accepted that in each of the parts of the business so divided decisions will be taken without reference to

---

[15] The precise origin of the expression 'Chinese Wall' is uncertain. The allusion is to the Great Wall of China but in modern times the expression has been used to mean an invisible and impenetrable barrier. Franklin D. Roosevelt is recorded as having used the phrase 'an old Chinese Wall policy of isolation'.

[16] E.g. the US Banking Act 1933 (the so-called 'Glass–Steagall' Act).

any interest which any other such part or any person in any other such part of
the business may have in the matter'.

On 27 October 1986 the Stock Exchange's rules on dual capacity and fixed
commissions were swept away. The anticipation of these changes resulted in
most of the independent stockbrokers and jobbers being taken over by
banks.[17] These banks were now able under one roof to offer such diverse
services as commercial lending, corporate finance, investment management,
stockbroking, and market-making in securities.

As these new financial conglomerates were considering how to structure
themselves a key question to be answered was whether to have separately
incorporated subsidiaries for activities regulated by the FSA. Many took this
route, which provided some measure of insulation against intra-group
conflicts of interest. Others, however, decided to opt for a single multi-
function organization, having regard in particular to the significant cost of
capitalizing separate subsidiaries at a level sufficient to satisfy the new capital
adequacy requirements applicable to investment businesses.

The need to regulate conflicts of interest within these conglomerates
became ever more critical. The era of Chinese Walls had arrived. A note of
caution was sounded by the 1985 White Paper, which said:

> The rapid increase in the number of firms engaging in more than one type of
> investment business and the blurring of demarcation lines (for example between
> brokers and jobbers) have made it more important than ever that investors are
> adequately protected against abuses arising from conflicts of interest within
> investment businesses. It has been suggested that 'Chinese Walls' offer this protection
> . . . The Government are not convinced that total reliance can be placed on Chinese
> Walls because they restrict flows of information and not the conflicts of interest
> themselves.[18]

Nevertheless, the FSA specifically enabled the rules to make provision
'enabling or requiring information obtained by an authorized person in the
course of carrying on one part of his business to be withheld by him from
persons with whom he deals in the course of carrying on another part and for
that purpose enabling or requiring persons employed in one part of that
business to withhold information from those employed in another part'.[19]

The rule books of the SIB[20] and certain SROs[21] adopted the concept of
Chinese Walls in order to qualify duties which flowed from actual or deemed
knowledge. The new framework introduced by the SIB in response to the
changes to the FSA introduced by the Companies Act 1989 has further

[17] By Feb. 1987, 15 jobbers and 90 brokers had been acquired by banks or other financial
institutions according to the Bank of England's *Quarterly Bulletin*, Feb. 1987, 54.

[18] Above, note 7, 19–20.

[19] s. 48(2)(h) of the FSA.

[20] See the Financial Services (Conduct of Business) Rules 1990 Part 5 Rules 5.01, 5.06, 5.08,
and Part 8 Rules 8.07 and 8.08 and the definition of Chinese Wall contained in the Financial
Services (Glossary and Interpretation) Rules and Regulations 1990.

[21] See e.g. The Securities Association Chapter IV Rules 350, 380, 410, 750, 760, 790, 1100
and the definition of Chinese Walls in Rule 1220.

developed the concept of Chinese Walls and arguably has greatly increased its importance.

The sixth principle in the Statement of Principles referred to above provides that a firm should either avoid any conflict of interest arising or, where conflicts arise, should ensure fair treatment to all its customers by disclosure, internal rules of confidentiality (i.e. Chinese Walls), declining to act, or otherwise. A firm should not unfairly place its interests above those of its customers and, where a properly informed customer would reasonably expect that the firm would place his interests above its own, the firm should live up to that expectation.

Turning to the Core Rules, Rule 36 specifically relates to Chinese Walls.[22] It contains four intricately drafted paragraphs. Paragraph 1 permits, pursuant to an 'established arrangement', the withholding of information which is obtained by the firm in the course of carrying on one part of its business from persons with whom it deals in the course of carrying on another part of its business and from persons employed in the second part of its business, but only to the extent that the business of one of the parts of the business involves investment business or business carried on in connection with investment business. Paragraph 2 provides that information may be withheld where this is required by an 'established arrangement' between different parts of the business of a *group* (i.e. between different companies within a group) but this is expressed not to affect any requirement to transmit information which may arise outside the Core Conduct of Business Rules.

Paragraph 3 provides that where the Core Conduct of Business Rules apply only if a firm acts with knowledge, the firm is not to be taken to act with knowledge if none of the relevant individuals involved on behalf of the firm acts with knowledge. This, for example, will qualify the duty of a firm under Rule 25 which says that, subject to anything to the contrary in the rules of a relevant SRO, a firm must not knowingly effect an own account transaction in an investment ahead of publication of a recommendation or piece of research affecting that investment by the firm or an associate. The qualification introduced by paragraph 3 is that if the dealer does not know of the intended publication the firm will not be in breach of the rule if it deals for its own account ahead of the publication. Paragraph 3 will similarly qualify Core Rules 2 (material interest) and 28 (insider dealing).

Paragraph 4 provides that nothing done in conformity with paragraph 1 of the core rule on Chinese Walls is to be regarded as a contravention of section 47 of the FSA, which is the wide-ranging section of the FSA dealing with misleading statements and practices.

It is understood that the SIB takes the view, as regards paragraph 1 of Rule 36, that it not only derogates from the Core Rules themselves but also operates so as to derogate from common law fiduciary duties (such as the duty of a fiduciary not to place himself in a position where his own interest or his

---

[22] The text of Core Rule 36 is set out below, p. 61.

duties to another conflict with the interests of his client) and the common law duty of care and skill. The SIB view is based on the premiss that in so far as section 48(2)(h) of the FSA permits rules to make provision enabling the withholding of information it must be taken to mean that the rules may derogate from a legal obligation to disclose that information (and not simply from a regulatory requirement to do so, breach of which would otherwise give rise to disciplinary proceedings).[23] If this view is right it might even be argued that this paragraph goes so far as to nullify an express contractual obligation. If this were true it would represent a significant change to the common law as regards investment firms which are authorized by an SRO or the SIB itself (but, perhaps anomalously, not investment firms authorized by an RPB because section 48 does not extend to them).[24]

This interpretation of paragraph 1 raises an interesting speculation as to the future use of Chinese Walls. Paragraph 1 of Rule 36 does not make it a prerequisite that the Chinese Wall be created in order to resolve conflicts of interest. This could be changed (e.g. by third-tier rules) but as matters stand now it would appear to be theoretically open to an investment firm to create a Chinese Wall for the sole purpose of limiting its contractual or fiduciary duties to customers. Since customers need not even know of the existence of a Chinese Wall because there is no express duty to disclose it, one may wonder whether Chinese Walls could one day end up seriously undermining the fundamental objectives of investor protection.

Until the courts have had an opportunity to consider the issues involved it will be a matter of debate as to whether or not the SIB view expressed above is correct. It is possible that the courts may be reluctant to conclude that the existence of a Chinese Wall offers not only a refuge from certain statutory-based rules but also a defence to an action for breach of duty or negligence, at least in the absence of any express agreement to the contrary. The SIB view, if upheld by the courts, would create an important exception to the well-known decision in *Harrods Limited* v. *Lemon*[25] in which it was held by the Court of Appeal that an agent was a single person at law and that the knowledge of each employee would be imputed to his employer.[26]

---

[23] It is interesting in this context to note the qualification incorporated in para. 2 of Core Rule 36 which assumes that the rules made under s. 48(2)(h) of the FSA cannot affect flows of information which are required or assumed by common law to take place between separate companies in a group as distinct from different parts of the business of the same company. It is questionable, however, whether the common law does require or assume information flows between different companies within a group.

[24] It is worth noting in this context that the FSA does contain provisions under which the conduct of persons, who need not be authorized persons, which conforms with certain rules made under the FSA can benefit from derogations from certain statutory prohibitions which would otherwise apply (e.g. s.s 48 (6) and (7), 58(1)(c), and 175 of the FSA) but these derogations are not expressed to affect the civil law consequences of such conduct.

[25] [1931] 2 KB 157.

[26] Two recent cases involving solicitors are also of interest in this context. The first is *David Lee & Co. (Lincoln) Ltd* v. *Coward Chance and Others* [1990] 3 WLR 1278 and the second *Re a Firm of Solicitors* [1992] 1 All ER 353. Both cases involved the propriety of a firm of solicitors

In a wider context, doubts have been expressed as to whether it is in any event sensible for a regulatory system to place too much reliance on Chinese Walls to regulate conflicts of interest, given the ever-present danger that the sheer weight of economic self-interest will create holes in the wall when the stakes are high enough.[27] It may also be questioned whether a regulator should be prepared to relax the operation of its rules in the case of investment firms which profess to maintain Chinese Walls where (*a*) the relevant internal rules do not conform to an industry standard (e.g. in relation to such matters as how high the wall should be within the firm and the circumstances in which and the conditions on which the wall may be crossed) and (*b*) the regulator itself is unable adequately to monitor their effectiveness.

In other areas, common law fiduciary duties are generally not explicitly affected by the statutory regulation of financial services. By way of example, an agent who complies with his statutory obligations under the FSA is not relieved by that Act[28] of his strict common law duty to account to his principal for any profit which he makes in his capacity as agent. It may be, however, that the courts will be prepared to review this particular duty having regard to the impact of statutory regulation. This is a subject which is considered in greater detail in Chapter 3.[29]

acting for a party to litigation when the firm was in possession of confidential information concerning the other party to the litigation. In each case the Court held that the firm could not properly act in the circumstances. In the first case the Court held that there was insufficient evidence of steps designed to produce a form of Chinese Wall which would ensure that there could be no leakage of the relevant information. In the second case a majority of the Court of Appeal cast doubt on the general effectiveness of Chinese Walls within a firm of solicitors. It is questionable, however, whether it is possible to discern from these cases a principle which is applicable to Chinese Walls generally as distinct from Chinese Walls which operate within a firm of solicitors. Solicitors are officers of the court and as such are subject to the special jurisdiction of the court. Their conduct is accordingly subject to considerations which are not necessarily of wider application. For a contrary view, however, see Berg, 'Chinese Walls Come Tumbling Down' (1991) 10 *International Financial Law Review* 23.

[27] See e.g. Norman S. Poser, 'Chinese Wall or Emperor's New Clothes' (1988) 9 *Company Lawyer* 119, 159, and 203.

[28] But note the power to issue regulations under (i) s. 55(2)(f) of the FSA authorizing the retention of clients' money representing interest which could have that effect in a limited way and (ii) s. 81 of the FSA relating to the constitution and management of authorized unit trust schemes and the powers and duties of the manager and trustee of such a scheme and the rights and obligations of participants therein.

[29] The writer wishes to acknowledge the helpful comments received from Jack Beatson and Andrew Whittaker in the preparation of this chapter.

3

THE RELATIONSHIP BETWEEN REGULATIONS GOVERNING THE FINANCIAL SERVICES INDUSTRY AND FIDUCIARY DUTIES UNDER THE GENERAL LAW

Jack Beatson

1. Introduction

This chapter concerns the approach courts are likely to adopt to regulatory rules made in the public law sphere which conflict with what, apart from the rules, would be required by the general law. Although it is difficult to consider this without also considering what approach they *ought* to adopt, as that question will be considered in the Law Commission's forthcoming Consultation Paper on this topic, I shall attempt to do so.

The topic was referred to the Law Commission by the Department of Trade and Industry and the Commission circulated an Issues Questionnaire in November 1990 to assess the extent to which the relationship between the two sets of rules is giving rise to practical difficulty. The reference is confined to public law regulation but although the question whether an activity is within the public law sphere can be a tricky one, this need not concern us since financial services clearly are.[1] Again, while the reference includes duties of care, as this part of the book is concerned with fiduciary obligations this chapter focuses on the relationship of regulatory rules with four overlapping equitable duties imposed on those who act on behalf of clients. These are the 'no conflict' rule, the 'no profit' rule, the undivided loyalty rule, and the duty of confidentiality.[2] One of the hallmarks of equity is its flexibility and the intensity of these duties varies according to the nature of the particular

---

[1] J. Beatson, (1987) 3 *Professional Negligence* 121; P. F. Cane, [1987] CJQ 324. Although the SIB's position has not been tested in the courts, at the time of *R* v. *Panel on Take-Overs, ex p. Datafin* [1987] QB 815 the SIB's then chairman, Sir Kenneth Berrill, stated that it accepted that it was subject to the judicial review jurisdiction. Cf, however, his views on SROs (1986) *Law Soc. Gaz.* 442. See also *SIB* v. *F.I.M.B.R.A.* [1991] 4 All ER 398. On SROs, see *Bank of Scotland* v. *I.M.R.O* [1989] SLT 432; *R* v. *F.I.M.B.R.A. ex p. Cochrane* [1990] COD 33; *R* v. *L.A.U.T.R.O., ex p. Ross The Independent* 11 July 1991.

[2] See Issues Questionnaire para. 2.1 for an outline statement of these.

relationship. This, however, makes it difficult to reduce them to a legislative code.

It is well known that, although the problems associated with conflicts of interest are not new, they were introduced to new situations as a result of the changes brought about by market developments and reforms in the structure of the financial markets in the 1980s. The abolition of single capacity in the trading of stocks and shares and the growth of large multi-function organizations, the development of the regulatory structure which is based on the Financial Services Act 1986 (FSA), and the scrutiny of practices in the light of scandals before and after its enactment have resulted in greater awareness of and concern about the problems. The Law Commission's Issues Questionnaire[3] gave two examples to illustrate the difficulties that might arise. Others are suggested by the questions asked.

The first example is where a broker-dealer deals on behalf of a client either with an associated company or off its own book. Where there is a customer agreement,[4] it will typically rely on a general consent in the agreement to the fact that it might execute transactions without prior notification of the fact that in so doing it *is or may be* acting as principal on its own account or for an associated company.[5] Unless such generalized consent at the commencement of the relationship suffices, this might be seen as infringing both the 'no conflict' and the 'no profit' rules.

The second example is where the private client department of a firm recommends purchasing shares in a company which the corporate finance department knows to be in serious financial trouble. Typically, the firm will have a 'Chinese Wall' clause in its client agreement which states that (*a*) it will provide services on the basis of the information known to the particular employees dealing with the individual client, (*b*) it is not required to have regard to any information known to it, its employees, or an associated company which is confidential to another client and (*c*) it might be unable to advise in relation to particular securities. The agreement may also seek to limit or define the extent of fiduciary duties owed to clients.[6] Again, unless generalized advance disclosure and consent clauses are effective, on a textbook formulation, the firm might be seen as infringing the undivided loyalty rule.[7]

---

[3] Para. 2.3.

[4] There may not be one in the case of an execution-only customer.

[5] Clause 25 of the British Merchant Banking and Securities Houses Association (BMBA) terms and conditions for discretionary fund management gives 13 examples of situations in which there may be a 'material interest', although note the limitation to 6 examples in Exception 3 to TSA Rule 750.01. See also Exception 1 to TSA rule 760.01 which obviates the need for pre-transaction disclosure of self-dealing and dual agency if the relevant customer agreement permits such transactions. See further the Securities and Futures Authority (SFA) Draft Guidance to Core Rule 2 on 'Material Interest' and to Core Rule 14 'customer agreements', esp. para. 14.4.

[6] BMBA Clause 25 state: 'The relationship is as described in the agreement. Neither that relationship nor the services nor any other matter shall give rise to any fiduciary or equitable duties which would prevent or hinder . . . [the adviser] . . . from acting as both market-maker and broker, principal or agent, dealing with other Associates . . .'

[7] The SIB's Chinese Wall provision, Core Rule 36, is discussed below.

How is one to respond to these problems? Paul Finn has considered the efficacy of traditional common law and equitable techniques of disclosure and consent[8] and Peter Graham has discussed the regulatory framework introduced as a result of the enactment of the FSA.[9] My task is to consider the effect of that system of public law regulation. Several situations should be distinguished.

1. There may be market practices which the rules assume to be, but do not explicitly make, legitimate. The position of the general consent in advance provisions in broker-dealers' client agreements about the capacity in which the broker-dealer may be acting falls into this category.[10]

2. There may be detailed rules about a particular matter. Core Rule 36 on Chinese Walls is an example of this.

3. There is a contrast between 'real' conflicts of regulatory and general law (in the sense that compliance with one would necessarily constitute breach of the other) and situations in which the regulatory rule sets a less onerous standard than the general law but does not prohibit compliance with the higher standard. We shall see that Core Rule 36 may raise the possibility of a 'real' conflict, while requirements about the timing and specificity of disclosure of commission and other remuneration in Core Rule 18(2) may not raise a 'real' conflict in this sense although they do raise the question of whether the rules offer a 'safe harbour' for those who comply with them.

Before turning to the possible judicial approaches, we should remind ourselves of a number of the features of the complex FSA structure.

2. The Statutory and Regulatory Framework

The primary regulatory power given to the Secretary of State for Trade and Industry was, as contemplated, delegated to the Securities and Investments Board (SIB) which recognizes self-regulating organizations (SROs) with responsibility for specific areas. Extensive executive and enforcement powers regarding the authorization of individuals, the recognition of SROs, and injunctive and restitutionary orders were given to the SIB by the statute. A new statutory damages remedy for breach of conduct of business rules was created by FSA, section 62, at first for all investors, but since 1991 only for private investors.[11]

---

[8] See Ch. 1 above.   [9] See Ch. 2 above.

[10] By FSA Schedule 8, para. 6 the rules of the SIB must make proper provision for requiring the capacity in which an authorized person enters a transaction to be disclosed. See SIB Principle 6 ('Conflicts of Interest'); Core Rule 2 ('Material Interest'); Core Rule 18(2) (disclosure of basis or amount of charges or either remuneration). By the proposed SFA Rules disclosure is not required of 'any profit made on a principal transaction (other than . . . [one] . . . effected in circumstances giving rise to similar duties as those arising on an *order* to effect a transaction as agent) or to any commission received from another *customer* as a result of a simultaneous matching transaction' (Draft Rule 18.4). This disclosure will normally be on the contract note; i.e. post transaction; SFA Draft Rule 19.4. Cf SFA Draft Rule 14.4. For the present position under the TSA rules see Exception 1 to Rule 760.01 (n. 6 above).

[11] For the definition of 'private investor' see SI 1991 No. 489.

As for rule-making powers, the SIB was to have extensive powers but the conditions for the delegation of regulatory powers by the Secretary of State included that he be satisfied that its rules provided an adequate level of investor protection and accorded with the principles set out in the Act. Recognized SROs are not given rule-making power directly by the FSA although the Companies Act 1989 gives them some power to modify or disapply certain of the SIB's core rules.[12] However, rules of recognized SROs are subject to statutory control and must satisfy certain requirements, in particular they must afford 'an adequate level of protection for investors'.[13]

Peter Graham has already pointed out that the FSA makes no overt reference to the relationship between rules made under it and parallel or overlapping duties arising in equity. There is also not much guidance in the two pre-legislative reports, Professor Gower's report[14] and the Government White Paper.[15] Professor Gower's report called for the regulatory rules to embody basic principles of law[16] but this could either require exact cloning or permit such variation as did not subvert the fundamental purposes served by the equitable rules. The White Paper contains a number of statements about the relationship including the following:

- 'Where an investment business acts as *agent* for a client, the general rules of agency and consequent fiduciary duties apply to the business' (para. 7.6).
- Specific conflicts of interest would need to be resolved in accordance with a 'best execution' principle and a 'subordination of interest' requirement (para. 7.6).[17] Apparently, although this is not expressly stated, this was to be done in regulatory rules, albeit not exclusively by rules concerning Chinese Walls, upon which the Government did not think total reliance could be placed since they restricted flows of information but not the conflicts of interest themselves (para 7.4).
- The law should provide a *clearly understood set of general principles and rules* to facilitate the objectives of the new framework for investor protection (para. 3.2).

Undoubtedly, fiduciary duties are part of this scheme of investor protection. So any separation of regulatory rules and 'ordinary' law could be an impediment to the achievement of a clearly understood body of law.

3. Three Models of Interpretation

The impact of rules made by the SIB and SROs on the common law and equitable rights and duties of those subject to regulation and their clients

[12] FSA, s. 63B (inserted by Companies Act 1989, s. 194).
[13] FSA Schedule 2, para. 3(1) as amended by Companies Act 1989, s. 203(1).
[14] Review of Investor Protection (Cmnd. 9125, 1984) hereafter 'Gower'.
[15] Financial Services in the United Kingdom: A New Framework for Investor Protection (Cmnd. 9432, 1985), hereafter 'White Paper'.
[16] Gower, para. 6.30.   [17] On this see FSA, Schedule 8, para. 3.

depends on two factors. First, there is the question of the regulators' authority to make rules altering such rights. Secondly, if there is such authority, the question is whether the regulators have in fact exercised it when making their rules. Although this chapter is primarily concerned with the first question, it is worth bearing in mind that it is not likely that the SIB would wish to make radical alterations to fiduciary duties, especially since the fundamental purpose of the FSA scheme is investor protection. What is more likely is an attempt to refine the requirements of a fiduciary duty in a given context in the light of the totality of the safeguards for investors under the regulatory scheme. This can be seen in the case of unit trust schemes, where the clear authority to modify equitable duties was exercised without covering the whole range of duties under the general law.[18]

Where a rule is made which appears to conflict with or modify fiduciary duties the court has several options. First, it can say there is no authority to make such a rule and invalidate it. Secondly, it can give the rule a restrictive interpretation so that it (*a*) does not affect common law and equitable duties or (*b*) only operates in the regulatory sphere. Thirdly, it can recognize that a rule made pursuant to statutory authority has statutory force and the same effect as if it was in the statute[19] and accept that it modifies the common law or equitable rule with which it conflicts. The common law or equitable rule is subsumed by the regulatory rule. This can occur in one of two ways: either simply because of the public law validity of the regulatory rule, or because the public law validity of the rule makes it relevant (although not conclusive) in the determination of the content of the common law or equitable rule in that particular context.

The approach taken will depend on the statutory context and the extent of the particular rule-making power. We have seen that recognized SROs are not expressly given rule-making powers by the FSA. For this reason, their rules, while instruments of public law and recognized by the FSA, may not be 'statutory' rules with statutory force[20] and may thus technically differ from the SIB's rules. In principle, however, the public law nature of rules of recognized SROs and the fact that they operate in an integrated way with the

---

[18] Financial Services (Regulated Schemes) Regulations 1991, regs. 7–16 (4–6) and 8–05(3). Cf. Financial Services (Regulated Schemes) Regulations 1991, reg. 7.12 which states that the regulatory duties of the manager and trustee are in addition to and nor in derogation from duties under the general law so far as they are not restricted by the regulations. The rule-making power is in FSA, s. 81, on which see below.

[19] F. Bennion, *Statutory Interpretation* (London, 1984), 133–5.

[20] The fact that the FSA expressly provides that they are to be treated as such in one context (withdrawal and suspension of a directly authorized person who is also a member of an SRO: FSA, s. 28 (read 28(3) together with 28(1)(b)) suggests that in other contexts they are not. The drafting of Core Rule 15 which prohibits firms 'excluding or restricting any duty or liability to a customer which it has under the Act or under the regulatory system' suggests that the SIB recognizes this difficulty since this is defined to include SRO rules; Financial Services Glossary 1991. See also M. Blair, *Financial Services: The New Core Rules* (1991), 91 (Mr Blair is General Counsel to the SIB).

SIB's rules[21] should mean that the court is able to take the same approach to their interpretation as it does to the SIB's rules.

The presumption that statutes do not alter the common law applies where statute accords power to public bodies including non-governmental ones such as the SIB. There is nothing special about financial services in this respect. As in other contexts, however, where the statute is not clear the court's choice between the options set out above may well depend on the strength of the presumption. This varies according to the context, whether personal liberty or property rights are affected, and the extent to which the statutory scheme is detailed and potentially self-contained.[22] The differing strengths of the presumption that statutes do not alter the common law can be represented by three models.

Where the presumption is strongest, 'special' regulatory law will be subject to 'general' principles of private law unless the common law principles are necessarily overridden by the statute. Under this 'private law model' there is no authority to make rules altering such rights and obligations save where the enabling statute, here the Financial Services Act, gives it expressly or by necessary implication. If there is no such authority, 'to the extent that the rules . . . are inconsistent with and do not comply with the general law, then they would obviously be improper'.[23]

Where the presumption is weakest, the facilitative aspects of the statute assume more importance. Under this 'public law model' it is the nature and scope of the statutory scheme rather than an express power to alter private law rights in the rule-making powers that is important in determining the scope of the rule-making powers. Although it might be *Wednesbury* unreasonable[24] or incompatible with statutory purposes for a rule to alter common law rights, this should be deduced from the words of the statute itself.[25]

A middle way would be for the court to give some recognition to the public law nature of the regulatory rules while keeping control over the content of

[21] See e.g. FSA, s. 61(1)(a)(iv) (SIB has power to restrain contravention of SRO rules) and the fact that the core rules treat a duty or liability to a customer under a SRO rule as a duty under 'the regulatory system' which cannot, under Core Rule 15(1), be excluded or restricted, see above.

[22] F. Bennion, *Statutory Interpretation*, 305.

[23] *Supasave Retail Ltd* v. *Coward Chance* [1991] 1 All ER 668, 672, per Browne-Wilkinson, V-C of the Law Society's rules on conflicts of interest arising on the amalgamation of firms of solicitors. There was in fact no incompatibility between the rules and the general law because the rules required all parties to consent if the amalgamated firm was to act for either and the statutory basis of the Law Society's rule-making power was not considered. Cf *Swain* v. *Law Society* [1983] 1 AC 598.

[24] In *Associated Provincial Picture Houses Ltd.* v. *Wednesbury Corporation* [1948] 1 KB 223 Lord Greene, MR stated the basic principles of judicial review of discretionary powers; i.e. propriety of purpose, relevance of considerations taken into account, and the residual ground of 'unreasonableness' or 'irrationality', on which, in the context of rule-making powers, see *Kruse* v. *Johnson* [1898] 2 QB 91; *Re Toohey* (1981) 38 ALR 439.

[25] *Kruse* v. *Johnson* [1898] 2 QB 91 (by-laws of public non-profit-making bodies to be benevolently interpreted); *Mixnam's Properties Ltd.* v. *Chertsey U.D.C.* [1965] AC 735, 755 (*per* Viscount Radcliffe, albeit in a minority).

common law and equitable obligations. Under this 'hybrid model', while 'general' principles of private law ultimately prevail unless the statute expressly or by necessary implication authorizes their modification or abrogation, in determining the content of those 'general principles' the court properly has regard to the custom and practice of the market and, in particular, to regulatory practices and rules, which should be taken to have effect if reasonable.

3.1. THE PRIVATE LAW MODEL

The rule-making powers under the FSA fall into a number of categories, only one of which, authorizing rules on matters affecting relations between authorized persons and those doing business with them,[26] concerns us. Within this category, the power to make rules concerning the management of unit trust schemes given by section 81 authorizes rules concerning 'the rights and obligations of the participants' and that concerning clients' money given by section 55 empowers rules permitting the retention of interest on clients' money and deals with authorized persons' liability as constructive trustee. Apart from these provisions there is no clear express authority to modify common law and equitable rights.

In particular, there are no similar references in section 48 which enables the making of rules governing the conduct of business. Does this preclude the power to modify common law and equity? Section 48(2)(a), the Chinese Wall provision, authorizes rules

enabling or *requiring* information obtained by an authorized person in the course of carrying on one part of his business to be withheld by him from persons with whom he deals in the course of carrying on another part and for that purpose *enabling* or *requiring* persons employed in one part of that business to withhold information from those employed in another part.

The SIB has exercised this power by making Core Rule 36, which provides:

(1) Where a firm maintains an established arrangement which requires information obtained by the firm in the course of carrying on one part of its business of any kind to be withheld in certain circumstances from persons with whom it deals in the course of carrying on another part of its business of any kind, then in those circumstances:
   a. that information may be so withheld; and
   b. for that purpose, persons employed in the first part may withhold information from those employed in the second;
   but only to the extent that the business of one of those parts involves investment business or associated business.
(2) Information may also be withheld where this is required by an established arrangement between different parts of the business (of any kind) of a group, but

---

[26] These concern conduct of business (FSA, s. 48); cancellation (FSA, s. 51); compensation where authorized persons unable to satisfy claims (FSA, s. 54); client's money (FSA, s. 55); unsolicited calls (FSA, s. 56); constitution and management of unit trust schemes (FSA, s. 81); publication of unit trust scheme (FSA, s. 85).

this provision does not affect any requirement to transmit information which may arise apart from the Core Conduct of Business Rules.

(3) Where the Core Conduct of Business Rules apply only if a firm acts with knowledge, the firm is not for the purposes of the Core Conduct of Business Rules to be taken to act with knowledge if none of the relevant individuals involved on behalf of the firm acts with knowledge.

(4) In addition, in order to avoid the attribution of information held within a firm to that firm for the purposes of section 47 of the Act, the effect of section 48(6) of the Act is that nothing done in conformity with paragraph (1) of the core rule on Chinese walls is to be regarded as a contravention of section 47 of the Act.

The question is whether Core Rule 36 authorizes the modification of a duty of disclosure pursuant to the fiduciary 'undivided loyalty' rule and the current law on attribution of knowledge within one corporate entity or partnership[27] so that knowledge will not, as it is now, be attributed between different parts of a firm. If so, unless the particular individuals dealing with a client actually have knowledge, the prohibition in Core Rule[28] on *knowingly* advising or dealing in the exercise of discretion will not apply.

On this interpretative model, there will be difficulties in finding authority for rules made under section 48 to have this effect, particularly where there is no 'real' conflict in the sense used above.[29] Where there is a 'real' conflict, however, as in the case of Core Rule 36 even on this model there is an argument favouring such authority. The argument is based on the use of the word 'enabling' and the undesirability of conflicting obligations,[30] the support of Chinese Walls in a number of legislative contexts, and the contrast between the approach of the 1983 Conduct of Business Rules and the FSA. Rule 14(4) of the 1983 Rules contained an express saving of the equitable 'no profit' rule and any rule enabling any contract between a licensed dealer and a managed account client to be avoided. There is nothing similar either in the FSA or in the Core Rules.[31]

---

[27] *Harrods Ltd* v. *Lemon* [1931] 2 KB 157. On attribution of knowledge in partnerships see the cases on lawyers discussed by Finn, Ch. 1 above, especially *National Mutual Holdings Pty Ltd* v. *Sentry Corp.* (1989) 87 ALR 539, 555 (Gummow, J.)

[28] This provides: 'Where a firm has a material interest in a transaction to be entered into with or for a customer or a relationship which gives rise to a conflict of interest in relation to such a transaction, the firm must not knowingly either advise, or deal in the exercise of discretion, in relation to that transaction unless it takes reasonable steps to ensure fair treatment for the customer.'

[29] See p. 57 above.

[30] An authorized person cannot be 'enabled' to withhold information if he is in any event free to do so, it can be argued that the subsection must be concerned with a situation in which there is an existing common law or equitable duty of disclosure. If this is correct, unless it empowers the modification of such duty, an authorized person would not be 'enabled'. In the case of a regulatory 'requirement' to withhold information he would be subjected to conflicting duties because withholding as 'required' by the rules would necessarily constitute breach of common law or equitable duties to disclose that information, while disclosure to satisfy the general law would necessarily involve breach of the regulatory 'requirement'.

[31] But see n. 18 above for the position under the Unit Trust rules.

3.2. THE PUBLIC LAW MODEL

This focuses on the nature and scope of the statutory scheme to determine the scope of the rule-making powers and without any presumption that a detailed scheme is incomplete. Account should be taken of the entire regulatory framework, the expertise of the regulatory body, and the fact that the court's role is limited to review or supervision. If regulatory rules are not empowered to modify common law or equitable duties, this is because of nonconformity to the statutory purposes (here the adequacy of the protection afforded to investors) and not of nonconformity to the common law.

An illustration of the way this model might work is provided by the approach of the House of Lords in *Swain* v. *Law Society*.[32] A statutory power to make rules concerning indemnity for losses arising from liability for professional negligence was held to empower the society to take out and maintain a master insurance policy which gave solicitors directly enforceable rights under the policy and to require solicitors to pay the premiums but without accounting for commission received. In a purely private law context there would have been no such enforceable rights (because of the doctrine of privity of contract) in the absence of agency or constructive trust which were not established but would have involved a duty to account. However, no duty to account arose because, in the exercise of its rule-making powers, the Law Society was acting in a public capacity. Lord Diplock stated that:

[W]hat it does in that capacity is governed by public law; and, although the legal consequences of doing it may result in rights enforceable in private law, those rights are not necessarily the same as those that would flow in private law from doing a similar act otherwise than in the exercise of statutory powers.[33]

The argument for applying this approach to financial services is based on the elaborateness and sophistication of the regulatory scheme created by Parliament to achieve the legislative aims of ensuring investor protection. The statutory controls over the rules of the SIB and SROs and, in particular, the role of the Secretary of State suggest that it was contemplated that rules which survived their scrutiny adequately protected investors. Investors benefit from active regulation and monitoring of investment business including the exercise of investigative and enforcement powers and in 1986 they were given a new statutory action for damages for breaches of regulatory rules.[34] On this approach, the argument that the rulemaking power in section 48(2)(h) permits modification of common law and equitable duties becomes easier and even the difference between 'real' conflicts and other 'safe harbour' situations may be less important.

---

[32] [1983] 1 AC 598. [33] Ibid. 608.
[34] See p. 57 above and pp. 66–67 below on the subsequent restriction of this to private investors.

3.3. The 'Hybrid' Model

This model draws on the process of implication of a term by custom. Such a term will be implied where it is notorious, certain, and reasonable, and is recognized in the market as creating legal rights.[35] Thus, regulatory rules would be evidence or guidance as to the expectations of the parties and of market usage.[36] The analysis may be put in one of two ways. The first is simply to see whether the regulatory rules are incorporated into transactions by custom. Alternatively, it may be said that here it is the public law validity of a rule that requires a court to give effect to it if reasonable, not the intentions of the parties. The difference between the two may be fine but the second analysis gives recognition to the public law validity of the rule while the first is exclusively contractual. However, the second analysis differs from the public law model because it presupposes separate spheres of operation for regulatory rules and 'ordinary' law.

Although a court could simply ignore the regulatory rule,[37] this is unlikely particularly in the case of public law regulation. Apart from the use of such rules as sources of custom and trade practice, there is a number of ways in which courts have used regulatory rules in determining whether an obligation under the general law exists or has been broken. First, non-compliance with the rules may assist a court in determining that a state of affairs exists or that conduct falls below the required standard.[38] Secondly, non-compliance with regulatory rules may be a ground upon which the court will refuse to enforce a stipulation of confidence.[39] Thirdly, compliance with regulatory rules or the regulator's directions may facilitate a finding that there has not been 'unreasonable' or 'unfair' conduct.[40] Although many of these examples concern standards that are often seen as more flexible than the equitable 'no conflict' rule, that rule is in fact formulated in terms of a 'reasonable man

---

[35] *General Reinsurance* v. *Fennia Patria* [1983] 1 QB 856. See generally *12 Halsbury's Laws*, 4th edn. (London, 1990), para. 450.

[36] *Benjamin* v. *Barnett* (1903) 8 Com. Cas. 244, 247–8; *Forget* v. *Baxter* [1900] AC 467, 479.

[37] *Warren* v. *Mendy* [1989] 3 All ER 103, 117 ('it is no answer to a claim in constructive trust to say that the . . . [British Board of Boxing Control's] . . . regulations permit a manager to act also as a promoter') but this did *not* concern public law regulation. In *North & South Trust Co.* v. *Berkeley* [1971] 1 WLR 470; [1970] 2 Lloyd's Rep. 467, the practice of Lloyd's brokers in acting for both the assured and the underwriter was not validated but (*a*) the practice was not sanctified by a Lloyd's by-law and (*b*) the practice was considered unreasonable.

[38] *Re St. Piran* [1981] 1 WLR 1300; *Re a Company* [1987] BCLC 382, 387 (ignoring the Take-Over Panel's Code may make it 'just and equitable' that a company be wound up or indicate that there has been 'unfairness' in the conduct of the company's affairs); *Stafford* v. *Conti* [1981] 1 All ER 691; B. Rider, C. Abrams, and E. Ferran, *Guide to the FSA*, 2nd ed., 1989 para. 608 (the SIB 'suitability' of investment rule may have the effect of imposing a duty on a broker to warn his customer against unsuitable investments whereas hitherto there was no such duty).

[39] *Dunford & Elliot Ltd* v. *Johnson & Firth Brown Ltd.* [1977] 1 Lloyd's R. 505 (stipulation of confidence infringed the Take-Over Code's provisions concerning equality of information). See also *Crabtree* v. *Hinchcliffe* [1972] AC 707, 730.

[40] See *Lloyd Cheyham* v. *Littlejohn* [1987] BCLC 303, 313 (*Likierman Report*, 319, 323); *Dawson* v. *Coats Paton* [1989] BCLC 233; [1990] BCLC 560 on the relevance of guidance prepared by Consultative Committee of Accountancy Bodies to auditors' liability.

looking at the relevant facts and circumstances of the particular case' thinking that 'there was a real sensible possibility of conflict'.[41]

4. The Advantages and Disadvantages of the Three Models

Both the public law and hybrid models take account of the approach of the courts to the interpretation of statutes which remit authority to a regulatory body. Where appropriate, the regulatory body may be given an appreciable margin by the court recognizing regulatory expertise, perhaps characterizing the meaning of statutory words as involving questions of 'fact and degree' rather than questions of law[42] and characterizing the relationship between the courts and the regulators as a partnership.[43] It might be objected that it is wrong for statute and regulations to affect the common law in this indirect way. On both the public law and the hybrid models, however, the court retains control; direct control if the hybrid model is used, indirect control by testing the regulatory rules against the statutory purposes if the public law model is used. We should not in any event be surprised at such indirect alteration of common law. After all, the Law Reform (Contributory Negligence) Act 1945, enabling apportionment of damages in tort, affected the courts' approach to the question of whether a plaintiff had been at fault, and the Unfair Contract Terms Act 1977's subjection of many exemption clauses to a 'reasonableness' test has led to a more natural and less restrictive approach to construction, even though neither Act addressed these issues.[44]

The advantage of the private law model is that it is based on the dominant approach to statutory interpretation and acts to preserve the rights investors would have had in the absence of statutory intervention. It reflects a view that the statute was giving investors an additional layer of protection. The disadvantages of the private law model are as follows. First, it does not appear to give any recognition to the expertise of the bodies to which Parliament has entrusted the regulation of financial services. Secondly, it either requires regulatory rules to clone common law rules or posits two independent systems of law; one operating in the regulatory context, the other in the ordinary courts. Although some complexity may be inevitable in this area, both alternatives are very confusing and complicated, not least

---

[41] *Boardman* v. *Phipps* [1967] 2 AC 46, 124. (Lord Upjohn). See Note 1 to TSA rule 750: an interest is 'material' when there is a 'serious possibility' (disregarding any independence policy) of an employee being induced to make a recommendation knowing it is contrary to the customer's interests or without giving proper consideration to whether it is in the customer's interests. Cf. the exclusive definition in the Financial Services Glossary 1991 and SFA's draft Guidance on Core Rule 2.

[42] *Puhlhofer* v. *Hillingdon L.B.C.* [1986] AC 484, 517–18.

[43] *R* v. *Panel on Take-Overs, ex p. Datafin* [1987] Q.B 815. See also *R* v. *MMC, ex p Argyll* [1986] 2 All ER 257; *R v. MMC, ex p Elders IXL* [1987] 1 All ER 451.

[44] P. S. Atiyah, (1985) 48 M.L.R. 1, 22–6. The evolution of general doctrines of 'unconscionability and unfairness' in Australia and Canada has been said to be in part due to the influence of the Australian Trade Practices Act 1974, s. 52, and the Canadian Charter of Rights.

because of the difficulty of accurately stating the equitable duties in a legislative form. Thirdly, it may imperil important aspects of the regulated system, for instance by concluding that Chinese Walls are ineffective to prevent the attribution of information or that because advance disclosure that would satisfy equitable requirements is impossible an authorized broker-dealer is always liable when he is buying or selling as a principal. These disadvantages were greater on the old SIB rules since the contrast between their detail and the broadness of the equitable principles was more likely to produce mismatch or conflict. While the difficulties are reduced by the new SIB principles and core rules, as the debate about the effect of Core Rule 36 shows, they have not disappeared and some of the complexity may well have been pushed into the third tier of regulations, the SRO rules.

The advantage of the public law model is that it facilitates the achievement of the regulatory purposes and the development of one clearly understood set of general principles and rules and thus promotes certainty. The regulators are not left with an unfettered hand because the courts retain power under their supervisory jurisdiction to hold that a rule is invalid for nonconformity to the statutory scheme, a central part of which is to ensure adequate investor protection.

The disadvantage of the public law model is that regulators might stop framing their rules in the shadow of and by reference to the principles of agency and fiduciary law which have a proven track record as effective protection for those who deal with an intermediary or fiduciary. Although the regulatory rules are subject to judicial review and to the control of SIB (in the case of SROs) and the DTI this might not be adequate. The scope of judicial review of delegated legislation may well be narrower than in respect of other administrative action[45] and the non-judicial controls on delegated legislation are limited even where there is a Parliamentary safeguard.[46] Where, as in this context, there are no Parliamentary safeguards, the dangers might be thought to be greater, particularly in view of the self-regulating elements of the system.

The public law model may also lead to differences between the position of different authorized persons which are not easy to justify. For instance, as Peter Graham's points out in Chapter 2, if Core Rule 36 empowers modification of the general law by the SIB the position of those authorized by membership of a recognized professional body (RPB) looks anomalous. The Core Rules do not apply and, unless the RPB is itself empowered to modify the general law and chooses to do so, the common law will apply. Again, it might be said that modification of the general law will create imbalance between private investors and others who do not have the protection of the

[45] See in relation to unreasonableness, wrong purposes and relevant considerations *Kruse* v. *Johnson* [1898] 2 QB 91; *City of Edinburgh DC* v. *Secretary of State for Scotland* 1985 SLT 551. See also *McEldowney* v. *Forde* [1971] AC 632. Cf. *Re Toohey; ex parte Northern Land Council* (1981) 38 ALR. 439 (High Court of Australia).

[46] Beatson, (1979) 12 Cornell I.LJ. 199; Haycroft & Wallington, [1988] Public Law 548.

statutory damages remedy under section 62.[47] On this last point, however, it can be said that the restriction in 1989 of the section 62 remedy to private investors is not relevant to the scope of the rule-making powers given under the 1986 Act. Furthermore, the force of the public law model comes from a comparison of the entirety of the regulatory system and not one isolated aspect of it. For instance, non-private investors will still have remedies under FSA, section 61, but will have to secure these by persuading the SIB to make an application for an injunction, restitution, or compensation.[48]

The advantage of the hybrid model is that the courts retain some control over the regulatory rules in the sense that they are not bound to give effect to them rather than the common law if they are considered unreasonable. Under this model the common law can be developed, not in a revolutionary way, but in the light of the experience gained in the regulatory system. However, this technique may not differ fundamentally from the application of the full *Wednesbury* test in the sense of determining the validity of the rule by assessing its adherence to proper statutory purposes, use of relevant considerations, and exclusion of irrelevant considerations as well as the residual 'unreasonableness' test. If so, the proliferation of similar tests to determine first whether the rule is a valid public law rule, and then whether it overrides private law rights, is a recipe for confusion and uncertainty.

5. Conclusion

The Law Commission's Issues Questionnaire dealt with a wide range of regulated contexts. The responses indicate the following.

(a) Many of the problems that undoubtedly exist do not arise from a mismatch or a potential mismatch between the regulatory rules and the fiduciary obligation. They arise from conflicts of interest which are prohibited by both the rules and the general law but which practitioners find it difficult to avoid.

(b) Serious practical problems do arise from mismatch between regulatory rules and fiduciary obligations.

(c) In one area, the investment activities of trustees, the regulator, IMRO, has disapplied all the rules which have been argued to conflict with trustees' obligations under the general law[49]

(d) The problems arising from mismatch (i) primarily concern financial services (ii) are concentrated within a narrow area, and (iii) are largely centred on the issues of generalized advance disclosure and the efficacy of Chinese Walls in relation to the attribution of knowledge within an organization so as to trigger positive duties to clients, including disclosure.

---

[47] By Companies Act 1989, s. 203 (introducing a new s. 62A to the FSA).

[48] Refusal to proceed will be subject to control by judicial review.

[49] I.M.R.O. Rules, ch. 12.

It is therefore likely that eventually the question of mismatch will come before the courts, perhaps in the context of the Chinese Wall or the efficacy of generalized advance disclosures. On the present state of the law it is difficult to predict the outcome but the relative merits and demerits of the three models considered show that difficult and sensitive policy issues are involved. The decisions on the use of Chinese Walls in lawyers' firms[50] suggest the courts are likely to be suspicious of them in the financial services context. Court decisions on similarly difficult issues in the last year—particularly the legality of interest rate 'swaps' by local authorities[51]—are said to have unsettled financial markets and to have led to the establishment by the Bank of England of the Legal Risk Review Committee to try to reduce uncertainty. Whatever the outcome of the Law Commission's study, an important objective is to make the law as certain as it can be without prejudicing the flexibility which has enabled it to respond adequately to new situations.

On the particular subject of Chinese Walls, while it is difficult to know what the courts' reaction will be, it should be remembered that the sceptical indications in the English cases involving law firms occurred in the course of an entirely private law approach to the matter. The public law aspects were not considered and did not need to be considered since the question of authorization by a regulatory rule did not arise. The cases also concerned what Paul Finn calls 'same matter' and 'former client' conflicts. There may be differences between these and 'separate matter' conflicts and it should be remembered that there are differences between legal and financial services— primarily the unique nature of the attorney–client privilege.

On a broader note, however, if it is concluded that FSA, section 48(2)(h) does empower rules which modify common law and equitable duties to disclose and rules governing the attribution of knowledge, this could have much wider consequences, despite what was said in the Gower Report and the White Paper. For, if section 48(2)(h) does provide such authority, it is arguable that so do the rule-making powers of section 48(1). By section 48(3), the particular powers in section 48(2)(h) are without prejudice to the generality of section 48(1) and it is surely at least arguable that if the particular rule-making powers give authority to modify duties owed to third parties under the general law, so does the general rule-making power. This may have implications for the efficacy of generalized advance disclosure since, as has already been said,[52] even if it has not explicitly legitimized, the rules assume prior disclosure of the capacity in which a broker-dealer may enter a transaction and post-transaction disclosure of the capacity in which he does so is sufficient.

---

[50] *Supasave Retail Ltd.* v. *Coward Chance* [1991] 1 All ER 668; *Re a Firm of Solicitors* [1992] 1 All ER 353; *National Mutual Holdings* v. *Sentry Corp.* (1989) 87 ALR 539; *Mallesons Stephen Jaques* v. *KPMG Peat Marwick* (SC of WA); *Martin* v. *Macdonald Estate (Grey)* [1991] 1 WWR 705; Reynolds, (1991) 107 *LQR* 536.

[51] *Hazell* v. *Hammersmith & Fulham L.B.C.* [1991] 2 WLR 372.

[52] See p. 56 above.

Finally, it is important to note that if regulatory rules in this context are capable of altering common law and equitable rights and duties to any degree, this is entirely a product of the construction of the FSA. In principle, as is shown by the examples given in the discussion of the 'hybrid' model, other regulatory contexts are susceptible to similar analysis. Whether their statutory or other public law framework in fact provides authority and whether, if it does, regulators have chosen to exercise it are different matters. For, although, as a matter of principle, there is nothing special about financial services, the FSA has created a very unusual regulatory structure, both in its scope and complexity and in the fact that the guiding purposes of and principles for regulatory rules are enunciated so elaborately in the enabling statute.

II
Directors' Duties to Share Holders, Creditors, and Employees

4

DIRECTORS, CREDITORS, AND SHAREHOLDERS

D. D. Prentice

1. Introduction

It is a generally accepted principle of company law that directors owe their duties to the company and not to the company's creditors or to its shareholders: 'no fiduciary duty is owed by a director to individual members of his company, but only to the company itself, and *a fortiori* . . . none is owed to a person who is not a member'.[1] It is important to appreciate what this means and what it does not mean. It does not mean that the interests of shareholders or creditors can be ignored—what it entails is that there is no 'free-standing' duty owed by directors because of their status to creditors or to shareholders entitling the latter to sue the directors directly without some involvement on the part of the company. Neither does it entail that the duties which directors owe to the company may not embrace the interests of either the shareholders or the creditors for, as will be seen, in certain circumstances the 'interests of the company' (that most protean of concepts) can embrace the interests of the creditors or the shareholders. There is of course no impediment to a director of his own volition assuming obligations towards shareholders or creditors, for example by agreeing to act as an agent for the shareholders in selling their shares or guaranteeing the debts of the company, but in such situations the duty of the director arises from the assumption of liability and not because of his status.[2] The focus of this chapter is status-based obligations. Lastly, statute can impose on the directors an obligation to consider the interests of any constituency affected by the affairs of the company as is the case in the United Kingdom with respect to employees.[3]

2. Justification for the Principle of No Free-Standing Duty

As a preliminary matter, it might be useful to determine what, if any, are the justifications for the general principle that a director's duties run to the

---

[1] Jenkins Committee Report, Cmnd.. 1749 (1962) at para. 89.

[2] See e.g. *Allen* v. *Hyatt* (1914) 30 TLR 444 (directors acting as agents for the shareholders in the sale of their shares); *Coleman* v. *Myers* [1977] 2 NZLR 225 (on the special facts directors held to have assumed fiduciary obligations towards shareholders).

[3] Companies Act 1989, s. 309. It is interesting to note that even in this case the duty is mediated through the company: see s. 309(2); D. D. Prentice, 'A Company and Its Employees: The Companies Act 1980' (1981) 10 *ILJ* 1.

company and that the interests of the creditors and shareholders must normally be mediated through the duty that the directors owe to the company. There is a number of reasons which at least cumulatively (if not individually) strongly favour the current position.

First, it prevents multiplicity of actions. If, for example, directors owed free-standing duties to shareholders the enforcement of such duties could result in a series of individual actions by aggrieved shareholders. It would not be beyond the wit of man to formulate a procedure for a representative action to curb multiplicity of actions, but this would not be easy since shareholders would not necessarily have an identity of interest.[4] Channelling recovery through the company acts as a form of representative action and avoids these difficulties. This brings out an important feature of the entity doctrine, namely, its mechanical efficiency in organizing claims by or against a company.[5]

Secondly, channelling recovery through the company eliminates problems that could otherwise arise with respect to double recovery or the ranking of claims to recovery. For example, in many situations the acts which allegedly caused harm to the shareholders or creditors may also have injured the company as an economic entity and the issue would inevitably arise as to whether all aggrieved parties had a right to bring an action and, if not, who had the preferred right of recovery.[6]

Thirdly, there is what one might refer to as the temporal element; this is particularly relevant with respect to shareholders. The persons who were shareholders at the time of the alleged wrong by the directors will not necessarily be the same persons who are shareholders at the time the wrong is discovered and any ensuing action is brought. If a direct action by shareholders against directors were to be allowed, a starting-point might be to vest the right of action in shareholders at the date on which the wrong is made public and has a material impact on the value of the company's shares. This would make sense where the public disclosure of the wrong depressed the price of the shares and where the price had not until this point impounded the effect of the director's wrongdoing. In this situation the value of the existing shareholders' shares would be depressed and the ex-shareholders would have received a price for their shares which had not been affected by the director's wrongdoing at the time they disposed of the shares. However, allowing the existing shareholders to recover would not be appealing where the recovery resulted in a windfall[7] for the existing shareholders because

---

[4] For example, there is the problem of harmonizing the interests of (i) pre-breach of duty shareholders (ii) shareholders at the time of breach, (iii) post-breach of duty shareholders, and (iv) shareholders at the time the breach is detected.

[5] See R. C. Clark, *Corporate Law* (Boston, 1986) at 19.

[6] The courts have been careful to ensure that wrongs to the company cannot be transmuted into harms to the shareholders: see *Prudential Assurance Co. Ltd.* v. *Newman Industries Ltd. (No.2)* [1982] Ch. 204, at 222–3. The Court also pointed out in that case that allowing a personal action would create difficult (if not insoluble) problems in showing a causal nexus between the alleged wrongdoing and the quantum of harm to the shareholder.

[7] This windfall problem also arises in the case of recovery by the company. For example, in

when their shares had been acquired the price had fully reflected the impact of the director's wrongdoing. This discussion also assumes that the point at which the effect of the director's wrongdoing on the value of a company's shares can be precisely identified, but this in many situations will be far from being the case.[8]

Fourthly, quantifying harm to the shareholders from a wrong committed by the directors in many situations will not be easy; a £100,000 loss to the company could cause a £1,000,000 loss to the shareholders where there was a fear that the wrong would be repeated in the future.[9]

Fifthly, if a direct action were allowed to creditors or shareholders, it could undermine the principles of insolvency law. It could do this in a number of ways. If a *shareholder* could bring an action in his own name this will entail that recovery is not channelled through the company with the consequence that the sums recovered will not be available in the first instance to satisfy the claims of creditors. This could prejudice creditors by depleting the asset pool that would otherwise be available to meet their claims.[10] Were a *creditor* to be allowed to bring a direct action, it might result in that creditor being paid its debt in full whereas other creditors might not so recover, something which would undermine the *pari passu* principle of insolvency law. In addition, the finality that is accorded to winding-up proceedings would be compromised (although perhaps not unacceptably) were a direct action by creditors or shareholders permitted since such an action could be brought even after the company had gone into liquidation.[11]

Finally, precluding direct action by a shareholder arguably underpins the policy relating to derivative actions. Most jurisdictions permit a shareholder in limited circumstances to bring an action in the company's name alleging that a wrong has been committed against the company and seeking redress on behalf of the company. Such an action is almost invariably subject to restrictions. The underlying rationale for these restrictions is not always clear but one justification is that shareholders should not in certain circumstances

Regal (Hastings) Ltd. v. *Gulliver* [1967] 2 AC 134 n. recovery by new controllers of a profit made by the previous directors of the company resulted for all intents and purposes in a reduction of the purchase price which the new controllers paid for their shares; *Abbey Glen Property Corp.* v. *Stumborg* (1978) 85 DLR (3d) 35. One way of dealing with this is by legislation: see e.g. Companies Act 1985, s.315.

[8] A theoretical argument could be made that the prospect of recovery would be impounded in the market price of the shares so that a selling shareholder could not be prejudiced. This would require the wrong to be known but, more importantly, it makes heroic assumptions about the efficiency of the market.

[9] J. C. Coffee, 'Litigation and Corporate Governance: An Essay on Steering Between Scylla and Charybdis' (1984) 52 *Geo. Was. LR 789*, at 807. There is also the *de minimiz* problem in that the amount of recovery by an individual shareholder may be so minimal that no action would be worthwhile (see n. 6). This could be overcome by allowing a pooling of claims.

[10] This assumes that there might be an overlap between claims by the company and the shareholder. The interests of the shareholder could be preferred but this could directly prejudice the interests of the creditors and as such has little to commend it. In fact it is a principle of insolvency law to subordinate the claims of members in liquidation: see Insolvency Act 1986, s. 74(2)(f).

[11] See *Butler* v. *Broadhead* [1975] Ch. 97.

be allowed to use corporate resources and tie up the time of management in situations where a majority of independent shareholders are against the action. Such a bar seems particularly justified where the costs of the litigation exceed any possible benefits.[12] If individual actions against directors were permitted this might undermine certain aspects of this policy since it would result in directors having to divert their energies to the defence of actions against them by shareholders; such an action would not easily be subject to a cost-benefit analysis in terms of the interests of the company. In all probability 'damage' to the company would be ignored or greatly discounted by the complaining shareholder.

3. Directors and Creditors: The Broad Debate

There has been a very active debate of long standing in company law involving the issue of to whom directors owe their duties. Writing in 1931, Professor Dodd put forward what is the classic case for directors being under a wider duty than merely furthering the economic interests of shareholders. He stated:

public opinion, which ultimately makes law, has made and is today making substantial strides in the direction of a view of the business corporation as an economic institution which has a social service as well as a profit-making function, . . . this view has already had some effect upon legal theory, and . . . it is likely to have a greatly increased effect upon the latter in the near future.

. . . A sense of social responsibility toward employees, consumers, and the general public may thus come to be regarded as the appropriate attitude to be adopted by those who are engaged in business . . . [13]

Not all have accepted this position[14] but the general rhetoric of company law is to recognise to some extent that in the carrying out of their duties the directors owe duties to a wider constituency than that of shareholders.[15] The case law and statutory developments, particularly with respect to creditors, favour this position.

[12] See *Smith* v. *Croft* (No. 3) [1987] BCLC 355; *Joy* v. *North* 692 F. 2d 880 (1982). This cost-benefit justification is somewhat question-begging. If the purpose of fiduciary rules is compensatory, then it provides useful guidance. However, if the rules are designed to deter then derivative actions would nearly always be justified irrespective of any gains to the company.

[13] E. Merrick Dodd, 'For Whom Are Corporate Managers Trustees?' (1932) 45 *Harv. L. Rev.* 1145, at 1148 and 1160 respectively.

[14] See A. Berle, 'For Whom Corporate Managers Are Trustees: A Note', (1932) 45 *Harv. L. Rev.* 1365; A. Friedman, *Capitalism and Freedom* (1962), at 133 ('In such an economy [that is a free market economy] there is one and only one social responsibility of business—to use its resources and engage in activities designed to increase its profits so long as it stays within the rules of the game, which is to say, engages in open and free competition, without deception or fraud.'). Subsequently, Berle conceded that the view of Dodd on the wider responsibilities of business had prevailed: see A. Berle, 'Corporate Decision Making and Social Control' (1968), 24 *Bus. Lawyer* 149, at 150.

[15] See generally, E. S. Herman, *Corporate Control, Corporate Power* (Cambridge, 1981), ch. 7; Lord Wedderburn, 'Trust, Corporations and the Worker' (1985) 23 *Osg. HLJ* 203, at 223–32;

It is not proposed to traverse ground that has been well ploughed. However, as regards the English debate a number of points need to be kept in mind. First, there has been a failure to appreciate fully that although fiduciary law operates as 'private law', it in reality performs public law functions: it provides a standard set of norms for regulating the proper discharge by directors of their duties and sets a standard of commercial morality.[16] Since these norms are on the whole judicially developed, there are institutional limitations on the competence of the courts to recognise interests within the framework of company law that would have the effect of radically restructuring the system. For example, in the context of take-overs, it would be difficult through the judicial process for the courts to oblige or permit the directors to take into consideration the types of interests that are recognised in some of the state take-over statutes in the United States.[17] Secondly, because fiduciary obligations are imposed in circumstances where the fiduciary has assumed to act in another's interest, or should be taken to have so assumed this obligation,[18] it is difficult to factor into this equation duties of a broad social nature. These difficulties are clearly illustrated by *Chase Manhattan Equities Ltd.* v. *Goodman*,[19] in which Knox, J. held that a failure by a director to comply with the Model Code for Securities Transactions by Directors of Listed Companies[20] could not constitute a breach of duty with the person with whom the director dealt.[21] If this type of duty cannot be made part of the fabric of company law by judicial development—in a situation where after all the Council of the Stock Exchange is the competent authority for the purpose of the Listing Directives[22]—then it is difficult to see how broader duties could be factored in other than by statutory

City Code on Take-Overs and Mergers, General Principle 9 ' . . . It is the shareholders' interest taken as a whole, together with those of employees and creditors, which should be considered when the directors are giving advice to shareholders.' See e.g., *Evans* v. *Brunner, Mond & Co Ltd.* [1921] 1 Ch. 359; Companies Act 1985, s. 719. There is no authority in the UK that goes as far as the American authorities: see e.g. *A. P. Smith Mfg. Co.* v. *Barlow* 98 A. 2d 581 appeal dismissed 346 US 86 (1953) ('modern conditions require that corporations acknowledge and discharge social as well as private responsibilities as members of the communities within which they operate'); *Theodora Holding Corp* v. *Henderson* 257 A. 2d 398 (Del. Ch. 1969).

[16] See Wedderburn, 'Trust', at 221: 'Fiduciary obligation is imposed by private law, but its function is public, and its purpose social.'

[17] See L. Johnson and D. Millon, 'Missing the Point About State Takeover Statutes' (1989) 87 Mich. L. Rev 846 (state statutes regulating take-overs permit directors of a target company to take into consideration the interests of employees and other groups affected by a take-over bid); Herzel and Shepro, *Bidders and Targets*, ch. 6. Cf. *Paramount Communications Inc* v. *Time Inc.* 571 A. 2d 1140 (Del. Supr. 1989).

[18] Finn, Ch. 1.

[19] (1991) BCC 308.

[20] See *Admission of Securities To Listing*, s. 5, ch. 2. This is conveniently set out in B. Hannigan, *Insider Dealing* (London, 1988), at 196–201.

[21] 'In my judgment there is too long and tenuous a chain of legal obligation between the duty of a director under the model code to report a proposed dealing in a security to the board at one end and a market maker in that security at the other end to justify the finding of a duty owed to the latter by the former to speak': (1991) BCC 308 at 335.

[22] See s. 142(6) of the Financial Services Act 1986.

development. Thirdly, the general debate on the reform of the structure of company law has been dominated by the issue of employee representation. The general position of the Government has been hostile to the imposition of a compulsory system of employee participation. The preoccupation with employee participation has meant that other aspects of the corporate governance debate have been neglected.[23]

4. Directors and Creditors: Judicial Developments[24]

However, an area in which there have been important developments relates to the manner in which the interests of creditors are factored into the duties that directors owe to companies. As good a starting-point as any is the Australian case of *Kinsela* v. *Russell Kinsela Pty Limited*[25] in which directors, with full approval of the shareholders, leased the company's property to themselves at below the current market rent and also gave the lessees the right to purchase the leased property at a highly advantageous price. At the time the transaction was entered into the company's affairs were in a highly parlous state. The company went into liquidation and the liquidator brought an action to have the lease set aside. In the course of his judgment, Street, CJ stated:

In a solvent company the proprietary interests of the shareholders entitle them as a general body to be regarded as the company when questions of the duty of directors arise. If, as a general body, they authorize or ratify a particular action of the directors, there can be no challenge to the validity of what the directors have done. But where a company is insolvent the interests of creditors intrude. They become prospectively entitled, through the mechanism of liquidation, to displace the power of the shareholders and directors to deal with company's assets. It is in a practical sense their assets and not the shareholders assets that, through the medium of the company, are under the management of the directors, pending either liquidation, return to solvency, or the imposition of some alternative administration.

This position has been adopted in other Commonwealth jurisdictions[26] and in the United Kingdom.[27] The question arises as to the nature of this doctrine and it would seem to involve the following:

1. It is triggered off only when the company is insolvent or on the verge of insolvency. Some cases suggest that the duty can arise even where the

[23] The appointment of the Cadbury Committee on Corporate Governance does not appear to be a harbinger of change or suggest that there will be a public debate on the wider responsibilities of directors. The initial issues to be addressed by the Committee are narrow and relate to reporting by directors and the respective roles of executive and non-executive directors: 'Committee on Corporate Governance', press release, 30 May 1991.

[24] D. D. Prentice, 'Creditor's Interests and Director's Duties' (1990) 10 *OJLS* 265; F. Oditah, 'Wrongful Trading' [1990] *LMCLQ* 205; R. Grantham, 'The Judicial Extension of Directors' Duties to Creditors' [1991] *JBL* 1.

[25] (1985–6) 10 ACLR 395, at 401.

[26] *Nicholson* v. *Permacraft (NZ) Ltd* [1985] 1 NZLR 242.

[27] *West Mercia Safetywear Ltd* v. *Dodd* [1988] BCLC 250.

company is solvent.[28] But this is difficult to accept. The only interest of a creditor is in being paid and if the company is solvent then this interest is protected. To extend the duty of directors to creditors in this situation is supererogatory. Where a company is solvent it is the prerogative of the shareholders to control the directors and ratify any breach of duty.

2. The duty is mediated through the company and is not free-standing.[29] One consequence of this is that there will be no recovery if the company has ceased to exist or, if in liquidation, the liquidator determines not to bring an action alleging breach of duty. The justification for this has already been set out in the first part of this chapter.

3. The principle has been applied mainly to situations where property has been recovered so as to swell the asset pool available for satisfying the claims of creditors and this entails that all creditors, not merely those who were prejudiced, can share in the recovery.[30] Such an outcome is normally justified on the grounds either that the wrong in question as a matter of fact has injured all creditors equally, or, alternatively, if the company is being wound up, the company's unencumbered assets constitute a pool that is available to meet the claims of all creditors on a pro rata basis.

4. As was pointed out above, the normal remedy granted where there has been breach of this duty to creditors is to restore to the company property that has been dissipated because of this breach. The doctrine could also be invoked to preclude directors proving for a debt in the company's insolvency; this would be particularly important where the director claims a proprietary interest.[31] The question arises as to whether one could go further and claim for what is a negligence-based liability; for example, incurring of debts by the company in circumstances where there was no reasonable likelihood that the company could pay the debts. It is doubtful if the duty would be extended in this way. At least as far as English law is concerned, the courts have imposed demanding fiduciary duties on directors but the duties of care and skill are relatively attenuated.[32] Whether as a matter of policy the duty should be so extended is a different question. Arguably it should. While honesty on the

---

[28] See *Winkworth* v. *Edward Baron Development Co. Ltd.* [1986] 1 WLR 1512; *Jeffree* v. *National Companies and Securities Commission* (1988–9) 15 ACL.R. 217.

[29] There is no authority specifically to this effect but it is grounded in basic principle.

[30] See e.g. *West Mercia*.

[31] See e.g. *Winkworth*.

[32] This is a very large topic which cannot be gone into here in any detail. Part of the reason for the lack of development of the duties of care and skill is that it is not possible to bring a derivative action with respect to a breach of this type of duty unless the breach involves the director obtaining the property of the company, that is negligence as gain as opposed to negligence as waste: see *Pavlides* v. *Jensen* [1956] Ch. 565 (negligence resulting in dissipation of assets, no derivative action); *Daniels* v. *Daniels* [1978] Ch. 406 (negligent sale of company's property resulting in gain, derivative action allowed). However, there are signs of change as regards the standard of the duty of care which directors owe to the company and s. 214, particularly subsec. 4, will have a considerable impact on the common law: see *Dorchester Finance Co. Ltd* v. *Stebbing* [1989] BCLC 498.

part of directors is an obvious good, so also is competence; both are of equal importance and should receive equal emphasis.

5. The question arises as to the issue of ratification; that is, where there has been breach of this duty can, for example, the shareholders ratify the breach?[33] As the duty is mediated through the company it might be possible as a matter of principle to argue that the shareholders as the company can ratify such breach. But this would be to drive the entity principle to absurd lengths and to overlook, at a point where it is of critical importance, that the phrase 'interests of the company' can be made to embrace the interests of the creditors. As the dictum quoted from the *Kinsela* case recognises, once the company becomes insolvent the shareholders cease to have any interest in the company and accordingly this should simply denude them of authority to ratify a breach of duty that affects the interests of others.

5. Directors and Creditors: Statutory Developments

For some outsiders, English insolvency law may appear to be both highly inquisitorial and punitive. Its inquisitorial features are reflected, for example, in the very wide powers vested in the court on the application of a liquidator to examine privately those who have been involved in the affairs of the company, and this information may be used in subsequent litigation against the person questioned.[34] Its punitive aspects are brought out, for example, by the growing use made of the power to disqualify persons from being involved in the management of the affairs of any company where their conduct in relation to the management of the affairs of a company shows them to be unfit to be so involved.[35] Another aspect of this punitive philosophy is section 214 of the Insolvency Act 1986—the so-called 'wrongful trading' section. To understand this section, a little background information is needed.

Since 1929, English company law has contained a provision whereby the court can impose liability on directors for the debts of a company which has gone into liquidation where the affairs of the company have been conducted so as to defraud the company's creditors or members, or for any fraudulent purpose.[36] This section did not prove particularly effective because of the requirement to show dishonesty. The Cork Committee reported that 'the difficulty of establishing dishonesty has deterred the issue of proceedings in

[33] This assumes that the company has not gone into liquidation since if it has the shareholders are *functus officio*.

[34] S. 236 of the Insolvency Act 1986. There is considerable case law on this: see *Re Cloverbay Ltd*. [1991] Ch. 90.

[35] See Companies Directors Disqualification Act 1986. Directions for the institution of proceedings for disqualification were authorized in 440 cases in 1989: see *Insolvency—1989 Annual Report*, (HMSO), Table 5. See also, 7 *Tolley's Insolvency Law and Practice* (London, 1990), at 41, Table 4. The courts have emphasized that the purpose of disqualification is not to punish but to protect the public. The *effect* of disqualification on the disqualified director is, however, punitive.

[36] The relevant provisions are now s. 213 of the Insolvency Act 1986 and s. 458 of the Companies Act 1985. Under s. 458 there is no need for the company to go into liquidation and the section provides for criminal sanctions rather than personal liability.

many cases where a strong case has existed for recovering compensation from the directo: s or others involved'.[37] At a result it recommended that directors should be made liable to compensate persons who have suffered loss as a result 'not only of fraudulent, but also of unreasonable, behaviour'.[38] The Committee was also concerned that the privilege of limited liability was being abused. Where a company is insolvent then the members have everything to gain and nothing to lose by continued trading; the principle of limited liability will protect them from any further loss but if the company proves profitable they will gain.

The proposals of the Cork Committee bore fruit in the form of section 214 of the Insolvency Act 1986—the 'wrongful trading' section—which provides that in certain circumstances a director[39] can be obliged to contribute to the assets of a company which has gone into insolvent liquidation. A director is potentially liable under this section where (*a*) a company goes into insolvent liquidation (*b*) the director knew or ought to have known that there was no reasonable prospect that the company could avoid going into insolvent liquidation, and (*c*) the director failed to take every step he ought to have taken with a view to minimizing loss to the company's creditors.[40] Australia has also a somewhat similar provision[41] which imposes liability for 'debts' incurred when a company is insolvent.

In *Re Produce Marketing Consortium Ltd (No. 2)*[42] the court held that the jurisdiction under section 214 was 'primarily compensatory' and that prima facie the amount that a director would be ordered to contribute to the assets of the company was the amount by which the company's assets could be discerned to have been depleted by the conduct giving rise to liability under section 214. This is tantamount to a negligence-based liability; it is the failure to take steps to avoid loss to creditors, where a reasonable director ought to have appreciated that loss would be caused to creditors, that gives rise to liability. Although there is no reason why equity should not develop a duty of care, for a fully fledged protection of the interests of creditors through negligence-based concepts, the intervention of the legislature is essential.

---

[37] *Insolvency Law and Practice—Report of the Review Committee* (Cmnd. 8558, 1982), para. 1776.

[38] Ibid., at para. 1777.

[39] This includes a shadow director (s. 214(7)) which is a director in accordance with whose instructions the board is accustomed to act (s. 251). The position has to be looked at from the point of view of the board since if the board fails to act on instructions that are issued to it the person giving the instructions will not be a shadow director. The extension of liability to shadow directors has important implications for (i) banks (ii) parent companies (iii) management agreements, and (iv) business advisers since these types of arrangement can give rise to a board acting on the instructions of someone else.

[40] The point in (*c*) is provided by way of defence. There is no indication on whom the burden of proof with respect to the defence is placed but it is probably on the director: see the position with respect to the burden of proof under s. 727 of the Companies Act 1985, *Re Kirbys Coaches Ltd* [1991] BCLC 414.

[41] Companies Act 1981 (Cth.), s. 556; *Statewide Tobacco Services Ltd.* v. *Morley* (1989–90) 2 ACSR 405; *Heide Pty Ltd* v. *Lester* (1990–1) 3 ACSR 159; *Commonwealth Bank of Australia* v. *Frederich* (1991) 5 ACSR 115.

[42] [1989] BCLC 520.

5

DIRECTORS' FIDUCIARY DUTIES AND INDIVIDUAL SHAREHOLDERS

Paul L. Davies

1. Introduction

The articles of association of companies whose directors and shareholders are not congruent groups, necessarily confer a wide range of discretionary powers upon the directors and senior managers of the company. This chapter, and its companions in this section of the book, are concerned with various aspects of the question of what role the law relating to the exercise of those discretionary powers plays in rendering directors and senior management accountable. To whom do the lines of accountability run in the law's eyes? How rigorous is the scrutiny that the law enforces? How easy is it to invoke the legal process if a breach of duty is thought to have been committed? These are the questions to which courts and commentators have addressed themselves when considering the law relating to directors' duties, and this chapter will examine some aspects of that debate.

The chapter will focus upon directors' fiduciary duties as defined by the common law. Although particular aspects of directors' duties, notably those applying where there is a possibility of conflict between the directors' personal interests and duty to the company, have been regulated by statute,[1] the 1970s plan[2] for a general statutory statement of directors' duties was never put into effect. Consequently, the fundamental propositions in this area have still to be derived from judicial decisions, upon which statute acts as a gloss, albeit an increasingly significant and complex gloss. Furthermore, this chapter will not consider the full range of duties imposed by the common law upon directors. Rather, the focus will be upon what is in at least theoretical terms the central common law duty, namely the duty placed upon directors to regard the welfare of the company as the central objective of their activities as directors. Our concern will be to ask what legally enforceable rights the duty placed upon directors to promote the interests of the company gives to individual shareholders.

At first glance, this last question does not appear to open up a fruitful line of enquiry. Standard formulations of directors' duties, at least in the legal

---

[1] See esp. Part X of the Companies Act 1985.
[2] The Conduct of Company Directors, Cmnd.. 7037 (1977), para. 2.

sources, place the shareholders *as a group* at the centre of the picture, rather than individual shareholders. This fact may be initially somewhat obscured because those conventional formulations begin by stating that, to quote a leading text, directors' duties 'are owed to the company and to the company alone'.[3] Nevertheless, one usually need read only the next sentence to discover that 'the company' means the shareholders as a group and the force of the statement that duties are owed to 'the company alone' is to make the point that, therefore, no duty is owed to *individual* shareholders.[4] My task in this chapter is to examine the basis for the doctrine that the duties of directors are owed to shareholders collectively rather than individually. I will suggest that the rationale for this view, although itself well founded, does not and should not exclude the possibility that directors owe legal duties directly to individual shareholders in appropriate situations, and that judicial decisions have increasingly recognised the force of this point.

A second, highly important feature of the directors' duties is that not only do they involve obligations owed to a collectivity, but also the group in question is widely defined. In particular, the group is not normally limited to the existing shareholders of the company. Thus, the same leading text, just quoted, itself quotes with approval the classic statement made by the inspector in the *Savoy Hotel* report that the company does not mean 'the sectional interests of some (it may be a majority) of the present members or even . . . of all the present members, but of present and future members of the company . . . on the footing that it would be continued as a going concern [balancing] a long-term view against short-term interests of present members'.[5] Thus, whereas a potential member of the company, considered individually, is not an object of the directors' duties, potential shareholders as a group are brought within the range of those whose interests the directors must promote. A distinct, but related, issue thus emerges of whether the courts do or should ever regard the appropriate group as the existing members of the company rather than both present and future members, and, if so, what the difference is between a duty owed to the existing shareholders individually and as a group.

One reason for being interested in these two issues (of duties owed to individual shareholders or current shareholders as a group) is that such duties are likely to be more constraining of managerial action than duties owed to a group widely defined in the *Savoy Hotel* style. It is notoriously difficult to demonstrate that directors have not acted in the best interests of the company defined in this broad way. Although the immediate beneficiaries of the directors' actions may appear to be themselves, the employees, its customers,

[3] L. C. B. Gower, *Principles of Modern Company Law*, 4th edn. (1979), 573.

[4] *Ibid.*: 'in general, the directors owe no duties to the individual members as such, or, *a fortiori*, to a person who has not yet become a member—such as a potential purchaser of shares in it.'

[5] Ibid. 577–8. See also *Gaiman* v. *National Association for Mental Health* [1971] Ch. 317, 330 *per* Megarry J.

or some other group, it will be a rare case where a plausible argument cannot be made that the shareholders will in the long run benefit from the course of action adopted. Given the reluctance of the courts to go behind such plausible arguments, for fear of ending up second-guessing business judgments,[6] it is only the rash management, that openly declares it has ignored shareholder interests, that is likely to be caught.[7] On the other hand, it is likely to be easier to demonstrate a breach of duty to even a non-interventionist court if the directors are required to focus on short-term shareholder utility (which is what a duty owed to current members seems to mean) or, *a fortiori*, on the utility of an individual shareholder.

Although it may be clear to lawyers that 'the company' means the shareholders (broadly defined), it is to be doubted whether most managers share this view. They are likely to take the statement that their duties are owed to the company at face value, and indeed a popular managerial theory developed some decades ago, associated with James Burnham,[8] sees managers as balancing the claims of various stakeholders in the company rather than as acting exclusively to promote shareholder interests. The chairman of United Biscuits has put the point in the following way.

The justification for incorporation of a business was, and is, that the enterprise gains strength from the legal differentiation of roles—the segregation of the rights and liabilities of shareholders, creditors, employees, investors, management, suppliers, customers, the community and the state. The role of management has traditionally been to derive optimum value from the financial, human and technological resources employed in the business—to serve the best interests of the company in its entirety.[9]

The fact that such theories can be developed and achieve much approval in society without a significant impact upon the common law formulation of directors' duties no doubt provides further proof of the weakness of the

---

[6] The English courts have not in terms developed a business judgment rule in the way that the US state courts have done, but the same function is performed, perhaps even more effectively, by formulating the directors' duties subjectively. Thus, in a classic statement, Lord Greene, M. R. said the duty of directors was to 'exercise their discretion bona fide in what they may consider—not what a court may consider—is in the interests of the company . . .': *Re Smith & Fawcett Ltd* [1942] Ch. 304. By way of contrast, see for the interventionism possible even under the business judgment rule the case of *Smith* v. *Van Gorkom* 488 A. 2d. 858 (1985), though it must be admitted that this case does not represent a typical application of the business judgment rule.

[7] The best-known example is from the USA. In *Dodge* v. *Ford Motor Co.* 170 NW 668 (1919) Henry Ford simply decided that the shareholders had done well enough already and announced that in future profit-maximising should be replaced by a policy of maximizing the output of the company and its employment levels. But a breach of this duty may arise from a simple failure to consider the interests of the shareholders (without any positive decision to act adversely to their interests). See *Re W & M Roith* [1967] 1 WLR 432. This case shows that a decision, here the provision of a pension for the managing director's widow as part of his service contract, can be in breach of duty (because the shareholder's interests were not in fact considered), even if the same decision (to provide the pension) might have been arrived at even if the company's interests had been properly assessed.

[8] J. Burnham, *The Managerial Revolution* (New York, 1941).

[9] National Association of Pension Funds, *Creative Tension?* (London, 1990), 60.

constraints, as suggested above, imposed upon management by a requirement to promote the interests of the shareholders when the shareholders'
interests are as widely defined as in the *Savoy Hotel* case. The *Savoy Hotel*
definition of duty, at least when applied by non-interventionist courts, is so
lacking in precise criteria to guide managerial decision-making that a whole
range of policies can be pursued consistently with it, at least by managements
that do not need to articulate too clearly the range of interests they are in fact
promoting.[10]

This is a prima-facie surprising and worrying state of affairs, for it suggests
that the central common law duty laid upon directors to promote the interests
of the shareholders is not a significant constraint upon the exercise of
managerial discretion and it raises the question of what lines of accountability, if any, for senior management and directors do in fact operate. Of course,
there may be mechanisms, other than the legal duties placed upon directors,
by which accountability to shareholders can be achieved and perhaps even
more effectively. Examples would be the market in corporate control via
take-overs or the greater exercise of membership rights by shareholders,
especially institutional shareholders, which seems to be the current panacea.
More radically, it may be suggested that the shareholder interest ought not to
have the centrality that legal theory presently assigns to it, and that the law
should recognise accountability to other groups.[11] Nevertheless, it is
submitted that, as part of that larger jigsaw, it is worth trying to analyse what
the proper scope is for a duty owed by directors to individual shareholders or
to current shareholders, if only because, as we shall see, some of the
alternative mechanisms of control, notably the market for corporate control,
may themselves depend for their full effectiveness upon a functioning system
of directors' legal duties.

2. The Rationale of Liability to Shareholders as a Group

Within the traditional model of shareholder supremacy, it is easy to see why
the duties of directors are prima facie owed to the shareholders collectively

---

[10] This may also explain the apparent lack of impact in practice of s. 309 of the Companies Act
1985, which provides that 'the matters to which the directors of a company are to have regard in
the performance of their functions include the interests of the company's employees in general,
as well as the interests of its members'. This formulation adds little to the current rule because
that rule is formulated in such a highly subjective way—the interests of the employees to which
the directors must have regard are, presumably, those interests as perceived by the directors, not
as perceived by the court—so that the statutory requirement will be broken only if it can be
shown either that the board did not consider the interests of the employees or that no reasonable
board could have arrived at the decision it did if it had considered these interests. In addition, of
course, there is no special enforcement mechanism for the employees. See generally D. D.
Prentice, 'A Company and Its Employees: The Companies Act 1980' (1981) 10 ILJ 1.

[11] See Ch. 4 above, in which Professor Prentice considers the position of creditors. The
position of employees is raised, of course, in the current Community debates on the proposed
Fifth Company Law Directive (OJ No. C 240 of 9.9.1983, pp.2–38) and on the proposed
Societas Europaea (COM (89) 268 FINAL-SYN 219).

rather than individually. After all, the purpose of the company is to enable a number, often a very large number, of people to come together in an association, for the purpose, usually, of promoting a business enterprise that would be beyond the financial means of any one of them (and probably beyond the means of a small group of them). It is therefore natural to think that the duties owed by those who manage the business enterprise on behalf of the investors should take as their starting-point the promotion of the group interest in the success of the venture, rather than the interests of any particular investor. Furthermore, since in a company with freely transferable securities it is expected that the normal method by which a particular shareholder will liquidate her investment is by selling the shareholding in the market, rather than by, say, a repurchase of the shares by the company, it is perhaps possible to see why that prima-facie duty is owed to both present and future shareholders and not just to the former. The amount of share capital available for issue is fixed (though capable, of course, of increase or decrease through prescribed procedures) but the composition of the shareholding body fluctuates, perhaps on a daily basis. So long, at least, as the company seems likely to continue as an independent entity, there would seem to be no reason in principle why the directors, in adopting their business policies, should be required by law to favour those shareholders who wish to sell their shares now or in the short term, as against those who see themselves as long-term holders. The *Savoy Hotel* formulation, as we have seen, gives the directors the discretion to balance long-term and short-term considerations and makes them the prisoners of neither set of objectives.

2.1. The Rule in *Foss* v. *Harbottle*

As is so often the case in English company law, these generalities are reflected most strongly in judicial decisions, not in relation to the definition of directors' duties, but in relation to their enforcement and, moreover, in relation to procedural rather than substantive law. Although by no means confined to serving a single policy objective, the rule in *Foss* v. *Harbottle*,[12] or at least its first limb, certainly stresses the collective nature of the process of enforcing directors' duties. The problem, it will be recalled, that this limb of the rule in *Foss* v. *Harbottle* addresses, is whether an individual shareholder should be allowed to enforce the duties owed by directors to the shareholders collectively. This limb of the rule is not concerned with the enforcement of rights vested in shareholders individually (a point to which we shall return below) but with the role of the individual shareholder in enforcing collective rights or, as it is nowadays usually expressed, of the individual suing derivatively to enforce rights vested in (and thus derived from) the company (i.e. the shareholders as a whole).

As is well known, even notorious, the thrust of the first limb of the rule in *Foss* v. *Harbottle* is to restrict severely the role of the derivative action, i.e. of

[12] (1843) 2 Hare 461.

the individual shareholder in enforcing the rights owed to the shareholders collectively. The individual shareholder (probably) cannot sue at all if the breach of duty by the director is ratifiable by an ordinary majority of the shareholders.[13] No doubt this provision helps to avoid wasted litigation, but it does also emphasize the role of the group: if the group can forgive the wrong, then equally the shareholders collectively should decide whether there should be litigation about the alleged wrongdoing. Group control of litigation is asserted even more clearly where the wrongdoing by the directors is not ratifiable. Here the rationale of preventing wasted litigation drops out of the picture—since the majority cannot forgive this class of wrong—but the individual shareholder, nevertheless, cannot sue unless she can further demonstrate that the alleged wrongdoers are in control of the company.[14] If they are not, then the collective decision-making body—the shareholders' meeting—is preferred to individual decision-making in respect of the initiation of litigation against the directors.

2.2. THE ROLE OF THE DISINTERESTED MINORITY

So much has long been clear (insofar as anything is clear in relation to that much-contested rule), but it is worth remarking that the recent judicial tendency has been to reinforce the importance of collective decision-making. In *Smith* v. *Croft (No. 3)*[15] Knox, J. applied the wrongdoer control requirement to *ultra vires* as well as fraud cases, thus suggesting that wrongdoer control is not a specific pre-condition for actions based upon fraud (in the equitable sense) by directors but is a general requirement of the derivative action, i.e. it applies wherever the individual seeks to enforce collective rights. A second and novel step taken by Knox J. in that case underscored the collective bias of the *Foss* v. *Harbottle* rule in a particularly effective way. The learned judge prevented the derivative suit from proceeding because it was shown that, even after one had discarded the views of the alleged wrongdoing majority shareholders, a majority of the remaining non-involved minority shareholders opposed the bringing of the litigation.[16]

[13] *Estmanco (Kilner House) Ltd.* v. *Greater London Council* [1982] 1 All ER 437, 444, *per* Sir Robert Megarry, V-C. The difficult cases to reconcile with this proposition are, of course, *Alexander* v. *Automatic Telephone Co.* [1900] 2 Ch. 56 and *Hogg* v. *Cramphorn Ltd.* [1967] Ch. 254. On the latter see below at p. 101.

[14] *Birch* v. *Sullivan* [1957] 1 WLR 1247; *Pavlides* v. *Jansen* [1956] Ch. 565.

[15] [1987] BCLC 355; or (No. 2) as it is reported on the All England Reports (see [1987] 3 All ER 909).

[16] *Ibid* at 403: 'Finally on this aspect of the matter I remain unconvinced that a just result is achieved by a single minority shareholder having the right to involve a company in an action for recovery of compensation for the company if all the other minority shareholders are for disinterested reasons satisfied that the proceedings will be productive of more harm than good. If the argument of counsel for the plaintiffs is well founded, once control by the defendants is established the views of the rest of the minority as to the advisability of the prosecution of the suit are necessarily irrelevant. I find that hard to square with the concept of a form of pleading originally introduced on the ground of necessity alone in order to prevent a wrong going without redress. I therefore conclude that it is proper to have regard to the views of independent shareholders.'

Although this decision stops short of requiring the individual shareholder, seeking to sue derivatively, to demonstrate that she has the support of the majority of the non-involved minority shareholders, it is at least clear that, if the defendants can show that the plaintiff does lack such support, then, according to Knox J., the individual should not be allowed to proceed. In other words, to demonstrate that the wrong is not ratifiable and that the wrongdoers are in control no longer provides the individual shareholder with a *laissez-passer* through the road-blocks set up by the rule in *Foss* v. *Harbottle*. On the contrary, if some disinterested[17] body of shareholders is available to take the decision as to whether litigation is to proceed, then, even if that collective decision-making mechanism does not represent the whole of the shareholder body, it is nevertheless preferable to individual shareholder decision-making.

In general, it is clear that stress on the desirability of collective enforcement of duties owed to shareholders collectively tends to reinforce the obstacles placed in the way of the derivative action. This judgment probably remains true overall, even though the same line of thought has made the individual shareholder's path easier if she can bring the case within the increasingly narrow range of circumstances in which *locus standi* will be conferred upon the individual to sue derivatively. Thus, in *Wallersteiner* v. *Moir (No. 2)*[18] it was the perception that the rights being enforced were collective in nature that led to the conclusion that, in appropriate cases, the company and not the individual should bear the costs of the derivative action, whether or not the action was successful. Indeed, it may not be fanciful to suppose that the prior decision in *Wallersteiner* on the company's liability to fund the derivative action had some influence on Knox J.'s decision to tighten the standing rules for individual suits. Subsequent courts have debated whether the *Wallersteiner* principle represents something in the nature of legal aid to the individual rather than a recognition of the true nature of the derivative action as the enforcement of a collective right,[19] so that the true basis of the principle cannot yet safely be said to have been determined. Nevertheless, I would suggest that the latter is the correct view and that it would therefore be appropriate, as the White Book hints,[20] if the idea, that in the derivative action the individual is acting as a sort of agent for the shareholders as a whole, were to lead to the imposition of fiduciary duties upon the individual as to her conduct of the derivative litigation and, especially, its discontinuance.

---

[17] The definition of disinterestedness is likely to be controversial, as it was in *Smith* v. *Croft* itself (in relation to the position of the Wren Trust). See also the note by Wedderburn in (1981) 44 *MLR* 202.

[18] [1975] QB 373.

[19] See e.g. the conflict between *Jaybird* v. *Greenwood* [1986] BCLC 319 and *Smith* v. *Croft* [1986] 1 WLR 580.

[20] *Supreme Court Practice* 1991, O.15, r.12, comment 5A.

2.3. LITIGATION AS AN INVESTMENT DECISION

It may be objected that restriction of the individual's right to sue derivatively is unnecessary for the protection of the collective nature of the duties owed by directors. Provided those duties are formulated substantively as duties owed to the shareholders collectively and provided, therefore, any remedy recovered in actions to enforce the duties enures for the benefit of the shareholders as a group, is it necessary, in order to protect the group interest, that the individual shareholder should be constrained in taking action on behalf of the group to enforce its rights? Indeed, it might be said that the group can only benefit in these circumstances from the individual share-holder's activities. A consideration of the views expressed by the Court of Appeal in *Prudential Assurance Co. Ltd.* v. *Newman Industries (No. 2)*[21] suggests, however, that this is too simple a view.

In that case the Court's remarks were only dicta, since at that stage the litigation had been adopted by the company and so the action was no longer derivative, but they were highly suggestive as to the rationale which might be thought to underlie the restrictive view on the *locus standi* issue. In the context of emphasizing the point that the question of the individual shareholder's standing to sue derivatively ought to be decided separately from, and in advance of, a hearing on the merits of the case, the Court said:

In the present case a board, of which all the directors save one were disinterested, with the benefit of the Schroder–Harman report, had reached the conclusion before the start of the action that the prosecution of the action was likely to do more harm than good. That might prove a sound or an unsound assessment, but it was the commercial assessment of an apparently independent board. Obviously the board would not have expected at that stage to be as well informed about the affairs of the company as it might be after 36 days of evidence in court and an intense examination of some 60 files of documents. But the board clearly doubted whether there were sufficient reasons for supposing that the company would at the end of the day be in a position to count its blessings, and clearly feared, as counsel said, that it might be killed by kindness. Whether in the events which have happened Newman (more exactly the disinterested body of shareholders) will feel that it has all been well worth while, or must lick their wounds and render no thanks to those who have interfered in their affairs, is not a question which we can answer.[22]

The purport of these remarks is the perhaps obvious point, though it has been ignored by many critics of the rule in *Foss* v. *Harbottle*, that the decision to resort to litigation to enforce the company's legal rights is far from unproblematic. It may not be clear that the company's legal rights have been infringed, either because the relevant law is uncertain or because persuasive evidence of what occurred is lacking. Even if there is no doubt that a breach of the company's rights has occurred, the potential defendants may not be worth powder and shot, or it may be thought that even successful litigation will cause the company harm in other ways, for example to its commercial

[21] [1982] 1 All ER 354. [22] At p. 365.

reputation. Whether to embark upon litigation can thus be regarded as an investment decision for the company: it may or may not be worth the company's while to devote the resources (financial and managerial) to suing the wrongdoing directors, and reasonable people might differ on where the balance of advantage lay in any particular case. If one were considering an investment decision other than the initiation of litigation, one would surely regard it as odd that an individual shareholder could commit the collective resources of the company in a particular direction. A derivative action is bound to cause a diversion of managerial time and effort and, after *Wallersteiner*, the company may even have to finance the litigation. From this perspective it is not difficult to understand the court's preference for collective rather than individual shareholder decision-making on the initiation of litigation by companies against directors alleged to have broken their duties.

The counter argument to this stress on collective decision-making, the argument which has generally prevailed in the academic literature, is that, if derivative actions initiated by individual shareholders are made too difficult, the result is likely to be no, or very little, enforcement of directors' duties through the legal process, rather than effective enforcement by some collective shareholder body. Certainly, after *Newman*, the Prudential, and other institutional shareholders, must feel that if they are to play a greater role in corporate governance, as they are constantly urged to do these days, derivative actions are unlikely to be an effective or attractive way of asserting the shareholder interest against inefficient or self-seeking management. It might thus be thought wise to complement the restrictions on derivative suits initiated by individual shareholders with some attempt to revive the collective decision-making mechanisms. A number of suggestions have been made. Vinelott, J. in *Prudential* v. *Newman* at first instance[23] proposed a radical alteration, viz. that the individual shareholder should always be able to sue derivatively unless the wrong had been ratified and, equally important, all wrongs should be ratifiable (but only disinterested shareholders should be entitled to vote). Although this might be thought simply to remove any *locus standi* requirement for individual suits (since after ratification no one can sue) and so amount to the opposite of what I propose, in practice this new rule might operate so as to give the wrongdoing directors a strong incentive to put the issue before the general meeting, i.e. the collective body. In other words, one might support a legal rule giving the individual apparently great freedom to act on behalf of the group to enforce its rights, if one could be sure that the practical operation of the rule would entail collective rather than individual decision-making on the initiation of litigation. Less radically, the latest version of the draft Fifth Directive proposes that legal action against the directors may be initiated by shareholders holding 10 per cent of the share capital, though the UK government is arguing that this should not be a

---

[23] [1980] 2 All ER 841.

free-standing right but confined to cases of alleged fraud by the directors.[24]
The purpose of this chapter, however, is not to examine these proposals
further but simply to point to the strength of the arguments in favour of
defining directors' duties as duties owed to the shareholders collectively and
in favour of taking enforcement decisions on a collective basis also. This is by
way of prelude to a consideration of the circumstances in which duties might
sensibly be said to be owed by directors to individual shareholders.

3. The Case for Individual Shareholder Rights

So far the argument has been that the duties directors owe to the company in
relation to the management of the assets of the company are in principle
correctly formulated as duties owed to the shareholders as a group and that
even derivative enforcement of those duties by individual shareholders
should be restricted to cases where no appropriate representative body is
available to take the decision over litigation. The rule in *Foss* v. *Harbottle* is
open to criticism, not because of its assertion of this principle, but for not
ensuring that the availability of an appropriate collective decision-making
body is an actual rather than a notional fact. However, mishandling of
corporate assets, whether through incompetence or self-dealing, does not
embrace the whole of the range of directorial acts of which an individual
shareholder may wish to complain. The complaint may concern a decision by
the directors that affects only the balance of advantage between or among
groups of shareholders and may be a complaint based either on the
substantive unfairness of the decision or on the inadequacy of the procedure
by which it was reached. Alternatively, the complaint may concern a decision
of the directors which affects the shareholders' property (the shares) rather
than the assets of the company. In both cases the rationale for collective
action, insisted upon above in relation to mishandling of the joint assets, may
not be applicable. In the latter case this is because individual rather than
collective assets are at risk; in the former case because of the inherent conflict
among the shareholders *inter se*.

   In these situations it may be appropriate to recognise that individual
shareholders have rights of action against the company or the directors. The
stress here is upon the word 'may'. In these cases the argument against
individual rights, derived from the collective nature of the corporate venture,
does not, it is suggested, operate. However, it does not therefore follow that
the shareholder interest in question should receive legal recognition or that, if
it is to be recognised, the most appropriate way of conferring that protection
consists in the imposition upon the directors of fiduciary duties owed to
individual shareholders. These questions need separate investigation.
Finally, even if these questions are both answered in the affirmative, one may

[24] Department of Trade and Industry, Consultative Document on the Amended Proposal for
a Fifth Directive . . . Jan. 1990, para. 15.2

need to address the further issue of how the boundary between individual and collective shareholder rights is to be drawn.

3.1. THE ROLE OF SECTION 459

It is clear that in UK law at present the question of which interests of individual shareholders are to be protected by the law, where the decision of the directors reflects a dispute among the shareholders *inter se*, is to be answered normally not through the mechanism of common law fiduciary duties, but through the statutory right of the individual shareholder to petition the court under section 459 of the Companies Act 1985 on the grounds that the affairs of the company are being conducted in a manner which is unfairly prejudicial to her. This section, at least potentially, provides a mechanism through which a wide variety of challenges to the exercise of directorial discretion may be mounted by individual shareholders, on grounds of both procedural and substantive unfairness. This is especially so since the amendment to section 459, effected by schedule 19, paragraph 11, of the Companies Act 1989, has made it clear that section 459 is apt for the consideration of directorial acts that formally affect all the shareholders equally as well as acts intended to affect the shareholders differentially. The function of the section in handling disputes between majority and minority shareholders is emphasized by those court decisions which have restricted the expenditure of corporate funds upon representation in section 459 cases. Since the dispute is normally between two groups of shareholders, the company has only a limited interest in the outcome of the litigation and the expenditure of company money must be similarly limited.[25]

Of course, one's optimism about the courts' likely actions under section 459 needs to be modified by one's knowledge of the historical failure of the courts to capitalize upon statutory discretions conferred upon them in the past to review some aspect or other of directorial decision-making.[26] Nevertheless, the current generation of Chancery judges seems to be cast in a more interventionist mould. At any rate, they have, in the end, avoided the more obvious interpretational traps that would have hobbled their discretion under section 459, notably by not insisting that unfairly prejudicial conduct be in some sense independently unlawful (i.e. when considered apart from section 459 itself), and by giving a flexible interpretation to the requirement that the prejudice be suffered by the petitioner in her capacity as a member and not in some other capacity.[27] Of course, these are essentially ground-clearing steps: we remain uncertain what positive use will be made of their

[25] See *Re Crossmore Electrical and Civil Engineering Ltd.* (1989)5 BCC 37; *Re Hydrosan Ltd.* [1991] BCC 19; *Re Milgate Developments Ltd.* [1991] BCC 24; *Re a Company ex parte Johnson* [1991] BCC 234.

[26] The remarks on this topic of the Lord President (Cooper) in *Scottish Insurance Corpn.* v. *Wilsons & Clyde Coal Co Ltd* 1948 SC 360 are too well known to need repeating.

[27] See *Re A Company* [1986] BCLC and the cases discussed in *Palmer's Company Law*, 25th ed. (London, 1992), para.8.1105.

discretion by the courts, at least in relation to medium-sized and large companies. The typical 459 case still concerns a quasi-partnership company where the petitioner alleges that the subsequent conduct of the company's affairs is in breach of an informal understanding, existing as betwen the incorporators when the company was established, as to how it would be run.[28] The cases reflect no more, perhaps, than the perception that the actual agreement among the incorporators in such cases is not fully reflected in the company's formal constitution. However, the door to a bolder use of section 459, by finding unfairness in the breach of a standard developed by the court rather than the shareholders themselves (even if informally), seems not to have been closed.[29] If the courts do prove capable of developing section 459 in a flexible way, it would seem a more appropriate method of handling allegations by shareholders of abuse of power by the company's controllers than the imposition of fiduciary duties upon directors *vis-à-vis* individual shareholders. This is because those duties, which are fully developed only in relation to directorial self-dealing, may not capture the full range of unfairness of which the individual shareholder wishes to complain in intra-corporate disputes.

However, the potential scope and flexibility of section 459 in protecting the legitimate expectations of minority shareholders must be subject to some restriction where the essence of the minority shareholder's claim is that a wrong has been done to the company. If the policy expressed in *Foss* v. *Harbottle* and elaborated in *Prudential* is a good one, it cannot be allowed to be subverted simply by the plaintiff shifting from an action begun by a writ to a petition under section 459. Herein lies the significance of the requirement that the petitioner be prejudiced as a member. Flexibly though that requirement is interpreted today by the courts, it nevertheless retains a crucial strategic significance as a tool to enable the courts to distinguish the intra-corporate aspects of a situation from the wrong done to the share-holders as a whole. The difficulties faced by the courts in these cases cannot be solved simply by the judges adopting a self-denying ordinance at the remedial level and confining the petitioner's remedy to the institution of civil proceedings in the company's name under section 461(1)(c). As *Prudential* stresses, the central issue is whether the individual should have control over corporate litigation and so the court cannot avoid taking an independent decision as to whether there has been unfair prejudice to the petitioner as a member or, in other words, whether the facts are such that the individual shareholder should be allowed to initiate litigation on the company's behalf.[30]

---

[28] *Palmer's Company Law*, para.8.1106, and *cf Re Blue Arrow plc* [1987] BCLC 585.

[29] *Re A Company [1986] BCLC 382 (use of standards derived from the City Code on Take-Overs and Mergers)*.

[30] See MacIntosh, 'The Oppression Remedy: Personal or Derivative?' (1991) 70 Can. B. Rev. 29; *Pennington's Company Law* (London, 6th edn. 1990) 683.

3.2. THE COMMON LAW

Even at common law, however, the absence of fiduciary duties owed by directors to individual shareholders does not leave the shareholder who regards herself as having been improperly treated by the directors in the company's internal procedures without remedy. By section 14 of the Companies Act 1985[31] (here doing little more than restating the general common law analysis of the legal status of the rulebooks of associations) the company's constitution constitutes a contract between the company and its members. Here, then, the question of which shareholder interests to protect is answered by examining the undertakings contained in the company's memorandum and articles of association, so that this principle ranges more narrowly than the section 459 claim. Legal protection is here provided through the law of contract, rather than the law of fiduciaries. However, the application of contractual law is somewhat restricted in this context, notably because it has been clear since the decision of the Court of Appeal in *MacDougall* v. *Gardiner*[32] that the second limb of the rule in *Foss v. Harbottle* prevents the individual shareholder from complaining of all breaches of the articles: some breaches, it is said, are mere internal irregularities, capable of being ratified by the majority in general meeting and so not to be complained of by the individual shareholder. Unfortunately or fortunately, in view of the nearly contemporaneous decision of the Master of the Rolls in *Pender* v. *Lushington*,[33] where the Court, in a case raising the same issue, analysed the situation as one where the plaintiff was asserting a personal contractual right on which the views of the wrongdoing defendant company in general meeting were irrelevant, it has never been clear of which breaches of the articles the individual shareholder may freely complain.

Some years ago Roger Smith argued trenchantly that *Foss* v. *Harbottle* ought to have no application to the personal action to enforce breaches of the articles and that 'it does not appear that any great harm would result from allowing personal actions to be unfettered'.[34] In other words, whereas the first limb of the rule in *Foss* v. *Harbottle* does a valuable job, as suggested in Section 2 of this chapter, in asserting the collective nature of wrongs done to the company, the second limb, as applied in *MacDougall*, seems entirely to mistake the relevance of the views of the majority of the shareholders where the company appears as potential defendant rather than as potential plaintiff. However that may be, all that needs to be asserted here is that where the directors' decision is a facet of a dispute among the shareholders, then, even in the absence of fiduciary duties owed to individual shareholders, the law

---

[31] '(1) Subject to the provisions of this Act, the memorandum and articles, when registered, bind the company and its members to the same extent as if they respectively had been signed and sealed by each member, and contained covenants on the part of each member to observe all the provisions of the memorandum and of the articles.'

[32] (1875) 1 Ch.D. 13.

[33] (1877) 6 Ch.D. 70.

[34] R. J. Smith. 'Minority Shareholders and Corporate Irregularities' (1978) 41 MLR 147, 160.

does provide remedial mechanisms. The common law contractual remedy, based on the articles, will remain, no doubt, something of a broken reed until the approach adopted in *Pender* is clearly preferred by the courts to that taken in *MacDougall* and recent decisions, such as *Devlin* v. *Slough Estates*,[35] do not leave one optimistic as to where the courts' preferences actually lie. Nevertheless, section 459 potentially provides, it is submitted, an adequate way of handling this class of dispute.

4. Indirect Enforcement of Directors' Duties to Individual Shareholders

4.1. DUTY TO CONDUCT THE COMPANY'S AFFAIRS IN ACCORDANCE WITH ITS CONSTITUTION

In spite of the shadow cast by *MacDougall* over the viability of the rights to be derived by the individual shareholder from her section 14 contract with the company, the existence of that contract does give rise to a possibility of individual shareholders indirectly enforcing some of the fiduciary duties owed by the directors to the company. It is important to stress that directors' duties cannot normally be enforced via the member's contract in this indirect way, and that, in the light of the arguments in Section 2 above, it would not be desirable to do so. Even where it is appropriate to accept the analysis, it is crucial at a remedial level to keep the distinction between the individual and the collective causes of action in mind.

Nevertheless, it is submitted that in some cases such an analysis is appropriate and a useful way of handling intra-company disputes and, in particular, that such an analysis will flow from an acceptance of the idea which appears to lie behind *Pender* and other cases that shareholders do have a contractual right to have the affairs of their company conducted in accordance with its constitution.[36] Since it is also one of the directors' duties to cause the company to conduct its affairs in accordance with its constitution and not to exceed their own authority,[37] it is likely that there will be a double aspect to liability where it is the directors' actions on behalf of the company which put the company in breach of its section 14 contract with the members. Between the company and the directors, the latter will be in breach of fiduciary duty; between the company and its members the former will be in

[35] [1983] BCLC 497. Here Dillon, J. refused to interpret an article requiring directors to prepare, lay before the company in general meeting, and distribute to shareholders individually proper accounts as conferring any right upon the individual shareholder; that duty was owed only to the company. *Cf Berlei Hestia (NZ) Ltd* v. *Fernyhough* [1980] NZLR 150, noted by Sealy in (1989) 10 *Company Lawyer* at 53.

[36] For an analysis of the 20th-cent. cases and strong argument in favour of the proposition that the shareholder has an individual contractual right to have the affairs of the company conducted in accordance with its constitution, see Wedderburn [1957] Camb. LJ 1984, 207–14, and (1968) 31 MLR 688.

[37] R. R. Pennington, *Directors' Personal Liability* (1987), 37–9, citing *Evans* v. *Coventry* (1857) 8 de GM & G 835, *Land Credit Co. of Ireland* v. *Lord Fermoy* (1869) LR 8 Eq. 7, and *Re Oxford Benefit Building and Investment Society* (1886) 35 Ch.D. 502.

breach of contract. The company appears as plaintiff or defendant according to which aspect of liability is in issue.

This twin aspect of liability has long been recognised in the case law in the *ultra vires* area,[38] and, even after the abolition of the third-party effect of that doctrine, these two other legal aspects of the requirements of the company's constitution remain important. Indeed, they have achieved legislative recognition in the Companies Act 1985 (as amended): s.35(1) abolishes the third-party effect of *ultra vires*, but s.35(3) states that 'it remains the duty of directors to observe any limitations on their powers flowing from the company's memorandum' (duty to the company), and s.35(2) provides that 'a member may bring proceedings to restrain the doing of an act which but for subsection (1) would be beyond the company's capacity' (company's duty to the member). Nevertheless, it is necessary to keep these two causes of action distinct and, in particular, to ensure that the remedy granted is appropriate to the cause of action asserted, lest otherwise the corporate claim come under the control of the individual shareholder.

A good recent example of the proper handling of this issue is provided by the decision in *Taylor* v. *NUM (Derbyshire Area)*.[39] The officers of the defendant union had committed the union to what the Court found to be an *ultra vires* strike and had expended the union's funds in pursuit of it. The individual member plaintiffs sought injunctions restraining the union and its officers from further expenditure of funds to this end and requiring the officers to restore to the union the sums already expended (some £1.7 million). In effect, there was an allegation both that the executive of the union had improperly favoured one side in the dispute between the working and the non-working miners and that the executive had misapplied collective assets. This situation (which cannot be uncommon) made the precise identification of the plaintiffs' cause of action and of their appropriate remedy crucially important. Vinelott J. granted the first injunction on the basis that 'every member of the union, as he has an interest in preserving the funds of the union, is, it seems to me, entitled to prevent the funds of the union being used in that way [i.e. in breach of its rules]'.[40] The claim for the second injunction involved, however, an assertion of a corporate claim—the funds misapplied were the funds of the union, not of the individual member—and that claim should be under the control of the majority of the members. Although an *ultra vires* act could not then[41] be ratified by even a unanimous

---

[38] Thus, in *Smith* v. *Croft* (No. 3) [1987] BCLC 355, 389, Knox J. said: 'Where what is sought is compensation for the company for loss caused by ultra vires transactions the wrong, in my judgment, is a wrong to the company which has the substantive right to redress. Where the minority shareholder is seeking to prevent an ultra vires transaction or otherwise seeking to enforce his personal substantive rights, the wrong which needs redress is the minority shareholder's wrong.' See also Wedderburn, 'Shareholders' Rights and the Rule in *Foss* v. *Harbottle*' [1957] Camb. LJ at 204–7.

[39] [1985] BCLC 237. [40] At 254.

[41] Or even now, since s. 35 of the Companies Act 1985 does not apply to trade unions. Query whether the *ultra vires* doctrine is in truth applicable at all to trade unions after the labour law reforms of 1974: see the note by Wedderburn (1985) 14 ILJ 127.

vote of the members, so that the ratifiability bar to a derivative action did not operate, nevertheless, in the absence of wrongdoer control, the majority rather than the individual should decide whether litigation to recover the money from the officers was in the union's best interests. The judge made an explicit reference to the applicability of this approach in the case of companies. 'The majority of the members of a trading company, for instance, might properly take the view that the publicity, costs and the inevitable loss, let us say, of the services of a managing director, who would be the defendant, would outweigh the benefit to the company of successfully prosecuting the action.'[42] At least as a matter of summary judgment he concluded that the second injunction should be refused.

It may seem odd at first sight that the shareholder should have an individual right to restrain future expenditure of corporate funds on an *ultra vires* purpose but no individual right to recover corporate funds already unlawfully expended. However, it is not difficult to see why a court would not order repayment of funds unlawfully disbursed from the company or association to the individual member, or even the member's aliquot share of these funds. To do so would be to ignore the separate legal entity of the company and to endanger the interests of those creditors whose claims lie only against the company and do not normally extend to its members. This rule could be seen, if you like, as the obverse of limited liability and as a corollary of the capital maintenance principle. It would be odd if the controls on the return of capital by the company to its shareholders were to be ignored simply because the context of the return was an initial wrongful disbursement of corporate funds by its directors.

If this is correct, then a member's claim for damages payable to herself would have to be posited upon a loss suffered personally by that member. In *Taylor* there presumably was no such loss, since the plaintiff's membership of the union had no market value, but the situation might be different with a trading company. This was a central issue raised in *Prudential* v. *Newman*. It was alleged that the directors, in conflict of interest and duty, had caused the company to buy assets at an overvalue from another company, in which the directors were interested, and had then issued a deliberately misleading circular to the shareholders to secure their approval of the purchase (that approval being required by the Stock Exchange's rules). The plaintiffs sued derivatively on behalf of the company but also personally, alleging the commission by the directors of the tort of deceit. The Court of Appeal robustly rejected the claim as 'misconceived', not apparently on the ground that deceit had not been practised, but rather on the ground that the plaintiffs had suffered no loss as a result. The main item of alleged loss was the drop in the value of the plaintiffs' shares, but this was not a loss distinct from that suffered by the company, and the latter was to be regarded, for the reasons given in the previous paragraph, as the primary loss.[43]

---

[42] At 255.   [43] [1982] 1 All ER 354, 366–7.

Thus, individual claims either for an aliquot part of the company's loss or for an individual loss represented by a consequential fall in the value of shares held seem not to be sustainable. The only alternative way of putting the individual's claim would be for individual control of the corporate claim, but, for the reasons discussed earlier in this chapter, and repeated by Vinelott J. in *Taylor*, there is good sense in having collective decision-making over corporate claims, if one takes the view that the initiation of litigation by the company is not an unproblematic decision. Consequently, the only acceptable way for the plaintiffs in *Taylor* to present their personal claim was one for an injunction to restrain a continuing breach of the union's rulebook.

4.2. DUTY NOT TO ACT FOR AN IMPROPER PURPOSE

The argument so far has been that the parallelism between the shareholders' contractual right against the company to have its affairs conducted in accordance with its constitution and the directors' fiduciary duty, owed to the company likewise to conduct its affairs, leads to a situation in which the directors' breach of their duty typically gives the individual shareholder a cause of action, albeit not against the directors as such or for breach of fiduciary duty. The area of controversial application of this theory concerns, however, not the duty of directors to conduct the affairs of the company in accordance with its articles, but their duty not to exercise the powers conferred upon them by the articles for an 'improper' or 'collateral' purpose, i.e. for a purpose other than that (or one of those) for which the power was conferred upon the directors in the articles. That it is a breach of duty for directors so to act, at least where that is their primary purpose, seems well established in UK law.[44] Equally well established, at least in practice, is the ability of individual shareholders to challenge directors' acts on these grounds, but the theory upon which this is done is far from clear. One possible explanation seeks to make use of a parallelism between directors' duties and shareholders' contractual rights along the lines described above.

Since it seems to be generally accepted that the purposes for which directors may exercise their powers are to be fixed by reference to the provisions of the company's articles of association, it has been argued that an exercise by the directors of their powers for an improper purpose is not simply a breach by the directors of their duty to the company (i.e. the shareholders generally) but constitutes also a breach of the articles of association. The issue has been debated, rather desultorily, in the courts. In the recent case of *Re A Company (No. 5136 of 1986)*[45] Hoffman, J., in an interlocutory decision, seemed to accept the argument. He refused to apply the *Wallersteiner* principle (of corporate finance for individual litigation) to an

---

[44] *Howard Smith Ltd* v. *Ampol Petroleum Ltd* [1974] AC 821, though it may be that in Australia the improper purpose need not be the dominant one in order to render the directors' action voidable: *Whitehouse* v. *Carlton Hotel Pty Ltd.* (1987) 11 ACLR 715 at 721 (High Court of Australia).

[45] [1987] BCLC 82.

unfair prejudice petition under s.459 of the 1985 Act, where the essence of the prejudice was alleged to be directors acting for an improper purpose in allotting shares. He said:

I am provisionally inclined to accept all of the submissions of counsel for the petitioner except (b). I do not accept (b) because whether brought by writ or petition under s.459 this is not, in my judgment, a derivative action. Although the alleged breach of fiduciary duty by the board is in theory a breach of its duty to the company, the wrong to the company is not the substance of the complaint. The company is not particularly concerned with who its shareholders are. The true basis of the action is an alleged infringement of the petitioner's individual rights as a shareholder. The allotment is alleged to be an improper and unlawful exercise of the powers granted to the board by the articles of association, which constitute a contract between the company and its members. These are fiduciary powers, not to be exercised for an improper purpose, and it is generally speaking improper—

'for the directors to use their fiduciary powers over the shares in the company purely for the purpose of destroying an existing majority, or creating a new majority which did not previously exist.'

(See *Howard Smith Ltd* v. *Ampol Petroleum Ltd* [1974] 1 All ER 1126 at 1136, [1974] AC 821 at 837). An abuse of these powers is an infringement of a member's contractual rights under the articles.[46]

This decision seems inconsistent with the view of the Court of Appeal in *Bamford* v. *Bamford*,[47] where the issue was whether the shareholders could effectively ratify a proposed issuance of shares by the directors which would defeat a proposed take-over bid. Russell, L. J., discussing the question of whether the directors' act was a nullity or not, said:[48]

In truth the allotment of shares by directors not bona fide in the interests of the company is not an act outside the articles: it is an act within the articles but in breach of the general duty laid upon them by their office as directors . . . The point before us is not an objection to the proceedings on *Foss* v. *Harbottle* grounds; but it seems to march in step with the principles that underlie the rule in that case . . . The harm done by the assumed improperly-motivated allotment is a harm done to the company of which only the company can complain.

The same result was arrived at, after full discussion and in an interesting set of judgments, by the Court of Appeal of New South Wales in *Winthrop Investments Ltd* v. *Winns*.[49] The reasoning in these two latter cases is the opposite of that adopted by Hoffmann J.: because the directors had only abused their powers, this was not a breach of the articles and so was only a wrong done to the company.

---

[46] At 84. This dictum comes close to denying entirely the collective aspect of the breach of the directors' duties.

[47] [1969] 1 All ER 969.   [48] At 976.

[49] [1975] 2 NSWLR 666, *cf. Provident International Corp.* v. *International Leasing Corp. Ltd* (1989) 89 WN (Pt. I) (NSW) 370, where however, the individual's *locus standi* was derived from statute, as was the case in *Grant* v. *John Grant Ltd* (1950) 82 CLR 1.

More recently and more boldly, the Supreme Court of South Australia has followed through the logic of Hoffmann J.'s dictum in its decision in *Residues Treatment and Trading Co Ltd* v. *Southern Resources Ltd (No.4)*.[50] That case, like *Howard Smith*, *Bamford*, and many others in this area, involved the issuance of new shares by the incumbent management of a target company in a take-over bid in order to destroy a majority the bidder had actually achieved or was threatening to achieve (an issue that in the UK has been rather overshadowed by the more stringent provisions of the City Code on Take-Overs).[51] The Court held that the plaintiff shareholder had a personal, equitable right to have the voting power of its shares undiminished by improper actions on the part of the directors, which personal right could be asserted against the company free of *Foss* v. *Harbottle* considerations.

However, whether one places the shareholder's action on a contractual basis (as in *Re A Company*) or finds a direct equitable relationship between the shareholders and the directors (as in *Residues Treatment*), the difficulty is to explain why the directors' actions should be ratifiable by an ordinary majority of the shareholders. Following *Pender* one can ask what relevance the opinion of the majority can have if the company is the wrongdoer (as on the contractual analysis) or not even a party to the relevant legal relationship (as on the *Residues Treatment* analysis). Indeed, in *Residues Treatment* the Court boldly accepted the consequences of its analysis and doubted the correctness of the decision in *Bamford* that breaches of directors' duties not to act for an improper purpose were ratifiable by the members in general meeting.[52] However, *Bamford* stands as part of English law and is probably correct in policy terms, at least in the typical case of share issues to defeat take-over bidders. The thrust of the City Code is that the fate of bids should be determined by a majority of the shareholding body.[53] It would thus seem undesirable that either collateral action by directors of the target should be lawful or that individual shareholders should be able to determine the success or otherwise of the bid. To view the directors' actions as a breach of a duty owed to the shareholders collectively and ratifiable by them reconciles the policy objectives in the required way.

What this approach does not explain, of course, is the basis on which the individual shareholder is able to sue. If the duty is owed to the shareholders collectively and breach of it is ratifiable by a simple majority, does not the first limb of the rule in *Foss* v. *Harbottle* (discussed in Section 2) deprive the individual shareholder of *locus standi*? Perhaps the best solution to this problem is that put forward by Wedderburn in relation to *Hogg* v.

---

[50] (1988) 14 ACLR 569, noted approvingly by Stapledon in (1990) 8 *Company and Securities Law Journal* 213.

[51] See General Principle 7 and Rules 21 and 37.3 prohibiting frustrating action by the target board.

[52] (1988) 14 ACLR 569, 576.

[53] Hence the ban on frustrating action by the target directors: see n. 50 above.

Cramphorn,[54] another take-over case and the first to put the collateral purpose doctrine on its modern footing. There the individual shareholder sued to restrain the allotment of shares and the Court heard and determined the substantive issue in his favour. However, before setting aside the scheme the judge gave the shareholders in general meeting an opportunity to ratify it (which they in fact did). Wedderburn's analysis was that the plaintiff's action had been a derivative one (to enforce the rights of the shareholders as a group) but that, exceptionally, the plaintiff would have *locus standi* to sue in this way unless the wrong was actually ratified, a solution which, as we have seen, Vinelott J. sought to generalize in *Prudential (No.2)*[55] at first instance.

4.3. DIRECTORS' DUTIES TO ACT FAIRLY AS BETWEEN SHAREHOLDERS

The third area of intra-corporate dispute that is worth considering is that put by Finn in the following way. 'When the board exercises a power which affects the rights of the members of differing classes of shares, and the company has no real interest in how that power is actually exercised, the board has a duty to act fairly as between the classes.'[56] Although admitting that the authority in favour of this duty is slender, Finn argues that it constitutes a prime example of a situation where directors ought to be recognised as owing a fiduciary duty directly to individual shareholders.[57] Even here, however, contractual analysis may be flexible enough to do the job. In *Mutual Life Insurance Co of New York* v. *The Rank Organization Ltd*[58] the defendant offered for sale to the public 20 million A ordinary shares, of which half were made available on a preferential basis to existing Rank A ordinary shareholders, except those resident in the USA and Canada, with whose securities laws the company did not wish to become involved. The plantiff's North American shareholders alleged this conduct by the company constituted a breach of an implied term in the articles of association that all holders of A ordinary shares were entitled to rank *pari passu* and be afforded equal treatment by Rank without discrimination between one and another.

Goulding, J. rejected the claim, but not, however, on the ground that it was impermissible to imply terms into the contract of association. On the contrary, he thought there was an implied term (which had not been broken)

---

[54] [1966] All ER 420, noted by Wedderburn in (1967) 30 MLR 77. In *Residues Treatment* the Court, assuming the breach to be ratifiable at all, was prepared to regard the potentiality of ratification as not depriving the plaintiff shareholder of *locus standi*, but, unlike Professor Wedderburn, it seems to have regarded the plaintiff's cause of action as asserting a personal right.

[55] [1986] 2 All ER 841, though doubt is cast upon his approach and that of Professor Wedderburn by the insistence of the Court of Appeal in the same case ([1982] 1 All ER 354) that the issue of *locus standi* be decided in advance of a hearing on the merits.

[56] P. Finn, *Fiduciary Obligations* (Sydney, 1977), 69.

[57] *Ibid*. 65 ff.

[58] [1985] BCLC 11. The facts occurred before the introduction of statutory pre-emption entitlements.

that the directors' powers must be exercised fairly as between different shareholders, but not that there was an implied term that shareholders of the same class be guaranteed equal treatment. It is clear from other areas of the law that, where a contractual relationship exists, implied terms can be used in a flexible way to ensure fair treatment[59] and there may even be a slight advantage in the implied term as against a fiduciary duty owed by the director. An implied term in a contract with the company catches corporate action whether it be effected by the board or the shareholders in general meeting. Indeed, the problem with the implied term may be its excessive flexibility. In *Mutual Life* Goulding J. thought there was an implied term based on 'the time-honoured rule that the directors' powers are to be exercised in good faith in the interests of the company'.[60] There may be a place for such a rule in intra-corporate disputes, but for the reasons given in Section 2 it would be a mistake to use such an implied term to create a set of duties, owed to individual shareholders, which is parallel to that owed to the shareholders collectively.

5. Duties Owed Directly to Individual Shareholders

In the previous section we considered situations where directors' decisions were an aspect of a dispute among the shareholders and we looked at various techniques that had been employed to confer upon individual shareholders rights to challenge those decisions. These techniques did not consist of conferring upon shareholders fiduciary rights exercisable against the directors but of contractual rights exercisable against the company. However, since the express or implied contractual entitlements of the individual shareholders were triggered by breaches of the fiduciary duties owed by the directors to the company, it seemed possible to characterize these situations as ones where directors indirectly owed fiduciary duties to the individual shareholders. At one level it might be regarded as fortuitous that this area of law had come to be dominated by contractual rather than explicitly fiduciary principles. On the other hand, the emphasis upon contractual rights might be seen as an appropriate way of conferring essentially constitutional protections upon individual shareholders as to how collective decisions should be taken within the company, without running the risk that directors' mishandling of the collective assets would be viewed as involving the breach of fiduciary duties owed to individual shareholders. That risk might be thought to be present in a scheme for viewing the relationship of directors and individual shareholders in explicitly fiduciary terms, because of the danger of slipping into the error of regarding the fiduciary duties owed to

---

[59] For a recent example arising out of complex three-way relationships between an employer, its employees, and a pension fund, see *Imperial Group Pension Trust Ltd* v. *Imperial Tobacco Ltd* [1991] IRLR 66.

[60] At [1985] BCLC 11, 21.

individual shareholders as fully replicating the range of fiduciary duties owed
to the shareholders collectively. Our concern in the previous section, by
contrast, was to argue that only a relatively limited range of breaches by
directors of duties to the company should be regarded as putting the
company in breach of contract with the individual shareholder—the most
controversial debate centres on the treatment in this regard of the directors'
duty not to act for an improper purpose—and, as our analysis of *Taylor* v.
NUM suggested, even within this restricted range it was important at the
remedial level carefully to distinguish individual and collective causes of
action.

In this section we consider cases where it is proposed that it *is* appropriate
to view the directors as owing fiduciary duties directly to the individual
shareholders, because the relationship between the two relates to individual
rather than collective property. For the same reason, there is no reason to
suppose that breach of the proposed duties owed to the individual
shareholder in these cases would necessarily arise out of situations in which
the directors were also in breach of duties owed to the shareholders
collectively. Furthermore, the recognition of fiduciary duties owed by the
directors to individual shareholders in respect of the latter's own property
interests should lead to no expectation of automatic parallelism with the
duties owed by directors to the shareholders collectively. Even in this area,
however, we shall see that there is a competitor (this time from tort law) to
the view that the director and individual shareholder relationship is best
characterized in fiduciary terms.

5.1. TORT DUTIES

In principle, acceptance of the proposition that directors may owe duties to
individual shareholders which are distinct from those owed to the shareholders collectively appears to pose no problems. Thus, in *Prudential* v.
Newman (No.2)[61] even the Court of Appeal seemed to accept that the
(equitable) fraud alleged to have been committed on the company by the
directors when they caused it to purchase property at an overvalue was
distinct from the (common law) fraud alleged to have been committed by the
directors against the shareholders when they sent out circulars in connection
with the proposition that the shareholders in general meeting approve the
purchase. The Court's concern was rather to keep separate the assessment of
loss in relation to each cause of action.[62] *Prudential* is in fact a good example
of the situation where it may be appropriate to recognise duties owed by

---

[61] [1982] 1 All ER 354.

[62] The Court said: 'It is of course correct . . . that [the directors], in advising the shareholders
to support the resolution approving the agreement, owed the shareholders a duty to give such
advice in good faith and not fraudulently. It is also correct that, if directors convene a meeting on
the basis of a fraudulent circular, a shareholder will have a right of action to recoger any loss
which he has been personally caused in consequence of the fraudulent circular; this might
include the expense of attending the meeting' ([1982] 1 All ER at 366).

directors to shareholders individually, in that it involved advice given by the former as to how the latter should exercise a power attached to their shares. The situation is even clearer where the advice is given by the directors, not in connection with a corporate scheme, but as to how the shareholders should react to an outside event, such as an offer from a take-over bidder to acquire their shares.

A duty in tort to be honest, owed by directors to individual shareholders, seems to be well established here. In *Gething* v. *Kilner*,[63] where the incumbent directors' advice to the shareholders had not revealed, or not revealed until very late in the day, that the target's stockbrokers thought the price offered by the bidder was based upon inadequate valuations of the target's substantial property holdings, Brightman, J. said: 'I accept that the directors of an offeree company have a duty towards their own shareholders, which in my view clearly includes a duty to be honest and a duty not to mislead.'[64] The action, brought by individual shareholders in the target company, failed, however, on the ground that the target company's board honestly believed that the bid ought to be recommended to its shareholders. The judge was clearly relieved to reach this conclusion since the principal relief sought lay not against the directors of the target, but was an interlocutory injunction to restrain the bidder from declaring its offer unconditional as to acceptances, on the ground that it had been implicated in the target management's wrongdoing.[65]

It seems likely that the directors' duty in such cases extends also to embrace negligence. In *Prudential* at first instance the judge referred to the 'application, to directors who assume responsibility for giving advice to shareholders, of the general duty to act honestly *and with due care*'.[66] Even after *Caparo plc* v. *Dickman*[67] it would seem that liability in negligence will flow where the plaintiff is the addressee of the advice (rather than a third party) and that the purpose of the advice is to influence the addressee to act in the way in which she did in fact act. Given the obligation placed by the City Code upon the directors of target companies to advise shareholders as to the merits of the bid and the responsibility directors of the target company must accept under the Code for the quality of the information provided,[68] the requirements for liability would seem to be satisfied. Indeed, in *Morgan Crucible Co plc* v. *Hill Samuel Bank Ltd*[69] the Court of Appeal upheld as a

[63] [1972] 1 All ER 1166.
[64] At p 1170. See also n. 61 above.
[65] There seems to be strong judicial reluctance to allow intervention by the courts while the bid is on foot; that is a task for the City Panel. See not only *ex parte Datafin plc* [1987] QB 815, but also *Re Ricardo Group plc* (1989) 5 BCC 388. The situation in *Gething* is now covered by Rule 3.1 of the City Code: 'The board of the offeree company must obtain competent independent advice on any offer and the substance of such advice must be made known to its shareholders.'
[66] [1980] 2 All ER 841, 858 (emphasis added).
[67] [1990] 1 All ER 568.
[68] See City Code, General Principle 5 and Rules 3, 19, 25, 28, and 29.
[69] [1991] 1 All ER 148 (noted 54 MLR 739).

possible claim (by refusing to strike it out) that the *bidder* was intended to act upon the defence documents (by raising its bid) and could thus sue the previous target management in tort for the loss caused by such reliance. It seems to have been taken for granted by the courts in this case, even by the judge at first instance who struck out the bidder's claim,[70] that the circumstances of a bid, where the City Code was applicable, would create a duty of care owed by the target directors to the individual shareholders of the target. However, it could be said that these cases involve no more than the application of general principles of tortious liability, albeit to the particular factual context of the director and shareholder relationship.

5.2. FIDUCIARY DUTIES

The decision in *Percival* v. *Wright*[71] is often said to stand for the proposition that directors of companies do not owe fiduciary duties to individual shareholders. From what has been said already, it will be clear that I think this is in general the correct rule. The question, however, is whether *Percival* v. *Wright*, only a first-instance judgment but one of long standing, contains sufficient flexibility to allow for those cases where the directors' dealings with the individual shareholders can be said to raise issues genuinely distinct from those arising from their dealings with the company (i.e. the shareholders as a group). The question is not simply a precedental one but raises issues of policy: what is it about any suggested exception to *Percival* v. *Wright* that makes it appropriate to impose a duty upon directors owed to individual shareholders, and should that duty be of a fiduciary character? The English courts have accepted that a fiduciary analysis of the relationship between individual shareholders and the directors is appropriate where that relationship has been overlaid by the relationship of principal and agent, typically where the shareholders have appointed the directors to negotiate with third parties for the sale of their shares.[72] The fiduciary character of the relationship derives in this case from the general fact of the agency rather than from the fact that the principal is a shareholder and the agent the directors. As with the torts of deceit and negligence, described above, it is no more than the application in a particular case of more general rules of liability, though none the less useful in practice on that account, especially in relation to small companies.

The question is whether and on what basis English law will develop a 'special facts'[73] exception to the no-liability rule of *Percival* v. *Wright* even where the special circumstance does not fit into some other legal category which is independently recognised as having a fiduciary character. Since

---

[70] See [1990] 3 All ER 330, 336. See also *Al-Nakib Investments (Jersey) Ltd* v. *Longcroft* [1990] 3 All ER 321; claim in negligence against the issuers of a prospectus struck out in respect of plaintiff's market purchasers but not in respect of plaintiff's decision to subscribe.

[71] [1902] 2 Ch. 421.

[72] *Allen* v. *Hyatt* (1914) 30 TLR 444; *Briess* v. *Woolley* [1954] AC 333.

[73] The phrase is American. See *Strong* v. *Repide* 213 US 419 (1909).

Percival v. *Wright* involved the sale by shareholders of their securities to directors who failed to disclose the fact that an offer for all the shares at a higher price had been made to them by a third party, the omens for such a development are not generally thought to be good. Indeed, *Percival* v. *Wright* constituted one (though only one) argument in favour of the introduction of statutory liabilities for insider trading. Nevertheless, the step of imposing liability has been taken by the New Zealand Court of Appeal in *Coleman* v. *Myers*.[74] Whilst accepting that it was not the case that the directors of even unquoted, private companies always stood in a fiduciary position *vis-a-vis* individual shareholders, the Court was prepared to hold that in appropriate cases (not confined to agency relationships) the imposition of fiduciary duties (and indeed tortious duties to take care) was proper. In the particular case the directors of a private company had recommended to shareholders a take-over bid, by a company which the directors wholly owned, without disclosing that the development value of the land owned by the target company, and which the bidder intended to develop, was very much greater than the value of the land in the target's books. In this case liability arose because of the family character of the company, the dominant position of the directors in both the company and the family, their high degree of inside knowledge, and their active role in persuading the shareholders to accept the bid. The liability was based upon the failure to disclose material matters as to which the directors knew or ought to have known the shareholders were inadequately informed and, in this case, amounted to the difference between the price paid and the value the shares would have had if the relevant information had been revealed. Interestingly, the City Code was prayed in aid to answer the question of what information was material.

Although English courts have not trodden a similar path in an ordinary common law case, some sympathy with this approach was evinced by Hoffmann J. in *Re a Company (No. 8699 of 1987)*[75] in the context of an unfair prejudice claim under s.459 of the Companies Act 1985. Here, there were competing bids for a private company and the directors strongly advised the shareholders to accept the lower bid (which came from a company owned by the directors), wrongly intimating that the rival bid was bound to fail. The learned judge held that, although in law the directors were not bound to advise the shareholders as to the merits of the bid (though the City Code, if applicable, would require this of directors[76]), if they did choose to issue advice, 'fairness requires that such advice should be factually accurate and given with a view to enabling shareholders (who, ex hypothesi, are being advised to sell) to sell, if they so wish, at the best price'.[77] The judge thought the directors' circular was open to the criticism 'that the board could not have advised the shareholders in such positive terms to accept the [lower] bid if they had placed their fiduciary duty to the shareholders before their own

---

[74] [1977] 2 NZLR 225.   [75] [1986] BCLC 382.   [76] See Rule 25.1.   [77] At 388.

interest in the success of that bid'.[78] This view seems to take the directors' duties beyond the realm of tort law and into that of fiduciary duties by emphasizing the directors' obligation, if they do advise, to advise in the interests of the shareholders concerned with the question of whether they should accept an offer for their shares, although it should be borne in mind that the issue in the case was only whether the section 459 claim should be struck out.

Although both *Coleman* and *Re A Company* involved private companies, where shareholders not involved in the management of the company are particularly dependent upon the directors for information and advice, it has been argued by successive editions of *Weinberg*[79] that the City Code creates a sufficient matrix between directors and shareholders for the establishment of fiduciary duties in the case of bids for public companies. Although the Code provides for its own extra-legal sanctions for breach of its extensive disclosure provisions, these do not include damages awards for individual shareholders. Consequently, the issue is of some importance. It would not seem to be an objection that this step would amount to attaching legal consequences to a breach of the Code. In respect of the provision of information required by the Code such liability is already quite widespread, for example, where a combination of the Code and the Yellow Book requires a paper bidder to issue listing particulars.[80]

In the above cases the establishment of a fiduciary duty, owed by the directors to individual shareholders, was seen as a necessary step in a process of reasoning designed to make the directors liable for non-disclosure of information to the shareholders. It is possible, however, to envisage a breach of fiduciary duty *vis-a-vis* individual shareholders that could be analysed more convincingly in terms of the diversion of an opportunity, originally intended to be presented to the shareholders, by the directors to themselves. The US case of *Brown* v. *Halbert*[81] is suggestive in this regard. A potential buyer of a company approached the managing director and majority shareholder of a company with an offer to purchase the company's business. The defendant said the company's business was not for sale, but that he would be prepared to sell his holding at $1,548 *per* share. Having agreed that sale, the defendant recommended strongly the buyer's offer to purchase minority shares at $300 *per* share, not disclosing the price he had obtained for his majority holding or the buyer's original proposal to buy the company's business. The Court held that the 'duty of the majority stockholder-director, when contemplating the sale of majority stock at a price not available to the other stockholders and which sale may prejudice the minority stockholders, is to act affirmatively and openly with full disclosure so that every

---

[78] Ibid.
[79] See now *Weinberg and Blank on Take-Overs and Mergers*, 5th ed. (London, 1989), para. 3–772.
[80] See Rule 24.9 and the Financial Services Act 1986, Pt. IV.
[81] 76 Cal. Rptr. 781 (1969).

opportunity is given to obtain substantially the same advantages that such fiduciary secured and for the full protection of the minority'.[82]

5.3. FIDUCIARY DUTIES TO THE CURRENT SHAREHOLDERS

In the previous sub-section we considered cases where the courts have held the directors to owe duties to individual shareholders. In this section we consider cases where the directors are said to owe duties to the shareholders as a group (rather than individually) but that group is defined as the current shareholders rather than both present and future shareholders, i.e. there are cases where the directors are required to maximize the short-term utility of the owners of the company. Having examined the cases, we shall than ask whether there is a significant difference conceptually between duties owed to shareholders individually and duties owed to the current shareholders as a group. Continuing with the practice of taking examples from the take-over area, we may use as the paradigm case the question of whether the directors of a target company, faced with two or more rival offers, are obliged to ensure that the shareholders are put in a position to accept, if they wish, the highest offer.

In two English cases the issue has arisen as a result of provisions in the company's articles giving the directors power to control the transfer of shares. In *Heron International Ltd.* v. *Lord Grade*[83] the non-voting ordinary shares of the target company (of which some 54 million had been issued) were listed on the Stock Exchange, but transfer of the 150,000 (necessarily unlisted) voting shares was under the control of the directors, who indeed owned or controlled the majority of the latter category of securities. The directors committed themselves to accepting a bid from a company (controlled by a director and shareholder of the target) at a time when they knew a rival bid at a higher price from another bidder might well be forthcoming. The Court of Appeal regarded the power vested in the directors under the transfer article as a fiduciary power. As shareholders they could have regard to their own interests in accepting the lower bid but as directors, in considering whether to permit the transfer of their shares to their favoured bidder, they must have regard to the interests of the company. 'The fact that the directors as individuals held between them a majority of the voting shares did not authorise them to reflect their individual inclinations. The directors as directors had a duty to consider whether, in the exercise of their fiduciary power vested in them by article 29, they should agree to voting shares being transferred to [the favoured bidder].'[84]

[82] At 793–4. As the defendant director was also the majority shareholder, the case is also an authority on the issue of whether such shareholders (irrespective of whether they are also directors) owe fiduciary duties to individual minority shareholders. This is the context in which the case is discussed in R C Clark, *Corporate Law* (Boston, 1986), 485–7. That issue is outside the scope of this chapter, but it is to be noted that the mandatory bid rule of the City Code (Rule 9) achieves, within its scope, the substance of what is often at stake in discussions of the fiduciary duties of majority shareholders.

[83] [1983] BCLC 244.   [84] At 264.

What is interesting from our point of view is the way in which the duty to the company was conceived of as a duty to promote the interest of the current shareholders.

Where directors have decided that it is in the interests of a company that the company should be taken over, and where there are two or more bidders, the only duty of the directors, who have powers such as those contained in Art 29, is to obtain the best price. The directors should not commit themselves to transfer their own voting shares to a bidder unless they are satisfied that he is offering the best price reasonably obtainable. Where the directors must only decide between rival bidders, the interests of the company must be the interests of the current shareholders. The future of the company will lie with the successful bidder. The directors owe no duty to the successful bidder or to the company after it has passed under the control of the successful bidder. The successful bidder can look after himself, and the shareholders who reject the bid and remain as shareholders do so with their eyes open, having rejected that price which the directors consider to be the best price reasonably obtainable. Thus, as a result of Art 29, the directors owed a duty to the general body of shareholders who were shareholders on 13 January 1982 to obtain for the shareholders the opportunity to accept or reject the best bid reasonably obtainable.[85]

This decision was followed by Hoffmann J. in *Re A Company (No. 8699 of 1985)*,[86] discussed above, in the doubtless more common context for this type of issue, of rival bids for a private company, where the directors preferred their own lower bid. The learned judge was, however, concerned to present the duty in negative rather than positive terms. The directors' obligation was to refrain from any exercise of their fiduciary powers that would prevent the unwelcome higher bid from being put to the shareholders, but the directors were not positively obliged to take steps to achieve this end. Thus, it would be a breach of duty for the directors to use their transfer powers to prevent shareholders, who wished to do so, from accepting the higher bid, but the directors were not obliged to use their transfer powers so as to secure the success of the higher bid.

What is not clear from these decisions is whether this duty, however defined, can be enforced by an individual shareholder who can recover for the loss suffered by her as a result of the breach of duty. If so, the situation seems to be that the duty is not owed to the shareholders as a group but is owed to the shareholders individually (though it is a right the shareholders have in common). In other words, the cases discussed in this section are in fact examples of a duty owed by directors to shareholders individually, as discussed in the previous section.

In *Re A Company* the issue did not have to be faced, partly because the claim, as we have seen, was under section 459 of the 1985 Act which itself confers *locus standi* on an individual shareholder and partly because the motion was to strike out the petition, so that the question of remedy was not

---

[85] At 265.   [86] [1986] BCLC 382.

reached. Again, in *Heron*, although that was a common law claim, the Court found that the directors had not broken their duty, so that the remedial issue did not arise. This was in fact a surprising conclusion. It was found as a fact that the directors had had regard only to their own interests when they committed themselves as directors to act so as to facilitate the transfer of their shares to the favoured bidder. Since the directors had not in fact considered the interests of the current shareholders, this ought to have been enough to invalidate their decision to permit the transfer.[87] However, the Court embarked on a hypothetical enquiry as to whether the decision was one a reasonable board of directors could have arrived at in the interests of the current shareholders and concluded that, on the facts, it was. It would have been reasonable for them to conclude that the higher bid could not succeed and that the lower bid would be withdrawn unless the directors committed themselves to it at once.[88]

The question of whose right it was sought to enforce could not be avoided entirely in *Heron*. The action was brought by the disappointed higher bidder but in its capacity as a shareholder in the target, suing on its own behalf and on behalf of all the other shareholders in the target (except the alleged wrongdoers). Was it enforcing a personal right (albeit in representative capacity because the other shareholders in the target held this right in common) or was it suing derivatively, seeking to enforce a right of the target company itself?[89] The Court seems to have thought both forms of action available. On the assumption (as we have seen, falsified by the facts) that the directors had acted in a way that no reasonable board would have acted, the Court saw two heads of loss as having resulted. The first was a decline in the value of the target's shareholding in a subsidiary company, but, following *Prudential* v. *Newman*, this was a loss to the company of which only the company could complain. The second was the loss by the individual shareholders of the opportunity to accept the higher bid. Since the first head of loss was unquantified, the Court thought it 'quite wrong to injunct the defendants at the instance of the shareholders purporting to sue in right of [the target], merely to prevent [the target] suffering this unknown loss, against the background of the fact that precisely the same loss may apparently be suffered by [the target] if the projected [higher] take-over comes about'.[90]

The essence of the claim was thus perceived by the Court to flow from the individual shareholders being deprived of the opportunity to accept the higher offer. That, the Court thought, 'is a loss suffered exclusively to the pockets of the shareholders, and is in no sense a loss to the coffers of the

---

[87] Cf. *Re W & M Roith* [1967] 1 WLR 432, and see n. 7 above.

[88] See the somewhat similar reasoning used by the Panel in the Irish Distillers case (Panel Statement of 17 Nov. 1988).

[89] Although a derivative action must normally be in representative form, not all representative actions purport to enforce corporate rights; the action may be representative because all the plaintiff shareholders share the same personal right.

[90] At 263.

company, which remain totally unaffected'.[91] From this characterization of the loss as loss suffered by the shareholders individually, it followed that the right to complain of the loss was an individual rather than a collective right. '*Foss* v. *Harbottle* has nothing whatsoever to do with a shareholder's right of action for a direct loss caused to his pocket as distinct from a loss caused to the coffers of a company in which he holds shares.'[92] On this basis the Court proceeded to examine the substantive merits of the plaintiff's claim and, as we have seen, eventually held it not to have been made out on the facts. However, from our point of view the important fact is that the duty to advance the interests of the current shareholders turned out to be a duty owed by the directors to the shareholders individually rather than to the shareholders as a group. This seems to be the correct approach. Where a loss can be identified as suffered by individual shareholders (even if they all suffer the same loss) and where the loss is clearly separate from any loss by the company, the arguments in favour of giving shareholders collectively control over the litigation to recover compensation fall away.[93]

5.4. The Basis of Fiduciary Duties to Individual Shareholders

It would thus appear that *Percival* v. *Wright* is not a complete block upon the recognition of fiduciary duties in English law, owed by directors to individual shareholders. To accept in principle that such duties may be imposed, however, does not take one very far in explaining why in particular cases such duties ought to be imposed. What do the cases discussed above have to tell us on this subject? The imposition of a fiduciary duty is perhaps easiest to envisage when the directors have made use of a power conferred upon them by the articles to act *vis-a-vis* the shareholders in a way that has caused them loss. Thus, in both *Heron* and *Re A Company (No. 8699 of 1985* the directors, unusually, were able to use their powers to permit or not to permit a transfer of shares in order to favour the lower of two take-over offers made for the company.

More commonly, however, as was also the case in *Re A Company*, the directors influence the shareholders' decisions simply via the advice that the former give the latter. In *Re A Company* Hoffmann J. thought that the giving of such advice attracted a duty, not simply to be accurate, but to give advice in the interests of the shareholders who were receiving it. The rationale for imposing a fiduciary duty in this situation, which is also the better rationale for imposing one where the directors use a power derived from the articles to influence the shareholders' decision, is the potential for conflict of interest or self-dealing arising in a situation where the directors are acting on behalf of

---

[91] At 262.   [92] At 263.
[93] Contrast *Gerdes* v. *Reynolds* 28 NYS 2d 622 (1941) where directors resigned their offices in order to facilitate a change of control to someone who subsequently 'looted' the corporation. The directors were held liable to compensate not the non-selling shareholders but the company itself.

the company *vis-a-vis* the shareholders. In *Heron* and *Re A Company* that potential was very clear, since the directors of the target were closely involved in the making of the lower bid, but there is always a potential for conflict of interest between directors of a target company, anxious to preserve their executive positions, and the shareholders of the target, concerned to maximize the values of their shares. Where directors, in such a situation of actual or potential conflict of interest, choose or are required by extra-legal regulation to give advice to the shareholders as to how they should exercise the powers attached to their shares (including the power of disposal), it is appropriate that they be required to give that advice on a fiduciary basis, i.e. not just carefully but in the interests of those who are to receive it. This principle applies *a fortiori* if the directors act *vis-a-vis* the shareholders, not simply by giving advice, but through the exercise of a corporate power.[94]

6. Conclusions

This paper began from the rather obvious point that the company, in traditional corporate law terms, is a form of collective capitalist endeavour, and that it is therefore natural to think of the duties of those who are responsible for running the enterprise, in so far as as they relate to the management of the collective assets, as being owed to its owners as a group, rather than to individual shareholders. It was then argued that this perception gives considerable support to the traditional learning underlying the first limb of the rule in *Foss* v. *Harbottle*, which restricts the freedom of individual shareholders to sue derivatively to enforce the corporation's rights. Although a derivative action lies to enforce the company's rights, and thus appears not to challenge the proposition that directors owe duties primarily to the shareholders collectively, even the derivative action involves a commitment of corporate resources, whose disposition one would expect to be a collective matter. Thus, the first limb of *Foss* v. *Harbottle* emphasizes the collective nature of the corporate endeavour at the level of enforcement of rights, so complementing the formulation of directors' duties as a matter of substantive law.

It was then argued that it was possible to identify two situations where the gravamen of the complaint was not the mishandling of collective assets, so that the rationale for group formulation and enforcement of the directors' duties was not necessarily applicable. The first concerned disputes between and among groups of shareholders where the complaint related to the procedural or substantive impropriety of the decision-making process. The protective techniques here, however, were statutory or contractual and led at

[94] Where the directors exercise a power conferred upon them by the articles, the possibility of providing redress through the s. 14 contract arises. See the discussion of *Mutual Life* v. *Rank* in Section 4 of this chapter. However, in the take-over situation the issue typically arises out of the advice directors give to the shareholders, advice which, where the City Code applies, the directors are required to provide.

best only indirectly to a situation in which duties owed by directors to the
company gave rise to a cause of action for individual shareholders.
Nevertheless, this approach, although technically somewhat complex,
seemed sufficiently flexible to provide even a degree of substantive fairness in
intra-corporate disputes. The second situation concerned dealings between
directors and shareholders in relation to the shareholders' own property (the
shares and the incidental rights attached to them). Here the imposition of
direct duties of a fiduciary character seemed appropriate where there was a
risk of self-dealing by the directors. However, it is not suggested that the
lines between mishandling collective assets and intra-corporate shareholder
disputes or between collective assets and individual assets can be neatly
drawn in particular factual situations, a point that has often revealed itself at
the remedial level. Nevertheless, it is suggested that these three broad
categories provide a useful approach to an analysis of individual and
collective shareholder rights *vis-a-vis* directors' decisions.

6

DIRECTORS' DUTIES TO SHARE-HOLDERS, EMPLOYEES, AND OTHER CREDITORS: A VIEW FROM THE CONTINENT

Klaus J. Hopt

Directors' duties and liability are topics discussed in many countries. Traditionally, this discussion has been restricted to national corporate law and its effects upon the behaviour of directors and upon recovery of damages from directors by the company itself and possibly by the company's shareholders and creditors.[1] Recently, however, there has been a growing interest in comparative law on the subject.[2]

There are several reasons for this change in perspective. First, better theoretical insight is gained when foreign experiences are taken into consideration. Since the nineteenth century the corporation has become a dominant form of business in all major Western countries and the laws of these countries all face similar problems.[3] In this sense, despite many legal differences in the details, there is a common European corporation law—much more so than in the field of stock exchange law and securities regulation, where the differences are much more marked. Second, the internationalization of business plays a decisive role in the rise of interest in comparative corporate law. For multinational companies it has become a matter of acute practical concern to know what duties and risks of liability the directors of their subsidiaries abroad will face under the law of the host country, and also the legal conditions for successfully suing the director of a foreign company in which the multinational company has invested or which

---

[1] For example, for Germany see Lutter and Krieger, *Rechte und Pflichten des Aufsichtsrats*, 2nd edn. (Freiburg, 1989); Schmidt-Leithoff, *Die Verantwortung der Unternehmensleitung* (Tübingen, 1989); for Switzerland see Forstmoser, *Die aktienrechtliche Verantwortlichkeit*, 2nd edn. (Zurich, 1987); for these and other countries, see the major treatises and commentaries on corporation law, for example Mertens in *Kölner Kommentar zum Aktiengesetz*, 2d ed. (Cologne, 1989), s. 93.

[2] Cf. Hopt and Teubner, eds., *Corporate Governance and Directors' Liabilities* (Berlin, 1985); Kreuzer, ed., *Die Haftung der Leitungsorgane von Kapitalgesellschaften* (Baden-Baden, 1991).

[3] Cf. Horn and Kocka, eds., *Recht und Entwicklung der Großunternehmen im 19. und frühen 20. Jahrhundert* [Law and the Formation of the Big Enterprises in the 19th and Early 20th Centuries] (Göttingen, 1979).

owes money to it. Finally, a third factor is often underestimated and sometimes even overlooked completely by national company law doctrine and practice: the impact of European Community law. The pace of the European harmonization of corporation law[4] and the movement towards a single internal market in Europe in 1992-3 will significantly change the traditional centres of gravity.

Comparative law work on directors' duties to shareholders, creditors, and employees turns out to be much more difficult than one would think at a first glance. The general rule in most European countries is that directors have direct duties and liabilities only to their company.[5] Furthermore, in many of these countries there is no strict personal liability of directors for wrongful trading as under section 214 of the English Insolvency Act 1986.[6] Yet this assessment, even though superficially correct, is misleading. A meaningful comparison of laws must reach further and take into consideration the different institutional and legal background of such duties.

1. Institutional and Legal Background of Directors Duties

1.1 FORM AND ORGANIZATION OF THE COMPANY

One of the most important points of comparison is the organization of the board of directors. In Germany and other European countries there is not just one board of directors, but a two-tier system, under which the managing board and the supervisory board are separated. Membership on the managing board nearly always entails full-time employment, while membership on the supervisory board is only a part-time occupation. European company law harmonization will probably adopt both systems as options for the national legislators.[7] In some countries, for example in France since 1966, the company itself has the choice between the one-tier system (*société à conseil d'administration*) and a two-tier organization along the German model (*société à directoire*).[8] Yet most companies have stayed with the traditional one-board system—probably more out of habit than for economic or legal reasons.

The duties of the members of the two boards are partly the same, partly different. Both kinds of directors have a duty of diligence and a duty of

---

[4] Cf. Buxbaum and Hopt, *Legal Harmonization and the Business Enterprise* (Berlin, 1988); Buxbaum, Hertig, Hirsch, and Hopt, eds., *European Business Law: Legal and Economic Analyses on Integration and Harmonization* (Berlin, 1991).

[5] Schlechtriem, 'Schadenersatzhaftung der Leitungsorgane von Kapitalgesellschaften', in Kreuzer, n. 2 above, 9 at 61. The situation as to rights of action may be more nuanced (see infra, Section 4), but it makes little sense to describe these very technical procedural remedies without the bases in substantive stock corporation law.

[6] But see infra, Section 2.2. As to s.214 see D. D. Prentice 'Creditor's Interests and Director's Duties' (1990) 10 *OJLS* 265, at 267 et seq.

[7] Cf. Second Amended Proposal of 20 Dec. 1990 for a Fifth EC Directive concerning the structure of public limited companies and the powers and obligations of their organs, OJEC 11.1.1991 C 7/4, Art. 3 ff., Art. 21a ff.; repr. in Hopt and Wymeersch, eds., *European Company and Financial Law, European Community Law-Text Collection* (Berlin, 1991), C. Pr. 6.

[8] Cf. Guyon, *Droit des affaires*, 5th edn. (Paris, 1988), 302 ff. and 340 ff.

loyalty. But the fact that the supervisory board members do not have the same function as the managing board members, and that they do not devote their full time to the company, makes an important difference regarding the duty of diligence as well as in the duty of loyalty. In countries with a one-tier system such as the United States, similar distinctions may be made as a consequence of the board-committee structure (outside directors, part-time directors).[9]

Another factor for comparison is free choice among legal forms of business associations. While comparing duties of directors in different jurisdictions seems to be an issue only in the realm of stock corporation law, and while indeed the legal form of the company may be less relevant for the duties of directors than the company's organization in a one- or two-tier board, one must still appreciate that the difference between public companies and close companies is of importance. In Germany there are only 2,500 stock corporations (*Aktiengesellschaft*), but 375,000 limited liability companies (*GmbH*). The duties of the directors in both kinds of companies are rather similar,[10] but the division of competences between the directors and shareholders or partners is quite different. The scope of activities expected from and allowed to a director depends, therefore, upon the legal form of the company. It also matters whether a supervisory board is mandatory, as in the stock corporation, or optional, as in the limited liability company. Accordingly, European harmonization of directors' duties would have a rather different meaning in the various EC Member States if it were confined only to stock corporation law.

1.2. Representatives of Shareholders Only, or Also of Other Constituencies

The harmonization of the structure of the stock corporation in Europe has been blocked for two decades by the issue of labour representation on corporate boards.[11] In some European countries, the directors of the board come from different constituencies. In major German companies since the mid–1970s, half the board members are elected by the shareholders, and the other half are labour representatives.[12] Even in smaller companies, at least

[9] Buxbaum, 'The Duty of Care and the Business Judgment Rule in American Law: Recent Developments and Current Problems', in Kreuzer, n. 2 above, 87.

[10] Drury, 'The Liability of Directors for Corporate Acts in English Law', in Kreuzer, n. 2 above, 103 at 104; cf. also Krebs, *Geschäftsführungshaftung bei der GmbH & Co. KG und das Prinzip der Haftung für sorgfaltswidrige Leitung* (Baden-Baden, 1991).

[11] As to the European Company (Societas Europaea), the EC Commission tried to unblock this deadlock in 1989 by splitting its proposal into two in order to avoid the unanimity requirement. See now Proposal of 25 Aug. 1989 for a Council Regulation: Statute for the European Company (S.E.) OJEC 16.10.1989, C 263/41, and Proposal of 25 Aug. 1989 for a Council Directive complementing the Statute for a European company with regard to the involvement of employees in the European company, OJEC 16.10.1989, C 263/69; both repr. in Hopt and Wymeersch, n. 7 above, C. Pr. 3 and C. Pr. 4.

[12] As to the manifold consequences see Hopt, 'New Ways in Corporate Governance: European Experiments with Labor Representation on Corporate Boards' (1984) 82 *Mich. LR* 1338.

one-third of the seats on the board are reserved for labour under traditional plant council legislation. Most of the labour representatives are members of the company's work-force and usually they are also members of the plant council. Under the co-determination law, a few seats are reserved for the trade unions, which may send representatives who have no contact whatsoever with the company. Legally, according to clear majority opinion, directors are not representatives of their different constituencies in the sense that they may or even should act only or primarily in their interest. Practically, however, there are substantial differences in outlook and professionalism between directors and their constituencies. From a functional comparison of law perspective, labour co-determination can be seen as an equivalent to directors' duties to employees, and indeed may even be a far more effective device.

Labour representation on corporate boards may also have a more direct impact on the duties of directors. It is true that the stock corporation laws in countries with labour co-determination do not distinguish between shareholder directors and labour directors apart from their election and revocation and on certain voting questions. Yet two examples show that the answer is not as easy as this.

First it is problematic whether the same standard of care can be expected, for example, from a banker elected by the shareholders and a blue-collar worker who, as spokesman for the plant council, has become a labour director on the board. This question of whether a lack of skill justifies a more lenient standard comes up not only in the context of labour representation on company boards as in Germany, but also in other countries: for example, in the case of unsophisticated spouses and honourary members.[13] The answer is usually that the standard of care may vary within the particular company and its business, but that it still is the standard of an average reasonable director.[14] However, in efforts to define this standard, courts in countries with labour co-determination may take into consideration the situation of a typical labour representative on the board, and accordingly apply a less stringent standard for directors than courts under a system with only shareholder representatives.

The second example concerns the duty of secrecy. Some argue that labour representatives should be free to pass on information on board matters to the plant council or the trade unions. The majority opinion is different: all directors have the legal duty to keep business secrets;[15] however the business secrecy must not be further extended by the by-laws.[16] Legally this view is clearly preferable since it maintains the equality of board members and better serves the functioning of the business enterprise with its need for a sphere of

---

[13] For the United States cf. Buxbaum, n. 9 above, at 86.
[14] Prentice, n. 6 above, at 269.
[15] Lutter and Krieger, n. 1 above, 74 ff.; see also infra Sections 3.2 and 3.3.
[16] Cf. BGHZ 64, 325 (Bayer AG); cf. also BGHZ 85, 293 (Hertie AG).

secrecy. Yet it remains a fact that the interest of the labour side differs from that of the shareholder side; accordingly, business practice shows that it is very difficult to keep boardroom information secret if it concerns issues which are of particular interest to labour.

1.3. LEGITIMATE CORPORATE AIMS AND ACTIVITIES

As stated earlier, the general rule in European countries is that the directors have no duties towards the employees. Yet there may be other mechanisms equivalent to or even more favourable to the work-force. One is institutional representation, treated above. Another is the incorporation of third-party interests into the legal concept of the 'interest of the company'. The scope of the interest of the company—i.e., whether the directors may or even must pursue interests other than those of the shareholders in the company—is one of the most famous and intricate questions of modern corporate law.[17] The German Stock Corporation Act of 1937 stated expressly that directors must pursue the interests of the shareholders, the company's labour force, and the public interest. The Stock Corporation Act of 1965 omitted the formula, which was discredited in the Third Reich, but respect for the interests of the company's workers and the common welfare was considered to be self-evident. In modern economic and company law theory there are many who plead for strict shareholder orientation in order to make the board more responsible both economically and legally. In other countries the duty to consider the interests of employees is laid down expressly by statute, as in Great Britain, for example.[18] In the United States, some states have gone further by enacting stakeholder statutes. The first such statute was passed in Pennsylvania in 1986; it provides that in discharging their duties, directors may 'in considering the best interests of the corporation, consider the effects of any action upon employees, upon suppliers and customers of the corporation, and upon communities in which offices or other establishments of the corporation are located, and all other pertinent factors'.

While the legitimacy of considering non-shareholder interests may make a significant difference in theory, the difference in the practical outcome is less significant, at least in the German experience. In modern society the company cannot, in the long run, afford to neglect the interests of its work-force or to act against the public welfare. Accordingly, the argument can be made that in most cases, the long-term interest of the company and its shareholders must also inevitably embrace third-party interests (i.e. interests of non-constituents) as well.[19]

This evaluation is confirmed by recent American experiences with the stakeholder statutes enacted by state legislators. These stakeholder statutes

---

[17] See Lord Wedderburn, 'The Legal Development of Corporate Responsibility', in Hopt and Teubner, n. 2 above, at 3 ff.

[18] S. 309 of the Companies Act 1985, cf. Prentice, n. 6 above, at 273.

[19] Schlechtriem, n. 5 above, 9 at 36 ff.

are part of the political take-over game between the federal authorities and
the state legislators: in enacting these statutes, state legislators appear to have
been less concerned with the interests of the work-force and other creditors of
the companies than with the state interest in maintaining the independence of
the companies incorporated and taxable in that state. The stakeholder
statutes have and are meant to have the effect of considerably broadening the
directors' discretion in trying to block take-overs, despite or even against the
interests of the shareholders.[20]

1.4. LEGAL TREATMENT OF GROUPS OF COMPANIES

In the rare instances that directors' duties are viewed from a comparative law
perspective, the comparison is usually made between the various duties of
directors which arise under traditional stock corporation law. This is an
appropriate analysis if the company is independent; but the reality of today is
characterized by groups of companies.[21] Some countries, like Germany have
responded to this reality by an elaborate system of statutory rules for groups
of companies, going far beyond traditional company law.[22] But most
countries try to cope with groups of companies through evolving case law and
by developing solutions for specific problems. These different approaches
also have far-reaching consequences for directors' duties. In the latter
countries, laws governing duties and liabilities are usually addressed
primarily to the dominant shareholders and the directors.[23] Sometimes
specific group-of-companies situations are dealt with by treating the parent
company as a *de facto* or shadow director.[24]

In contrast, the primary goal of the German law of groups[25] is to regulate
the relationships between the companies in the group for the sake of the
minority shareholders and creditors of the subsidiary and also, under certain
circumstances, of the parent. Furthermore, difficult questions of sharing and
apportionment between the members of the group arise. Under this legal
approach to groups of companies, the duties of directors both of the
subsidiary and of the parent are important, but must follow the primary rules
for the member companies. Therefore a meaningful and comprehensive
comparison of the directors' duties would imply a comparison of the different

[20] Cf. R. S. Karmel, 'The Duty of Directors to Non-Shareholder Constituencies in Control
Transactions: *A Comparison of US and UK Law*' (1990) 25 *Wake Forest LR* 61.
[21] Cf. C. Schmitthoff and F. Wooldridge, eds. *Groups of Companies* (London, 1991);
Sugarman and Teubner, eds., *Regulating Corporate Groups in Europe* (Baden-Baden 1990); Hopt,
ed., *Groups of Companies in European Laws* (Berlin, New York 1982).
[22] ss. 291 ff. of the German Stock Corporation Act 1965; an English translation can be found
in Schmitthoff and Wooldridge, n. 21 above, appendix III.
[23] Cf. A. Tunc, 'The Fiduciary Duties of a Dominant Shareholder', in Schmitthoff and
Wooldridge, n. 21 above, 1 ff.
[24] Prentice, n. 6 above, at 267 ff.
[25] Cf. Wiedemann, *Die Unternehmensgruppe im Privatrecht* (Tübingen 1988); Wiedemann,
'The German Experience with the Law of Affiliated Enterprises', in Hopt, ed., *Groups of
Companies in European Laws*, n. 21 above, 21 ff.; Hopt, 'Legal Elements and Policy Decisions in
Regulating Groups of Companies', in Schmitthoff and Wooldridge, n. 21 above, 81 ff.

approaches to groups of companies, which is not possible in this context.

As stated previously, in most countries directors have duties only to the company, not directly to the shareholders and creditors. In the context of groups of companies, however, this principle would have clearly negative effects: it is unlikely that the claims of the subsidiary against the directors of the parent would be enforced by the directors of the subsidiary because they are dependent on the former. Therefore it makes sense either to create personal duties for directors of the parent to the minority shareholders and creditors of the subsidiary, or to give each shareholder of the subsidiary the right to assert the claim of the subsidiary against the directors of the parent. The German law of groups follows the second approach.[26]

2. The Duty of Diligence

In most European jurisdictions, the directors' duty of diligence and the duty of loyalty are clearly distinguished. From a comparative law perspective as used in this chapter, there is little use emphasizing the distinction between duty and liability, even though this distinction is of course a valid concept. One author has remarked that the English system is concerned more with duties than with liability.[27] On the other hand, an American authority on the subject finds that, under American law, substantive standards are less relevant than the liability itself.[28] It will be left to English and American lawyers to judge whether this difference is real. For most Continental European laws, the approach taken is that violation of duty and liability are considered as opposite sides of the same coin, except in unusual situations. Therefore, it seems more helpful to examine the duty of diligence in specific situations and its meaning for shareholders and creditors.

2.1. DUTY TO ACT WITHIN THE LIMITS OF THE LAW: NATIONAL DIFFERENCES

The duty of diligence is just a general formula for more specific duties which have been concretized by case law and legal literature. One of these is the duty to act within the limits of the law. In the United States, this is sometimes called the duty of obedience.[29] The organization of a company and the decision-making within it must be in accordance with the law. At first glance this looks like a truism. Yet what seems self-evident in the national context,[30] namely that the directors must respect the law of the land, is a

---

[26] ss. 309 (4), s. 317 (4) of the German Stock Corporation Act 1965. See also infra, s. 4.2.

[27] Drury, n. 10 above, 104.

[28] Buxbaum, n. 9 above, at 79.

[29] Cf. Samson-Himmelstjerna, 'Persönliche Haftung der Organe von Kapitalgesellschaften, Vergleichende Darstellung von amerikanischem und deutschem Recht' (1990) 89 *ZVglRWiss* 288, at 296.

[30] But see e.g. s. 93 (3) and (5) of the German Stock Corporation Act 1965. Under these sections the directors are subject to actions by the creditors more readily if they have breached particular duties imposed upon them expressly by company law. See also infra, s. 4.3.

difficult problem in the international context. While there has been a considerable harmonization in the European Community,[31] there are still many important differences between the laws of EC Member States.

This is true even in company law, which is harmonized by nine directives enacted and several other draft directives pending. Some of the major differences concern the delineation of competences between company organs, particularly between the directors and the general assembly;[32] corporate finance, with its many difficult limits set up by law;[33] the general attitude towards disclosure;[34] and the whole area of take-over regulation.[35] Further inter-Member State differences arise over such defences against take-overs as green mail, golden parachutes, voting right restrictions, use of authorized capital with denial of pre-emptive rights of the old shareholders in favour of a white knight, etc.[36]

Even more important legal differences to be taken into consideration by directors exist outside company law: for example, in securities regulation, commercial law, labour law, and tax law. The EC Commission is not even aiming at a full European harmonization in these fields.

Regarding directors' duties to shareholders and creditors, the duty to act within the limits of the law and the very considerable differences of the laws to be respected in the various countries have a further consequence. In Germany and in a number of other European countries, the rights of certain creditors, particularly employees, are spelt out in considerable detail within statutory and sometimes judge-made law outside company law; for example, for safety on the job. Disregarding such a provision may result in liability not only on the part of the company, but also of the directors personally, if they had the duty to oversee the rights of the employees and if this legal duty is construed as third-party protection within the meaning of tort law.[37] The latter situation is a tort law question irrespective of the general company law principle that the director owes his duties only to his company.

2.2. STANDARD OF CARE, BUSINESS JUDGMENT RULE, RESCUE AND INSOLVENCY SITUATIONS

Directors have the duty to manage the business of the company and to supervise its officers in the best professional way. The standard of care which the director must meet is not just a subjective one, but is determined by the

---

[31] See most recently the comprehensive European Community Law-Text Collection by Hopt and Wymeersch, eds., *European Company and Financial Law* (Berlin, 1991).

[32] Cf. the German Holzmüller case, BGHZ 83, 122; more generally Schlechtriem, n. 5 above, at 43 ff.

[33] Cf. from a German–American perspective Kübler, *Aktie, Unternehmensfinanzierung und Kapitalmarkt* (Cologne, 1989).

[34] Cf. Meier-Schatz, *Wirtschaftsrecht und Unternehmenspublizität* (Zuric, 1989).

[35] This has been the general view of the participants in the Brussels Take-over Symposium, cf. Hopt and Wymeersch, eds., *European Take-overs-Law and Practice* (London, forthcoming).

[36] Cf. Maeijer and Geens, eds., *Defensive Measures Against Hostile Take-overs in the Common Market* (Dordrecht. 1990).

[37] s. 823 (2) of the BGB. Cf. Putzo in Palandt, *BGB*, 50th edn. (Munich, 1991), s. 618 annot. 8.

behaviour of a diligent and prudent director. The German Code concretizes this formula under its two-tier system by stating that in managing the company, the members of the managing board shall act with the care of a diligent and prudent executive.[38] The United States Model Business Corporation Act is more specific without being different in substance.[39]

It has been remarked that the duty of diligence is much more demanding in German law than in English law.[40] This observation is based upon the assumption that under common law the duty of care is essentially subjective in its application, while in German law the standard is an objective one. But an English individual who accepts the task of directorship of a company without personally having the necessary qualifications could possibly (even though not in all cases) be considered, from a subjective standpoint, to have acted negligently; even if it is true that a subjective standard is less severe, the law in action (i.e. factually applied by the court) may be more important than the theoretical standard applied.

Under the business judgment rule, the duty to manage the business of the company is not violated merely because a decision turns out to be harmful to the company. In most jurisdictions, the business judgment rule is not part of the corporate statutes but has been developed by the courts, sometimes with the help of legal literature. Clearly, the bad economic outcome of a business transaction is not sufficient to establish a breach of duty on the part of the directors. Quite the contrary, directors may even be in breach of their duty if they let a good business opportunity for the company, which is seldom completely without risks, pass by. In any case, a court cannot use hindsight and is not qualified to judge whether or not a business decision would have been better had it been made in a different fashion.

Sometimes it is said that this formula sets gross negligence as a precondition for liability, but this argument is misleading. Of course the business judgment rule never covers a grossly negligent decision. But the director who is simply negligent is also barred from seeking haven within the limits of the business judgment rule. The reason for such a rule is the uncertainty under which decisions must be taken in real business life. Yet this uncertainty does not exist, at least not to the same degree, in, for example, the preparation of the decision, the general supervision of the officers, or—in the case of a two-tier board—the supervision of the management board or the enquiry into facts in case of suspicion. This issue has been discussed particularly in the United States in the aftermath of *Smith* v. *Van Gorkom*,[41] a Delaware Supreme Court decision of 1985 which has

---

[38] s. 93 (1) of the German Stock Corporation Act 1965.

[39] 'A director shall discharge his duties as a director . . . (1) in good faith; (2) with the care an ordinarily prudent person in a like position would exercise under similar circumstances; and (3) in a manner he reasonably believes to be in the best interests of the corporation.' American Bar Association, Committee on Corporate Laws, Model Business Corporation Act, (1984), s. 8.30.

[40] Cf. the discussion by Drury, n. 10 above, at 105.

[41] 488 A. 2d 858 (Del. 1985).

been followed by other American courts. But in substance, a similar stand is taken in many European jurisdictions, allowing for a degree of discretion on the part of directors making business decisions, regardless of their eventual outcome.

In rescue and insolvency situations, things change dramatically for the directors and their duties to shareholders and creditors, even in those countries where there is no wrongful trading provision such as section 214 of the English Insolvency Act 1986 or the *action en comblement du passif*, available (with certain differences) in France and in Belgium.[42] These changes may be illustrated by three examples.

1. Usually directors still have a fair amount of business discretion as far as the ways and means of looking for rescue are concerned. Yet disclosure to the general assembly and, finally, the filing of the bankruptcy petition cannot be avoided as a matter of business judgment. If upon proper consideration it is assumed that the company has incurred a loss amounting to one-half the stated capital, the managing board must meet without delay and call a shareholders' meeting to report this fact.[43] This is the directors' duty, irrespective of the fact that such a shareholders' meeting does not pass unnoticed by the press and the general public and may further damage the company's business.

It is quite controversial to whom this duty of disclosure is owed. The majority opinion holds that the duty is owed only to the company itself, the general assembly being a company organ. But others regard this provision as tort law protection for the shareholders, the future buyers of the shares, and even the creditors of the company.[44] Accordingly, in the case of violation of this duty, the directors could be personally liable not only to the company but directly to those persons who could have avoided damage if they had known earlier of the company's disastrous situation; for example, by avoiding further losses, by not buying new shares, or by successfully insisting upon having their debts paid by the company.

2. The duty to file a bankruptcy petition is even more crucial. Again, a reasonable line must be drawn between giving ample room for trying to rescue the company and the necessity of finally facing the economic facts. The creditors' interests suffer if the petition is filed too early as well as too late. The German Stock Corporation Act gives an example, not necessarily a model: 'If the company becomes insolvent, the managing board shall, without undue delay and not later than three weeks after the insolvency arose, file a bankruptcy or composition petition . . . The petition shall not be deemed to have been unduly delayed if the managing board proceeds to

[42] Cf. Zahn, *Geschäftsleiterhaftung und Gläubigerschutz bei Kapitalgesellschaften in Frankreich: eine rechtsvergleichende Untersuchung* (Frankfurt, 1986); Hopt in Birk and Kreuzer, eds., *Das Unternehmen in der Krise: Probleme der Insolvenzvermeidung aus rechtsvergleichender Sicht* (Frankfurt, 1986), 11 at 32 ff.

[43] s. 92 (1) of the German Stock Corporation Act 1965.

[44] Cf. the references given by Mertens, n. 1 above, s. 92 No. 24.

initiate the composition proceedings with the care of a diligent and prudent executive.'[45]

Here the situation is different from mere disclosure to another organ of the company, as mentioned in (1) above. This duty can hardly be understood as a duty to the company since its substance is to put an end to the company (however, one may argue that in the case of a timely filing of the bankruptcy petition the company may still have a chance of reorganization).[46] Nor can the duty to file for bankruptcy be categorized as a duty to future shareholders since all shareholders, the ones already present and the buyers of shares, form the company which has become bankrupt. Instead, the duty is clearly meant to protect the creditors. It follows that the creditors who have suffered a loss due to the delayed petition in bankruptcy have a viable claim.

Yet there are two restrictions: first, these claims cannot be asserted by the creditors themselves, since in the case of bankruptcy all actions are concentrated in the person of the receiver;[47] second, the amount of the damages recoverable is restricted to the difference between what the creditor got and what he would have received if the bankruptcy petition had been filed in time, i.e. the so-called quota damage. In contrast, creditors cannot recover damages if in the case of a timely bankruptcy petition they would not have entered into business with the company at all. The latter has long been highly disputed, but has been settled for good in a landmark case and is generally accepted today by legal doctrine.[48]

3. In the context of rescue and insolvency, it is sometimes mentioned that specific rules may apply to a director who is a bank or the representative of a bank.[49] In some jurisdictions, particularly in the United States but also in France and Belgium, there is a tort law doctrine of lender's liability which could make directors liable not only to the company but also to the other creditors of the company. In Great Britain there is discussion whether the director who has given credit to his company breaches his duty if he pays back the credit to himself before other creditors.[50]

In other countries banks may be prevented by law from recovering their debt and even their share in the bankruptcy proceeding if, as shareholders of the company, they have extended credit to it instead of increasing the share capital. This is the German doctrine of the so-called capital replacing credit (*eigenkapitalersetzende Darlehen*).[51] The peculiarity of this rule is that

---

[45] s. 92 (2) of the German Stock Corporation Act 1965. Cf. Schlechtriem, n. 5 above, at 51 ff.; Drury, n. 10 above, at 119 ff.; Prentice, n. 6 above, at 267 ff.

[46] BGHZ 96, 231 at 237; Mertens, n. 1 above, s. 92 No. 50.

[47] s. 93 (5) last sentence of the German Stock Corporation Act of 1965 applied by analogy.

[48] BGHZ 29, 100 at 106 and the references given by Mertens, n. 1 above, s. 92 No. 52 ff.

[49] Cf. the case mentioned by Prentice, n. 6 above, at 268 n. 20: bank as a shadow director.

[50] Prentice, n. 6 above, at 274.

[51] This was developed for limited liability companies and was then extended to the stock corporation. It applies to all partners of the limited liability company, while in stock corporation it applies only to those shareholders who have an entrepreneurial interest in the stock corporation, i.e. usually more than 25% of the shares. Cf. BGHZ 90, 381; Hopt and Mülbert, *Kreditrecht* (Berlin, 1989), s. 607 No. 106 ff.

although there is a duty to maintain orderly financing of the company, there is no liability for damages. The legal sanction is instead the forfeiture of the credit extended to the company.

These duties and liabilities are problematic both in practice and in theory. In practice, if extended too far they are counterproductive. Banks and other potential creditors might be willing to give fresh money in order to save the company provided they have some say and control as directors or as members of the supervisory council. But this willingness disappears quickly if they are forced to bear the risk of failure of the rescue operation. Theoretical evaluation of these duties shows that they are not really directors' duties, but duties of banks or duties of partners and shareholders as such.

2.3. DIRECTORS' DUTIES IN SPECIFIC CONTEXTS

More problems of directors' duties arise in specific contexts which cannot be treated here in great detail. The most pertinent example is provided by takeover contests. The key question is whether directors may take their own stand in the battle instead of leaving this fully to the shareholders.[52] If they may be or even are required by law to pursue the interests of the company as distinct from the interests of different shareholders, it is questionable what is this interest of the company, and whether it comprises the interests of other stakeholders.[53]

A further question is whether, at least under certain circumstances, these stakeholders have a direct claim against the directors. They may have a valid claim under tort law if the directors wilfully act against the interests of the workforce or of the bondholders,[54] or possibly even under contract law if the directors have promised the offeror in a legally valid way[55] to advocate the take-over in the general assembly and later change their minds.

Another difficult situation arises where the directors want to make contributions to political parties or for social, ecological, or charitable purposes[56] and the shareholders or a faction thereof are opposed to this. Again, the question whether the directors may make such contributions is one concerning legitimate corporate aims and activities, as seen above.[57] The answer may be once more that, at least to a certain extent, such contributions are valid if they are in the long-term interests of the company.

---

[52] Assmann, 'Director's Duties and Liabilities in Transfer of Control under the Continental Legal Systems', in Brussels Takeover Symposium, n. 35 above.

[53] Supra, Section 1.3.

[54] Cf. Note, 'Debt Tender Offer Techniques and the Problem of Coercion' (1991) 91 Colum. L. Rev. 846; Karmel, n. 20 above, at 71 ff.; Mark M. Weber, *Schutz der Anleihensgläubiger bei kreditfinanzierten Unternehmensübernahmen (leveraged buyouts)* (Zurich, 1990).

[55] The problem is whether the directors can bind their own discretion, which they are compelled to exercise in the interest of the company.

[56] Cf. Mertens, n. 1 above, s. 76 comments 32 ff. with many references.

[57] Supra Section 1.3.

But from the perspective of directors' duties to shareholders there is a particular problem beyond this: namely, whether all or a minority of the shareholders may stop such contributions. As a general rule they would not be able to because such an action would constitute undue interference by the shareholders in management. But could there be an exception in the case of company assets being given away without consideration? If not, the only way to stop the directors would be to dismiss them. Yet dismissal may often occur too late and, in countries with a two-tier system, it is not even within the competence of the shareholders to dismiss the culpable directors; it is in the exclusive competence of the supervisory council.

3. The Duty of Loyalty and Secrecy

Conflicts of interest and loyalty give rise to specific and very complex legal problems which cannot be treated here.[58] Only a few remarks must suffice.

3.1. CONFLICTS BETWEEN THE INTERESTS OF THE COMPANY AND OF THE DIRECTOR

The duty of loyalty is of course recognized in all company laws. But in Germany,[59] France,[60] and some other European countries it is less developed and concretized than, for example, the fiduciary duties in the United States[61] and also in Great Britain.[62] The director must act in the interest of the company and may not pursue his own interest against the interest of the company. Usually there are quite extensive rules and prohibitions against self-dealing with the company. In some countries competition with the company is of particular concern for the legislator and has given rise to a body of rules apart from the duty of loyalty. In this context the two-tier system is relevant.[63] Competition with the company is prohibited for managing directors, but is allowed for supervisory board members (of course within the limits of anti-trust law). The corporate opportunity doctrine has been developed only recently and is not yet very refined. Particular attention should be paid to the law of groups of companies.[64] There are special rules and cases concerning competition and conflicts of interests in the stages of both the formation of the group and later on in its operation.

[58] See Ch. 1–3 above.

[59] Hopt, 'Self-Dealing and Use of Corporate Opportunity and Information: Regulating Directors' Conflict of Interest', in Hopt and Teubner, n. 2 above, 285; Kübler, 'Erwerbschancen und Organpflichten', in *Festschrift für Werner* (Berlin, New York 1984), 437; Kübler and Waltermann, 'Geschäftschancen der Kommanditgesellschaft' (1991) *ZGR* 162.

[60] Cf. Giesen, *Organhandeln und Interessenkonflikt: vergleichende Untersuchung zum deutschen und französischen Aktienrecht* (Berlin, 1984).

[61] Cf. Brudney and Clark, 'A New Look at Corporate Opportunities' (1981) 94 *Harv. LR* 998.

[62] Drury, n. 10 above, at 105.

[63] See supra, Section 1.1.

[64] See supra, Section 1.4.

3.2. CONFLICTS BETWEEN THE INTERESTS OF DIFFERENT CONSTITUENCIES

Conflicts between the interests of different constituencies often arise for deputized bank representatives. Such conflicts are particularly acute in countries with an all-purpose or universal banking system as, for example, in Germany; this issue has been discussed there in quite some detail.[65] Similar conflicts have arisen more recently as a consequence of labour representation on corporate boards.[66]

3.3 BUSINESS SECRECY, DISCLOSURE, AND INSIDER DEALING

Traditionally in Continental Europe, corporate law provides for a special duty to keep secret all business affairs, while the issue of disclosure, even to the shareholders, has been neglected. This has changed somewhat in recent years, partly due to EC directives. But as stated above,[67] the European countries are still well behind as far as disclosure is concerned. Nevertheless, under company law each shareholder has a right to information from the company. Obviously the information must be provided by the directors. Therefore, according to the majority view, directors have a personal duty to the shareholders breach of which can give rise to personal liability for damages. However, a more rational approach might be to stick to the general principle that such duties of the directors are owed only to the company.[68]

It is not surprising that on the Continent, maybe with the exception of France, it has taken some time for the prohibition against insider trading to be recognized. Under the recent European Insider Dealing Directive, provisions against insider dealing are now mandatory for the Member States.[69] But details are still very controversial. This is particularly true for civil sanctions on insider dealing. If such sanctions are enforced, the director who has used inside information may be liable not only to the company, but also to the shareholder from whom he has bought or to whom he has sold the shares.

4. The Rights of the Company, the Shareholders, and the Creditors to Bring an Action

In Continental European countries, the procedural side of the problem of suing is (usually, but not always) the equivalent of the substantive side; i.e.

---

[65] Cf. BGH NJW 1980, 1629 (Schaffgotsch case); Lutter, 'Bankenvertreter im Aufsichtsrat' (1981) 145 *ZHR* 224; Lutter, 'Interessenkonflikte durch Bankenvertreter im Aufsichtsrat' (1987) *RdW* 314; Hopt, 'Inside Information and Conflicts of Interests of Banks and Other Financial Intermediaries in European Laws', in Hopt and Wymeersch, eds., *European Insider Dealing* (London, 1991), 219.

[66] Supra, Section 1.2 and Kübler, 'Dual Loyalty of Labor Representatives' in Hopt and Teubner, n. 2 above, 429.

[67] See supra, Section 2.1 and Meier-Schatz, n. 34 above.

[68] Mertens, n. 1 above, s. 131 comments 100 ff. with references to the majority opinion.

[69] Cf. Davies, 'The European Community's Directive on Insider Dealing: From Company

the right to bring an action follows the duty and its beneficiary, and the beneficiary of this duty is usually the company.

4.1. ACTIONS BY THE COMPANY

In the case of violation of a director's duty, the company itself can bring an action. Technical problems arise from the fact that the action must be brought for the company by its directors against a fellow director. This is easier to solve in a two-tier system then in a one-tier system, since in the former the task of asserting a claim by the company against a member of the managing board can be given to the supervisory board.[70]

In most jurisdictions only the company may sue its director for breach of duty, even if that duty also affects the interests of the shareholders, the employees, and, more generally, the creditors. The reasons are threefold: the danger of interfering with company policy and decision-making, the wish to avoid double recovery, and the policy of treating all shareholders alike (at least all those who belong to the same class).

4.2. ACTIONS BY SHAREHOLDERS

According to the aforementioned principle, shareholders themselves have a right to sue in their own name only if the director has injured them in their personal rights. Possible examples given above concern tort law situations, the shareholder's right to information, and insider dealing.

In exceptional cases the shareholders have a right to sue on behalf of the company. Such a right exists particularly under the German law of groups of companies.[71] In France and Switzerland, derivative suits by shareholders are more generally feasible, but for practical reasons this option is seldom used.[72] Class actions by shareholders as in the United States are traditionally unknown in civil law countries.

In some countries, damages claims by the company against its directors (both members of the managing board and members of the supervisory board) relating to its management must be asserted upon request of a minority of shareholders holding at least 10 per cent of the stated capital.[73] Upon application by the minority the court appoints special representatives to assert the claim for damages against the directors. While this is obviously not the same as a direct action by individual shareholders against the directors, this provision, part of general minority protection, is an equivalent device.

Law to Securities Markets Regulation? (1991) 11 *OJLS* 90; Hopt, 'The European Insider Dealing Directive' (1990) 27 *CMLR* 51.

[70] s. 112 of the German Stock Corporation Act 1965.

[71] s. 309 (4), sentences 1 and 2 on which ss. 310, 317, 318, 323 of the German Stock Corporation Act 1965 refer. Cf. also the right of each shareholder to apply to the court for appointment of a special auditor, s. 315 of the German Stock Corporation Act.

[72] Schlechtriem, n. 5 above, 64 ff.

[73] So-called *Klageerzwingungsverfahrung*; s. 147 (1) of the German Stock Corporation Act 1965.

Beyond this, at least in Germany, the so-called shareholder action is very controversial.[74] The Bundesgerichtshof in its famous Holzmüller decision[75] did affirm the possibility of such an action in a case where the directors acted without the necessary approval of the general assembly. But a general acceptance of this approach in other situations has still not been extended.[76]

4.3. ACTIONS BY CREDITORS

For creditors, basically the same arguments apply as for shareholders. Only in very exceptional situations do the creditors of the company have a personal claim against the director and are able to sue in their own name.

1. Creditors can sue in their own name if they have special statutory protection; for example, investors in securities regulation and under capital market law.

2. Apart from such statutory rights, a creditor may also assert a claim for direct and personal injury to his rights through the director's fault. In many jurisdictions, specific tort situations may give rise to such actions.

3. In some countries creditors may assert their rights even in particular contractual and pre-contractual confidence relationships; for example, if the directors when concluding a contract for the company made false representations to the contracting party. German courts have gone very far in acknowledging such personal claims by the contracting party against the director and have given basically two criteria for determining such liability: first, there must have been personal trust and confidence between the parties beyond the mere fact that one was a director of the company; and second the director must have acted in his own self-interest in the deal. The doctrine has been more restricted on such subjects as personal duties and liabilities.[77] Indeed, the criterion of self-interest is clearly too vague since directors always have some self-interest in promoting the affairs of the company. The personal trust and confidence criterion is more acceptable, but should be confined to exceptional cases. The personal confidence which every contracting partner places in his counter-party is certainly not enough.

---

[74] A very restrictive view is taken, for example, by Zöllner, 'Die sogenannten Gesellschafter-klagen im Kapitalgesellschaftsrecht' (1988) *ZGR* 392; Mertens, 'Der Aktionär als Wahrer des Rechts?' (1990) *AG* 49; cf. also von Gerkan, 'Die Gesellschafterklage', (1988) ZGR 441. Others writers plead for a more generous approach towards the shareholder action, e.g. Brondics, *Die Aktionärsklage* (1988); Wiedemann, *Organverantwortung und Gesellschafterklagen in der Aktiengesellschaft* (1989) See generally Raiser, 'Das Recht der Gellschafterklagen', (1989) 153 *ZHR* 1.

[75] BGHZ 83, 122 at 133 ff.; cf. Großfield and Brondics, 'Die Aktionärsklage—nun auch im deutschen Recht' (1982) *JZ* 589.

[76] Contra the minority view of Mertens, n. 1 above, s. 93 comments 171 ff. According to Mertens the shareholder's right of membership may be violated by the director in such cases.

[77] Cf. Medicus, 'Zur Eigenhaftung des GmbH-Geschäftsführers aus Verschulden bei Vertragsverhandlungen', in *Festschrift für Steindorff* (Berlin, New York 1990), 725.

In certain circumstances a creditor can sue in his own name, but on behalf of the company.[78] Under German law the company's claim for damages can be asserted by its creditors to the extent that they cannot obtain satisfaction from the company.[79] But apart from some clear-cut mismanagement cases, this rule applies only where directors grossly breach their duty to act with the care of diligent and prudent directors. Swiss and French law open up similar possibilities for the creditors.[80]

In practice, however, this derivative suit by creditors against directors is not very important, because most often the company is bankrupt. As soon as an order subjecting the assets of the company to bankruptcy proceedings has been issued, the receiver exercises the rights of the creditors against the directors during the pendency of the proceedings.

5. Summary and Outlook

Altogether, the risk of liability suits against directors of a company is still much less acute in Continental Europe than in the United States, but it is clearly increasing.[81] Waiver is usually no way of escape, particularly not in the case of creditors suing on behalf of the company.[82] Ratification is not excluded, but is rather difficult.[83] Indemnification and insurance are not yet as common as in the United States, but they are gaining importance quickly despite the problems connected with them.[84]

Returning to the institutional questions treated in the beginning of this chapter, it seems important to underline once more the corporate governance aspect. Clearly the duties and liability of directors to shareholders, employees, and other creditors are but one means of making directors responsible; they are not necessarily the most effective way of achieving this result. Other means might be more disclosure to the shareholders and the

---

[78] This is to be distinguished from the obvious possibility of a creditor whose claim has been affirmed by court order seizing the claim of the company against its director and then suing the director on the basis of the seized claim.

[79] s. 93 (5) of the German Stock Corporation Act 1965; similarly s. 117 (5) of the same Act which deals with the abuse of influence on the company and s. 309 (4) sentences 3–5 of the same Act, which deals with groups of companies, see supra, Section 1.4.

[80] Schlechtriem, n. 5 above, 68.

[81] For Germany see the BGH NJW 1980, 1629, Schaffgotsch case: conflict of interest; LG Düsseldorf AG 1991, 70, Girmes AG: inactivity of supervisory council in rescue situation; BGHZ 79, 38 touches of the Poullain case, but not the liability part of it. Quite a number of cases are pending, e.g. Harpener AG Dortmund/Omni (Rey): alleged looting by the Swiss parent, involvement of directors, FAZ No. 193 21.8.1991, p. 15, No. 195 23.8.1991, p. 16; Hornblower Fischer AG Frankfurt: activities of director for the competitor, FAZ No. 191 19.8.1991, p. 15; Co op AG: fraudulent balance sheets, FAZ No. 86 13.4.1991, p. 15. As to the situation in the USA see Buxbaum, n. 9 above, at 97 ff.: 'capping' statutes as a response to the host of litigation and the exodus of qualified persons from their boards.

[82] s. 93 (5) sentence 3 of the German Stock Corporation Act 1965.

[83] Drury, n. 10 above, at 106 ff., 145 ff.

[84] Cf. 'mehr Rechtsschutz für Top-Manager', *Süddeutsche Zeitung*, No. 181 7 Aug. 1991, p. 29; Drury, n. 10 above, at 147 ff.

general public, the development of duties and liabilities of auditors and certified public accountants, a functioning take-over market without undue restrictions, and possibly also legal responsibility on the part of the financial intermediaries which would correspond with their role taken *de facto* towards companies and in the financial markets.

III
Trusts in the Recovery of Misapplied Assets

7

THE RECOVERY OF A DIRECTOR'S IMPROPER GAINS: PROPRIETARY REMEDIES FOR INFRINGEMENT OF NON-PROPRIETARY RIGHTS

Roy Goode

1. Introduction

1.1 THE SCENARIO

D is a director of a development company, P, a public limited liability company in which D holds a substantial block of shares. He is also the chairman and controlling shareholder of X, a large private limited liability company engaged in a similar line of business. During the course of his travels D meets Charles, a wealthy landowner, who is impressed by D and some months later approaches him to see whether he would be interested in buying a substantial area of land suitable for residential development. A price is agreed and D arranges for X to purchase the land and to construct a high-class residential estate. Several of the houses on the estate are sold, part of the proceeds being used by X to pay for equipment and the rest placed on deposit with X's bank. D also arranges for P to place a contract for the purchase of a substantial quantity of materials with a company owned by Charles's son, for which D receives a secret commission from Charles of £50,000. This sum D invests in quoted securities which rapidly increase in value. He sells some of these for £20,000, which he pays into his bank account, then in credit.

The question examined by this chapter is whether, and in what conditions, P can assert proprietary claims to the land and properties comprising the residential estate still held by X, the equipment purchased with part of the proceeds, the money fund constituted by X's deposit with the bank, and the securities still held by D or the £10,000 in his bank account.

The present section of this chapter deals with certain fundamental concepts and considerations. In Section 2 I shall examine English law as I currently understand it to be. Though set in the context of claims against a director and his associated company much of the analysis applies with equal force to ordinary equitable tracing rights. In Section 3 attention will be focused on what appear to me to be weaknesses in the conventional analysis.

In particular, it will be contended that in what has become known in America as the 'corporate opportunities' situation P's rights against X and D are not proprietary rights (or rights *in rem*) but rather rights in *personam ad rem*, that is, personal rights to a proprietary *remedy*. It will be argued as a corollary that in situations of the kind described above the English-type institutional constructive trust is inappropriate and that what is required is the American-style remedial constructive trust. Hence the word 'non-proprietary' in the very title to this chapter must be regarded as controversial.

It will be assumed throughout that D's actions constituted a breach of his fiduciary obligations to P and that for one reason or another P wishes to pursue proprietary rather than personal claims. Thus the scope of the duty will not be examined, nor will the range of personal remedies available to P. But a brief comment about each of these excluded questions will help to set the scene.

1.2. The Existence of the Obligation

Quite apart from rules governing infringement of confidentiality, tort claims for improper use of a company's tangible property, and dereliction of contractual obligations, there are a number of distinct but interrelated doctrines under which D could be held in breach of duty. First, there is the rule that a director as a fiduciary must not put himself in a position where his personal interest conflicts with his duty to the company.[1] Secondly, he is not allowed to retain for himself a benefit he obtains in the course of his activities on behalf of the company, even if it is clear that the company itself could not or would not have obtained the benefit.[2] Thirdly, there may be a distinct principle under which a director who exploits for himself a business opportunity which he ought to have exploited for his company is accountable for any benefit received.[3]

Yet there are several questions which English law has yet to answer satisfactorily. Given the width of the second of the principles referred to above it is hard to see what independent scope there is for the third. Indeed, the latter, so far as it exists or may develop as a distinct principle, is more likely to operate as a qualification of the other two.[4] The relationship between these various doctrines, which overlap and are often treated as interchangeable, is a matter of uncertainty. It is reasonable to suppose, but not clear from the case law, that an executive director is under more stringent fiduciary duties than a non-executive director, that a full-time director will more

---

[1] *Cook* v. *Deeks* [1916] AC 554.

[2] *Regal (Hastings) Ltd.* v. *Gulliver* [1942] 1 All ER 378, [1967] 2 AC 134 n. *Industrial Development Consultants Ltd.* v. *Cooley* [1972] 2 All ER 162.

[3] Whether English law possesses a distinct rule of this kind is not clear. Subsequent references to the pursuit of business opportunities by D are intended to identify the fact situation under consideration, not to point to the existence of a separate corporate opportunities doctrine.

[4] All these questions are admirably treated by Professor R. P. Austin, 'Fiduciary Accountability for Business Opportunities,' in P. D. Finn, ed., *Equity and Commercial Relationships* (Sydney, 1987), ch. 8.

readily be held accountable than a part-time director, and that a benefit obtained by a director from an activity wholly unconnected with the existing or imminent business of the company is less likely to be susceptible to a restitutionary claim than a benefit derived from dealing in an area covered by the company's business. But these are issues which English courts have yet to work out.

1.3 PERSONAL REMEDIES

The pursuit of proprietary remedies in situations of the kind described above tends to be the exception rather than the rule. In the typical case the asset wrongfully acquired by D for himself has been disposed of or, in the case of money, spent, so that proprietary relief is not available. This does not, however, mean that proprietary issues are irrelevant; on the contrary, it is often to P's advantage to establish an initial proprietary entitlement in order to be able to take into account in quantifying its personal claim any enhancement in the value of the asset or its products or proceeds.

The remedy most commonly sought against a director who is considered to have breached his fiduciary obligations to his company is an account and payment of the profits derived from his allegedly improper conduct. Sometimes a claim is laid to particular assets in his hands, or even to the entirety of a business developed from the infringing activity, on the basis of a constructive trust,[5] but even then it is not always clear whether the remedy sought or granted is a true proprietary remedy or merely a personal order for transfer of the assets or business in question.

The personal remedies against a director who misuses his position are bewildering in their diversity and have been the subject of extensive examination by numerous scholars. The complexity arises not only from the different sources of legal obligation—restitution, tort, and contract—each with its own distinctive rules for liability and measure of recovery, but from the fact that in relation to personal restitutionary claims the plaintiff has the option of suing for what my colleague Professor Peter Birks has conveniently labelled the first measure of restitution (value received) or the second measure of restitution (value surviving)[6] and the defendant may receive different forms of value at different times. In the case of X, this would be the contract for the acquisition of the land, the subsequent interest in the land itself, the houses subsequently built on the land, the proceeds of sales, the equipment purchased with them, and the claim by X on its bank in respect of the sum deposited.

Thus where D improperly receives money he may be ordered to pay over the amount received, either by way of equitable account or in a common law quasi-contractual claim for money had and received to P's use. Where he

[5] See e.g. the unsuccessful claim to the constructive trust of an entire business in *Hospital Products Ltd.* v. *United States Surgical Corp.* (1984) 156 CLR 41, a decision of the High Court of Australia.

[6] *Introduction to the Law of Restitution* (Oxford, 1985), 75 ff.

receives a tangible asset, then whether or not he still holds it he may be ordered to pay an amount equal to the highest value of the asset during the period it was in his hands;[7] whilst if he has disposed of the asset he can be ordered to pay the amount or value of any tangible or intangible proceeds received in exchange. In all these cases D is entitled to an allowance for the cost to him of acquiring and maintaining the asset, so that the claim is in substance for the profit or gain he has made. Where D has not made an outright appropriation of the asset but has merely used it for his own purposes or where there is no 'hard' asset at all but merely a 'soft' asset such as information, P may at its option claim an account and payment of the profits derived from the use or a sum equal to the use-value of the asset for the period of use.

1.4. WHY PROPRIETARY CLAIMS?

Given that the establishment of a proprietary claim is inherently more arduous than that of a personal claim, since it often raises difficult questions of the nature of the obligation owed with respect to an asset and its identifiability after changes in form, why would a plaintiff seek property rights instead of merely claiming an account of profits? One reason is the fear that the defendant has become or might become bankrupt, leaving the plaintiff who obtains a purely personal order for payment to prove as an unsecured creditor in competition with other creditors. Curiously, this is a consideration which has rarely featured in the reported cases, which almost invariably involve a defendant who is assumed to be or is in fact solvent. Secondly, there may be difficulties in valuing a money claim which are avoided by recovery of the asset *in specie*. Thirdly, the plaintiff may anyway wish to have the asset *in specie* rather than mere payment of its value, as where it consists of a business which he wishes to take over.

It might be thought that once the asset had been disposed of so as to become irrecoverable[8] P would have no incentive to spend time and money demonstrating that until such disposal it had a proprietary right to the asset. This, however, is not the case, for a proprietary right to the asset, unlike a purely personal claim, carries with it a proprietary right to any proceeds, products[9] and accretions still in the hands of D. Moreover if the proceeds, etc., were worth more than the asset or have increased in value P may be in an even better position than if it had been able to claim the original asset. So

---

[7] This is on the basis that since from the time of receipt he was under a continuing duty to transfer it to P it is to be assumed in favour of P that he could have had and resold the asset at the most favourable time and price.

[8] E.g. because it is not physically traceable or has been destroyed or has passed into the hands of an innocent purchaser for value who acquires an overriding title.

[9] To the extent that these reflect the contribution made to them by the asset to which P had a proprietary claim. Where the product results from a commingling of that asset with the assets of D or third parties P normally becomes a co-owner of the product to the extent that its asset forms part of it.

establishing the proprietary base may be important even if the base itself has disappeared.[10]

There is no doubt that over the years the courts have shown an increasing willingness to grant *in rem* relief through the medium of the constructive trust, D being deemed to receive and hold the improperly acquired asset as trustee for P. However, it will be suggested later that because English law has hitherto treated the constructive trust as exclusively institutional—that is, as an ordinary property trust which treats P as the beneficial owner of the asset from the time of its acquisition by D—and has not been willing to accept that it may have an alternative use as a court-imposed *remedy*, there has been an unfortunate tendency to regard P as having a proprietary *right* to deemed agency gains, to the potential detriment of D's creditors, when it would have been more appropriate to grant it a proprietary remedy to enforce what should more properly have been characterized as an *ad rem* personal right.[11]

1.5. TWO IMPORTANT DISTINCTIONS

A particular feature of the above scenario is that the assets to which P lays claim were not previously its property, nor did they result from any appropriation of its property rights, so that the relief P seeks is not the recovery of assets, or products or proceeds of assets, to which it had a pre-existing beneficial title,[12] but the disgorgement by the defendants of assets acquired as the result of a breach of duty owed by D to P to which, in relation to the development, D's company X was a party.

The distinction is of fundamental importance, for to give a plaintiff back what has always been his, or what has become his as the result of his election to avoid a voidable transfer to the defendant or another person, has no impact on the defendant's general creditors, whereas to remove from the defendant an asset which (however improperly acquired) formed part of his beneficially owned estate may have implications for his creditors for it reduces the quantum of assets which would otherwise have been available to meet their claims. Unfortunately this distinction has not been observed in English case law or, indeed, in that of other common law jurisdictions, a point to which I shall return in the concluding section of this chapter.

---

[10] Where D has not appropriated the asset outright or where the asset is a 'soft' asset such as information, P ought not in principle to be granted a proprietary right or remedy for it still has the asset. The question whether P has suffered a subtraction from its estate for the purpose of a *personal* restitutionary claim against D, e.g. for the value derived from the improper use of P's property, is a separate issue which is well discussed by J. Beatson, *The Use and Abuse of Unjust Enrichment* (Oxford, 1991), 230 ff. For some of the difficulties arising from the assimilation in legal analysis of fact situations which should be differentiated in determining the appropriate remedy, see Roy Goode, 'Property and Unjust Enrichment', in A. Burrows, ed., *Essays on the Law of Restitution* (Oxford, 1991), 221–31.

[11] See *infra*, pp. 146 ff.

[12] A subject dealt with in Ch. 8 below.

It is also necessary to differentiate cases in which the defendant was unjustly enriched by undertaking for his own benefit activity which, if he undertook it at all,[13] should have been undertaken for the plaintiff from cases in which the defendant's benefit is derived from conduct in which he should never have engaged at all, as where he took a bribe or secret commission. In the former case the plaintiff can legitimately claim that the defendant should be treated as if he had acted on the plaintiff's behalf so that he should be given a proprietary remedy (though not a proprietary right[14]) for what I have referred to elsewhere as the defendant's 'deemed agency gains'.[15] In the latter case the benefit received by the defendant, though wholly improper, cannot be treated as acquired for the plaintiff, so that there is no basis for proprietary relief. This distinction, which bears on the plaintiff's entitlement to the proceeds of and accretions to the benefit originally received by the defendant, *is* observed in the cases, though its validity is considered by many commentators (not, however, by the present writer) to be unsound.

1.6. THE DISCRETIONARY NATURE OF NON-MONEY REMEDIES

There is one final preliminary point to be made. It is a characteristic of English procedural law that whilst the court must recognise proprietary rights established by law, all judicial remedies other than for the payment of money (and certain forms of monetary relief also) are discretionary. A plaintiff who has a proprietary right to an asset will not necessarily be granted a proprietary remedy but may be required to accept a money judgment instead. As I have pointed out elsewhere,[16] the effect of the court's decision on P and D's creditors is economically neutral, for P's substantive proprietary right is neither dependent on nor extinguished by the judgment and continues in force until the judgment is satisfied. By contrast the conferment of a proprietary remedy to support a purely *ad rem* right is far from neutral, for it confers on P an asset which it did not have before and in so doing removes from D's estate an asset which previously belonged to it.

2. The Conventional Analysis of P's Rights

2.1. THE CLAIM TO THE UNSOLD LAND AND HOUSES

There is clear authority for the proposition that X, as a participant in D's breach of fiduciary duty, took the contract for the acquisition of the land as constructive trustee for P. The leading case is *Cooks* v. *Deeks*,[17] in which three directors managing a company negotiated for a contract with a third party with whom the company had many previous dealings but at the last moment diverted the contract to themselves and had the work carried out by a newly formed company which took over the contract and received the

---

[13] It is not necessary that he should have been under a duty to undertake it for P; it suffices that he should not have done it for himself.

[14] See section 3, below.

[15] Above, n. 10 at p. 219.

[16] Ibid. 223–4.

[17] (1916) AC 554.

profits. The Privy Council held that the contract concluded by the defendants had belonged in equity to the original company, and the directors, having obtained it for themselves in breach of their duty to that company, held it for the company.[18] Similarly in *Carlton* v. *Halestrap*[19] where it was alleged that the director of a company had taken for himself a development opportunity comprising three properties as the result of information received as such director, Morritt, J. granted an interlocutory injunction to restrain a sale of the properties by the defendant, holding that if the facts were established at the trial then the defendant would be a constructive trustee of the property itself, with an entitlement to reimbursement of the purchase price and expenses, and that the plaintiff was not limited to an account of profits.

In effect, the property is treated as if it had always belonged to the plaintiff and is treated as a form of enrichment by subtraction from the plaintiff's estate[20] rather than as an enrichment resulting solely from a wrong done to the plaintiff. Thus English law currently draws no distinction between this form of 'interceptive' subtraction[21] and that which derives from D's collecting from T money or property which T was legally obliged to pay or transfer to P; indeed, both forms of interceptive subtraction are apparently equated with the two-party situation in which D acquires title to an asset from P himself to which he was never entitled or to which he has ceased to be entitled and can therefore be regarded as part of P's patrimony. Whether this equation is justified is a controversial question that will be considered later.

2.2. The Claim to the Equipment

Once P is recognised as having a proprietary right to an asset this right carries through to identifiable proceeds and products in accordance with the normal rules of equitable tracing. Where the disposition of the asset by D to a third party, T, does not take place in such circumstances as to override P's title it is probably the case that P's interest in the proceeds is *ad rem* rather than *in rem* unless and until it elects to look to the proceeds rather than the original asset.[22] But where T acquires an overriding title, P's interest attaches to the proceeds automatically under the equitable rules.[23] This does, of course, presuppose that P has a proprietary *right* to the original asset, not merely a proprietary *remedy* to enforce a right *ad rem*. If English law were to take the position, as I later suggest it should take, that P's entitlement to deemed agency gains is only *ad rem*, then by the same reasoning its entitlement to proceeds could at most be *ad rem*.

---

[18] The contract having been completed, there could not, of course, be any question of pursuing a proprietary claim to the contract itself; an account of profits was ordered.

[19] (1988) BCC 538.

[20] Aptly termed 'interceptive' subtraction (Birks, above, n. 6, pp. 133 ff.).

[21] This useful term was coined by Birks (ibid.) to denote a situation in which D receives an asset 'at the expense of' P—that is, by subtraction from P's estate—not by way of transfer from P itself but from a third party who was legally liable to make it over to P or who would certainly have done so if D had not intercepted it.

[22] Birks, *supra*, n. 6, pp. 70, 92, 393.

[23] Goode, *supra*, n. 10, pp. 233 ff.

2.3. THE DEPOSIT WITH X'S BANK

The sum which X placed on deposit with its bank represented the balance of the proceeds of sale of the properties which X must be considered to have held on a constructive trust for P. The effect of the deposit was to create in favour of X a claim against the bank. Accordingly P is entitled to trace the above balance into the bank account and claim that the deposit is held by X on trust for P. It is important to appreciate that this is a claim not to money itself but to the chose in action represented by X's claim as a creditor of its bank. In the unlikely event that physical money had been paid into the bank the bank as borrower would have acquired ownership of it. But almost certainly the bank will have received the deposit not in physical money but by transfer from another bank which itself will not have been in money but, directly or indirectly, by an in-house transfer in the books of the Bank of England. Hence what the bank will have received is a claim on another bank, and that claim it holds for its own benefit. A further possibility is that the original payer—i.e. a buyer of one of the properties—also banked with X's bank, in which case what the bank acquires is a claim on that payer, which again it holds for its own benefit. The essential point is that P's tracing right attaches not to what the bank received but to the claim that X has upon it.[24]

2.4. THE SECURITIES AND PROCEEDS DERIVED FROM D'S SECRET COMMISSION

I have earlier drawn attention to the distinction drawn by English law between gains made from activity which, if undertaken by D at all, should have been undertaken for P and gains resulting from activity which D should never have undertaken in the first place. To gains of the first type, and their proceeds and value enhancements, P has a proprietary claim; to gains of the second it has merely a personal claim to the amount of money represented by the receipts in their original form. The *locus classicus* is the decision of the Court of Appeal in *Lister* v. *Stubbs*.[25] In that case Stubbs, an employee of the plaintiff company, Lister & Co., responsible for buying materials on its behalf, accepted a bribe from Varley & Co., a firm of suppliers, to place orders with them and invested the bribe in securities and property for his own benefit. The plaintiffs' application for an interlocutory injunction to restrain dealings with the property and securities on the ground that they had a proprietary right to them was rejected by the Court of Appeal, which held that the right enjoyed by the plaintiffs was merely a personal right to the amount of the bribe as money had and received or alternatively by way of equitable debt, so that the plaintiffs had no beneficial interest in the money itself or in the assets purchased with it. The issue was put with his customary lucidity by Lindley, L.J.:

[24] The most recent decision on tracing into (and indeed through) a bank account into the hands of a stranger as constructive trustee is *Agip (Africa) Ltd.* v. *Jackson* [1991] 3 WLR 116.
[25] (1890) 45 Ch. D. 1.

The relation between Messrs. Varley and Stubbs is that of debtor and creditor—
they pay him. Then comes the question, as between Lister & Co. and Stubbs,
whether Stubbs can keep the money he has received without an accounting for it?
Obviously not. I apprehend that he is liable to account for it the moment he gets it.
It is an obligation to pay and account to Messrs. Lister & Co., with or without
interest, as the case may be. I say nothing at all about that. But the relation
between them is that of debtor and creditor; it is not that of trustee and *cestui cue
trust*. We are asked to hold that it is—which would involve consequences which, I
confess, startle me. One consequence, of course, would be that, if Stubbs were to
become bankrupt, this property acquired by him with the money paid by him to
Messrs. Varley would be withdrawn from the mass of his creditors and paid over
bodily to Lister & Co. Can that be right? Another consequence would be that, if
the Appellants are right, Lister & Co. could compel Stubbs to account to them, not
only for the money with interest, but for all the profits which he might have made
by embarking in trade with it. Can that be right? It appears to me that those
consequences show that there is some flaw in the argument. If by logical reasoning
from the premises conclusions are arrived at which are opposed to good sense, it is
necessary to go back and look again at the premises and see if they are sound. I am
satisfied that they are not sound—the unsoundness consisting in confounding
ownership with obligation.[26]

After a hundred years the decision continues to generate controversy,[27] yet
it has recently, and in my view rightly, been followed both in England[28]
and elsewhere.[29] To treat P as having a proprietary right to the bribe and its
fruits is to breach the line between restitution by subtraction and restitution
for wrongs. Indeed, even to allow a personal claim to the proceeds of the
bribe, and to their proceeds, *ad infinitum*, faces the serious objection that it
treats the initial breach of a personal obligation as if it were a continuing
breach, thus giving P a claim of the same value as if it had a proprietary
entitlement.

In the present case we are not told whether the secret commission was in
truth a bribe, that is, offered in advance, or merely a large gift by way of
appreciation and without any intention to influence future transactions. In
the former case the amount of the commission it is clearly forfeited to P; in
the latter, the position is less clear, since the commission is not linked to any
improper conduct, but it is likely that P could lay a personal claim to a large
gift,[30] though the basis for this is not clear.[31]

---

[26] *Ibid.*, at p. 15.

[27] For good recent discussions which put the case against *Lister* v. *Stubbs*, see T .G. Youdan,
'The Fiduciary Principle: The Application of Proprietary Remedies', in Youdan, ed., *Equity,
Fiduciaries and Trusts* (Toronto, 1989), ch. 3; and David Hayton, 'Constructive Trusts: Is the
Remedying of Unjust Enrichment a Satisfactory Approach', Ibid., ch. 9, at pp. 210, 222–26.

[28] *Attorney General's Reference* (No. 1 of 1985) [1986] QB 491; *Islamic Republic of Iran
Shipping Inc.* v. *Denby* [1987] 1 Lloyd's Rep. 367.

[29] *Daly* v. *Sydney Stock Exchange Ltd.* (1986) 160 CLR 371.

[30] *Bowstead on Agency*, 15th edn. (London), 186.

[31] Where there is a prospect of future contracts between the parties the court is likely to infer
from the size of the gift that it was in fact intended to influence the award of such contracts.

3. A Critique of the Legal Treatment of Deemed Agency Gains

There are four possible judicial responses to P's claim in respect of an asset held by D representing what I have called deemed agency gains. The first is to restrict P to a money claim, which might, according to the circumstances, be for the value of the asset, the profits derived from it by D, or damages for the loss suffered by P. The second is to make an *ad rem* order, that is, a personal order directing D to transfer the asset to P. Such an order would not in itself change the ownership or protect P from the consequences of D's insolvency; P would acquire a real right in the asset only through enforcement of the order or D's compliance with it prior to bankruptcy. The third possible response is to treat P, as in the first two cases, as having only a personal *right* but to protect that right by conferring on it a proprietary *remedy* by imposing a constructive trust, operative from the date of the order.[32] Such a judicial remedy can be qualified by such conditions as the court thinks just for preventing unfairness to other creditors. The fourth response is to treat P as having a proprietary right to the asset from the beginning, which is the present rule in English law.

There is no consensus as to the proper approach in policy terms. At one end of the spectrum are those who favour the first response and argue that P should not be given either a proprietary right or a proprietary remedy but should be treated like any other unsecured creditor. At the other are those who support the existing rule embodied in the fourth response. As a matter of policy there seems no good reason to restrict P to a purely personal remedy. D was under an equitable duty to transfer the asset to P; why should D not be compelled to perform his equitable obligation?

There are equal difficulties with the fourth response. The law of restitution draws a clear distinction between the unjust enrichment of D by subtraction from P's estate and enrichment resulting solely from a wrong done to P, which benefits D but not by reducing P's estate. In the former case P is in principle accorded a proprietary right; in the latter, its remedy may not lie in restitution at all but in contract or tort, and even in those special cases where restitution is available the right infringed is only a personal right and the remedy available ought thus to be either purely personal or at most *ad rem*.

Thus where D has been enriched at P's expense by appropriating to himself an asset, or the proceeds of an asset, received from P to which D was never beneficially entitled[33] or to which he had a voidable title which has been avoided,[34] the law rightly treats the asset or proceeds as not forming

---

[32] American jurisprudence gives a court-imposed constructive trust effect retrospective to the time of the unjust enrichment. The effect of this approach is that while the constructive trust is remedial, in the sense that it is for the court to determine whether and in what conditions it should be imposed on the asset, the effect where it is imposed is virtually indistinguisable from that of the substantive institutional trust in English law.

[33] E.g. where D receives from P a payment of money sent in discharge of a debt which P has forgotten he had already paid, or wrongfully disposes of P's goods and retains the proceeds for himself.

[34] As where the contract under which D received the asset from P has been rescinded by P for misrepresentation.

part of D's estate, for in the first case D never acquired a beneficial interest in the asset at all and in the second he took it subject to the equity of avoidance which has been exercised against him. Hence to recognise P's right as proprietary does not remove from D's estate any non-voidable asset which previously formed part of it and causes no loss to D's creditors. The same is true of cases where D receives from T money or property which T was legally obliged to pay or make over to P, for again the right to the money or property was vested in P from the beginning and D was at no time beneficially entitled. In both types of case D's enrichment is clearly by way of subtraction from P's estate. By contrast, D's receipt of a bribe from T does not remove from P anything to which he was entitled, so that to accord P a proprietary right in the bribe and its fruits is to remove from D's estate retroactively an asset which would otherwise have been available for his creditors.

The difficult case is the one I have termed 'deemed agency gains,' benefits derived by D from pursuing for his own advantage a business opportunity which he should have pursued for his company, P. Are such benefits to be treated as derived from an appropriation of P's asset, and thus a subtraction from its estate? Or are they to be treated as derived purely from a wrong done to P, so that P's claim ought properly to be for disgorgement by D of an asset which has become his but which he ought not in equity to be allowed to retain?

Those who contend that this is simply another case of enrichment by subtraction, in principle indistinguishable from cases in which D's benefit is derived directly from P, argue that since D should not have pursued the business opportunity on his own behalf but only for P, any benefits he derives should be treated as held on trust for P from the beginning. One can extend the argument in this way. If D had been instructed by P to pursue the business opportunity there can be no doubt at all that in so doing D will be treated as if he had acted in accordance with his instructions and obtained any resulting benefit for P. Why should it make any difference if the duty to act in P's interests rather than his own is imposed by law by reason of the fiduciary relationship? Does not equity treat as done that which ought to be done? Indeed, is not that the whole basis on which uncompleted agreements for the transfer of an asset are treated in equity as completed?

The short answer to this is that there is a great deal of difference between D's diverting to himself an asset to which P was legally entitled—as where he collects from T a debt due from T to P—and D's conduct in preventing a *potential* asset (e.g. a putative contract right) from ripening in favour of P so as to constitute an addition to its wealth; and there is an even greater difference between D's appropriation of P's asset and his acquisition of gains through activity which he was under no obligation to undertake for P and which P would not have undertaken for itself, so that P's complaint is not that it has been deprived of anything but simply that D should not have acted to his own advantage and should therefore forfeit the gain he has made.

There can, of course, be no doubt that in all these cases D's breach of fiduciary duty should expose him to an *in personam* claim for the amount or value of his initial improper receipt. But why should P be held the beneficial owner *ab initio* of that which never belonged to it? Admittedly no great harm is done where P's claim is to a particular asset bought by D for himself which he should have bought for P, for D's creditors are adequately protected by the requirement that as a condition of securing restitution P must reimburse D for the price and other acquisition costs, thus restoring lost value. But this is not true of the more complex case where the original asset has changed form, perhaps several times, and grown in value in the process. If, for example, D's improper behaviour led, mediately or immediately, to the acquisition of a business which he proceeds to develop, why should future creditors of the business be exposed to loss through proprietary claims by P to the assets of the business which in effect place P in a position of absolute priority? Indeed, where D acted in good faith (and several of the reported cases have teetered on the borderline between breach and no-breach of fiduciary duty), why should he himself suffer such exposure?

I have suggested elsewhere[35] that there is a *via media* between treating P as having a proprietary right on the one hand and a purely personal right on the other, namely that its entitlement should be characterized as a *ius ad rem*, a personal right to the delivery up of the asset in the hands of P, and of its proceeds and enhancements in value, and that the remedy, as always, should be discretionary and if granted should be by imposition of a remedial constructive trust under an order which provides adequate protection for D's secured and unsecured creditors.[36] An alternative approach is to make the remedy as well as the right *ad rem* and to give P an order *in personam* requiring D to make over the asset he has obtained through his improper conduct. This puts P in much the same position as any other judgment creditor who is left to convert his personal right into a real right by a process of execution. The remedial constructive trust is somewhat more favourable to P, since it gives immediate protection from D's insolvency as well as the benefit of any increase in the value of the asset between judgment and compliance with or enforcement of the judgment.

The above conclusions are based on the present state of English insolvency law. If our rules of preference were more rational and embraced involuntary transfers, including those effected by a judicially imposed constructive trust, the problem of fairness in relation to the general body of creditors would disappear, for the right conferred on P by the constructive trust would be vulnerable to a preference claim, in the event of D becoming bankrupt within the specified statutory period, in just the same way as if D had voluntarily made over to P, in discharge of a personal obligation, an asset forming part of D's estate.

---

[35] *Supra*, n. 10.
[36] As to the different ways in which this might be done, see ibid. 242–44.

8

TRUSTS IN THE RECOVERY OF MISAPPLIED ASSETS: TRACING, TRUSTS, AND RESTITUTION

Peter Birks

The title of this chapter could include almost the whole of the law of restitution. Hence it is important in the first instance to establish a clear picture of the kind of situation in which we are interested. The key is the word 'misapplied', which has both a broad and a narrow sense. It might be taken to include, for example, even mistaken payments. It will be as well to set out one case which is within the broader meaning but of a kind with which we are not immediately concerned.

In *Chase Manhattan Bank N.A. Ltd.* v. *Israel-British Bank (London) Ltd.*[1] the plaintiff bank mistakenly paid more than $US 2 million to the defendant bank. It meant to pay one such sum, but because of a clerical error it repeated the payment. This misfortune was compounded when the recipient, the defendant bank, almost immediately went into liquidation. There was no doubt whatever that the plaintiffs were entitled to restitution. They obviously had a claim *in personam*, a personal claim that the defendants ought to repay the amount received. But that would have required them to join the queue of unsecured creditors. They wanted to trace the money and to claim an equitable proprietary interest in the traceably surviving proceeds. Goulding J. held that, if the exercise of identification could be successfully done—that is, if they could on the facts trace—they would indeed be entitled to assert an equitable proprietary interest.

For the purpose of defining our subject it is necessary to distinguish between the types of claim in play in *Chase Manhattan* and the facts upon which they arose. With the species of restitutionary claim illustrated in that case we are indeed directly concerned. But the *Chase Manhattan* facts are not directly in our sights because they involve only a simple two-party payment. The money was indeed misapplied, in the sense that it ended up where it was not intended to go, but it was not misapplied by any third hand. For present purposes, 'misapplied' will be used only in the narrower sense which supposes a misapplication by some third party not now before the court. The

[1] [1981] Ch. 105.

central issue is whether the person entitled to the misapplied fund can leap over the misdirector and get restitution from the recipient. And the analytical or semantic question to be answered in tandem with the discussion of that issue is what, if any, role the language of trusts has in the solution of this kind of problem.

1. What Kinds of Fact Situation?

Our concern therefore is with the situation in which someone, usually not worth suing and often on his way to prison, has misdirected to the defendant value, usually money, to which the plaintiff was entitled. The primary question is whether the plaintiff, the victim of the misapplication, can recover from the recipient or some other person. And the secondary question, of general importance but given extra prominence here by the theme of this volume, is what part, if any, the law of trusts has to play. Historically the law and language of trusts have been prominent. The argument will be that the time has now come for them to assume a much lower profile.

The misdirector may on occasion not be dishonest, as where he himself is the victim of some mistake or misunderstanding. The most obvious example is the trustee or other fiduciary who honestly misdirects the fund in his keeping because he interprets the law incorrectly or makes an error of fact.[2] Much more often the third hand is engaged in fraud.[3] As Sir Peter Millett has recently written in the *Law Quarterly Review*, it is the fact that large-scale commercial fraud has become a growth industry that makes it imperative for the law to make intelligible and efficient its weapons of restitution.[4]

2. What Kinds of Claim?

A golden rule, not always adhered to in the past, is to distinguish very clearly between claims against the recipient and claims against someone who is alleged to have helped, the accessory to the misdirection. This can best be illustrated by drawing on the two leading cases which will repeatedly be used as models throughout this chapter. One is *Agip (Africa) Ltd.* v. *Jackson & Co.*,[5] which was decided at first instance by Millett J. and was indeed the immediate stimulus to his writing the article in the *Law Quarterly Review* which has already been mentioned. The other is *Lipkin Gorman* v. *Karpnale Ltd.*, a recent decision of the House of Lords which is likely in due time to be

[2] *Re Robinson, McLaren* v. *Public Trustee* [1911] 1 Ch. 502; *Re Diplock* [1948] Ch. 465; *In re Montagu's Settlement Trusts* [1987] 2 WLR 1192.
[3] *Banque Belge pour l'Étranger* v. *Hambrouck* [1921] 1 KB 321; *Transvaal & Delagoa Bay Investment Co. Ltd.* v. *Atkinson* [1944] 1 All ER 579; *G. L.Baker Ltd.* v. *Medway Building & Supplies Ltd.* [1958] 2 All ER 532 (Danckwerts J.), [1958] 3 All ER 540 (CA). See also *Agip* and *Lipkin Gorman* discussed in the text immediately following.
[4] Sir Peter Millett, 'Tracing the Proceeds of Fraud' (1991) 107 *LQR* 71.
[5] *Agip (Africa) Ltd.* v. *Jackson* [1990] Ch. 265 (Millett J.); [1991] 3 WLR 116 (CA).

regarded as the case which set the modern English law of restitution on a new and sound foundation.[6]

2.1. Accessories and Recipients

Agip (Africa) Ltd. v. *Jackson & Co.* conveniently shows that the same person may be attacked both as recipient and as accessory. There the misdirector was a fraudulent senior accountant called Zdiri who was employed by Agip in Tunis. He was in the habit of altering the name of the payee in cheques and other payment orders signed on behalf of Agip. The fraud cost Agip tens of millions of dollars. This litigation concerned one of many incidents. Zdiri had sent money from Agip's bank account to a dummy company. The defendants, who were chartered accountants on the Isle of Man, had set up the company for him and his associates on anonymous instructions. They therefore indubitably helped the misdirection, and the only question was whether they had done so with the degree of fault which was required if they were to be liable. But the accountants had also received the misdirected funds from the dummy company into their own bank accounts. Hence there was room for an enquiry whether they were liable, not only *qua* accessories, but also *qua* recipients.

In *Lipkin Gorman* v. *Karpnale Ltd.* the Playboy Club (Karpnale Ltd.) was attacked as recipient. The plaintiffs were solicitors. One of their partners, Cass, played the part of misdirector. He was addicted to gambling. At the Playboy Club in Mayfair he gambled away more than £200,000 from their client account. The alleged accessory to this misdirection was the bank at which the plaintiff solicitors held their client account. Cass was an authorized signatory, but the solicitors maintained that in letting him withdraw these huge sums the bank had helped the misapplication of their funds and had done so with the requisite degree of knowledge.

We are not at the moment concerned with the details of the outcome of these model cases, but they will work better as models if their results are known. The Playboy Club, as the recipient from the misdirector, Cass, had to repay the solicitors, but it was conceded a partial defence based on the change of position which consisted in their paying out money on the occasions when he placed a successful bet. A defence based on their having given value in good faith failed. Even though the Club did not have notice that Cass had no right to be using the money, all the gambling transactions were null and void (though not illegal) and could not therefore support the assertion that value had been given.[7] By contrast, the Isle of Man chartered accountants escaped liability as recipients of Agip's money, because their receipt was merely ministerial, not beneficial—they were mere agents for

---

[6] *Lipkin Gorman* v. *Karpnale Ltd.* [1987] 1 WLR 987 (Alliott, J.); [1989] 1 WLR 1340 (CA); [1991] 3 WLR 10 (HL). The importance of the case is assessed by Peter Watts in 'Unjust Enrichment and Misdirected Funds' (1991) 107 LQR 521. Cf. Birks, 'The English Recognition of Unjust Enrichment' [1991] *LMCLQ* 473.

[7] This conclusion that value had not been given is suspect. Further discussion in Birks, n. 6 above, 490–6.

others and had passed the money on in accordance with their principals' instructions. However, they were caught by the other species of personal liability: they had to answer for Agip's loss as accessories.

The basic difference between the recipient's liability and the accessory's liability should now be clear. The recipient's liability is purely restitutionary, based on the unjust enrichment of the recipient at the plaintiff's expense and aimed at recovering that enrichment. The accessory's liability is not based on a receipt and is not restitutionary. In *Agip* the defendants were accessories who did also receive, but that was a peculiarity of the facts of that case. The accessory's liability is not in any way dependent on the receipt of an enrichment. It is a liability to make compensation, not restitution, and it is based on a wrong—wrongfully helping a misdirection of the plaintiff's funds. We would call it a tort if we were not so anxious to limit the law of tort to common law wrongs.

2.2. Two Measures of the Recipient's Liability

In the case of the recipient we now have to make a secondary distinction. There are claims, always personal *(in personam)*, that the defendant ought to make restitution of the value received (first measure claims).[8] And there are claims, usually proprietary *(in rem)*, that the recipient is liable in respect of as much of that value as still survives in his hands at the time of the action (second measure claims). *Agip* exemplifies both, for the defendant chartered accountants still traceably held rather less than one-tenth of what they had received. Laying claim to that relatively small surviving enrichment, the plaintiffs at the same time made their claim in the first measure, for the whole sum received. *Lipkin Gorman*, by contrast, did not involve any claim in the second measure. The question was whether the Playboy Club was liable to make restitution of the sums which it had received from Cass. There was indeed a question whether it might have a defence which would diminish its ultimate liability, but there was no question of claiming 'what the club had left': nobody suggested that the Club traceably retained any of the money so received.[9]

It was the same in *In re Montagu's Settlement Trusts*.[10] The deceased Duke of Manchester had received many valuable assets from his trustees, as a result

---

[8] For this distinction see further, P. Birks, *Introduction to the Law of Restitution*, rev. ed. (Oxford, 1989), 75–77, 358–59. It must be noted that there is no perfect correlation between the two measures and the analytical labels *in rem* and *in personam*, though all first measure claims are *in personam*. The picture is further complicated if one admits, with Professor Goode, a third analytical label, namely *ad rem* (which, however, is in the writer's view reducible to a claim *in personam* to a specific *res*): see R. M. Goode, 'Property and Unjust Enrichment' in A. S. Burrows, ed., *Essays on the Law of Restitution* (Oxford, 1991), 215, esp. 221–2.

[9] It is necessary to emphasize 'traceably' for there is a passage in the speech of Lord Templeman, especially his comment on *Transvaal & Delagoa Bay Investment Co. Ltd* v. *Atkinson* [1944] 1 All ER 579, which might be understood as contemplating only a claim in the second measure, for money still retained: [1991] 3 WLR 10, 22B. But Lord Templeman is using 'retained' in an unusual sense.

[10] [1987] Ch. 264.

of a breach of trust by them. No attempt was made to establish by tracing that his estate still held any of the value so received. The question was whether, assuming the assets to have been dissipated, the estate should make restitution of the value which the Duke had received. In other words, it was a personal claim in the first measure of restitution.

It will be helpful to say, expressly, that this chapter does not consider claims in tort which may be maintainable when funds are misdirected, as for conversion of a cheque or other chattel. However, it is evident from *Lipkin Gorman* that there is work to be done on the relationship between the claims maintainable in tort and the claims maintainable in restitution, especially in relation to money. This is not at all easy, but it requires a separate study.[11]

3. When Is the Language of Trusts Used?

Both the recipient's liability and the accessory's liability are commonly handled in the language of constructive trusts. The accessory's liability always takes us first to the books on equity or trusts, in which it is known as 'knowing assistance'. It is usually said that one who knowingly assists in a fraudulent misdirection is liable as a constructive trustee or, more specifically, is liable to account as a constructive trustee.

3.1. THE PERSONAL LIABILITIES: SUPERFLUOUS TRUST ANALOGIES

The latest edition of *Snell's Equity* still indexes the accessory's liability only under 'constructive trust'. In the text, it includes it as a form of constructive trusteeship arising from intermeddling: 'The responsibility of an express trustee may be extended to those who, not being appointed trustees, receive the trust property or assist others to do so.'[12]

And a few lines later it affirms:

A person who does not actually receive the trust property may also incur liability to the beneficiaries if he knowingly assists in a fraudulent design on the part of the trustee. But 'strangers are not to be made constructive trustees . . . unless they assist with knowledge in a dishonest and fraudulent design on the part of the trustees'.[13]

Although it is not condemned by Sir Peter Millett,[14] it is not clear that this language of trusteeship is anything but a nuisance. It is rooted in the days of the institutional separation of common law and equity, and it reflects the fact that equity frequently extended the scope of the relief that it could offer by working outwards from the central case of the trustee. *Hanbury and Maudsley*

[11] In *Lipkin Gorman* conversion comes in only in respect of one item, a banker's draft which Cass endorsed over to the Playboy Club. See [1991] 3 WLR 10, 23 (Lord Templeman) and 41–2 (Lord Goff). And cf. *Midland Bank plc* v. *Brown Shipley & Co. Ltd.* [1991] 1 Lloyd's Rep. 576 (Waller, J.).

[12] P. V. Baker and P. St. J. Langan, eds., *Snell's Equity*, 29th edn. (London, 1990), 193.

[13] Ibid. 193–4. The quotation is from Lord Selborne in *Barnes* v. *Addy* (1874) 9 Ch. App. 244, 251.

[14] 'Tracing the Proceeds of Fraud', n. 4 above, esp. 80, 83, 85.

reveals the consequential tensions. Like *Snell*, it indexes 'knowing assistance' only under 'constructive trust', but it then expressly says in the text that it should really be treated elsewhere. However, having struggled to that admission, it finally decides not to act on it:

> It may be said however that, as there is no trusteeship, the matter should not be considered in this chapter [on constructive trusts], but hereafter; that is so; but because the cases are closely allied with those of trusteeship *de son tort*, it will be convenient to discuss the question here.[15]

It is time something was done about this. The phrase 'as a constructive trustee' is crutch which we can now throw away. The accessory's liability is merely a personal liability to compensate the victim for a loss which the accessory helped to inflict. The notion that this liability arises 'as a constructive trustee' is not only surplusage; it also forces us into the additional falsehood of talking all the time about 'trust money', thus concealing the true scope of the liability.[16]

The truth is that in most big fraud cases, unless one desires with perverse intensity to retain the echo of jurisdictional arrangements which passed away more than a hundred years ago, there is no 'trust' and no 'trust money'—and no need to pretend that there is. For example, in *Agip* and in *Lipkin Gorman*, there is simply money which, before the fraud began, belonged to the plaintiff now seeking some remedy for its loss. It is perhaps more accurate in most modern cases, and certainly in these, to say that the story begins not with money as such but with a chose in action—the plaintiff's bank account, which the fraudster then pilfers. We should take care to use language which describes things as they really are. But, before we can attend properly to accurate discrimination between money and the personal claim to money colloquially referred to as a bank account, we have to expel the notion that our problems are incapable of solution unless first located in the non-existent context of an imaginary trust.

Let us turn from the liability of the accessory to the liability of the recipient in the first measure (value received). The characterization of the liability as that of a constructive trustee is no less misleading in this case. We actually need no description of the liability beyond saying that it is invariably personal and that the content of the obligation, subject to defences which may

---

[15] Jill E. Martin, ed., *Hanbury and Maudsley's Modern Equity*, 13th edn. (London, 1989), 289–90. The same refusal to act on the correct analysis is found in D. J. Hayton, *Underhill and Hayton's Law of Trusts and Trustees*, 14th edn. (London, 1987), 355.

[16] *Jacob's Law of Trusts in Australia*, still, like *Snell* and *Hanbury and Maudsley*, retaining the discussion under the traditional head, points out that the fraudulent scheme need not be a scheme of 'trustees' and that the defendant need not in any sense be 'an agent' of the 'trustees': 5th edn. ed. R. P. Meagher and W. M. C. Gummow (Sydney, 1986), 1333. cf. R. P. Meagher, W. M. C. Gummow, and J. R. F. Lehane, *Equity, Doctrines and Remedies*, 2nd edn. (Sydney, 1984), 4122. This position amounts to a plain admission that we are talking about a liability in which the trust case is no more than a central example, and, if that is so, it must be more accessibly described. The law is usually more interested in marking the boundaries of liabilities, leaving the central case to take care of itself.

diminish the sum finally payable, is to pay over the value initially received, without regard to what happened to it afterwards. Neither 'account' instead of 'pay', nor the addition of 'as a constructive trustee', can further elucidate the nature of the liability. However, in relation to the recipient's liability *Hanbury and Maudsley* shows no reluctance to use the language of constructive trust. Rather to the contrary, it uses it with emphasis. But it employs it to describe, not so much the nature of the liability, as the circumstances in which the liability comes into existence:

So long as [the recipient] retains the property he is bound to return it, and the proprietary remedy of tracing is available in respect of the property or its identifiable proceeds. However this is different from the question whether the recipient should be under a *personal* liability as constructive trustee. The distinction is important if he no longer has the property. If he is a constructive trustee, his liability remains. If he is not a constructive trustee, his liability is confined to the return of the property or its proceeds while still in his possession.[17]

This passage distinguishes between liability in the second measure of restitution, with which it starts, and liability in the first measure, to which it moves in the sentence containing the emphasized 'personal'. It then asserts that the personal liability in the first measure (value received, irrespective of retention) depends on constructive trusteeship. This makes some historical sense but, analytically, it is manifestly unhelpful. Whether the liability in the first measure attaches must depend on whether the facts are such that it should. And constructive trusteeship is not a fact. As a matter of logic, therefore, the characterization of the recipient as a constructive trustee can only be a conclusion of law intermediate between certain constitutive facts and the liability in question. And that logical argument also suggests, without however proving, that that intermediate label is likely to be redundant.

It is redundant. Let it be assumed for the sake of the argument at this stage that the fact which supports the intermediate conclusion that the recipient is a constructive trustee is, as Megarry, V.-C. suggested in *In re Montagu's Settlement Trusts*, that he was dishonest, at least in the sense that he recklessly shut his eyes to the defect in his entitlement.[18] Knowing the nature of the recipient's liability—that it is personal and measured by the value received, irrespective of retention—and now knowing the fact which triggers that liability, namely dishonest receipt, we have no need whatever to insinuate a mystifying intermediate conclusion between the two. The proposition of law should be, on this assumption as to the nature of the relevant constitutive fact: one who dishonestly receives another's money comes under a liability to make restitution of the amount so received, whether or not he still retains it at the time at which that other makes his claim. Any mention of constructive trusteeship can only muddy the waters. Nothing here denies, of course, that the phrase 'another's money' requires sustained and refined exposition, nor

[17] *Hanbury and Maudsley*, n. 15 above, 292.   [18] [1987] Ch. 264, 285-6.

that in the course of that exposition it will certainly always be necessary to consider the case in which the would-be plaintiff's entitlement to the money arises under one or other species of trust.

The redundancy of the language of constructive trust in relation to the first measure liability of the recipient of misapplied funds is confirmed by the fact that the same configuration of facts can be analysed purely at common law. When it is, there is absolutely no recourse to any equivalent language. Nobody would now accept the invitation, implicit in the old language of the forms of action, to characterize the liability at common law as that of a constructive receiver to the plaintiff's use.

As it happens, certain concessions puzzlingly made by counsel in *Lipkin Gorman* v. *Karpnale Ltd.* did allow the House of Lords to keep the case entirely within the common law, though it had initially been pleaded in equity as well.[19] The effect of *Lipkin Gorman* is to make a modern restitutionary enquiry turn on the questions implicit in the language of unjust enrichment, which the House of Lords approves.[20] These questions are: (1) Was the defendant enriched? (2) If so, was it at the expense of the plaintiff? (3) If so, was the enrichment actionably 'unjust', in the sense that it was in the circumstances reversible as a matter of positive law? (4) Is there any defence or other countervailing factor requiring restitution none the less to be denied in whole or part? If these questions are worked through in a scientific manner, the answers being drawn from the cases, they will always yield a clear and intelligible conclusion. Those who say that equitable analysis must include the digression through constructive trusteeship bear the onus of proving why that continues to be necessary.

3.2. THE ROLE OF THE TRUST IN SECOND MEASURE CLAIMS

There remain claims in the second measure. These are usually proprietary, though there is no logical necessity for the claim to be made *in rem* except in the case where the reason, or at least a reason, for the plaintiff's making a second measure claim is to obtain priority over other creditors of an insolvent defendant. In that case it is the proprietary nature of the claim that gives the plaintiff his priority. The fact that the claim is also in the second measure of restitution is really only incidental: a plaintiff cannot assert a proprietary interest against an insolvent except in respect of assets still held. Hence, one who wants priority has to settle for the second measure, value surviving, not value received.

Personal claims in the second measure need not detain us. It is important that they should be recognized,[21] but so far as concerns the need to use the language of trusts they raise no issues not already addressed above. The same conclusion applies, that an obligation to repay value—value surviving no less

---

[19] [1987] 1 WLR 987, 990, 996–1008.
[20] [1991] 3 WLR 10, 15F–H, 23C (Lord Templeman); 27F, 32F–H, 33A–B (Lord Goff). Agreeing: 14H (Lord Bridge), 23DE (Lord Griffiths), 23F (Lord Ackner).
[21] Further discussion, Birks, *Introduction*, n. 8 above, 394–401.

than value received—cannot be in any way better understood through a redundant analogy with a trustee's liability. Hence anything like 'as a constructive trustee' should be struck out.

When a proprietary claim in the second measure is successfully made against the recipient in equity, it can take one of two forms. It is best to describe them by reference to a concrete illustration. Suppose the fraudster misdirects £1,000 of *P*'s money to *D*, a volunteer. *D* adds £2,000 of his own and invests the £3,000 in shares which he still holds and which are now worth £9,000. *P*'s two possible proprietary claims are, first, an equitable lien for £1,000 or, secondly, a beneficial interest proportionate to his one-third contribution.[22]

The proportionate share will always be more attractive unless the asset into which the value is traced has depreciated. Thus, if the shares were now worth less than £3,000, the lien for £1,000 would yield more.[23] Where the proprietary interest is a lien, English courts find it unnecessary to invoke the language of trusts, though the American usage appears to be different.[24] But the case in which the plaintiff has a beneficial interest proportionate to his contribution cannot but be described in terms of trust. On the other hand, even there it is probably easier to conduct the enquiry in terms of a question which omits the language of trust and trustee until it reaches its conclusion and instead asks only whether the plaintiff is entitled to a proprietary interest and, if so, of what kind. If that enquiry reaches the conclusion that he has a beneficial interest proportionate to his traced input, it will follow, as part of that conclusion, that the defendant holds on trust for him. That approach seems to minimize the danger of confusion.

4. When Is Tracing Necessary?

It is important that tracing should be understood as a process of identification and no more. It is not in itself a remedy. And successful identification of the location of value at some relevant moment tells us nothing of the kind of

---

[21] Further discussion, Birks, *Introduction*, n. 8 above, 394–401.

[22] A third possibility, reflecting the thinking in *Lupton* v. *White* (1808) 15 Ves. 432, is to give the entire beneficial interest to the plaintiff, subject to payment of the defendant's quantifiable contribution or subject to lien for that contribution. American cases have followed that line on occasion: *Nebraska National Bank* v. *Johnson* 71 NW 294 (1897); *Atlas* v. *US* 459 Fed. Supp. 1000 (1978). See D. Oesterle, 'Deficiencies in the Restitutionary Right to Trace' (1983) 68 *Cornell LR* 172, 196.

[23] Whether the plaintiff has a free choice between the two is a difficult and undecided point. The US authorities appear to limit the free choice to the case in which the defendant is a conscious wrongdoer. See G. E. Palmer, *The Law of Restitution*, 4 vols. (Boston, 1978, with supplements), i. 180–6, 224–25; ii. 521–2. But it is not clear that this limit, laudable though it may be, is easily reconciled with the law relating to resulting trusts based on contributions, where the contributor is entitled to a proportionate interest because of the contribution, not because of the moral quality of the defendant's conduct. Goff and Jones do not appear to embrace the US position: see Lord Goff of Chieveley and Gareth Jones, *The Law of Restitution*, 3rd ed. (London, 1986), 76, citing *Re Tilley's Will Trusts* [1967] Ch. 1179.

[24] Palmer, n. 23 above, ii. 520.

right, if any, which the person tracing may be entitled to demand in respect of it. There is, in particular, no necessary link between tracing and proprietary claims. The phrase 'the proprietary remedy of tracing' which we encountered above[25] in a quotation from *Hanbury and Maudsley* is doubly wrong, or at best dangerous shorthand, since it both makes the proprietary link and calls tracing a remedy. All the rules of tracing do is to locate value in time. If a particular claim requires the court to find where the value represented by such and such a sum of money was at some particular moment of time, it is by tracing that that finding is made.

Though the rules of tracing are difficult, the difficulty being aggravated by the fact that they are also incomplete, it is elementary that if the claim is in the second measure the plaintiff must trace not merely to the moment of the defendant's receipt but down to the time of the claim, to show that the value received is still held by the defendant in some form or other. But tracing is also necessary in first measure claims, though it is usually so unproblematic as to escape mention. In our three-party situations, however, it is anything but unproblematic. Consequently, it is in these claims that it becomes evident that a plaintiff must trace even to bring a personal claim against a recipient. Whatever may be the first impression or the layman's assessment, if the plaintiff cannot trace the value which left him to the receipt by the defendant, there will be no connection between him and the value received by the defendant and the assertion that the defendant was enriched at his expense will turn out to be illusory.[26]

Thus, if a plaintiff wants to make a personal claim in the first measure against a recipient from the misdirecting third hand, he must identify the value received by the defendant as the same value as that to which he, the plaintiff, was entitled at the beginning of the story. Both our model cases exemplify this. In *Lipkin Gorman* v. *Karpnale Ltd.* the solicitors, maintaining a personal claim in the first measure, had to show that the money received by the Club was traceably their money.[27] They had, that is, to trace to the moment of receipt, an exercise in which they were helped by concessions made by the Club. And in *Agip (Africa) Ltd.* v. *Jackson* the plaintiffs had to trace through the dummy company which was the first recipient to the receipt into the Jackson account. They could do this in equity but not, in Millett J.'s view, at law.[28] Both these cases, especially *Agip*, raise problems on this score to which we must return below.

---

[25] Text to n. 17 above. Sir Robert Megarry, V-C has said, with some emphasis, 'Tracing is primarily a means of determining rights of property', *In re Montagu's Settlement Trusts* [1987] Ch. 264, 285. That is not to be denied, but it requires the word 'primarily' to be given weight, and the words 'determining property rights' to be understood as a compression for 'identifying assets preparatory to asserting property rights in them'.

[26] There are very difficult issues latent here. Cf. n. 46 below and text thereto.

[27] [1991] 3 WLR 10, 28–9, Lord Goff.

[28] [1990] Ch. 265, 285–6, 289–90.

5. What Are the Worst Confusions in the Law?

There is one area of chaos. Subject to any defences that may be available, is the recipient's liability in the first measure in principle strict or based on dishonesty—or somewhere in between, so as to be based on a species of fault less than dishonesty or to require dishonesty in some cases but not others? Of other difficulties, two in particular stick out. One relates to the title to sue, one to defences.

5.1. Strict or Fault-Based Liability

In *Lipkin Gorman* v. *Karpnale Ltd.* the Club's liability was strict. There was an unchallenged finding of fact that the club was innocent, in the sense that it had not the least reason to suspect that the gambler was gambling with money other than his own. This has never been in doubt so far as common law is concerned. A Scots case has recently taken the same line.[29] However, on the same configuration of facts, the equity cases are in disarray. Some, agreeing with all the cases at law, say the personal liability of the recipient in the first measure is strict;[30] others go so far as to hold that it requires dishonesty;[31] while yet others seem to take a *via media* by requiring fault but not dishonesty.[32]

This equitable confusion is thinly disguised by accepting, without analysing, the validity of the distinction between a claim to recover value

[29] *M. & I. Instrument Engineers Ltd.* v. *Varsada* (Outer House, 6 Feb. 1990) 1991 SLT 106. There the fraudster gave his ill-gotten gains to the woman with whom he lived and she used them to buy the house in which they were still living. He was insolvent, but she was personally liable to repay the amount received, without proof of fault. It was not a proprietary claim against the house as the asset in which the value traceably inhered.

[30] *Re Diplock* [1948] Ch. 465; *G. L. Baker Ltd.* v. *Medway Building & Supplies Ltd.* [1958] 2 All ER 532 (Danckwerts J.), [1958] 3 All ER 540 (CA); *Eddis* v. *Chichester Constable* [1969] 1 All ER 566, aff'd [1969] 2 Ch. 345 (not dealing with this issue); *Butler* v. *Broadhead* [1975] Ch. 97.

[31] In re *Montagu's Settlement Trusts* [1987] 2 WLR 1192, possibly explicable on the ground that dishonesty was needed to overcome the lapse of time. Cf. *Re Robinson, McLaren* v. *Public Trustee* [1911] 1 Ch. 502. *Montagu* was followed by Alliott, J. at first instance in *Lipkin Gorman* v. *Karpnale Ltd.* [1987] 1 WLR 987, 1005–6, where there was no limitation point. More recently Vinelott J., applying the principle of *Manchester Trust* v. *Furness* [1895] 2 Q.B. 539, at 545 *per* Lindley, L. J., has held that, in a commercial context, dishonesty must be shown while in non-commercial situations a more strict standard may apply: *Eagle Trust PLC* v. *SBC Securities*, [1991] BCLC 438, 458–61. This case is, however, open to the interpretation that what was in issue was the degree of activity to be required, according to the circumstances, on the part of a defendant who, having given value, wanted to take advantage of the defence of *bona fide* purchase. It is doubtfully necessary to speak of two different standards. It may be better to say, more simply, that the reasonable man makes fewer enquiries in the context of commercial dealings. Cf. *Cowan de Groot Properties Ltd* v. *Eagle Trust plc*, 19 July 1991, Knox, J. as yet unreported.

[32] *Agip (Africa) Ltd.* v. *Jackson* must be in that category: [1990] 1 Ch. 265, 291F (constructive notice only), though Millett J. later expressed himself agnostic as to the correctness of *Montagu*, *ibid.*. 293C. The recent New Zealand case *Powell* v. *Thompson* [1991] 1 NZLR 597, on the other hand, attenuates the fault requirement almost to the point of making the liability strict. Ungoed Thomas, J.'s important *Selangor United Rubber Estates Ltd.* v. *Cradock* (No.3) [1968] 1 WLR 1555 is strong and much-followed authority against a requirement of dishonesty, though marred by a failure to distinguish clearly between the recipient's liability and the accessory's liability.

misdirected from a deceased person's estate (recipient strictly liable) and a claim to recover value misdirected from an *inter vivos* trust (recipient not liable unless dishonest).[33] This will not bear examination. If there were any substance at all in the distinction, it would none the less be embarrassed by the position taken by the common law, where the liability is strict despite the fact that the context has nothing to do with the administration of estates. And this shows that the courts were not in error when in *G. L. Baker Ltd.* v. *Medway Building and Supplies Ltd.* they accepted, admittedly with some surprise, that the equitable claim based on misdirection from an estate could be brought in respect of funds misdirected, not by an executor or administrator, but by a fraudster.[34] This case forms a bridge between *Re Diplock*[35] and *Lipkin Gorman*, and makes it quite impossible to sustain the view that the personal claim in *Re Diplock* can be locked up in the law relating to the administration of estates.

A last but important argument is provided by the need to maintain consistency between the law of restitution for mistake and the law relating to the three-party configuration of facts now under discussion. There is not the least doubt that mistaken payers, even if at fault, recover from innocent payees. In other words the liability of the recipient is strict.[36] Though the courts never say so, that which in our cases parallels 'mistake' is 'ignorance' —the plaintiff is wholly unaware that his money is passing to the defendant recipient. It would be very remarkable if a plaintiff who knew he was paying but whose knowledge was vitiated by error could have restitution on the basis of strict liability, while a plaintiff who did not know at all that his money was passing to the defendant—that is, the more absolutely non-intending plaintiff—had to bear the extra burden of proving fault on the part of the recipient. Any conclusion for a fault-based liability thus not only breaks the unity between the cases of 'ignorance' and the cases of 'mistake' but does so counter to the logic of the reason for allowing restitution, namely the deficiency in the plaintiff's consent to the enrichment of the defendant at his expense.

The House of Lords has not yet had, or has not yet taken, the opportunity to harmonize these conflicting authorities, but it is clear that, subject to

[33] This distinction is textured into Re Diplock [1948] Ch. 465 and is realized in the contrast between it and *Re Montagu's Settlement Trusts* [1987] 2 WLR 1192. It is an extraordinary fact and one which stands witness to the intellectual confusions in this area of law that *Underhill and Hayton*, n. 15 above, can present these two cases as entirely consistent with each other (308 n. 14 and text thereto), from which one would have to infer that the charities escaped personal liability. The technical defence that they did escape *qua* constructive trustees is not available to this text in view of its perception, cf. n. 15 above, that 'as a constructive trustee' is surplusage or a misnomer or both.

[34] [1958] 3 All ER 540 (CA). The court reversed Danckwerts, J. only on a pleading point which was irrelevant except on the assumption that the equitable claim in the first measure of restitution was in principle strict, albeit subject to defences.

[35] [1948] Ch. 465.

[36] Of many examples: *Kelly* v. *Solari* (1841) 9 M & W 54; *R. E. Jones Ltd.* v. *Waring & Gillow Ltd.* [1926] AC 670; *Barclays Bank Ltd.* v. *W. J. Simms & Son Ltd.* [1980] QB 677.

defences, strict liability must now prevail. There is no dispute between law and equity. The common law is for strict liability, and so are some of the equity cases. The way forward is to develop the defences while acknowledging the strict nature of the liability. This accords with the position taken by Sir Peter Millett, writing extra-judicially: 'The liability of the recipient is receipt-based and should be strict. The basis of his liability should be the same whether or not he has parted with his money, but should be subject to a change of position defence.'[37]

A similar question as to the principle of liability must be asked in relation to the accessory's liability, though nobody is there found to suggest that that could be strict: does it require dishonesty or carelessness? Sir Peter Millett takes the view that it must be founded on dishonesty but acknowledges that there is fine-tuning still to be done: 'The liability of the accessory is necessarily fault-based, and should depend on dishonesty. . . . [T]he difficult question which is still to be explored concerns the extent of knowledge which is required.'[38] In *Agip (Africa) Ltd.* v. *Jackson* he held the defendants liable as accessories to the fraudulent misdirection because they were dishonest in the sense that they were 'at best indifferent to the possibility of fraud'.[39] This view that dishonesty is required is now gaining support,[40] although it requires heavy reinterpretation of a number of rather careful judgments which appeared to be satisfied with something more like carelessness.[41]

5.2. Title to Sue

We have already touched upon this in discussing the reasons why tracing is necessary. To bring a restitutionary claim against the recipient, the plaintiff must be the person at whose expense the recipient was enriched. 'At the expense of' has two senses. In one the plaintiff identifies himself as the victim of a wrong: the defendant was enriched by committing a wrong against him. In the other the plaintiff identifies himself as the person whose minus accounts for the defendant's plus: the defendant was enriched by subtraction from him. Where a plaintiff relies on the wrong sense of 'at the expense of' he is complaining of that wrong, and the enquiry is essentially remedial: is that a wrong for which a gain-based remedy is available? We are not concerned with that kind of enquiry here. We are concerned only with the subtractive sense

[37] 'Tracing the Proceeds of Fraud' (1991) 107 *LQR* 71, 85. Note, however, the contrary position taken by A. S. Burrows, 'Misdirected Funds: A Reply' (1990) 106 *LQR* 20 (replying to Birks [1989] *LMCLQ* 296–341, and (1989) 105 *LQR* 352, 528).

[38] Ibid.

[39] [1990] Ch. 265, 293–95. Cf. in Australia *Consul Development Pty. Ltd.* v. *D. P. C. Estates Pty. Ltd.* (1975) 132 CLR 373, 410–11.

[40] It is adopted by *Snell's Equity*, n. 12 above, 194.

[41] Chiefly *Selangor United Rubber Estates Ltd.* v. *Cradock* (No.3) [1968] 1 WLR 1555; *Karak Rubber Co. Ltd.* v. *Burden* (No. 2) [1972] 1 WLR 602; *Baden, Delvaux and Lecuit* v. *Société Générale* [1983] BCLC 325. The Court of Appeal's judgment in *Agip* is somewhat ambiguous. It says that the question is whether the defendants were honest but there is no clear repudiation of the sufficiency of constructive notice (points 4 and 5 on the *Baden Delvaux* scale): compare [1991] 3 WLR 116, 133G and 134E with 131G.

of the crucial phrase. When a plaintiff relies on that substractive sense, the enquiry is essentially substantive: does the plaintiff have a ground for getting back the plus to the defendant which is a minus to himself?[42]

In *Agip (Africa) Ltd.* v. *Jackson* did Agip have any title to sue?[43] There the fraud of a third party led Agip's bank, without Agip's knowledge, to debit Agip's account and transfer money to the account of a dummy recipient, from whose account it was further transferred to the defendants. Did the defendants receive Agip's money? There was no doubt that, at the beginning of the story, Agip had a balance standing to its credit in its account at its Tunis bank. That is, it had claim against the bank for that amount. But could it be said that the money which arrived in the defendants' hands was received at Agip's expense? There was more than one problem, but the most difficult was at square one. Was the legal effect of the third party's fraud that the bank paid out its own money, not in any sense at all the money of Agip?[44] If yes, the recipients were enriched at the expense of the bank, not at the expense of Agip.

There was an additional reason why Agip needed to be able to sue. It had tried to obtain a remedy against its bank in the Tunisian courts, and it had failed. We do not know the reason why. It was obviously desirable that Agip be allowed to recoup on its own initiative from the payees and subsequent recipients. Could its title to sue be satisfactorily explained? The answer given by the courts was that on these facts it was sufficiently 'Agip's money'. It was necessary to look to the substantial reality of what had happened. The bank had as a matter of fact debited Agip and, given that fact, Agip was entitled to say that it had paid out their money, even though as a matter of law the bank might indeed have had no right as against Agip to do so.[45] This answer needed the confirmation of the House of Lords, but leave to appeal was refused. It is good that Agip should have been able to sue, but the exact nature of their title to do so requires elaboration.[46]

It will be recalled that Agip actually won the case on the basis of the defendants' having dishonestly assisted the misdirection. It is unlikely that

---

[42] Further discussion of the distinction between these two senses in Birks, *Introduction*, n. 8 above, 132–9.

[43] *Agip (Africa) Ltd.* v. *Jackson* [1990] 1 Ch. 265, 283–84, [1991] 3 WLR 116, 126–8.

[44] These difficulties are excellently explored by E. McKendrick in 'Tracing Misdirected Funds' [1991] LMCLQ 378, esp. 379–81. An important contribution to the point in issue is also made in an article by Lionel Smith 'Three-Party Restitution: A Critique of Birks's Theory of Interceptive Subtraction' (1991) 11 *OJLS* 481.

[45] [1990] 1 Ch. 265, 283 C–F, [1991] 3 WLR 116, 127–8. It is not clear whether the Court of Appeal thought it crucial (*semble*, no) or merely supportive (*semble*, yes) that Agip had failed in the attempt to get redress from the bank in the Tunisian courts: *ibid.* 126D, 127F.

[46] It is a further complication that, if the factual nexus approach is sufficient, a question arises whether it operates within the rules of tracing or as an alternative to them. It is said above that a plaintiff who cannot trace cannot show that the defendant was enriched at *his* expense. Given the factual nexus approach, that statement is only true if the enquiry into factual nexus between the enrichment and the minus to the plaintiff is a tracing enquiry or, in other words, if tracing is ultimately explained in terms of factual causation.

the title to maintain that cause of action could or should be developed differently from title to sue the recipient in unjust enrichment.

There are similar but not identical problems in *Lipkin Gorman* v. *Karpnale Ltd*. There was Privy Council authority, which the House of Lords was invited by the solicitors to review, to the effect that property in the money drawn from the bank passed to the gambler.[47] If the money gambled belonged to the gambler, the Club could not easily be said to have been enriched at the solicitors' expense. Lord Goff, refusing to overrule the troublesome cases, shows that the money, though the gambler's, was none the less caught by the *Taylor* v. *Plumer* principles of common law tracing.[48] The chose in action against the bank was the firm's property,[49] and the money was obtained in substitution for part of that chose in action.[50] On this analysis what the solicitors had was not an immediate property in the money but a right—more accurately a power—to trace and claim. That power was a sufficient interest to support the claim against the Club. The power itself evidently sufficed, for there was no attempt to exercise it in relation to any traced asset. It was not that the solicitors did vest the money in themselves but that it was money which was liable to be vested in them on their election. They had no immediate property in the money, but in the gambler's hands it was all the time liable to be vested in them on their election. Lord Goff describes the election as analogous to ratification, albeit not a ratification.[51] It will remain to be seen whether this unexercised power will continue to be regarded as a sufficient nexus between the plaintiff and defendant to satisfy the words 'at the expense of' and to give the plaintiff a title to sue. It is to be hoped that it will. If so, it will not automatically answer the *Agip* problem, for there, other than 'factually', there had been no drawing on Agip's bank account at all.

5.3. DEFENCES

The last main point relates to defences. The defence of change of position for which Sir Peter Millett argued in his article in the *Law Quarterly Review* has since been recognized by the House of Lords in *Lipkin Gorman*, though it has

---

[47] *Union Bank of Australia Ltd.* v. *McClintock* [1922] 1 AC 1; *Commercial Banking Co of Sydney Ltd.* v. *Mann* [1961] AC 1.

[48] *Taylor* v. *Plumer* (1815) 3 M & S 562.

[49] 'Property' is here used as 'asset', not in the narrower sense of interest in *rem*, much as the Roman lawyers used *res* ('thing') to include rights *in personam* (see Gaius, *Institutes*, 2. 1 and 2. 12–14; Justinian, *Institutes*, 2. 2), but there can be no objection to applying *Taylor* v. *Plumer* to assets initially obtained from or in substitution for the plaintiffs' personal claim against a bank: it is already perfectly clear that common law can trace to and through such a claim, as in *Banque Belge pour l'Etranger* v. *Hambrouck* [1921] 1 KB 321.

[50] *Agip (Africa) Ltd.* v. *Jackson* [1990] Ch. 265 differs in that Zdiri did not in law exchange any asset of Agip's for the money, the bank's indebtedness to Agip remaining the same.

[51] [1991] 3 WLR 10, 28GH, 29AB. It is important to emphasize the unexercised nature of this power, which may well cause trouble in the future. Cf. n. 9 above. The note by Watts, n. 6 above, does not explicitly take this point: see esp. 525–6.

deliberately been left less than fully formed.[52] We cannot at the moment see how the defence will work. It must not be left to intuitive justice. That was precisely what an earlier generation of judges feared.[53] Lord Goff puts the question which has to be answered: 'Why do we feel that it would be unjust to allow restitution in cases such as these (*scil.* in cases where there has been a change of position)?'[54]

The secure case for a defence will be that in which the change of position calls for the measure of the defendant's enrichment to be reassessed. That is to say, the defendant will have a defence where he can show that, although he was enriched at the expense of the plaintiff, there was also an outflow of wealth from him which was causally determined by the inflow from the plaintiff, as where, in Lord Goff's example, he received £10,000 and, by reason of that receipt, gave £3,000 to charity.[55] When the change of position does not bear directly on the enrichment in this way it will be necessary to proceed very cautiously, taking care to make articulate the factor which renders recovery 'inequitable'. Otherwise intolerable uncertainty will supervene.

The recognition of change of position as a defence carries with it another task. We have to relate it to defences which were recognized before. In some cases there is now a question whether we had in fact recognized special types of change of position, albeit under other names. If so, these nominate special cases can fall back into the larger whole. This question arises in relation to 'bona fide purchase', also 'counter-restitution essential' and 'ministerial receipt'.

In *Lipkin Gorman* itself the relation between bona fide purchase and change of position was of first importance. Once again Sir Peter Millett appears to have been blessed with prophetic powers, for in his article he suggested that bona fide purchase be seen as a paradigm of change of position.[56] In fact, however, the House of Lords did not attempt any such reintegration. Rather to the contrary, Lord Goff took care to say that the two defences were separate.[57] The club was not a bona fide purchaser, because, its contracts

---

[52] [1991] 3 WLR 10, 15A (Lord Bridge), 23F (Lord Ackner), 34G (Lord Goff). For the background, see Goff and Jones, n. 23 above, 691–9, and J. Beatson, *Use and Abuse of Unjust Enrichment* (Oxford, 1991), 145–6, 153–60. The English Law Commission also favours the development of the defence: Consultation Paper No. 120 (1991).

[53] *Baylis* v. *Bishop of London* [1913] 1 Ch. 127, 137 (Farwell, LJ), 140 (Hamilton, LJ); *Holt* v. *Markham* [1923] 1 KB 504, 513 (Scrutton, LJ); *Ministry of Health* v. *Simpson* [1951] AC 251, 276 (Lord Simonds).

[54] [1991] 3 WLR 10, 34B.

[55] Ibid. 34.

[56] (1991) 107 *LQR* 71, 82. My own attempt to find an explanation in 'counter-restitution essential' is wrong because it uses the wrong generalization: [1989] *LMCLQ* 296, 301–5. More likely, counter-restitution is simply another response to a species of change of position. In other words, 'counter-restitution essential' is no more than the form which the defence of change of position takes when the way in which the defendant's position has changed is that, in exchange for the value which the plaintiff now wants back, the defendant himself conferred a benefit on the plaintiff.

[57] [1991] 3 WLR 10, 35.

being void, it had not given value. But it did have a limited defence of change of position.

The separate identities of these defences is a matter to be debated more fully. It is not easy to see how the defence of bona fide purchase works if not as an enrichment-related defence of change of position. The fraudster who spends my money at a restaurant enriches the restaurant at my expense but, against that inflow of value, the restaurant sets the causally related outflow of value to precisely the same amount—the meal supplied at the price which was paid.[58]

6. Conclusion

The law relating to the recovery of misapplied funds is developing very fast. It is growing away from its false dependence on trusts and, at the same time, it is being emancipated from the grip of the common law forms of action. This is the yield, in this one area, of the recognition of the independence of the law of restitution, based on unjust enrichment, which, though it has its own additional internal complications, may in turn be seen as a part of the larger task of unifying law and equity. We are perfectly familiar with the notion that, say, the law of contract draws on both law and equity. In the same way there is no contrast between restitution and equity. The law of unjust enrichment—and it is the name 'unjust enrichment', rather than the remedially oriented 'restitution', which aligns with a subject such as contract —similarly draws on, and unites, fragments from law and equity.

The advantages which flow are simpler language, clearer principles, and the fewer contradictions. But it is not all plain sailing. We have identified patches of choppy water. The defence of change of position will have to be analysed and restrained. Also, careful attention must be paid to defining the plaintiff's title to sue. It is relatively easy to say that he must be the person at whose expense the defendant was enriched, but, as we have seen, that requires interpretation and explanation. Again, conflicts as to the requirement of fault on the part of the recipient need to be resolved. These are only the most obvious problems. For example, the rules of tracing and the preconditions for recourse to them are also in urgent need of rationalization.[59]

As for the relevance of the law of trusts, in most cases to invoke analogies with the remedies available against trustees is to insist on attaching a fifth

---

[58] Cf. [1991] 3 WLR 10, 16 where Lord Templeman gives the case of a car dealer who sells a car to a thief. The enrichment is cancelled.

[59] Regrettably, the *Agip* Court of Appeal took a very cautious line in relation to the modernizing judgment of Atkin LJ in *Banque Belge pour l'Étranger* v. *Hambrouck* [1921] 1 KB 321: see esp. [1991] 3 WLR 116, 131 AB. It would seem that English law may have reverted to the situation in which recourse to the more resourceful equitable rules will depend on the property having passed through fiduciary hands, a position which is known to produce intolerable results. On other problems in the law of tracing, see Oesterle, 'Deficiencies of the Restitutionary Right to Trace Misappropriated Property', n. 22 above.

wheel to a vehicle which will run better on four. Describing the defendant as a constructive trustee does nothing to help, has indeed a record for hindering. If there is an exception, it is the case where the restitutionary claim is made against an insolvent defendant. There, in order to gain priority over unsecured creditors, what the plaintiff needs to establish is of course a proprietary interest in assets held by the defendant. If the plaintiff has an equitable beneficial interest in such assets, then there must be a trust. This is the subject which is explored in Chapter 9.

9

THE TREATMENT OF TRUST ASSETS IN ENGLISH INSOLVENCY LAW

Hamish Anderson

It is in the context of insolvency law that the distinction between proprietary rights and personal monetary obligations is likely to be most significant. The personal rights of beneficiaries may be of no value against an insolvent trustee; beneficiaries may be wholly dependent on their proprietary rights to the trust assets. This chapter is concerned with the treatment of property held by an insolvent person on trust for one or more third parties. It is not concerned with the situation in which a beneficial interest in property, held on trust by a third party, constitutes part of an insolvent estate. The existence of a perfected trust obligation enforceable by or on behalf of a *cestui que trust* will necessarily be assumed. Such questions are discussed elsewhere.

The treatment of trust assets will be examined in the context of the six principal English insolvency procedures which are the subject matter of the Insolvency Act 1986: liquidation, administrative receivership, administration, corporate voluntary arrangements, and, in the context of personal insolvency, bankruptcy and individual voluntary arrangements. With the exception of administrative receivership, these are collective insolvency procedures. The purpose of liquidation is to realise the assets of a company and to distribute the proceeds to creditors (and to shareholders if there is a surplus) in accordance with a statutory scheme. Liquidation is a terminal procedure; it results in dissolution of the company, that is the extinction of its legal personality. There is no concept of discharge from liquidation. Liquidation occurs either as a result of judicial process (compulsory liquidation) or in an extra-curial form initiated by shareholders' resolution (voluntary liquidation). Bankruptcy is the personal insolvency equivalent of compulsory liquidation. There is, however, a distinction which is very significant in the context of this chapter. Apart from rare cases under s. 145 of the Insolvency Act 1986 where property is vested in the liquidator, a liquidator always acts as an agent of the company.[1] Bankruptcy differs from compulsory liquidation (and from all other insolvency procedures described in this chapter) because the assets of the bankrupt automatically vest in the

---

[1] *Knowles* v. *Scott* [1891] 1 Ch. 717.

trustee in bankruptcy under s306 of the Insolvency Act 1986.[2] The bankruptcy of a trustee, therefore, raises special questions which are dealt with in a separate section later in this chapter (1.1).

Administration is a corporate insolvency procedure which imposes a moratorium for the purposes of achieving either survival, implementation of a voluntary arrangement (or scheme of arrangement), or the more advantageous realisation of assets. Whilst an administration order is in force the affairs of the company are managed by an administrator who is an officer of the court.[3] Administration is a means to an end. The end may be either terminal or reorganizational.

It is difficult to generalize about voluntary arrangements, which are the least structured of all formal insolvency procedures under the Insolvency Act 1986. A voluntary arrangement is either a composition in satisfaction of debts or a scheme of arrangement of the debtor's affairs. The proposal for a voluntary arrangement must provide for some person (first 'the nominee' and then, if the proposal is approved, 'the supervisor') to act in relation to the arrangement either as trustee or otherwise for the purposes of supervising its implementation. There are important differences between the provisions governing corporate and individual voluntary arrangements but the underlying purpose of both sets of provisions is the same: these are re-organisational procedures.

Administrative receivership is not a collective insolvency procedure. It is a security enforcement mechanism undertaken primarily for the benefit of the security holder. It is a special form of receivership applicable only to corporate mortgagors. The appointment of an administrative receiver must relate to the whole or substantially the whole of the company's property. It must be an extra-curial appointment by or on behalf of the holders of debentures of the company secured by a charge which, as created, was a floating charge, or by such a charge and other securities. The significance of all this lies in the nature of the issues which will arise in relation to trust assets in administrative receivership. In collective insolvency procedures, any issue as to whether a trust asset constitutes part of the property divisible amongst creditors will normally be a bilateral issue between the office holder in the insolvency proceedings (representing the general body of creditors) and the beneficiary. In administrative receivership, the primary issue will be between the debenture holder (i.e. one secured creditor) and the beneficiary. Generally speaking, the derivative rights of a security holder cannot be more extensive than the rights of the mortgagor but, exceptionally, the rights of the secured creditor can take precedence. The exceptions are dealt with later in this chapter.

Although English law has readily recognised that trust assets stand outside an insolvent estate, such assets are not sacrosanct. Thus, for example, the doctrine of reputed ownership under the Bankruptcy Act 1914 demon-

---

[2] See also s. 61(5) of the Land Registration Act 1925.
[3] *Re Atlantic Computer Systems plc* [1990] BCC 859.

strated a willingness to take trust assets into a bankrupt's estate in appropriate circumstances.[4] The basis of the doctrine was that goods not owned by the bankrupt but in his possession could be property divisible amongst creditors if in the possession of the bankrupt in his trade or business with the consent and permission of the true owner and in circumstances that the bankrupt was the reputed owner thereof. A beneficiary who allowed the possession of the trustee to have the character of that of a reputed owner was liable to have trust assets brought within the insolvent estate, in particular in cases where the beneficiary himself had created the trust.[5] Under modern insolvency law it is appropriate to consider ss 234 and 304 of the Insolvency Act 1986. Under these provisions an office holder (excluding supervisors under voluntary arrangements) who seizes or disposes of property not forming part of the insolvent estate but which, at the time of seizure or disposal, he believes (on reasonable grounds) that he is entitled to seize or dispose of, is absolved from liability for resultant loss or damage except in so far as the same is caused by his negligence. There seems no reason preventing these provisions being applied to trust assets in suitable cases. There is a proviso that the office holder should have a lien on the property or its proceeds for his expenses. The existence of a lien implies that the original owner's proprietary claims attach to the proceeds (subject to lien).

There are three more substantial areas of risk in modern law, namely avoidance of trusts under the provisions regulating malpractice prior to insolvency, exhaustion of beneficial interests through permitted dealing, and subordination of beneficial interests to the costs and expenses of the insolvency. Each of these will be considered in turn later in this chapter.

The general recognition of trust assets by English insolvency law has been exploited in commercial situations through arrangements made to protect classes of 'creditors' and to prevent funds forming part of the insolvent estate. Such arrangements are frequently encountered in construction industry contracts. The technical difficulties of those contracts, and the trust provisions which they tend to incorporate, have raised some problems in the context of insolvency proceedings. Any agreement which conflicts with the statutory scheme for the distribution of assets in liquidation is void.[6] A similar principle applies in bankruptcy.[7] However, an analysis of the building cases[8] shows that it is possible for contracts to include effective

---

[4] Abolished by the 1985–6 reforms of English insolvency law and forming no part of the Insolvency Act 1986 but still applicable to bankruptcies in which the petition was presented (or a receiving order or adjudication made) before 29 Dec. 1986—see sched. 11 para. 10 of the Insolvency Act 1986.

[5] See generally *Ex parte Moore* (1842) 2 MD & D 616; *Ex parte Burbridge* (1835) 1 Dea. 131; *Kitchen* v. *Ibbetson* (1873) LR 17 Eq. 46.

[6] *British Eagle International Airlines Ltd.* v. *Compagnie Nationale Air France* [1975] 1 WLR 758.

[7] *Re Jeavons ex parte MacKay* (1873) 8 Ch. App.643.

[8] *Re Tout & Finch Ltd.* [1954] 1 WLR 178; *Rayack Construction Ltd.* v. *Lampeter Meat Co. Ltd.* (1979) 12 Build. LR 34; *Re Arthur Sanders Ltd.* (1981) 17 Build. LR 125; *Re Jartay Developments Ltd.* (1983) 22 Build. LR 134; *Henry Boot Building Ltd.* v. *The Croydon Hotel and Leisure Company Ltd.* (1985) 36 Build. LR 41.

provisions requiring retention money to be held as trust money for the contractor and even diverting that money to subcontractors and other third parties. Apart from doubts about the extent to which such trusts can be established without constituting registrable charges, trust arrangements appear to provide opportunities for protection from insolvency. Examples of trusts being used for similar commercial purposes can be found in other areas. In *Re Chelsea Cloisters Ltd.*[9] tenants' deposits were received and paid into a separate bank account which was not designated as a trust account. The Court of Appeal none the less held that the fund was trust money unavailable to the general body of creditors.[10] Following *Carreras Rothmans Ltd.* v. *Freeman Mathews Treasure Ltd. & Anor.*[11] it is possible to establish a conduit for payment to third parties by means of a trust.

The law imposes limits on the extent to which trust devices can be used to protect third-party interests. There is an overriding principle that no person may agree to be divested of property, which previously has been owned absolutely, on the occurrence of bankruptcy or liquidation. In *Re Harrison ex parte Jay*, James, LJ said:

a simple stipulation that, upon a man's becoming bankrupt, that which was his property up to the date of the bankruptcy should go over to some one else and be taken away from his creditors, is void as being a violation of the policy of the bankrupt law.[12]

Such divesting arrangements made by a debtor must be distinguished from arrangements imposed by creditors or third parties upon the debtor at the time when any initial interest in property was acquired by the debtor. In the earlier case of *Whitmore* v. *Mason*, the following statement of the rule was adopted by Page Wood, V-C:

the general distinction seems to be, that the owner of property may, on alienation, qualify the interest of his alienee by a condition to take effect on bankruptcy; but cannot, by contract or otherwise qualify his own interest by a like condition, determining or controlling it in the event of his own bankruptcy, to the disappointment or delay of his creditors. The *jus disponendi*, which for the first purpose is absolute, being in the latter instance subject to the disposition previously prescribed by law.[13]

Although the application of these principles to bankruptcy and, by analogy, liquidation is settled, their application to other forms of insolvency proceedings is not entirely clear. Arguably, there are good policy reasons why

[9] (1981) 41 P & CR 98, discussed further at pp. 176–80.
[10] But contrast *Re Multi Guarantee Co. Ltd.* [1987] BCLC 257.
[11] [1985] Ch. 207. In *Re Northern Developments (Holdings) Ltd.* (6 Oct. 1978, unreported) it was held that persons intended to benefit from the carrying out of a primary trust have enforceable rights.
[12] (1880) 14 Ch. D. 19 at 25; *Re Walker ex parte Barter ex parte Black* (1884) 26 Ch. D. 510; see further *Re Johns* [1928] Ch. 737.
[13] (1861) 2 J & H 204 at 210.

such principles should protect creditors of companies in administration. The case for extension to voluntary arrangements is weaker. The normal armoury of statutory remedies to attack antecedent transactions is not available to supervisors under either individual or corporate voluntary arrangements. The absence of such rights may constitute good reason why creditors should not agree to proposals averting bankruptcy or liquidation in some cases. The last procedure to be considered is administrative receivership. Here there appears to be no policy consideration requiring the interests of a secured creditor to be protected. Bankruptcy case law demonstrates that, even where the principle applies, the arrangements are good between the parties although void against the trustee in bankruptcy.[14] There seems no sound reason why the validity of contractual rights acquired by third parties under this particular type of contract should be treated any differently from any other form of contractual rights for receivership purposes.

Finally, by way of introduction, a distinction must be drawn between assets held by an insolvent party on trust for third parties as a result of pre-insolvency events and the 'statutory trust' which is sometimes said to arise upon liquidation. Liquidation divests a company of its beneficial ownership. *Ayerst* v. *C & K (Construction) Ltd.*[15] shows that there can be no question of a trust in the traditional sense of a trust as recognised by the Chancery courts but equally recognises the concept of a statutory trust. In that case Lord Diplock said of the relevant authorities:

All that was intended to be conveyed by the use of the expression 'trust property' and 'trust' in these and subsequent cases . . . was that the effect of the statute was to give to the property of a company in liquidation that essential characteristic which distinguished trust property from other property, viz., that it could not be used or disposed of by the legal owner for his own benefit, but must be used or disposed of for the benefit of other persons.[16]

This chapter is concerned with assets which are trust assets by virtue of pre-insolvency events and not with the fiduciary obligations of office holders in insolvency proceedings.

1. General Principles

It is a fundamental principle of English insolvency law that assets belonging to third parties do not constitute part of the property divisible amongst creditors of the insolvent party. Trust assets are merely one example of this principle in operation. Although there are many other examples of assets in the possession of insolvent parties which will not form part of the property

---

[14] *Re Harrison ex parte Jay* (1880) 14 Ch. D. 19 at 26.
[15] [1976] AC 167; see further *Re Ashpurton Estates Ltd.* [1983] Ch. 110; *R* v. *Registrar of Companies ex parte Central Bank of India* [1986] QB 1114; *Re Lines Bros Ltd.* [1983] Ch. 1; *Re Stetzel Thomson & Co. Ltd.* (1988) 4 BCC 74.
[16] [1976] AC 167 at 180.

divisible amongst their creditors, for example, leased goods or goods purchased under retention of title agreements, the application of the general principle to trust assets is particularly interesting because such interests may arise not only through the express agreement of the parties but also through the intervention of equity imposing constructive trusts and through the presumed intention of the owner in the case of implied or resulting trusts.

At its simplest, the general principle that trust assets form no part of an insolvent estate is exemplified by the doctrine that a trustee in bankruptcy takes subject to any equities affecting the property comprised in the estate in the bankrupt's own hands.[17] Section 283(3)(a) of the Insolvency Act 1986 provides that any property held by the bankrupt on trust for any other person does not constitute part of a bankrupt's estate for the purposes of the Act. There is no equivalent express statutory provision relating to any of the corporate insolvency procedures or to individual voluntary arrangements. However, there can be no doubt that assets or interests held on trust for a third party do not constitute divisible property. The point was considered by the House of Lords in a Scottish appeal in *Heritable Reversionary Company Ltd.* v. *Millar*.[18] The case concerned the meaning of the word 'property' in s102 of the Bankruptcy (Scotland) Act 1856[19] and Lord Watson said:

An apparent title to land or personal estate, carrying no real right of property with it, does not, in the ordinary or in any true legal sense, make such land or personal estate the property of the person who holds the title. That which, in legal as well as conventional language, is described as a man's property is estate, whether heritable or moveable, in which he has a beneficial interest which the law allows him to dispose of. It does not include estate in which he has no beneficial interest, and which he cannot dispose of without committing a fraud.[20]

This reasoning is directly applicable to English collective insolvency procedures under which available assets are realised for the benefit of creditors and distributed according to a prescribed order of priority. In the context of non-collective procedures, for example administrative receivership, where the issue lies between the beneficiary and a third party, it is perhaps more correctly characterized as an example of *nemo dat quod non habet*—a creditor can generally assert no better claim to assets than that of the debtor from or through whom the creditor's rights arise.

1.1. COMPLICATIONS IN BANKRUPTCY

As previously stated, the fundamental difference between bankruptcy and the other collective procedures under the Insolvency Act 1986 is that the bankrupt's estate vests in his trustee in bankruptcy under s306. The

---

[17] *Ex parte Holthausen* (1874) LR 9 Ch. App.722.
[18] [1892] AC 598; see also *Mettoy Pension Trustees Ltd.* v. *Evans & Ors* [1990] 1 WLR 1587 to the effect that a fiduciary power is not an asset of any company in which it is vested.
[19] See now s. 31 Bankruptcy (Scotland) Act 1985.
[20] [1892] AC 598 at 614.

exclusion of 'property held by the bankrupt on trust *for any other person*'[21] in s283(3)(a) of the Insolvency Act 1986 gives rise to some doubt about whether property held by the bankrupt on trust for himself and another vests. The general view (supported by earlier authority[22]) is that it is necessary for the bankrupt to be a 'bare trustee' that is a trustee with no beneficial interest, in order for the legal title to a trust asset to escape vesting in the trustee in bankruptcy. (The beneficial interests of other beneficiaries are not affected except by any change of trustee.) The distinction is somewhat arbitrary and exclusion of assets held as bare trustee from the vesting provisions owes more to the purposes of the bankruptcy jurisdiction in administering assets for the benefit of creditors than to any concern for the protection of beneficiaries in a situation where the trustee may be unfit. The difficulties do not extend to joint trusteeship of a legal estate which is not severable. Where the bankrupt jointly owns, for example a matrimonial home, with another person, the legal estate remains vested in the trustees for sale and the trustee in bankruptcy has no legal title.[23]

In any case where an insolvent party is a trustee there is clearly scope for conflict of interest. English insolvency law makes little overt recognition of this potential difficulty but it is addressed, in the context of pension funds, by the Social Security Pensions Act 1975.[24] Under that legislation there is a requirement for the appointment of an independent trustee of a pension fund where the scheme employer becomes insolvent. Such funds are controversial because over-funded schemes may afford a prospect of repayment to the employer which would constitute a realisable asset in the insolvency. In principle, this is not a different problem to that posed by other trust assets except to the extent that the scheme rules vest a discretion in the employer which would otherwise be exercisable by the office holder.[25] Generally speaking, issues will centre on whether a given asset has trust asset status with consequences which will flow naturally from that determination. In such circumstances there is no reason to suppose that the preservation of the trust asset itself is exposed to additional risk because the affairs of an insolvent trustee are being conducted by a licensed insolvency practitioner. On the contrary, such an appointment is more likely to reduce risk. However, in situations where beneficiaries find the continued trusteeship of the insolvent party intolerable, English insolvency law offers no special remedies; the matter must be dealt with either by conventional court applications in the insolvency proceedings or by invocation of general principles of trust law.

[21] Emphasis added.

[22] See *Morgan* v. *Swansea Urban Sanitary Authority* (1878) 9 Ch. D. 582; *Governors of St Thomas' Hospital* v. *Richardson* [1910] 1 KB 271; but see *Re A Solicitor* [1952] Ch. 328.

[23] *Re McCarthy (A Bankrupt)* [1975] 1 WLR 807; the legal estate in land cannot be severed— s. 34 of the Law of Property Act 1925—but a tenancy in common of chattels is still possible. Presumably an individual share in chattels would vest.

[24] As amended by the Social Security Act 1990 sched. 4.

[25] See further *Icarus (Hertford) Ltd.* v. *Driscoll* [1990] 1 Pensions Law Reports 1; *Mettoy Pension Trustees Ltd.* v. *Evans & Ors* [1990] 1 WLR 1587.

Section 36 of the Trustee Act 1925 confers a statutory power, exercisable by the persons specified for that purpose in the Act, to appoint a new trustee or trustees in place of a trustee who is unfit to act. A bankrupt would probably be regarded as 'unfit' to continue as a trustee for these purposes unless his continued trusteeship would be with the consent of bene-ficiaries.[26] Further, the court has power to remove a bankrupt trustee under s41 of the Trustee Act 1925 and this power will be exercised where the trust property is at risk.[27] In conjunction with these provisions for the removal of trustees, it should be borne in mind that under s281 of the Insolvency Act 1986, discharge from bankruptcy releases a bankrupt trustee from liability for a breach of trust provided that the breach was not fraudulent.[28]

1.2. RIGHTS OF DEBENTURE HOLDERS IN ADMINISTRATIVE RECEIVERSHIP

Administrative receivership and the floating charges on which such appoint-ments depend are a concept of English law not always readily recognised in civil jurisdictions. This chapter presupposes a valid and enforceable appointment. It does not address the more complicated (and variable problems) that arise if the title of the debenture holder is not recognised by a foreign court. Such problems are more the province of private international law than English insolvency law.

As a matter of general property law, equitable interests in land can sometimes be overreached by a disposition of the legal estate even where the disponee is on notice of the existence of the rights.[29] Such provisions are unlikely to be relevant to the position of the holder of a common form debenture (typically a bank).[30] It is much more likely that a debenture holder taking a legal charge on land will rely on the general doctrine that a purchaser (which includes a person taking a mortgage or charge) for valuable consideration without notice, takes free of equitable interests.[31] In many cases the operation of the rule may be disguised by registrability of interests and deemed notice, but the essential rule is clear although there are doubts about the degree of notice required. The doctrine of constructive notice operates in respect of transactions in land.[32] However, the courts have

---

[26] *Re Hopkins* (1881) 19 Ch. D. 61.

[27] *Re Barker's Trusts* (1875) 1 Ch. D. 43; *Re Adams' Trusts* (1879) 12 Ch. D 634.

[28] S. 281 should be read in conjunction with s. 382.

[29] See e.g. ss2 and 27 of the Law of Property Act 1925.

[30] Similarly the issues in *Williams and Glyn's Bank* v. *Boland* [1981] AC 487 and subsequent cases dealing with the rights of occupiers are a feature of general mortgage law less likely to be encountered in administrative receivership—but see further *Midland Bank Ltd.* v. *Farmpride Hatcheries Ltd. & Another* (1981) 260 EG 493.

[31] *Pilcher* v. *Rawlins* (1872) 7 Ch. App.259. This is subject to s136 of the Law of Property Act 1925 (legal assignments of things in action) as to which see further *E. Pfeiffer Weinkellerie, Weinkauf GmbH & Co.* v. *Arbuthnot Factors Ltd.* [1988] 1 WLR 150 and *Compaq Computers Ltd.* v. *The Abercorn Group Ltd. & Ors* [1991] BCC 484.

[32] See further s. 199 of the Law of Property Act 1925.

the courts have resisted the extension of that doctrine to chattel dealing or to general commercial transactions.[33]

In the more common situation where the security takes the form of all-embracing equitable interests and the issue is whether the rights of the secured creditor prevail over the beneficiary in respect of a trust asset ostensibly caught by the ambit of the security, then the relevant maxim is *qui prior est tempore potior est jure*, although this too can be displaced by the statutory effect of registration. Subject also to equities being in other respects equal, interests rank in order of creation.[34] A pre-existing beneficial interest will, therefore, be upheld in normal circumstances. Although a floating charge is present security[35] it does not attach to any individual asset unless and until the charge crystallizes. The effect of crystallization is not retrospective and so it appears sufficient for the beneficial interest to be created in the ordinary course of business prior to crystallization for it to take priority to the interests of a debenture holder under a floating charge. Even though a legal estate is necessary in order to achieve priority to other equitable interests, an equitable interest can achieve priority to mere equities.[36] 'Mere equities' are not proprietary rights but rights which are ancillary to proprietary rights, for example rights to have transactions set aside or rectified.

Bankers' rights of set-off or combination of accounts are related issues but not strictly ones of priority between the security under which the administrative receiver has been appointed and the beneficial interest. None the less, *Barclays Bank Ltd.* v. *Quistclose Investments Ltd.*[37] and *Neste Oy* v. *Lloyds Bank Ltd.*[38] illustrate how easily these questions can arise in the same factual nexus. In both cases trust money was preserved on the ground that the recipient bank had received the fund in issue with notice of the relevant circumstances constituting it trust money.

Although in administrative receivership the principal issue is whether a trust asset has been subject to any transaction or dealing which confers priority on the debenture holder, it is possible for there to be a separate issue to be resolved between the beneficiary and a liquidator if the claims of the secured creditor fail or a surplus is realised.

[33] *Manchester Trust* v. *Furness* [1895] 2 QB 539; *Feuer Leather Corp* v. *Frank Johnstone & Sons* [1981] Com. LR 251.

[34] *Cave* v. *Cave* (1880) 15 Ch. D. 639; *Walker* v. *Linom* [1907] 2 Ch. 104; *Coleman* v. *London County and Westminster Bank Ltd.* [1916] 2 Ch. 353. The rule in *Dearle* v. *Hall* (1828) 3 Russ. 1, which qualifies the ordinary rule of priority when applied to successive equitable assignments, does not apply to competition between a declaration of trust and an assignment—*Hill* v. *Peters* [1918] 2 Ch. 273; *B. S. Lyle Ltd.* v. *Rosher* [1959] 1 WLR 8.

[35] *Evans* v. *Rival Granite Quarries Ltd.* [1910] 2 KB 979.

[36] *Westminster Bank Limited* v. *Lee* [1956] Ch. 7; *National Provincial Bank Ltd.* v. *Ainsworth* [1965] AC 1175.

[37] [1970] AC 567 where the case for the beneficiaries was advanced on the basis that notice was required to preclude bank combination of accounts and Lord Wilberforce gave his opinion on an assumption to that effect.

[38] [1983] 2 Lloyd's Rep 658.

2. Avoidance of Trusts

The first of three areas of difficulty considered in this chapter which can lead to a beneficiary's interest being defeated in whole or in part, concerns the provisions for avoidance of antecedent transactions contained in the Insolvency Act 1986. Specifically, the relevant provisions are those dealing with transactions at an undervalue, preferences, or transactions defrauding creditors.[39] Although these provisions may loosely be described as part of the provisions of the Act regulating malpractice in the period prior to the commencement of insolvency, it is important to appreciate that it is only in the context of the provisions dealing with transactions defrauding creditors that the existence of an illicit purpose goes to jurisdiction. In the case of transactions at an undervalue and preferences, the debtor may have been motivated by morally acceptable considerations.

Inevitably, these provisions will tend to be invoked in the context of express trusts although, as acknowledged by Oliver, LJ in *Re Chelsea Cloisters Ltd.*,[40] there may not be an 'express trust' in the sense of an explicit declaration attended by any particular degree of formality. Implied or resulting trusts arising out of the presumed intention of a third party and constructive trusts imposed by way of equitable remedy are fundamentally inconsistent with the notion of malpractice prior to the commencement of insolvency.

Put simply, a transaction at an undervalue occurs when an insolvent party makes a gift or otherwise enters into a transaction for no consideration or for a consideration which is not commensurate with that given by the insolvent. On any basis, the creation of a trust conferring a beneficial interest on a third party will constitute 'a transaction' for these purposes.[41] It follows that any voluntary settlement is liable to be set aside if made within prescribed time limits before the onset of insolvency. In the case of a transaction at an undervalue entered into for the purpose of delaying or defeating creditors' claims there are no time limits and proof of insolvency at the time of the transaction is not required (although it may be relevant to establishing purpose). The application of these principles to express trusts in favour of third parties is straightforward. The application of the preference rules is more complicated.

The essence of preference is some event (again within a prescribed period prior to the onset of insolvency) which puts a creditor or surety in a better position than that person would otherwise have had in an ensuing bankruptcy or liquidation. It is necessary to show that the insolvent party was influenced by a desire to produce that effect in favour of the recipient of the alleged preference. Preference is capable, therefore, of attacking quite different situations to those likely to be challenged under the provisions relating to transactions at an undervalue or transactions defrauding creditors. Whereas

[39] ss. 238–41 (ss. 339–42 in bankruptcy cases) and s. 423.
[40] (1981) 41 P & CR 98.　　　　　　　　　　　　[41] s. 436 of the Insolvency Act 1986.

the former provisions are concerned with the preservation of net value in the insolvent estate,[42] the preference provisions are directed to upholding the principle of *pari passu* distribution in collective insolvency procedures. Here questions will arise if an insolvent party endeavours to use a trust device to protect a pre-existing class of creditor or to make good a previous breach of trust. Relevant examples can be taken from cases under the pre–1986 legislation.

In *Re Kayford Ltd.*[43] the issue was whether deposits paid by customers of a mail order company which were held in a separate bank account constituted trust money. The facts of the case were strong. Although the bank account was an ordinary pre-existing deposit account utilized for the purpose, the company was acting on professional advice that a trust account should be operated. The case was decided on the footing that there could be no question of 'fraudulent preference' (that being the language of the earlier legislation) because the question was not of preferring creditors but of preventing those customers paying money from becoming creditors by making them beneficiaries under a trust. The status of the fund as trust money was upheld. Under the modern legislation it seems clear that it is possible to create a scheme under which money advanced by way of pre-payment will always be impressed with a trust in the hands of the recipient company with the consequence that the creation of a trust fund and tenure of a pre-payment in that fund will not amount to a preference. The narrow point on which fraudulent preference was thought to be unarguable in *Re Kayford Ltd.* is more questionable. Whilst it is clear that there can be no preference unless the payer is a creditor or surety, it is not clear that a person who has entered into a contract for the supply of goods is not a creditor for the purposes of the Act. 'Creditor' is not defined by the Act for the purposes of its corporate insolvency provisions but the term is widely defined in s383 for the purposes of the individual insolvency provisions. In that context, 'creditor'[44] includes any person who is owed any debt or liability to which the bankrupt is subject at the commencement of the bankruptcy or may become subject to thereafter by reason of any pre-existing obligation. Such debt or liability may be present or future, certain or contingent, and fixed in amount or unliquidated. This appears wide enough to cover customers under pending contracts. It is submitted that the narrow ground on which fraudulent preference was decided in *Re Kayford Ltd.* is not available under the Insolvency Act 1986. On the other hand, it does not necessarily follow that the constitution of such a fund will result in a preference. If the money is received in circumstances in which the court would hold the recipient accountable as a constructive

---

[42] *Re M. C. Bacon Ltd.* [1990] BCC 78.

[43] [1975] 1 WLR 279.

[44] The definition applies in the context of an individual who is already bankrupt or to whom a bankruptcy petition relates. It is thought that it should none the less be applied to s. 340 (preferences)—to do otherwise would lead to anomalies. Consider Re *Blackpool Motor Car Company Ltd.* [1901] 1 Ch. 77.

trustee, then there will be no preference because the creation of the fund will not have put the customer in a better position than that customer would have enjoyed in an ensuing bankruptcy or liquidation; that is, there is no factual preference regardless of whether there was the requisite desire to produce that effect. Equally, the customers' rights will be upheld if their money has been paid pursuant to some arrangement under which it ranks as an advance made for a specific purpose[45].

It is not clear from the report of *Re Kayford Ltd.* why the company was advised to open the account in question. The judgment of Megarry, J. states that the object of the account was to provide a fund out of which customers could be repaid. The open question is the extent, if any, to which those concerned thought they were under a legally binding obligation to create such a fund or were exposed to liability if they did not.[46] However, these questions are touched on in *Re Chelsea Cloisters Ltd.*[47]—the case where tenants' deposits were paid into a separate bank account which was not designated as a trust account. The account was opened with some £11,000 already held but the Court of Appeal decided that the whole of the resultant fund was trust money and did not form part of the company's funds available to the general body of creditors.[48] Preference appears to have been considered primarily in terms of ascertaining the intention behind creation of the account. It was held that the person responsible had acted in the belief that there was an obligation to protect the deposits, thereby implicitly rejecting any suggestion of an intention to prefer.[49] Here the new legislation is materially different from the old. Under the earlier legislation the question was whether there was a dominant intention to prefer. Persons could be taken to 'intend' the natural consequences of their acts. The new test is whether the insolvent party was 'influenced by a desire' to effect a preference. In *Re M C Bacon Ltd.*[50] it was held incorrect to assume that persons desired all the necessary consequences of their acts. Millett, J. held that 'intention' is objective but 'desire' is subjective. Even if desire was established it is still necessary to show 'influence', that is that the perceived consequences of a given course of action actually influenced the decision taken.[51] On this analysis it seems likely that *Chelsea Cloisters*[52] would be similarly decided under the 1986 Act. *Re Vautin*[53] is an example under earlier legislation of intention to prefer not

---

[45] [1975] 1 WLR 279 at 282.

[46] Following *Neste Oy* v. *Lloyds Bank Ltd* [1983] 2 Lloyd's Rep 658.

[47] (1981) 41 P & CR 98.

[48] But contrast *Re Multi Guarantee Co. Ltd* [1987] BCLC 257.

[49] (1981) 41 P & CR 98 at 103.

[50] [1990] BCC 78.

[51] These tests were further considered by Robert Wright, QC in *Re Beacon Leisure Ltd.* [1991] BCC 213 where he expressed the view that the distinction between the objective test of intention and the subjective test of desire might in many cases be small. Referring again to the old test of dominant intention, he further expressed the view that in many cases it would be easier to draw an appropriate inference under the new legislation than the old.

[52] (1981) 41 P & CR 98.

[53] [1900] 2 QB 325.

being established because of an honest and reasonable belief that there was a legally binding obligation to pay.

The problem of a defaulting trustee seeking to make restitution arose in *Re Lake ex parte Dyer*.[54] In this case the trustee of a settlement who had misappropriated the fund deposited some free assets very shortly before his bankruptcy together with an admission of breach of trust. Understandably, a fraudulent preference claim ensued. However, the Court of Appeal held that the bankrupt's dominant motive was not to prefer the *cestuis que trust* but to remedy his own breach and refused to set aside the transaction. It is no longer necessary to establish a dominant motive.[55] It is now sufficient that the bankrupt was 'influenced' by the requisite 'desire'. Although a bankrupt is not to be taken as desiring all the necessary consequences of his actions, the new requirement is satisfied if the desire was merely one of the factors which operated on his mind. It is unnecessary for it to have been the only factor or even the decisive one. On that basis, it seems unlikely that *Re Lake* would be decided in the same way under the 1986 Act. It appears that the Court of Appeal thought that the dominant motive was a sense of obligation to make good a breach of trust and a sense of shame. However, the recognition of mixed motives would probably be the undoing of the *cestuis que trust* under modern law.

Further possibilities for avoidance arise from the creation of trusts by an insolvent party as a form of security. The difficulty here arises from the registration requirements attending to certain classes of security and the consequence of non-compliance that the security is void. It is possible that trusts by way of security could be created requiring registration under the Bills of Sale legislation and the Agricultural Credits Act 1928. However, in practice, the point is most likely to arise under the Companies Act 1985.[56] In a series of retention of title cases, the courts have considered and rejected, on grounds of lack of registration, attempts to secure obligations to pay the price of goods through trusts on proceeds of sub-dealing.[57]

On examination, this subject appears to owe more to confused terminology than difficulties of fundamental principle. It is perfectly possible to create a valid trust as a conduit for the payment of money.[58] Where such a trust is correctly constituted, no question of the registration of charges arises. Further, it has been held that a single transaction can include a loan and a

---

[54] [1901] 1 KB 710.

[55] *Re M. C. Bacon Ltd.* [1990] BCC 78 at 87.

[56] Shortly to be amended by Part IV of the Companies Act 1989 but with no material distinction for present purposes except that 'charge' will be defined under s. 395(2) of the Companies Act 1989 (as amended) as meaning 'any form of security interest (fixed or floating) over property, other than an interest arising by operation of law'. Under s. 396 (unamended) 'charge' includes 'mortgage'.

[57] See generally *Robert Horne (Midlands) Ltd.* v. *The Liquidator of Rioprint Ltd.* (6 Nov. 1978, unreported); *Re Bond Worth Ltd.* [1980] Ch 228; *Tatung (UK) Ltd.* v. *Galex Telesure Ltd.* (1989) 5 BCC 325.

[58] *Carreras Rothmans Ltd.* v. *Freeman Mathews Treasure Ltd. & Ors* [1985] Ch 207.

trust.[59] Of the various forms of consensual security known to English law only a mortgage involves the transfer of ownership to the secured creditor. Since the creation of a trust by way of security entails the creation of a beneficial interest vested in a beneficiary/creditor but defeasible by discharge of the underlying obligation, it would appear that the creation of a trust asset ranks as a species of equitable mortgage which will require registration under the Companies Act 1985 in the same circumstances as any other form of equitable mortgage.[60] In *Re Bond Worth Ltd.*,[61] Slade, J. appeared to acknowledge the concept of a trust by way of charge. It is difficult to see how a true charge, that is the mere appropriation of property to the satisfaction of a debt but unaccompanied by the transfer of ownership necessary to constitute a mortgage, could arise out of a genuine trust relationship where there is a vested beneficial interest. If this analysis is correct, there is no real overlap between the doctrine that trust assets do not form a divisible part of an insolvent estate and the creation of security interests requiring registration. If a 'trust' is created by way of security then the trust asset does form part of the insolvent estate subject only to the prior beneficial interest of the secured creditor (assuming due compliance with all formalities).

3. Exhaustion of Beneficial Interests

Beneficial interests can be lost through breach of trust resulting in the trust asset being destroyed or dissipated. However, the problem of exhaustion of beneficial interests can also arise out of legitimate dealings by the insolvent party. Thus in *Space Investments Ltd.* v. *Canadian Imperial Bank of Commerce Trust Co. (Bahamas) Ltd.*[62] trust asset status was lost where trust funds were put on bank deposit. Under general principles, the banking relationship was that of debtor and creditor and, on the failure of the bank (which was both trustee and bank and was permitted to receive deposits made by it in its former capacity to it in its latter capacity), the claims in respect of the deposit money were ordinary unsecured claims. The logic of this decision is unassailable if the premiss is accepted that the insolvent bank *qua* trustee must be regarded separately from the insolvent bank *qua* banker. If a trustee lawfully deposits trust money with a third-party bank, the trustee is an unsecured creditor ranking *pari passu* with the claims of other customers of the bank in the event of insolvency. On the other hand, if a bank trustee lawfully receives funds *qua* trustee or wrongly appropriates trust money, then the principles in *Re Hallett's Estate*[63] can be invoked to protect the beneficiaries. The case turned on the express authority which allowed trust

---

[59] *Barclays Bank Ltd.* v. *Quistclose Investments Ltd.* [1970] AC 567; *Re EVTR Ltd* (1987) 3 BCC 389.

[60] See further R. M. Goode, *Legal Problems of Credit and Security*, 2nd edn. (London: Sweet & Maxwell, 1988), 14 and 15.

[61] [1980] Ch. 228 at 247, 250 and 266.

[62] [1986] 1 WLR 1072.

[63] (1880) 30 Ch. D. 696.

money to be treated as if it were customers' money, thus precluding the intervention of equity. This is all very well but the fact remains that the bank *qua* trustee and the bank *qua* banker were one and the same legal entity. Equity has been more vigilant in other cases.

In *Re EVTR Ltd.*[64], the Court of Appeal had to deal with the consequences of money being paid to the company for a specific purpose which, on established principles,[65] gave rise to a resulting trust. The money in question had been advanced to finance the purchase of equipment. The company entered into two contracts, the first with the supplier of the equipment and the second with a leasing company under which the latter agreed to take over the company's obligations by purchasing the equipment and then leasing it to the company. The money advanced was paid to the supplying and leasing companies pursuant to the contracts. The Court was in no doubt that, prior to payment, the money was impressed with a trust. Similarly, there was no doubt that if the contracts had proceeded as intended, the lender would have become an unsecured creditor. There was no suggestion of unauthorised dealing. In the event, the scheme became abortive and led to refunds by both the supplying and leasing companies. A unanimous Court of Appeal, whilst acknowledging the difficulty of the point, held that the refunded money was impressed with a resulting trust in favour of the lender.

Chronologically, the next case was *Re Berkeley Applegate (Investments Consultants) Ltd.*[66] The case arose out of the creditors' voluntary liquidation of a mortgage investment vehicle. At the commencement of liquidation there were some 125 mortgage advances amounting in total to approximately £10.2 million together with a further £1.2 million in client account and an additional sum for accrued interest on the client account money. The principal business of the company was described by directors as being to act as agent in the placement of funds on behalf of individual investors and taking first mortgages over freehold security. Investors paid money to the company which was held in client account until used. In practice it was generally aggregated with money from other investors for the purposes of making advances. The records identified the investors separately. Interest was paid by the borrowers direct to the investors whose funds had been utilized in a particular loan. The company accounted for interest earned on investors' money in client account pending utilization in lending, minus interest at the rate of 2 per cent which it retained for itself. When a borrower repaid, the redemption money was held in client account until used on another advance with interest being paid to the investor. Investors had a right to give notice and withdraw their funds. If this occurred at a time when the money had been utilized in an advance, another investor's money would be

---

[64] (1987) 3 BCC 389.
[65] *Barclays Bank Ltd.* v. *Quistclose Investments Ltd.* [1970] AC 567.
[66] (1988) 4 BCC 274.

substituted. All this was covered by book entries. Questions naturally arose as to whether the client account money and the benefit of the mortgages were held on trust for the investors and these questions were answered in the affirmative. Although there had been some irregularity in the conduct of the clients' accounts, there was no question of the mortgage lending activity itself being unauthorised dealing. It was the *raison d'être* of the investments.

The next case is *Re Eastern Capital Futures Ltd.*,[67] which concerned an application for directions by liquidators as to how they should deal with money received from brokers in respect of futures transactions carried out by the company on behalf of its clients. Client accounts were maintained into which money received by the company from its clients was paid. Money was paid out of the accounts to the brokers with whom the company dealt to pay for futures contracts and margin calls. Money was paid back into the accounts by the brokers representing the proceeds of futures contracts. The trust status of the client accounts was not in issue and the only question was whether the futures contracts themselves and balances with brokers prior to payment into client account were also trust assets. Morritt, J. said:

> In my judgment, as between the company and its clients, they were. The company was authorised by the client to deal in futures contracts on behalf of the client and was authorised to disburse moneys out of the segregated accounts for that purpose. The company dealt with the brokers as principals but this is quite consistent with the company being a trustee of the benefit of the contract for its clients, a point which is confirmed by the clients' obligation to take delivery of the commodity if the contracts matured.
>
> The futures contracts were no more nor less than the authorised form of investment of the trust moneys in the bank account. As such, in my judgment, the benefit of the contracts and the balances in the hands of the brokers, prior to payment into the segregated bank accounts, were assets held by the company in trust for its clients and not assets available for payment of the company's own creditors.[68]

The crucial distinction between this case and *Space Investments Ltd.* v. *Canadian Imperial Bank of Commerce Trust Co (Bahamas) Ltd.* [69] is that the relevant assets were either in the hands of solvent parties or consisted of rights against solvent parties. Unfortunately, none of the judgments in any of the four cases reviewed refers to any of the other cases in the sequence. Accordingly, none contains any attempt to rationalize the principles, which appear to be as follows:

1. Trust assets held as such for the purposes of permitted dealing do not constitute property divisible amongst creditors.
2. The rights of an insolvent trustee against third parties arising out of permitted dealings with trust assets are themselves held on trust and do not form part of the property divisible amongst creditors.
3. Where money is advanced for a specific purpose the trust will be

---

[67] (1989) 5 BCC 224.   [68] *Ibid.* 225.   [69] [1986] 1 WLR 1072.

exhausted by satisfaction of that purpose but derivative rights will be impressed with the trust if the purpose is not achieved.

4. If permitted dealing results in trust assets being in the hands of an insolvent third party who is not accountable as trustee, equity will not intervene to protect those interested in the trust asset as such (there could be other proprietary rights) and the same will be true if the trustee itself has dual capacity.

4. Subordination of Beneficial Interests

The possibility of the claims of a debenture holder to a trust asset taking priority to the claims of a beneficiary have already been examined. Recent case law has developed a separate question of subordination of trust assets which involves no third party. The problem arises when application is made to pay liquidation costs—typically arising in the winding-up of some form of investment vehicle—out of trust assets. The basic rule is that a trustee may not profit from its trusteeship[70] but there is inherent jurisdiction to allow a trustee remuneration even where none is provided for under the terms of the trust.[71] Equally clearly this is a jurisdiction which will be sparingly exercised. Charging trust assets with any of the expenses of insolvency proceedings entails an extension of the jurisdiction exercised in favour of trustees.

The issue arose in *Re Exchange Securities & Commodities Ltd. & Ors. (No. 2)*.[72] The case concerned the liquidation of a series of companies which had taken deposits from the public for commodity investment and which had undertaken transactions in the commodity markets. Claims by depositors gave rise to complicated trust and inter-company claims which had to be resolved in order to determine the true beneficial ownership of the assets held by the companies. Applications were made by the official receiver as provisional liquidator seeking orders that fees and expenses (and those of a special manager) be paid out of the assets held by each company, even if it later should appear that those assets were trust assets beneficially owned by the depositors. A submission that statutory fees could be paid out of trust assets was rejected. An alternative submission on behalf of the official receiver that the court had an inherent jurisdiction to direct payment was accepted by counsel for the representative defendants—a concession which Vinelott, J. thought rightly made. The substantive issue in respect of inherent jurisdiction turned on how a just allowance to the official receiver was to be calculated and the incidence of that allowance. This issue was thought premature and was not decided. The decision was, therefore, poor authority for the proposition that liquidation costs could be debited to trust assets.

[70] *Vyse* v. *Foster & Ors* (1874) LR 7 HL 318.
[71] *Re Masters* [1953] 1 WLR 81; *Re Worthington, Leighton* v. *MacLeod* [1954] 1 WLR 526; *Re Duke of Norfolk's ST* [1982] Ch. 61.
[72] (1986) 2 BCC 98, 932.

The issue returned to the Chancery Division in *Re Berkeley Applegate (Investment Consultants) Ltd. (No. 2)*[73], a case in which counsel for the liquidator accepted that Vinelott, J. had not had before him authority which established the inherent jurisdiction on which he relied, but none the less argued for the existence of such jurisdiction. A previous decision[74] had already determined that assets representing investors' funds were held on trust for the individual investors. The free assets were unquantified but insufficient to meet the fees and expenses of the liquidator. The liquidator sought an order for payment of his fees and expenses out of the assets of the company and the trust assets or alternatively an order that the company was entitled to be paid remuneration as trustee. One of the particular objections taken on behalf of investors was that the liquidator, operating as agent of the company, was not a trustee for anyone. The issue was whether any part of the fees and remuneration could be paid out of trust assets either directly or indirectly by payment to the company. In this case it was common ground that there was no statutory authority for payment.

It was held that authority established that when a person claimed to enforce an equitable interest in the property, the court had a discretion to require an allowance for costs incurred and skill and labour expended in connection with the administration of that property. In a case strongly influenced by practicalities, the court further held that the beneficial interests of investors could not have been established without some investigation along the lines actually carried out by the liquidator. Although his efforts had not added directly to the value of the trust asset his work was none the less essential before the trust estate could be realised. Ensuring that fair compensation was made to the liquidator was, accepting one of the maxims invoked on the liquidator's behalf, an application of the rule that he who seeks equity must do equity. Particular objections, including that to the effect that the liquidator was not personally a trustee, were rejected. Edward Nugee, QC said:

The authorities establish, in my judgment, a general principle that where a person seeks to enforce a claim to an equitable interest in property, the court has a discretion to require as a condition of giving effect to that equitable interest that an allowance be made for costs incurred and for skill and labour expended in connection with the administration of the property. It is a discretion which will be sparingly exercised; but factors which will operate in favour of its being exercised include the fact that, if the work had not been done by the person to whom the allowance is sought to be made, it would have had to be done either by the person entitled to the equitable interest . . . or by a receiver appointed by the court whose fees would have been borne by the trust property . . . and the fact that the work has been of substantial benefit to the trust property and to the persons interested in it in equity . . . In my judgment this is a case in which the jurisdiction can properly be exercised.[75]

[73] [1989] Ch. 32.
[74] *Re Berkeley Applegate (Investment Consultants) Ltd.* (1988) 4 BCC 274.
[75] [1989] Ch. 32 at 50.

Of the argument that the liquidator was not personally a trustee, he went on to say:

First it was said that the liquidator was not in the position of a trustee, in that the legal interest in the trust assets remained throughout in the company and did not vest in him. In my judgment this does not preclude the court from making an allowance to him out of the trust assets in respect of his expenses and remuneration, although it is no doubt a factor to consider when determining to what extent compensation for his expenditure of money, skill and labour should be borne by the trust assets rather than the company's own assets.[76]

Although providing reassurance to the liquidator that fees and remuneration would be paid, if necessary, out of trust assets, the further question of the incidence of those claims was deferred.

Re Exchange Securities & Commodities Ltd. & Ors. (No.2)[77] was a case of compulsory liquidation. Counsel for the investors in *Re Berkeley Applegate (Investment Consultants) Ltd. (No.2)*[78] sought to distinguish that decision on the grounds that an official receiver, by virtue of his office, automatically became liquidator until another was appointed. The submission was to the effect that a liquidator in a voluntary liquidation has an opportunity of considering the position before acceptance of appointment and that the intervention was, therefore, officious interference. This is a somewhat unrealistic line of argument to advance in the case of a failed investment vehicle where the trust issues arising are likely—as demonstrated by the decided cases—to be exceedingly complex. In any event, the judgment in *Berkeley Applegate* refused to accept this distinction. Having established inherent jurisdiction exercisable in favour of a liquidator in creditors' voluntary liquidation, it would appear, *a fortiori*, that the jurisdiction would extend to the official receiver and any other liquidator (or provisional liquidator) appointed in a compulsory liquidation. This view is supported by the next decision, which was that in *Re Eastern Capital Futures Ltd.*[79] The decision of Edward Nugee QC in *Berkeley Applegate* does not explore the question of whether office holders appointed in other forms of insolvency proceeding can benefit from the inherent jurisdiction asserted in that case. The general principle quoted previously is sufficiently widely expressed to apply to strangers. Indeed, a liquidator is a stranger in the sense that he is neither a trustee of the trust asset or a beneficiary. On the other hand, a liquidator can scarcely be considered unconnected. The inherent jurisdiction merely gives rise to a discretion; it does not follow that the discretion will necessarily be exercised. It is submitted that the correct approach is to avoid delineating classes of persons who fall within or outside the jurisdiction and to concentrate merely on how the discretion will be exercised. For these purposes, the analogy between bankruptcy and liquidation is close enough. Subject to complications about the identity of the trustee due to the operation

[76] *Ibid.* 52.   [77] (1986) 2 BCC 98, 932.   [78] [1989] Ch. 32.   [79] (1989) 5 BCC 224.

of the vesting rules, it would seem likely that the discretion would be exercised in favour of a trustee in bankruptcy as freely as in the case of a liquidator. The position in other forms of insolvency proceeding is more complicated. In favour of an administrator it may be said that he is an officer of the court and that he has a statutory duty to take possession of assets which are or appear to be the property of the company.[80] A prudent administrator will seek directions[81] as soon as he perceives that he is, or may be, in possession of trust assets. Provided that he does so (and subsequently acts in accordance with any directions given) he can reasonably anticipate a sympathetic exercise of the jurisdiction. By contrast, it seems relatively unlikely that the jurisdiction will benefit an administrative receiver. Such a receiver is entitled to disregard assets covered by the security if he does not consider it in the interests of the appointing debenture holder to pursue those assets.[82] It follows that an administrative receiver dealing with trust assets will bring the 'officious interference' objection sharply into focus. Administrative receivership is a commercial operation designed to realise a security to best advantage. There seems no reason why costs wrongly incurred intermeddling with assets which turn out to be trust assets should not simply constitute part of the costs of the receivership debited to the receivership fund. This severe approach might be tempered in the case of floating charge assets. Here there is a statutory duty to pay preferential creditors[83] and an administrative receiver might find himself in a position more analogous to that of a liquidator. Finally there is the question of supervisors under voluntary arrangements. It is no more realistic to suppose that issues concerning beneficial interests can be finally resolved before proposals are approved in a voluntary arrangement, than it is to suggest that they can be determined before the commencement of liquidation. On the other hand, the existence of significant issues of that type might be thought to render a case an unsuitable subject for a voluntary arrangement. A more meritorious claim to invoke the inherent jurisdiction would arise in a case where there had been no reasonable ground for supposing that a beneficial interest existed prior to acceptance of appointment. Beyond that it is difficult to generalize because the circumstances will differ widely from case to case. Given that the circumstances which give rise to exercise of the inherent jurisdiction are now not uncommon, it is a matter for further discussion whether it is appropriate that office holders should have to rely upon the discretion of the court in the exercise of its inherent jurisdiction. Here a legitimate distinction could be drawn between cases in which the beneficial ownership of assets is initially in doubt and those where it is clear from the outset that the asset in question is a trust asset. The arguments for a statutory right to remuneration are stronger

---

[80] s. 17 of the Insolvency Act 1986.
[81] s. 14(15).
[82] *Newhart Development Corporation Ltd.* v. *Co-Operative Commercial Bank* [1978] QB 814.
[83] s. 40 of the Insolvency Act 1986.

in the former case than the latter. However, the practical interests of beneficiaries might best be served by statutory provision in all cases. The alternative is the ever-present risk that trust assets will be left unadministered in the hands of insolvent trustees, thereby placing the assets in jeopardy and necessitating court applications by the beneficial owners.

In *Re Eastern Capital Futures Ltd.*[84] Morritt, J. held that the liquidators should retain out of trust funds remuneration equal to what they would have got if the trust money had been a free asset of the company. He applied a prescribed scale, holding that trust money should notionally be aggregated with the company's free assets, applying the scale to the aggregate with the incidence being borne proportionately between the trust assets and the free assets but without prejudice to the ability of the liquidators and the creditors' committee to agree some other basis for remuneration out of free assets, that is, solely directing as to the quantum to be borne out of trust assets.

The question of incidence had been left open in *Re Berkeley Applegate (Investment Consultants) Ltd. (No.2)*[85] but was brought back to the Chancery Division in *Re Berkeley Applegate (Investment Consultants) Ltd. (No.3)*.[86] On this occasion the case was heard by Peter Gibson, J. The decision illustrates very clearly the difficulties of laying down precise rules in this situation. At the time of the hearing the company's own assets amounted to between £45,000 and £80,000. The total costs and expenses amounted to about £686,000 of which only some £41,500 was estimated by the liquidator to represent liquidation expenses as distinct from the expenses of administering trust assets. It was held that remuneration, costs, and expenses incurred in administering trust assets should not be paid out of the free assets and that any surplus company assets over and above liquidation expenses should go to unsecured creditors. That left the question of incidence between two classes of investor, namely those whose money was invested in mortgages at the time of liquidation and those whose money was in client account. On behalf of the first class it was argued that remuneration and expenses should be borne *pari passu* except to the extent that specific expenditure was attributable to specific assets. On behalf of the second class it was submitted that this would be prejudicial to client account investors since their interests had occasioned less work. The liquidator submitted that costs might be borne *pari passu* for the initial period when his work had been for the benefit of all and, that for the remaining period, 90% should be borne *pro rata* by those who remained mortgage investors and 10% divided between the rest. The liquidator's suggestions were accepted on the basis that they were the fairest.

In *Acoma (Bilston) Ltd.* v. *Comer & Ors,*[87] the issue was again quantum following an earlier '*Berkeley Applegate*' order. Judge Micklem rejected submissions that *Re Eastern Capital Futures Ltd.* asserted any general statement of principle that liquidators should retain remuneration out of trust funds equal to what they would have got if the trust money had been a free

[84] (1989) 5 BCC 224.   [85] [1989] Ch. 32.   [86] (1989) 5 BCC 803.   [87] 1 Mar. 1990, unreported.

asset (although that was, in terms, what Morritt, J. had ordered that the liquidators in that case should receive) and it is submitted that this is a correct interpretation of the earlier decision. He went on to reject the scale applied by Morritt, J. as an appropriate method of quantification in the instant case which entailed the liquidation of a company which was trustee of a pension fund and where, in contradistinction to the *Berkeley Applegate* situation, there had been little difficulty in getting in and preserving the trust fund and no initial confusion between free assets and trust property.[88] Accordingly he distinguished both *Berkeley Applegate* and *Eastern Capital* as cases where the actions of the liquidator *qua* liquidator were intimately bound up with what had to be done in the administration of the trust asset. He therefore upheld the order under appeal, namely that the assessment of remuneration was intended to be on a time basis. The decision is determined in terms which owe much to the constitution of the original '*Berkeley Applegate*' order in the case but the observations on calculation of reasonable and proper remuneration are of more general application. The liquidator was ordered to bear personally the costs of the appeal.

On a review of the authorities it is possible to advance the following propositions about the exercise of the inherent jurisdiction upheld in *Berkeley Applegate*:

1. Tne scope of the jurisdiction is not limited to any predetermined class of persons involved in the administration of trust assets.

2. Although not determinant, the capacity in which a person has been involved in the administration of trust assets will be relevant to the exercise of discretion in his favour.[89]

3. Discretion will more readily be exercised in cases where payment is sought in respect of costs (or time) and expenses which would have been incurred in any event if beneficial owners had sought relief by another route.

4. Those seeking exercise of the inherent jurisdiction in their favour should demonstrate benefit to those beneficially interested in the trust assets.

5. The benefit need not take the form of an enhancement of value; it may consist of the good administration of the trust asset.

6. The discretion will more readily be invoked in favour of persons who find themselves dealing with a situation not originally foreseen and in the circumstances where action is required.[90]

7. Any contractual provisions governing the rights as between the trustee and beneficiary will be a relevant factor to the exercise of discretion but will not preclude jurisdiction to award costs and remuneration in favour of the office holder.[91]

---

[88] Although there appear to have been difficulties in dealing with beneficiaries.
[89] *Re Berkeley Applegate (Investments) Ltd. (No.2)* [1989] Ch. 32 at 52.
[90] *Ibid.*
[91] *Ibid.*; see further *Re Eastern Capital Futures Ltd.* (1989) 5 BCC 224.

8. It is not a prerequisite to the exercise of discretion that free assets should first have been exhausted.[92]

Re Westdock Realisations Ltd.[93] exemplifies a different line of authority. Here questions arose as to entitlement to a receivership surplus. The receiver sought directions as to how to deal with the surplus and liquidators sought orders that their costs in determining the issues raised on the receiver's summonses be paid out of the funds held by the receiver. The surplus was payable to the liquidators in the ordinary way subject to a claim by the Export Credits Guarantee Department that it was subrogated to the bank's security. The liquidators had no funds with which to litigate and submitted that the litigation was analogous to litigation concerning beneficial interests in a trust fund. It was held that the proper approach in litigation between rival claimants was the costs should normally follow the event; but if it was necessary for the proper execution of a receiver or liquidator's duties to obtain a decision from the court and the applicant joined a representative respondent to argue on behalf of a class, then that respondent's costs could properly be paid out of the fund in issue. In rather special circumstances, it was decided that the liquidators should have the orders for costs which they sought. On jurisdiction Browne-Wilkinson, V-C said *(inter alia)*:

The other jurisdictional point relates to the question where the court has jurisdiction to make an order for payment out of the moneys which at the end of the day are found to belong to some other person. If a trustee, liquidator or receiver, or any other person in a neutral capacity is holding moneys which belong to others but it is not known who is beneficially entitled, the court frequently makes orders that the costs of determining who is beneficially entitled to those moneys are to be paid out of the moneys held. The ordinary order for costs in the case of an express trust fund is one example. In addition, orders are frequently made in the Companies Court where there are issues as to beneficial ownership that the costs come out of the fund . . . It is in my judgment much too late to put forward a contention that there is no jurisdiction to make such an order. However, of course, in considering whether such an order should be made the fact that in one event the fund will be held not to belong to the liquidators is a most relevant matter to take into account.[94]

Re Westdock Realisations Ltd. can be contrasted with the slightly earlier decision of Harman, J. in *Re Stetzel Thomson & Co. Ltd.*[95] In that case liquidators, in a voluntary liquidation, applied for directions as to the ownership of a fund where there was a possibility that some or all of it was held on trust. The business of the company had been the conduct of syndicates writing reinsurance business in London and it was unclear how the fund had come into existence. The judgment is principally concerned with the rejection of applications for directions and for representation orders

---

[92] *Re Berkeley Applegate (Investment Consultants) Ltd. (No.3)* (1989) 5 BCC 803, see further *Re Eastern Capital Futures Ltd.* (1989) 5 BCC 224.

[93] (1988) 4 BCC 192.

[94] *Ibid.* 197. See further s. 51 of the Supreme Court Act 1981.

[95] (1988) 4 BCC 74.

in relation to the various classes of claimants to the syndicate funds, but there are other points of interest. Echoing the 'officious interference' line of argument, Harman, J. held that the voluntary liquidators has assumed office of their own free will and had available funds, as did the claimants to the syndicate fund. Prospective orders for costs and remuneration were refused. The liquidators had to take their own view, administer the fund as they thought fit, and resist any adverse claims subsequently brought against them as best they could.

5. Conclusion

The traditional principle that a trust asset does not form part of the property divisible amongst creditors still applies. However, the interests of the beneficiaries are not inviolable. Apart from the acquisition of rights over trust assets by innocent third parties (the particular problem of administrative receivership), the areas of risk divide. Trust interests created at the expense of creditors prior to the onset of insolvency are liable to be set aside under the provisions of English insolvency law applicable to all antecedent transactions. This is a general consideration but the other areas of risk are more specifically applicable to trust assets. Unauthorised dealings by an insolvent trustee may result in the destruction or dissipation of the trust asset and even authorized dealings may result in an asset ceasing to have trust status. Finally, equity may exact a price for its intervention in upholding a beneficial interest, by requiring prior payment of associated costs and expenses in an insolvency. Whereas the avoidance of antecedent transactions and the loss of trust status through authorized dealings entails balancing the interests of the beneficial owners of trust assets against those of ordinary creditors, the final issue is approached differently. Here the issue will be between the office holder and the beneficial owner of the trust asset, and the interests of creditors are only relevant to the extent of ensuring that the costs of administering trust assets for the exclusive benefit of those interested therein do not erode free assets. It remains a matter for continuing debate whether the final issue should remain solely a matter for the discretion of the courts in individual cases.

IV
Asset Protection for Multinational Companies and Their Shareholders

10

ASSET PROTECTION FOR MULTINATIONAL CORPORATIONS

Harry Wiggin

1. Introduction

Individual and corporate investors throughout the world have, in recent years, become increasingly aware of the potential adverse commercial consequences of political and economic instability. This is especially so at the present time.

The risks have, of course, been apparent since the advent of international trade. Indeed, as early as the Magna Carta in 1215, a principle similar to that enshrined in more recent Trading with the Enemy legislation was recognized, namely that the property in Britain of subjects of an enemy government could be attached until and unless it was established that their country recognized the property rights of aliens. However, down the centuries, and especially in the eighteenth and nineteenth centuries, numerous international treaties were entered into with the object of *protecting* the sanctity of private property; it was not until the American Civil War that Trading with the Enemy legislation as we now know it came into its own.

An examination of various countries' Trading with the Enemy legislation which developed during the two World Wars and subsequently would occupy a treatise in its own right and will not therefore be attempted in this brief chapter. Suffice to say that, although protection from the impact of Trading with the Enemy legislation was the principal motivating factor leading to the creation of corporate asset protection trusts in the past, this is no longer likely to be the case.

Professor Jeffrey Schoenblum will explain, in Chapter 11, the many obstacles to protecting assets against United States expropriation, confiscation, or freezing. Not only these obstacles, but also recent changes in the world political picture also, will militate against the perceived utility of and need for asset protection mechanisms for United States situs assets.

As this chapter will seek to establish, however, there are many risks other than United States vesting and freezing against which corporations operating internationally will wish to secure protection for their assets. It is submitted that, with careful planning, such protection is something to which they can reasonably aspire.

It is a general principle of international law that the courts of one state will not sit in judgment on the acts of another sovereign state, expropriating or confiscating property located within its own territory,[1] even if the property belongs to an alien.[2] In the United States, this principle is known as the Act of State doctrine. As Professor Schoenblum will explain, the United States judiciary will apply the doctrine to assets situate within the United States, unless the political (as distinct from judicial) branch of government certifies that there is no foreign policy justification for recognizing an extraterritorial expropriation or confiscation by the foreign government concerned (the *Bernstein* exception).[3]

In addition to the problems presented by the United States vesting or freezing powers, the scope of the Act of State doctrine remains uncertain,[4] raising yet another obstacle to any ambitions foreign nationals might have for seeking to protect their assets situated in the United States.

Having regard to these uncertainties in the United States, this chapter will proceed on two basic assumptions. The first is that in any case where Trading with the Enemy legislation or the Act of State doctrine is potentially material, the efficacy of any solution will be regarded as an open question as regards assets situate in the United States. The second is that, in relation to any proposed solution, it is to be taken as read that the potential problems enumerated by Professor Schoenblum in relation to the integrity and enforceability of the trust mechanism must first be satisfied.[5] There must, for example, be no doubt about the choice of law governing various aspects of the trust, no doubt about the validity of the transfer of assets into trust, and no doubt that the best-protected trusteeship structure available has been selected.

In the light of these assumptions it seems difficult to escape the conclusion that it is most unlikely that the forum of administration selected for a corporate asset protection trust, or the situs of incorporation of the chosen trustee, will be located in the United States; and this is likely to be the case even where the majority of the assets to be comprised within the structure are situated in the United States.

In devising any method of asset protection it has to be borne in mind that it is a general principle of international law that property situate in one state cannot normally be affected by purported expropriation or confiscation by another state, even if such property belongs to a national of that other state.[6] However it has to be recognised that this principle in turn conflicts, in certain

---

[1] *Aksionairnoye Obschestvo A M Luther* v. *James Sagor & Co* [1921] 3 KB 532; *Princess Paley Olga v. Weisz* [1929] 1 KB 718

[2] *Re Helbert Wagg & Co Ltd* [1956] Ch. 323.

[3] Discussed at p. 254. This should be contrasted with the approach of other countries. The courts of the UK, for instance, are not prepared to recognise an extraterritorial expropriation or confiscation. *Bank Voor Handel en Scheepvart NV* v. *Slatford* [1953] 1 QB 248.

[4] See further p. 255.

[5] See further p. 218.

[6] *Re Russian Bank for Foreign Trade* [1933] Ch. 745.

circumstances,[7] with the common law principle that a foreign state cannot be impleaded.[8]

Thus the efficacy of any proposed solution will be dependent upon the principles of territoriality and jurisdiction applicable in the jurisdictions relevant to the particular circumstances of the case and the proposed solution must, therefore, take such principles into account. As has already been noted, the English courts will recognise an expropriation or confiscation by another state of property located within its own territory at the time of the decree, even if it is subsequently brought to the United Kingdom.[9] This principle will apply whether the decree provides for just compensation ('expropriation') or not ('confiscation').[10]

The judgments in *Williams and Humbert Ltd* v. *W and H Trade Marks (Jersey) Ltd*, both at first instance[11] and in the Court of Appeal,[12] provide perhaps the most important relatively recent discussions of the application under English law of foreign confiscatory laws.[13] Furthermore, it is worth quoting in full the analysis by Nourse, J. (as he then was) at first instance, which was adopted by the Court of Appeal in *Settebello Limited* v. *Banco Totta*.[14] He propounded the following classification.[15]

First, there are laws which are not recognised at all and are, by a legal fiction, deemed not to exist. Second, there are laws whose validity and effect within the territory of the foreign state are recognised but which will not be directly or indirectly enforced in England. . . .

I am not concerned with penal or revenue laws simpliciter. I confine myself to expropriatory laws of duly recognised states, principally to confiscatory laws, that is to say expropriatory laws which do not provide for payment of any or any proper

---

[7] e.g. if the expropriating state has possession of the property, rather than the putative owner

[8] Now governed by The European Convention on State Immunity (1973) (Cmnd 5081) and, in the United Kingdom, by the State Immunity Act 1978. Under the latter there are exceptions to the general immunity conferred by s. 1 in the case, *inter alia*, of proceedings relating to (i) rights in the United Kingdom in respect of any patent, trade mark, design, copyright, or trade or business name (s. 7) and (ii) ships used for commercial purposes and commercial cargoes (s. 10). Application of the Act is also expressly excluded in respect of proceedings relating to taxation (s. 16(5)), other than VAT and commercial rates (where it is expressly provided that the immunity shall not apply—s. 11).

[9] *Aksionairnoye Obschestvo A M Luther* v. *James Sagor & Co* [1921] 3 KB 532; *Princess Paley Olga* v. *Weisz* [1929] 1 KB 718.

[10] *Williams and Humbert Ltd.* v. *W and H Trade Marks (Jersey) Ltd.* [1986] AC 368, applied *Luther* v. *Sagor*, supra, in all three courts up to and including the House of Lords, despite the fact that at first instance and in the Court of Appeal the nationalization of a Spanish holding company (Rumasa) was considered to be confiscation, whereas the House of Lords treated it as expropriation with compensation. (It should also be noted that the nationalization of Rumasa resulted in the *indirect* expropriation of an English wholly owned subsidiary of Rumasa, Williams and Humbert Limited.)

[11] [1985] 2 All ER 208.

[12] [1985] 2 All ER 619.

[13] As is observed by Cheshire and North, *Private International Law*, 11th edn. (London: Butterworths, 1987), 124.

[14] [1985] 1 WLR 1050 at 1056.

[15] [1985] 2 AII ER 208, 213.

compensation. In this regard the existing authorities appear to me to support the following propositions.

(1A) English law will not recognise foreign confiscatory laws which, by reason of their being discriminatory on grounds of race, religion or the like, constitute so grave an infringement of human rights that they ought not to be recognised as laws at all: see *Oppenheimer* v. *Cattermole*.[16a] These are class I laws.

(1B) English law will not recognise foreign laws which discriminate against nationals of this country in time of war by purporting to confiscate their moveable property situated in the foreign state: see *Wolff* v. *Oxholm* (1817) 6 M&S 92, [1814–23] All ER Rep 208, *Re Fried Krupp AG* [1917] 2 Ch. 188 and *Re Helbert Wagg & Co Ltd* [1956] 1 All ER 129 at 138, [1956] Ch. 323 at 345. These are also class I laws.

(2A) English law, while recognising foreign laws not falling within class I which confiscate property situated in the foreign state (see (3) below), will not directly or indirectly enforce them here if they are also penal: see *Banco de Vizcaya* v. *Don Alfonso de Borbon y Austria* [1935] 1 KB 140, [1934] All ER Rep 555, in some respects a puzzling case which has sometimes been misunderstood. These are class II laws.

(2B) English law will not enforce laws which purport to confiscate property situated in this country: see *Frankfurther* v. *W L Exner Ltd* [1947] Ch. 629 and *Novello & Co* v. *Hinrichsen Edition Ltd* [1951] 1 All ER 779, [1951] Ch. 595. This can now be seen to be an application of the wider rule that English law will not enforce foreign laws which purport to have extra-territorial effect: see *Bank voor Handel en Scheepvart NV* v. *Slatford* [1951] 2 All ER 956, [1953] 1 QB 248. Thus the rule would just as much apply to expropriatory laws which provided for payment of proper compensation: see *Oppenheimer* v. *Cattermole* [1975] 1 All ER 538 at 566, [1976] AC 249 at 276 *per* Lord Cross. All these are class II laws, although the first two cases cited might now be decided on the ground that the laws there in question were class I laws falling within category (1A).

(3) English law will recognise foreign laws not falling within class I which confiscate property situated in the foreign state and, where title is perfected there, will enforce its incidents in this country: see *Aksionairnoye Obschestvo A M Luther* v. *James Sagor & Co* [1921] 3 KB 532, [1921] All ER Rep 138, *Princess Paley Olga* v. *Weisz* [1929] 1 KB 718, [1929] All ER Rep 513; and *Frankfurther* v. *W L Exner Ltd* [1947] Ch. 629 at 644. The nationality of the owner is immaterial: see *Re Helbert Wagg & Co* [1956] 1 All ER 129 at 140, [1956] Ch. 323 at 348–349.

2. The Risks

This chapter is concerned with a number of risks. The principal risks can be divided into the following categories.

Home risks: the confiscation of assets located in, and owned by citizens or residents of, the state concerned. The United Kingdom courts 'will not enquire into the legality of acts done by a foreign government against its own subjects in respect of property situate in its own territory'.[16] In general it can be said that such confiscation cannot extend extra-territorially (though United States exceptions to this principle are mentioned by Professor Schoenblum).[17]

[16] *Princess Paley Olga* v. *Weisz* [1929] 1 KB 718 at 725.
[16a] [1976] AC 249.   [17] Ch. 11, pp. 253–5.

The majority of local business assets will invariably be locally owned and the risks this entails cannot for the most part be avoided. What can be avoided, however, subject to technical problems such as local exchange control, is the extended ownership chain where foreign assets are owned through local companies.

This is particularly relevant in the case of shares of overseas affiliated companies, which should, if possible, be structured under different (foreign) ownership (and therefore not subject to confiscation by the home country of the principal company), so that expropriation or confiscation of the principal company will not subsume the affiliated companies. An emergency trust, described later, may be an ideal vehicle for this purpose.

This protective principle had not been adopted in the case of the St Gobain Glass Company, nationalized by the French government in 1982, where the Belgian courts held that the corporate ownership of the Belgian subsidiaries by the principal company resulted in title remaining with the (nationalized) French principal company and that the claim of shareholders that the nationalization should not have extra-territorial effect in relation to the subsidiaries could not be sustained. The implication, however, was that had the French nationalization law been contrary to public policy the court might have considered piercing the corporate veil as regards the interests of the shareholders in the subsidiaries—the 'split company' principle referred to below.

In contrast, other countries have taken a different view and have considered that where a company has assets outside the host country, the company may retain its corporate personality outside such country—the 'split company' principle.[18] It will be readily appreciated that, if it could be relied upon, this principle would provide important opportunities for advanced strategic planning to protect not only affiliated companies but also industrial property rights such as patents, trade marks, and business and corporate names, which for many companies represent the life-blood of their business.

A classic example of this situation is the Zeiss Optical Foundation, which was originally based in East Germany. After the Second World War its senior management moved to West Germany and purported to move the seat of the Foundation to that country. They started to make optical products using the Zeiss name and trade marks. Litigation over their entitlement to do so took place in over fifty countries. Before German unification, the West German courts had consistently upheld the proposition that, *vis-à-vis* assets held

---

[18] This principle has found greatest favour in Germany where the Federal Tribunal has stated that a split company will come into existence at the moment of confiscation in any country where there are corporate assets. The principle rests on the fundamental assumption that corporate rights have a situs wherever there are corporate assets. It has, however, been heavily criticized and few countries have actually adopted the principle. See F. A. Mann, 'The Confiscation of Corporations, Corporate Rights and Corporate Assets, and the Conflict of Laws', (1962) 11 *ICLQ* 471.

outside the Eastern Bloc (e.g. the business name, its trade names, and trade marks registered in its name), the Zeiss Foundation retained its separate identity, despite expropriation of its business after the Second World War in its original country of domicile, East Germany. Since that time, two separate brands of Zeiss products have been on the market, one brand emanating from a Zeiss Foundation in West Germany and the other emanating from a Zeiss Foundation in East Germany. This has caused immense complications for the businesses of the two organisations, because courts throughout the world have not taken a consistent view of the situation. For example, the courts in the USA and France supported the view of the West German courts that the Zeiss Foundation situated in West Germany was the only body entitled to use the Zeiss name and trade marks. Other courts elsewhere (e.g. in India and Pakistan) have taken the opposite view.

In litigation before the English courts to determine the entitlement to use the Zeiss name and trade marks the House of Lords held, on a preliminary application of the East Germans to strike out the case, that it was for the courts of East Germany to decide whether the Zeiss Foundation continued to exist there. The litigation continued for some years but was compromised by agreement, after lengthy interlocutory proceedings which reached the House of Lords, before any decision was reached as to the use of the trade marks, etc.

This has all become history during 1991, however, as the western Carl Zeiss, based in Heidesheim, with the aid of the Treuhandanstalt—the German privatization agency—and of the eastern federal state of Thuringia, have rescued Carl Zeiss Jena from virtual bankruptcy (albeit with a massive reduction in output and jobs), with integration of ownership of the two businesses in a new joint foundation.

It will be apparent that there can be no hard and fast rules in this area; it is thus all the more important to structure an international business appropriately *before* a problem arises.

The law in the United States in particular is highly complex. The leading case for many years on the Act of State Doctrine was *Banco Nacional de Cuba* v. *Sabbatino*.[19] The decision in this case gave rise in 1964 to what is generally known as the 'Hickenlooper amendment' (amending the Foreign Assistance Act 1961), which placed limitations on the application of the Act of State doctrine to governmental confiscations which violate principles of international law or certain prescribed criteria, except where the political branch considers its application to be in the best interests of United States foreign policy.

Professor Schoenblum acknowledges that there is 'general American hostility to foreign takings', but draws attention to the present problematical position of the United States courts in relation to the Act of State doctrine. While it is evident that the outcome of cases which actually come before the American courts cannot be predicted with certainty, the writer's view would be that, provided care has been taken to ensure that assets have been validly

[19] [1963] 376 US 398.

vested in a well designed and implemented asset protection structure, whose proper law and forum of administration is located outside the United States, it is most unlikely that a claim would be brought in the United States courts in respect of any such assets which are located outside the United States, and that so far as United States situs assets are concerned their vulnerability to the Act of State doctrine will at least not be increased—and may well be substantially lessened—by their inclusion in the asset protection structure.

Home risks: the imposition of exchange controls or investment restrictions in respect of foreign assets owned by citizens, residents or corporations of the state concerned. A corporation operating in international markets may be dependent for its business on acquiring raw materials, know-how, or other rights externally, for which it is essential that it has access to foreign currency, either belonging to itself, or belonging to an associated or affiliated entity, or through its ability to raise external finance. Businesses located in countries with major debt problems have evinced particular concern in this respect and have been wise to take steps to protect such sources of overseas trade finance.

Exchange control regulations have not been viewed by the courts in the same way as confiscatory or expropriatory legislation, though there have been instances where they have amounted to concealed means of accomplishing the latter objectives. The United States courts have seldom seen them in such light,[20] however, and a challenge nowadays to their efficacy in the United States courts would be unlikely to be successful. The United Kingdom courts have traditionally been more robust in this area, the question generally turning on whether the transaction itself is subject to the law of the country purporting to impose the controls[21] and whether or not such controls were of a penal or confiscatory nature.[22] The Swiss courts have, not surprisingly, steadfastly resisted attempts by other states to reach, through exchange control requirements, assets banked in their country.

In 1944 the International Monetary Fund agreement known as the Bretton Woods Agreement sought not only to impose criteria by which exchange control regulations should be judged but also, where such criteria have been complied with, to provide for co-operation between member states in their enforcement.[23] Where assets are located outside the state imposing the controls, such exchange controls can of course, however, apply only to residents of such state, and accordingly legitimate planning *before* such controls have been imposed may normally be undertaken. Here again, various permutations of the emergency trust may often prove appropriate.

---

[20] *Ida Werfel* v. *Zivnostenska Banka* 23 NYS 2d 1001 (1940); see also Dr Walter Kolvenbach, *Protection of Foreign Investments—A Private Law Study of Safeguarding Devices in International Crisis Situations*(Kluwer, 1989), 262.

[21] *Re Helbert Wagg & Co Ltd* [1956] Ch. 323. see also *Re Lord Cable* [1977] 1 WLR 7 at 13–14.

[22] *Re Helbert Wagg & Co Limited* supra; *Empresa Exportadora De Azucar* v. *Industria Azucarera Nacional SA, the Playa Larga* [1983] 2 Lloyds Rep 171 at 190.

[23] Second Amendment to Articles of Agreement of the International Monetary Fund (1976) Article VIII s. 2(b).

Foreign or outward investment risks (for the non-resident alien): compulsory acquisition or nationalization by the acquiring country of assets belonging to non-resident alients with ('expropriation') or without ('confiscation') just compensation. Such expropriation or confiscation may be imposed either by a legitimate government seeking to pursue the reasonable economic objectives of its country, or by a revolutionary or corrupt government seeking unjust enrichment. Confiscation may take an indirect form or to some extent be concealed under the guise of excessive or penal taxation.

If the assets concerned are located in the legislating country (e.g. a company incorporated or resident there), this is a most difficult risk to protect against. Local situs assets may include either underlying assets or shares in a company incorporated in the jurisdiction but holding assets elsewhere. Underlying assets are of course vulnerable, while in the case of a local company the expropriation or confiscation may affect the entire share capital of that company (and, therefore, on the principle described above, all assets owned by that company, including any subsidiary companies, whether or not local). Again it may well be possible to interpose a protective mechanism to protect assets of the company located elsewhere. If the legislating country is merely the host country where a foreign company is doing business, the expropriation or confiscation may reasonably be expected to affect only assets of the company having their situs in that host country, not the company itself.

In some countries it may not be necessary to adopt contrived protective mechanisms, however. Beginning in the early 1960s, a number of major European trading nations and the United States entered into bilateral agreements with many developing countries of a type designed to protect against political risk, in the host country, foreign investment emanating from the supposedly safe home country. Such agreements generally provide for fair compensation in the event of expropriation or nationalization and give guarantees of freedom to repatriate capital and profits subject to appropriate conditions. In 1967 the OECD produced a draft Convention on the Protection of Foreign Property and in 1972 the International Chamber of Commerce produced Guidelines on International Investments with the same objects in view. In addition, the European Community has entered into agreements with a number of countries.

Home risks (for the resident alien), foreign or outward investment risks (for the non-resident alien): investments in supposedly non-risk host countries becoming suject to freezing, vesting, expropriation or even confiscation under Trading with the Enemy legislation. This is the risk against which protective mechanisms have in the past been most widely used. It can result in both capital and profits of a locally- or foreign-owned business being locked in by the host country. The freezing of assets may be of such long term duration that, in the final analysis, it proves virtually if not equally as damaging as expropriation or confiscation would have been.

Companies owned or incorporated in countries which stand at risk of becoming, at some indeterminate time in the future, in conflict (whether at war or merely in diplomatic conflict, e.g. sanctions) with the prospective host country should consider ownership of their investment via an indirect entity such as an emergency trust. This consideration might also be regarded as important by third country joint venture investors or financiers who would be concerned to ensure that their investment was not jeopardised by future sanctions against the country of origin of their partner.

Recent examples of this type of risk include United States sanctions against interests emanting from Cuba, North Korea, China, Vietnam, Afghanistan, Iran, Libya, Iraq, and, of course, the sanctions against South Africa. Likewise, in 1982 the United Kingdom blocked Argentinian assets located in the United Kingdom and Argentina retaliated by blocking most United Kingdom assets located in Argentina. More recently, Iraqi assets in the United Kingdom and in other countries have been frozen.

Such sanctions are rationalized not only on the grounds of economic warfare but also, in many instances, with a view to protecting assets belonging to individuals resident in the foreign country concerned.

A crucial aspect of protection against risks of this nature is that arrangements should be in place to ensure that continued management of the business can be undertaken in the non-risk host country, by ensuring that the investment is structured in such a way that the provisions do not apply in the first place. If, for example, the business is managed by aliens of the non-risk host country who may themselves become *persona non grata* or whose movements from their home country may become restricted, two considerations arise. The first is that that fact of itself is likely to trigger the Trading with the Enemy provisions. The second is that, even if that does not occur, it is essential to have made provision for alternative management in the host country so that the business does not come to a grinding halt in the event of a crisis situation arising.

Home risks (for resident investors), foreign or outward investment risks (for inward investors): the imposition of exchange controls or investment restrictions in respect of local assets. Companies owned or domiciled in countries with unstable economies will be concerned to protect their local assets from becoming subject to home country expropriation or exchange controls. A version of emergency trust[24], located overseas, coupled with legitimate investment mechanisms, may provide the ability not only to protect against such controls but also to insulate (from the home country parent) foreign currency appreciation resulting from a crisis devaluation of their home country currency.

The imposition of new and/or penal or confiscatory taxes or the withdrawal, cancellation or restriction of current exemptions or reliefs without warning or

[24] Discussed below at pp. 209–11.

opportunity to take avoiding action. The principal means of guarding against such risks is to minimize the assets retained within resident entities, as far as possible diverting both capital and revenue resources to separately owned entities.

The imposition of a moratorium in respect of the obligations of state-owned banks. Again, the only possible advice must be to minimize exposure, if such an eventuality seems possible.

3. Assets at Risk

Having briefly reviewed the types of hazard to be guarded against it is appropriate to consider the principal types of asset which may be at risk. These include the following

1. Cash—domestic or foreign currency. It should be borne in mind that debts will normally have a legal situs where the debtor is resident[25] or the debt payable.[26]

2. Securities and other commercial investments. It should be borne in mind that the situs of bearer shares is normally where the share certificate is located, whereas that of registered shares is either where the company is incorporated or, if there is more than one share register, where the relevant share register is located.[27] It should be further borne in mind that in devising protective mechanisms it may be possible to refine the protective mechanism if classes of shares are issued having different rights; for example one class of shares may carry the right to dividends representing revenue profits while another class, which may be subject to a lock-away protective mechanism, could carry rights to capital profits and underlying principal. In this way profit and loss figures would flow through to the parent, whereas disposal or liquidation value could be preserved for the ultimate shareholders. A third class of shares could control voting rights as regards both distributions and winding up, the terms of which could ensure the accrual of profits to the parent under normal conditions but the diversion of underlying capital value in a crisis situation.

The possible permutations are of course virtually infinite and must be adapted to the particular circumstances of the group concerned. Furthermore, very careful consideration will need to be given to the taxation and reporting requirements resulting from the structure adopted.

3. Other financial instruments. Negotiable instruments, bonds, and

---

[25] *Swiss Bank Corporation* v. *Boehmische Industrial Bank* [1923] 1 KB 673; *Sutherland* v. *Administrator of German Property* (1933) 50 TLR 107.

[26] Specification of the place of payment is usually irrelevant (*Re Helbert Wagg & Co Ltd.*, supra) but if the debtor is resident in more than one country the situs will be where payment is made in the normal course of business (*Jabbour* v. *Custodian of Israeli Absentee Property* [1954] 1 WLR 139).

[27] *London and South American Investment Trust Limited* v. *British Tobacco Company (Australia) Limited* [1927] 1 Ch. 107; *R* v. *Williams* [1942] AC 541.

securities transferable by delivery are located where the instrument or document is to be found.[28]

4. Real estate and other fixed assets. In so far as these are located within the risk jurisdiction, the scope for their protection is limited. Possible approaches may include financing by means of local borrowing against the security of the property or assets concerned or, in certain circumstances, put options to sell for an external consideration.

5. Exported cargoes in transit, e.g. oil from Iran and Libya; copper from Chile.[29]

6. Ships. The location of ships will depend upon whether they are within territorial waters or on the high seas.[30]

7. Industrial property rights.[31] Although such rights are mentioned last, they are perhaps one of the most important categories of asset calling for protection.

Two rights are worthy of further comment in this context. The first is patents. During both the First and Second World Wars the United States made use of Trading with the Enemy legislation not only to inflict damage on Germany's industrial base in the long term but also to build up its own industries. In the First World War, for example, the United States chemical industry grew out of all proportion from its original size on the strength of German patents bought at bargain prices by the Chemical Foundation Inc., a corporation formed for the express purpose of acquiring patents from the Alien Property Custodian for the 'Americanization' and 'advancement of chemical and allied science and industry in the United States'. In 1926 the Supreme Court upheld the validity of such sales.[32] During the Second World War the United States confiscated many thousands of patents and also German-owned companies holding patents, and granted licences for their use to American companies for very low or nominal royalties. It should, however, be borne in mind that patents have a limited life, since they expire after the statutory period for which they may be registered in the relevant country concerned.

The second right worthy of further comment relates to trade marks and business names. Unlike patents, trade marks are renewable and, as we have noted, may be the life-blood of the business concerned. An example early in the present century relates to Chartreuse liqueur, which was distilled in France by the Carthusian monks. The monastic order was dissolved by French legislation, following which the monks moved to Spain, taking the

---

[28] *Winans* v. *AG* (No 2) [1910] AC 27; *AG* v. *Glendining* (1904) 92 LT 87; *Winans* v. *R* [1908] 1 KB 1022.

[29] For a discussion of the treatment of goods in transit see Cheshire and North, *Private International Law*, 800–1

[30] When within territorial waters, ships are situated where they are actually located (*Trustees, Executors and Agency Company Limited* v. *IRC* [1973] Ch. 254. When on the high seas, they are deemed to be situated at the port of registration.

[31] For a more detailed discussion, see Kolvenbach, *Protection of Foreign Investments, 421–36.*

[32] *United States* v. *The Chemical Foundation Inc*. 272 US 1, 11 Oct. 1926.

taking the process with them. Although their right to use their trademark outside France was challenged by the French liquidator of the original order, the monks were successful in several jurisdictions, including the United Kingdom, the United States, Switzerland, and Germany, in establishing the territorial nature of the trade marks in the geographical markets concerned and that the rights to their use could not be expropriated by another state.[33]

However, the territorial inviolability of trade marks and business names has by no means been consistently upheld—indeed, where precautions have not been taken by proper advance planning there have been many instances where expropriation of such assets has been unsuccessfully challenged. Examples of this have been the trade marks outside France of the Mumm Champagne Company, which had been expropriated during the First World War by the French government under Trading with the Enemy legislation, since the company was German-owned.

The Bayer name and trade mark were confiscated by the United States in the First World War, the company being German-owned, and it was only in the early 1970s that the Bayer company's attempts to recover their trade marks and the use of their trade name were finally concluded, subject to substantial payments by Bayer to the United States owner who had bought them many years before from the Alien Property Custodian. Likewise the Osram light bulb trade mark, which was expropriated in the First World War, was only re-acquired by the Osram Company within the 1980s, having been held by the English General Electric Company during most of the intervening period.

In litigation in the United States the courts have normally held that expropriations have not dispossessed the rights of former owners to use United States trade marks, thus confirming the territorial nature of such trade marks. This serves to emphasize the importance of not only registering trade marks in all relevant geographical market-places, but also, since the attitudes of various courts are inconsistent, of paying close attention to contractual arrangements as to the use of such trade marks and, indeed, of patents. If their use is to be by affiliated companies, it may be that ownership can be vested in a neutral entity (such as a protective trust) and licensed to the prospective user on terms enabling termination of the licence in certain prescribed circumstances. This will not, however, be possible in the case of all trade marks since the trade mark laws of many countries preclude their transfer other than in parallel with the business for which they have been registered. If this proves a practical obstacle in any particular instance, or if (as may be the case) there are other technical problems such as anti-trust laws, an alternative approach may be for the company owning the trade marks, or holding a licence to use them, to appoint an attorney whose power in respect of the industrial property rights concerned would survive an expropriation or confiscation of the company granting the power.

---

[33] *Lecouturier* v. *Rey* [1910] AC 262.

4. Choice of Mechanism

The nature of the protective mechanism to be selected will be dependent upon:

(i)   the nature and location of the assets to be protected;
(ii)   the possible actions of the host country, the home country, or even a third country; and
(iii)   the country of residence of the company concerned, of its beneficial owner(s), and of any affiliated companies at the time when the crisis occurs.

Turning now to the choice of protective mechanisms, the fundamental rule in setting them up is to ensure that the *underlying assets* are not held in any jurisdiction whose stability is suspect, if that can be avoided, whether or not the company (or a trust structure designed for its protection) is itself so located. Furthermore, the mechanism must ensure that the *legal right* to control the assets of the trust or company is removed from the volatile jurisdiction, *before* the emergency occurs. Where, however, a company has assets both within and outside the volatile jurisdiction, and may be capable of being treated as a split company, the assets outside the volatile jurisdiction should ideally be held in a separate entity or alternatively be the subject of a power of attorney enabling the external assets to be claimed on behalf of the shareholders.

Before a company creates an emergency trust, it is important to establish that the intended means of transferring the relevant assets will be *intra vires* and valid. This principle goes to the heart of one of Professor Schoenblum's main concerns, as I understand it, and I endorse his view by emphasizing that if this first condition cannot be satisfied, then no useful purpose will be served by seeking to establish an asset protection trust.[34]

The structure must be flexible and capable of variation or termination in the event of unforeseen circumstances or changes in the law and it must not be so cumbersome as to render impracticable the proper, efficient, and continuing administration of the business. The set-up and annual running costs must be justifiable in the light of the value of the assets being protected and the tax consequences of the mechanism, both on its creation and on its 'triggering', must be considered.

As regards secrecy, in some jurisdictions companies are required to file accounts. In few, if any, are trusts required to do so. Thus the trust mechanism has an additional advantage where non-disclosure might result in the avoidance of subsequent dispute. The non-disclosure should not of course ever be relied upon as a protective mechanism *per se* and should certainly not be adopted as a means of evading legitimate legal obligations. A further advantage of trusts is their additional flexibility in that they are more easily modified than is the case with companies.

[34] See *Williams & Humbert Ltd* v. *W & H Trade Marks (Jersey) Ltd* and *Rumasa SA* v. *Multinvest (UK) Ltd* [1986] AC 368.

In considering the choice of mechanism for corporate interests it would be relevant to consider the following questions.

(i)   What is the law of the relevant jurisdiction on such matters as reduction of capital, thin capitalization, share premium account?

(ii)   Can redeemable shares can be issued? If so, how can they be redeemed?

(iii)   Can bearer shares can be issued?

(iv)   Is the company a trading or investment company?

(v)   What constitutes a taxable distribution?

(vi)   How active is the company?

(vii)   Are its shareholders related or connected?

(viii)   What is its management structure?

(ix)   Does the company have (or is it likely to have) substantial creditors? Who are they?

(x)   Can the company change its 'domicile'?

(xi)   Can the company have directors resident in more than one jurisdiction?

5. Types of Mechanism

5.1 TRANSFER OF CORPORATE SEAT

One means of corporate protection is the transfer of the corporate seat. Different jurisdictions have different concepts of corporate residence, nationality and domicile. The concept of 'nationality' has little relevance to companies. In common law jurisdictions, a company is 'domiciled' in the country in which it was incorporated. For instance, under United Kingdom law, a company incorporated in the United Kingdom retains a United Kingdom domicile throughout its existence and this cannot be changed.[35] It is generally accepted that any purported change is deemed to effect a constructive dissolution.

In most civil law jurisdictions, the domicile of a company is determined by the location of its principal establishment or its *siège social effectif*, i.e. the centre of its administration. Under civil law there is, therefore, little distinction between the concepts of residence, nationality, and domicile. Under the civil law concept of domicile, a company is able to transfer its corporate seat from one country to another merely by moving its centre of administration. Alternatively, as in Italy, it may do so by resolution of a quorum of shareholders. Whether such a transfer will be sufficient to protect the assets of the corporation will be determined by the law of the jurisdiction in which an action to protect or claim those assets is brought or by the law which that country's conflict rules may apply.[36]

---

[35] *Gasque* v. *IRC* [1940] 2 KB 80.

[36] The potential conflict between the common law and civil law jurisdictions is evidenced by the Belgian case of *W Lamot* v. *Societe Lamot Limited*, Cour de Cassation 12.11.65 No 5321, in which a company which had moved its Head Office and centre of administration from England

The companies legislation of a number of jurisdictions contains specific provision dealing with the ability of companies incorporated in that jurisdiction to transfer their corporate seat to another jurisdiction or for companies incorporated in another jurisdiction to immigrate and be treated as if they had been incorporated in the accepting jurisdiction.

The legislation differs from country to country in a number of respects.

(i)   Most such countries will allow emigration if the prior consent of a governmental authority is obtained and proper notices (for the protection of creditors) are given. However, in the British Virgin Islands, for example, a directors' or members' resolution is sufficient.[37]

(ii)   Some jurisdictions will only allow emigration to particular jurisdictions.[38]

(iii)   There are limited provisions relating to corporate migration in the laws of other European countries.[39]

(iv)   A number of 'accepting jurisdictions' require the consent of the jurisdiction from which the company has emigrated.[40]

(v)   Some 'accepting jurisdictions' are prepared to adopt a stand-by procedure enabling the formalities to be completed in advance so that, upon the occurrence of an emergency, the transfer of corporate seat can take place as speedily as possible.[41]

(vi)   The British Virgin Islands will recognise the immigration of a company notwithstanding non-recognition of its emigration by the source country.[42] Other jurisdictions have introduced or are in the course of introducing similar provisions.

(vii)   Certain jurisdictions, while not specifically providing for a company to transfer its corporate seat, allow an effective transfer inwards by enabling a foreign corporation to merge with a domestic corporation.[43]

(viii) The efficacy of a transfer of corporate seat is likely to be tested in the courts of the country where the corporation's assets are situated and thus, in a country where the theory of a split company is recognised by the courts, such as in Germany, the migration of the domicile of the company itself may accordingly be unnecessary.

5.2. The Emergency or 'Wartime' Trust

The emergency trust was a concept originally developed to protect against Trading with the Enemy legislation, for example the United States Philips

to Belgium was held to be subject to both Belgian and English law.

[37] Article 88 of The International Business Companies Ordinance 1984.
[38] e.g. The Netherlands to The Netherlands Antilles.
[39] Such as Belgium, Luxemburg, France, and Switzerland.
[40] e.g. Nauru.
[41] e.g. Antigua, the British Virgin Islands, and the Turks and Caicos Islands.
[42] s. 84(2) of the International Business Companies Ordinance 1984.
[43] e.g. s. 10.5 of the Liberian Business Corporation Act 1976.

Trust. While it is still used for that purpose, it is now also used to protect against the following:

(i)   expropriation or exchange controls in respect of the overseas assets of a corporation by the government of its home country;

(ii)   the protection of a holding company's assets in an offshore risk jurisdiction;

(iii)   the potential inability of individual managers to leave the home country to manage overseas investments; and

(iv)   risks potentially threatened against inward investments into a risk country, beneficially owned by a company or investors in a more secure country.

The mechanism commonly involves the transfer of some or all of the assets of the company to a trustee which, during the 'peacetime' period, holds the assets primarily for the benefit of the company. It is vital to ensure that this transfer is permissible and validly effected. On the occurrence of an 'emergency' (whether objectively defined in the trust instrument and/or determined by a Protector or Advisory Committee), the emergency trust provisions bite and thereafter the assets are held by the trustee for the benefit of the shareholders or of an entity capable of benefiting the same shareholders. Any such other structure would be situated in another jurisdiction.

The trustee should be a company incorporated and resident in a different jurisdiction, and legal title to the assets should be transferred to the trustee upon creation of the trust. The identity and location of the trustee must be carefully chosen, in order to avoid encountering the same problem at one remove. A particularly secure type of trustee, as well suited as any for the trusteeship of emergency trusts, is what has become known as an International Trust Corporation or ITC.[44]

Regard must be had to the common law principle of maintenance of capital,[45] which developed in order to afford a measure of protection to creditors of a company. In any case where, on the creation of an emergency trust, the company will be effectively giving away some or all of its assets (not necessarily always the case) it should be considered whether the members of the company need to give their consent; further, the terms of the trust should protect creditors, so that the expropriatory authority cannot allege that the declaration of the trust was either *ultra vires* or fraudulent, i.e. with a view to defeating the company's creditors. It may be somewhat more difficult to structure an emergency trust for a trading company than for an investment holding company, in regard both to creditor protection and to ease of administration.

Since it is essential that the trust should not be held void for uncertainty of objects, care will need to be taken in defining the beneficiaries, especially in

---

[44] Discussed below in section 7.
[45] *Trevor* v. *Whitworth* (1887) 12 App. Cas. 409.

cases where the company is not closely owned, where the shares are dealt in on a stock exchange, or where there are bearer shares in issue.

The emergency trust should not provide that, upon the occurrence of an emergency, the shareholders in the company become absolutely entitled to the assets of the trust, as this may result in adverse tax consequences for the shareholders. Where Trading with the Enemy legislation is applicable, such a provision might actually bring such legislation into play even if there is only one enemy alien amongst the shareholders. Alternatively, where changes in the home-country legislation of some or all of the shareholders is one of the risks sought to be guarded against, their freedom to benefit from an absolute interest is likely to be impaired. The trust should be capable of continuing in existence after the state of emergency has arisen.[46]

It must always be borne in mind that, especially in the case of a publicly quoted company, it will normally be necessary to refer to the existence of an emergency trust in the company's accounts or in any prospectus. This is a perfectly acceptable and understandable procedure, though in some jurisdictions it may be desirable to camouflage the reference as far as possible.

5.3. Conditional Sale of Assets to a Mirror Company

A conditional sale of assets to a mirror company may be an appropriate mechanism for a trading company in respect of which an emergency trust is unworkable; however there are formidable drafting problems in ensuring that the agreement will become unconditional (and legal title pass) prior to the occurrence of the emergency.

5.4. Redeemable Preference Shares

The companies legislation of a number of tax havens is based originally on the Companies Act 1929 of the United Kingdom. The relevant provisions of each country's legislation concerning reduction of capital and the ability to issue redeemable shares, or the purchase by a company of its own shares, needs to be considered individually, the status of the share premium account being all-important.

Subject to the suitability of the relevant legislation, Redeemable Preference Shares may be issued; this entails the inclusion in the Articles of the company of a power to issue preference shares, redeemable at the discretion of the holder for the time being of those shares and/or of the directors upon the lodgement of a valid redemption notice, together with the relevant share certificate, at a suitable place outside the jurisdiction in which the company is incorporated. Redemption notices should be lodged by the holder immediately but should be expressed to take effect on the occurrence of an emergency, which would be defined to include not only certain specified events but also the receipt of an appropriate notice from a Protector or non-

---

[46] In this connection, beware the rule in *Saunders* v. *Vautier* (1841) Cr. & Ph. 240.

resident director, nominated by the directors of the company for this purpose.

If one is dealing with a jurisdiction which still rigidly applies the maintenance of capital principle, it may be worthwhile considering whether the laws of that jurisdiction allow preference shares to be redeemed at a premium if issued at a premium, or at all.

5.5. PARALLEL OR TWINNED COMPANIES

Where a mirror company is required (e.g. as beneficiary of an emergency trust, or under a conditional sale mechanism, share twinning or stapled stock of the kind normally used for withholding tax purposes may be adapted to requirements. Very briefly this entails provisions designed to ensure that the transfer of shares or shares of a class in one company are only capable of transfer together with corresponding shares or shares of a class in another company. The other company may be a subsidiary of the first—the arrangement being designed to provide dividend income access from a different jurisdiction, more tax-efficiently for the shareholders concerned— or it may be a sister company.

In the case of a sale to a mirror company, for example, the acquiring company would enter into an arrangement with the disposing company whereby it would issue special preference shares to the shareholders of the disposing company, conferring the right to elect to receive any distributions either from the disposing company or from the acquiring company. These shares and the shares in the disposing company would be twinned or stapled for transfer purposes. This type of arrangement is obviously impractical in any case where a company wishes to set up effective mechanisms on a secret basis.

A public example of twinning was the Nestlé Group, which in 1936 was twinned with a Panamanian company, Unilac Inc., although this arrangement has subsequently ceased. The purpose of the arrangement was to provide protection against political risks and the nature of the twinning was that the rights in the common stock of the main company were dependent upon the corresponding bearer shares being attached to the certificate for the registered shares.

Likewise stapled stock was issued[47] on the merger of SmithKline Beckman of the United States and SmithKline Beecham of the UK. 'Equity Units' in SmithKline Beecham were issued as stapled stock to US shareholders in SmithKline Beckman at the time of the merger. Although these units will shortly become convertible into shares, the company has said that it will not exercise its right to convert, so the arrangement will continue for the foreseeable future. A plan on the part of British Petroleum to issue stapled shares in its subsidiary, Britoil, to save Advance Corporation Tax, was blocked by the announcement[48] of legislation to eliminate the tax advantage

---

[47] In 1989.   [48] In May 1991.

of such an arrangement. These examples illustrate that the concept of stapled stock or share twinning is well established.

It perhaps goes without saying that it is most desirable for tax purposes that if a parallel structure is to be adopted it should be put in place before the businesses become too valuable; the tax consequences of the necessary transfer of assets may otherwise be too high a price to pay for the results achievable by this method, though in some cases it might be possible to devise an alternative solution.

5.6. CONTRACTUAL DUAL STRUCTURES

A variation of the parallel company can be devised by contractual means, such as is the case with the United Kingdom and Dutch Unilever businesses. These businesses are effectively unified by means of contractual arrangements but there are two quite separate parent companies, the chairmen of which, for example, regard themselves as joint chairmen of the whole.[49] The shares are not twinned, but shareholders in one company possess equivalent rights to those in the other company, such rights being accomplished by means of a so-called Equalization Agreement. The shares of Unilever plc are listed in London and, as American Depositary Receipts, in New York. The shares or certificates (depositary receipts) of Unilever NV are listed in Amsterdam, London, New York, Austria, Belgium, France, Germany, Luxemburg and Switzerland. From this it will be seen that, unlike twinned shares, the shares in each company have a separate life of their own.

5.7. OTHER MECHANISMS

Other mechanisms which may be used include the use of a voting trust, where share ownership may prove a threat under Trading with the Enemy legislation, but it is vital to ensure in this case that the arrangements are so structured as to provide for co-ordinated management.

Specialized means of employing corporate assets may be devised which may exploit exchange rate or commodity volatility, or other risk elements. Thus, when the crisis to be guarded against occurs, the effect of the investment structure is to divert the exchange difference or commodity fluctuation into a separate beneficial ownership chain, to the advantage of the ultimate beneficial owners. Great care must be taken in these instances to ensure that such arrangements are not in conflict with the corporate or other laws of the home or host country.

6. Trustees

The stability of the trustee of any emergency trust structure is, of course, a prerequisite. As we have noted,[50] certain jurisdictions allow a company

---

[49] The chairman of Unilever plc (English) is vice-chairman of Unilever NV (Dutch), and vice versa

[50] At p. 209.

incorporated in that jurisdiction to emigrate and continue in another jurisdiction (which is prepared to accept such immigrating company) as if the company had been incorporated under the laws of that other jurisdiction, so that the laws of the first jurisdiction cease to apply. However, many of the statutory provisions do not allow a company to change its corporate base instantaneously. Any requirement to apply for consent or to serve notice will render the provision of no assistance in the circumstances with which this chapter is concerned.

It is possible in certain jurisdictions (notably Canada, and more particularly the provinces of New Brunswick and Prince Edward Island) to apply to the Legislature of that jurisdiction for a private Act to be passed conferring on the company the ability to emigrate. The advantage of such an Act is that it can be drafted in such a way as to ensure that the emigration can be effected speedily. Naturally, the expense of obtaining a private Act of the relevant Legislature is beyond the means of most trustees. However, a few International Trust Corporations (ITCs) have gone to this expense and, to illustrate the extra measure of protection that such a trust corporation can offer, we shall analyse the structure of one of these trust companies.

The company concerned was originally incorporated by a private Act of the New Brunswick Legislature. A private Act was necessary as the Foreign Resident Corporations Act only permitted emigration 'in time of war or other emergency'. The company is owned (and correspondingly controlled) by six shareholders—all major international banks—resident in various countries. As a result, shareholder control does not lie in any one jurisdiction and any pressure exerted on the shareholders by the authorities in those countries will have no effect unless it is concerted. For Canadian tax reasons, no trust administration takes place in Canada.

All administration is carried out by branches, which are located in some seven trust jurisdictions where there is an established common law tradition of trusts. It is important that the local branches are seen to be properly established so that there is no argument that any trust administered by such branches is in fact a Canadian trust. The place of administration can be moved from one branch to another speedily and without reference to the manager of the local branch where the trust is currently administered. Duplicate records are maintained elsewhere than in the country in which a trust is currently being administered, so that continuity is assured and confiscation or destruction of such records is of no consequence. The income of the trusts under administration is not liable to Canadian federal taxes nor is there any requirement to report details of such income to the Canadian authorities.

It is suggested that such a structure affords the best protection of the trustee's functional integrity currently available. Canada must be considered a more stable jurisdiction than any tax haven but there is the ability to relocate the trust company speedily should the need arise. The administration of trusts is carried out in tax havens, thus ensuring favourable tax treatment, but such administration can be switched speedily without involving a change of trustee. Maintenance of duplicate records ensures continuity.

Such a structure is not cheap to maintain and accordingly an ITC's charges tend to be higher than those of conventional trust companies. For trusts with substantial assets, as will always be the case with corporate emergency trusts, the additional protection is likely to be worth the additional cost.

7. Conclusion

In conclusion, it is suggested that it is unwise for any company with substantial assets, operating internationally, not to give serious consideration to the use of protective mechanisms. The retention of *de facto* control over the assets of the trust or company is essential for practical commercial purposes but, if an expropriatory action ever has to be considered in the courts, it must be possible to show that *legal title* to the relevant assets has been transferred by the trust or company subject to the expropriatory decree *before the decree became effective*.

No mechanism is guaranteed to work and much will depend upon the law of the country in which the action is brought. This is likely to be the country in which the assets are situate. Notwithstanding the general uncertainty as to the efficacy of protective mechanisms, the courts are likely to have sympathy for trusts or companies that have taken legally valid steps to protect themselves against expropriatory action.

11

THE ADAPTATION OF THE ASSET PROTECTION TRUST FOR USE BY THE MULTINATIONAL CORPORATION: THE AMERICAN PERSPECTIVE

Jeffrey Schoenblum

1. Introduction

During major international conflagrations and internal political disruptions in the past, corporate and individual capital has sought refuge in the United States and, to a lesser extent, the offshore Caribbean Islands. The conditions that have fostered the flight of capital to these jurisdictions persist and, thus, there is a continuing demand for fail-safe mechanisms for the preservation of the assets of corporations operating around the world.[1]

The common law trust has been regarded by some as an instrumentality that is capable of assuring the protection of such capital, while preserving flexibility of management and perpetuating corporate control, even though the corporation itself may be under siege. A careful analysis suggests, however, that there needs to be far more evolution in the law and focus on the underlying problem before one can truly claim this new role for the trust. Presently, the asset protection trust may actually be less appealing in many situations than the alternative of inaction or reliance upon certain other protective devices discussed in Chapter 10.

The focus of this chapter is on the United States. It functions as a giant receptacle for assets from abroad. The United States and the sovereign island nations offshore serve as well as the administistive centres for trusts and other entities. The purpose of many of these entities is to hold and administer assets already invested in the United States and, possibly, elsewhere in the Western Hemisphere. The purpose of others is to exist in a dormant state, to stand by until a specified emergency arises that triggers the transfer of assets to the waiting trust or other management vehicle.

[1] This chapter focuses exclusively on non-tax matters. While tax considerations are beyond the scope of this chapter, they do play an extremely important role in structuring asset protection vehicles.

Six fundamental assumptions are often made in connection with the use of trusts in North American havens as asset protection vehicles:

(1) that the local law of the American trust situs, rather than the law of an undesirable jurisdiction, such as the corporate domicile, will invariably apply to issues of trust creation, administration, and construction;[2]

(2) that American and English trust law are compatible, coherent bodies of law, yielding predictable outcomes and that the recent Hague Convention on the Law Applicable to Trusts and on their Recognition will assure the extension of this system of law to civil law systems in which multinational corporations have assets and operations;[3]

(3) that illegal or offensive foreign Acts will not be given effect by American courts with respect to trust assets situated in the United States;[4]

(4) that the American trust can afford protection for corporate assets and operations situated in third countries;[5]

(5) that local American law is itself invariably favourable and protective of trust assets, as well as facilitative of the proper operation of the multinational enterprise;[6] and

(6) that the protective trust, if properly conceived, can be drafted and implemented without undue practical impediments.[7]

The subsequent sections of this chapter consider these assumptions in depth and demonstrate that they are largely exaggerated, if not faulty.

2. Choice of Law

The fact that a trust is situated and administered from the United States or some other North American jurisdiction does not assure that the hostile law jurisdiction from which corporate assets or equity have fled will be avoided. In many instances, the real possibility exists that the American state in which a trust is being administered will apply the law of the corporate domicile, thereby defeating the very purpose of the asset protection trust. In some instances, the common law jurisdiction will be required to ignore the trust altogether, because the country that is having its law applied does not recognize the trust.

2.1. AMERICAN CHOICE OF LAW IN GENERAL

Trust law in the United States is not national in character, but has developed independently in each of the fifty states. While there are common threads that run through these autonomous laws, the consequence of independent

---

[2] See below, text accompanying nn. 7–91.
[3] See below, text accompanying nn. 91–146.
[4] See below, text accompanying nn. 147–76.
[5] See ibid. and below, text accompanying nn. 271–3.
[6] See below, text accompanying nn. 177–220.
[7] See below, text accompanying nn. 221 ff.

judicial decision-making and statutory enactments has been a variety of outcomes on a wide range of issues. Thus, even if a trust is situated within the United States, and trust assets are as well, unless they are all in one state, there will be a multistate dimension to the governing law issue, in addition to the inevitable multinational issue.[8]

A second point of significance with respect to American choice of law is that certain states, traditionally more international in their economic orientation, have sought to market themselves as trust havens.[9] These few states stand in sharp contrast to the majority of states, which have adhered woodenly to less favourable choice of law rules.

Third, broad generalizations cannot safely be drawn about choice of law rules applied by various states with regard to *inter vivos* trusts. Great care must be exercised in identifying and properly characterizing the issues likely to arise. Without such analysis, it will be impossible to predict the outcome should the transfer of assets to the trust, its validity, or its administration ultimately be challenged.

Finally, a conflicts revolution and current counter-revolution, which have shaken American choice of law theory in areas such as contracts and tort law, have largely left trust choice of law unscathed. That choice of law is, however, currently under some challenge.[10] There can be no assurance that the choice of law principles prevalent today will still be the dominant ones years down the road when the asset protection trust is called upon to perform its intended function.

Having taken these essential considerations into account, the remaining portion of this segment of the chapter deals with the particular issues of choice of law raised by the asset protection trust for the multinational corporation and how they are addressed in American jurisprudence.[11]

2.2. The Choice of Law Problem: An Overview

The basic choice of law problem with *inter vivos* trusts of personal property has been posed succinctly by Professor Scott, perhaps the foremost American

[8] For detailed consideration of the multistate dimension, see J. Schoenblum, *Multistate and Multinational Estate Planning* (1982 and 1991 Supp.) ch. 17. Portions of this section of the Chapter are derived in part from ch. 17. See also E. Scoles and P. Hay, *Conflict of Laws* (1984), ch. 21.

[9] See e.g. below, text accompanying n. 41.

[10] See Restatement (Second), Conflict of Laws (1971) (hereinafter referred to as the Restatement). In an effort to accommodate diverse trends, the Restatement sets forth a series of traditionally accepted rules, but also takes account of gravity of contacts and governmental interests considerations.

[11] In addition to choice of law, matters of jurisdiction, *forum non conveniens*, and enforcement of judgments may play central roles. Although these topics are beyond the scope of this chapter, they are not likely to work in favour of aggrieved companies and investors. Indeed, American courts might not even afford a forum. See Foreign Sovereign Immunities Act, 28 USC s. 1601 ff. See also *Islamic Republic of Iran* v. *Pahlevi*, 62 NY 2d 474, 467 NE 2d, 245, 478 NYS 2d, 597 (1984), *cert. denied*, 469 US 1108 (1985). A recent extensive analysis suggests substantial barriers to suits against foreign sovereigns for acts of expropriation. See M. Gordon, *Foreign State Immunity in Commercial Transactions* (1991), ch. 11.

scholar of trust law. In determining which jurisdiction's law to apply, the forum faces the following conundrum:

Should it be the state of the situs of each of the assets included in the trust estate at the time of its creation, if they have a situs? Or should the law of one state be applicable to all of the assets no matter where they are situated? If so, the law of what state should be applicable? Should it be the law of the settlor's domicile at the time of the creation of the trust? Should it be the law of the place of execution of the trust instrument? Should it be the law of the domicile of the beneficiary? Should it be the law of the forum? Should it be the law of the state, if any, in which the trust is to be administered? Is it material whether the settlor expressly or impliedly designates the law of a particular state as that of the applicable law? Does the application depend upon the ground for invalidity, so that the law of one state may be applied to one issue of validity and the law of another state applied to another issue? Should the court apply the law of a state which renders the trust or a provision of the trust valid, rather than that of a state which would render it invalid? Finally, if the law of a particular state is held to be applicable, should it be the local law of that state or should it be the whole law of the state?[12]

Many of these questions remain unanswered and thus raise serious doubts about reliance on the trust device to protect assets, whether of an individual or corporation. While general guidance may be ascertainable on some questions with regard to trusts created by individuals, so little attention has been paid to trusts created by corporate settlors that few, if any, safe conclusions can be drawn. This is particularly the case when the matters are international, and jurisdictions with diverse trust jurisprudence and conflicts rules or no trust jurisprudence and minimal conflicts rules in the trust realm are involved.

This portion of the chapter will not focus in great detail on immovables. In American jurisprudence the nearly uniform choice of law rule is that the law of the situs controls.[13] While there have been certain departures from this rule, especially where personal jurisdiction is obtained over the trustee or other relevant parties,[14] the assumption ordinarily should be that the law of the situs of a fixed asset will be applied by the forum. Thus, while a corporation may be viewed as a unitary economic entity, the attempt to protect its assets by the application of a single, favourable law may be thwarted by a scission in choice of law between movables and immovables and the unwillingness of the situs of the immovable to give effect to a foreign judgment regarding the immovable asset's fate.

[12] See A. Scott, *The Law of Trusts*, rev. Fratcher (1989) s. 597, at 298, Professor Scott was the principal architect of modern American trust law. His treatise, which has recently been updated, continued to exercise considerable influence among lawyers and judges. Professor Scott also played a vital role in the drafting of the Restatement's provisions on trusts. Accordingly, his work is often regarded as having authoritative significance.

[13] See Restatement, Topic 2, Land, prefatory to s. 276, at 203.

[14] See e.g. discussion and cases cited in Restatement s. 276, Comment b and Reporter's note.

2.3. TRANSFERS INTO TRUST

When a single asset is conveyed outright, the local law of the situs at the time of the transfer generally governs the validity of that transfer.[15] This is true of movables as well as immovables. A severe problem is presented by this choice of law principle. Some assets may not be deemed validly transferred to the trust, while others may be, depending on the law on conveyances to trusts of the country in which the asset is originally situated. Furthermore, the forum's choice of law rules regarding characterization of the asset and identification of its situs will prove crucial, as will the existence of an opportunity to move the asset from an invalidating to a validating jurisdiction prior to transfer to the trust. The drawing into the trust of assets from diverse jurisdictions could present additional difficulties were a challenge to be subsequently mounted. Reinvestments and gains would have to be traced back to ascertain their source in what might well prove a complex, if not impossible, task.

To the extent that shares or other evidences of equity ownership are placed in trust, the foregoing problem may not be as pronounced. If shares transferred are those of a single corporation, the conveyance law of one jurisdiction, the corporate domicile, is likely to be applied to determine the validity of the transfer. However, if it is an inhospitable jurisdiction, and a change of corporate domicile was not a viable option, the adverse law of the corporate domicile may be unavoidable, thus preventing a valid transfer of share into trust in a safe haven.

2.4. SUBSTANTIVE VALIDITY

Which jurisdiction's law will determine the validity of the trust itself? To the extent that immovables, such as buildings and land, are involved, the law of the situs will control, with certain exceptions.[16] The traditional view, expressed in the maxim *mobilia sequuntur personam*,[17] was that movables, everything from shares to bank accounts to intellectual property, precisely because of their mobility, had no fixed situs. Because control over the location of movables could largely be determined by the owner, the law of his domicile was considered appropriate to control his movable wealth.[18]

This reliance on the law of the settlor's domicile has largely been repudiated in the trust area in the United States.[19] Recognizing the increasing mobility of individuals, many courts have tended to look to the situs of administration. This appears to be a sensible course. Nevertheless, the Restatement §270(b), influenced by developments in areas of choice of

---

[15] Scott, above, n. 12, at 299.

[16] See Restatement s. 278.

[17] That is, the movables are deemed to follow the owner and to be governed by the law of his domicile.

[18] See Scott, above n. 12, s. 597, at 300.

[19] See e.g. *Hutchison* v. *Ross*, 262 NY 381, 187 NE 65 (1933).

law where predictability is not as vital, introduces a process-oriented approach. In other words, the law of the jurisdiction with 'the most significant relationship' is to be applied. Restatement §6 sets forth the factors is to be relied upon in determining the jurisdiction with the 'most significant relationship'.[20] The analysis involved here assures little predictability. Thus, it may be establishing a more flexible choice of law process at the very high price of impracticability and unpredictability.

When considering the appropriate choice of law rule for a corporation, the distinctive character of this entity suggests, however, that the traditional respect accorded the law of the domicile may hold sway. Corporations are creatures of state law. They are firmly rooted in the jurisdiction from which they derive their legal status. Change of domicile cannot be as easily effectuated as in the case of individuals who, at least theoretically, have certain internationally recognized 'human' rights in this regard. Under these circumstances, the law of the corporate domicile might be relied upon to determine the substantive validity of the trust. Certainly, to the extent that a settlor corporation explicitly or implicitly retains control over the trust, the corporate domicile is likely to be regarded as the strongest, most sustained nexus, and its law applied. This would present severe problems for a corporation that had established the trust for the purpose of avoiding the expropriatory or other hostile laws of the jurisdiction of corporate domicile, but insists on retaining control.

One further option sometimes considered is that the intent of the corporate settlor ought to control, and its choice of law should prevail. However, even if this rule were followed, the manifestation of that intent may give rise to very practical problems. For example, in explaining in the trust instrument its intent to have the law of some other jurisdiction apply, the corporation could not openly set forth its concerns about political instability at its domicile.[21] Otherwise, its status at home could be undermined, as might be the transfer into trust.

In the current atmosphere of uncertainty as to the proper choice of law rule or process in matters of trust validity, the place of execution of the trust instrument has also been deemed a relevant factor. The rationale for reference to this factor is not clear. The validity of a trust should not hinge on the law of the place of execution when that place was selected fortuitously or simply as a means of avoiding the restrictive provisions of a jurisdiction

---

[20] These factors include the needs of the interstate and international system; the relevant policies of other states and their interest in having their law applied to the particular issue; the protection of party expectations; the basic policies underlying the particular field of law; the objectives of certainty, predictability, and uniformity of result; and the ease of determining and applying the law previously identified as applicable. See also Hay and Scoles, above n. 8, s. 2.13. Among other cases taking a gravity of contacts or most significant relationship approach, see *First National Bank* v. *Shawmut Bank*, 378 Mass. 137, 389 NE 2d 1002 (1979) and *Ford* v. *Newman*, 77 Ill. 2d 335, 396 NE 2d 539 (1979). See also *Rudow* v. *Fogel*, 12 Mass. App. 430, 426 NE 2d, 155 (1981).

[21] See below, text accompany nn. 268–70 relating to the statement of trust purposes.

having a greater connection with the trust over the long term.[22] Certainly, with regard to contracts, the place of execution has largely been abandoned as a choice of law talisman. Nevertheless, reliance on this factor suggests the considerable planning that must enter into the process of settling the asset protection trust and the great weight that may be accorded certain formal details. Indeed, the less familiar a jurisdiction is with the trust as a legal construct, the more likely its courts are to take a hypertechnical approach in analysing validity. Especially if the place of execution is also the corporate domicile, the scales could be tipped in favour of the jurisdiction's law being applied.

One final factor that is occasionally taken into account is the domicile of the beneficiaries. This factor is mentioned in §269 of the Restatment as establishing the trust's substantial relation with a jurisdiction. As was noted in Chapter 10 and is discussed later in this chapter,[23] the shareholders of the parent corporation seeking to establish an asset protection trust are typically its beneficiaries. If these beneficiaries were a relevant choice of law factor, the validity of the trust might be contingent on any number of domiciles, each of which would be subject to constant change. Furthermore, the domiciles of unborn or unascertained beneficiaries for whose benefit shares were held in trust could not possibly be anticipated at the time of the asset protection trust's creation or initial administration. Moreover, the trust might be valid with regard to some benefciaries but not with regard to those in countries refusing to recognize trust validity.

It would seem fair, then, to state the general 'American' approach to the validity of *inter vivos* trusts of movables as follows: the principal elements for consideration are the place of administration, the domicile of the settlor, the situs of the corpus, and the place of execution of the trust instrument. Typically, the greatest weight will be given to the place of administration, but many courts will not consider this factor conclusive.[24] For these courts, the process may well be one of identifying the state that has the most significant contacts with or governmental interest in the trust. Of course, no clear-cut method for evaluating the relative weights of various contacts or interests has yet been developed. Here, corporate domicile or subsidiary and marginal factors such as the domicile of beneficiaries may prove decisive. In a positive vein, courts have been inclined to emphasize those factors which will result in the application of a law that validates the trust.

Of course, little will have been accomplished if a law is applied that validates the trust, but the majority of corporate shareholder-trust beneficiaries remain under the control of a hostile authority. That authority can

[22] See generally Cavers, 'Trusts Inter Vivos and the Conflict of Laws', 44 Harv. LR 161 (1930). See also Note, 'Trusts of Movables in the Conflict of Laws', (1961) 36 NYULR, 713; Note, 'Trusts of Personalty and Conflict of Laws' (1941) 89 U. Pa LR 360.

[23] See e.g. below, text accompanying nn. 289–90.

[24] See e.g. *Wilmington Trust Co.* v. *Wilmington Trust Co.* 26 Del. Ch. 397, 24 A. 2d, 309 (1942).

accomplish indirectly by way of power over equity what it could not achieve through direct acts of expropriation or the like.[25] Moreover, the very fact that beneficiaries are subject to the authority of a hostile power may not engender a sympathetic American response. If the country is also in conflict with the United States, the United States may vest or freeze whatever interests it can reach in the corporation or its controlled trust.[26]

Finally, it should be recognized that a choice of law rule that looks to the law of the corporate domicile permits courts to avoid deciding controversial issues relating to the propriety of a foreign government's expropriatory action. For example, if the corporate domicile's law is controlling, and that law does not recognize trusts, an American trust created by the corporation could be held invalid by an American forum applying the foreign law. The property, at least if it is intangible, will then have no substantial connection with the United States, and there will be no basis for applying a validating rule that conflicts with the law of the country from which the corporation derives its existence or in which its seat is located.[27]

2.5. INDIVIDUAL VERSUS CORPORATE TRUSTEE AND INSTABILITY AT THE SITUS OF ADMINISTRATION

Often, the jurisdiction in which a corporate trustee is organized and doing business will be considered the place of administration. When an individual trustee is involved, the place of administration will typically be his domicile. However, the trustee's domicile may be assigned less weight under these circumstances, since an individual is likely to move about far more than a corporate trustee. Moreover, the trustee's personal domicile is more likely to differ from the place where the trust is managed.[28] Ordinarily, a corporate settlor will not utilize individual trustees. None the less, there is a significant history of the use of individuals who are highly placed present and former corporate officers or members of the board of directors to constitute a governing committee that functions as a co-trustee or in a directory capacity.[29] To the extent that such individuals play an active role in the affairs of the trust, their domiciles may also be taken into account, thereby creating difficulties in pinpointing the situs of trust administration.

Despite the difficulties associated with the appointment of individual fiduciaries, the utilization of a sole corporate trustee is problematic as well. To the extent that a corporate trustee is constrained in changing its domicile when circumstances warrant, corporate assets will face an additional risk.

[25] See also text accompanying nn. 55, 82, and 163.

[26] See below, text accompanying nn. 177–220.

[27] For a comparison of common and civil law concepts of corporate domicile, see Hadari, 'The Choice of National Law Applicable to the Multinational Enterprise and the Nationality of Such Enterprises', (1974) *Duke LJ* 1. The common law tends to emphasize place of incorporation, while the civil law focuses on the corporate seat.

[28] See Scott, above, n. 12, s. 612, at 351.

[29] See below, text accompanying n. 239.

The exposure of corporate assets is increased by the introduction on to the scene of a corporate trustee, because the trustee may also be subject to expropriatory acts at *its* home, just as the settlor faces this prospect at its corporate domicile. The difficulties associated with the transfer of a corporate domicile makes this added risk most pertinent. Accordingly, the creation of a trust in a foreign jursidiction may thus be a source of danger as well as protection for the multinational corporation.

To avoid the risk of governmental intrusion at the trustee's domicile, great care has gone into developing a structure for some highly sophisticated trusts for individuals which have multiple corporate trustees in several different countries. Administration is shared, but may be eliminated from one trustee, as a result of certain undesirable occurrences at its situs. This structure may, in fact, accomplish its goal and is discussed in Chapter 10 by Harry Wiggin, who played an instrumental role in its development. Alternatively, a strategy may be pursued of situating assets and administration in a perceived safe haven, such as the United States, with the thought that its laws are favourable and the trustee will never have to move. This is the United States Philips Trust model for corporate assets.[30] Modern American history, however, suggests that the perception that an American trustee will be absolutely safe from governmental interference is simply incorrect.[31]

2.6. THE RULE OF TRUST VALIDATION VERSUS PUBLIC POLICY CONCERNS AT THE SITUS OF ADMINISTRATION

American courts have sought, on the whole, to follow a rule of validation in the case of *inter vivos* trusts of movables. Still, the view that a strong affront to public policy should outweigh a general interest in validating trusts has been adopted by a number of courts. For example, this has been the stance of the New York courts when trusts have been used to deny spouses their otherwise lawful rights.[32]

The potential invocation of 'public policy' is troublesome for other reasons as well. Public policy changes over time and this would seem especially true with regard to attitudes toward large, multinational corporations in a local economy. Thus, there is no way to assure the continued validity of the trust. Moreover, the absence of public policy concerns at the state level does not mean that they will not arise at the national level, especially if American foreign policy is involved. Indeed, national policy concerns have sometimes involved the endorsement of foreign expropriations.[33]

Finally, a fundamental distinction between individuals and corporations drawn earlier should be reiterated. A local American forum may be less concerned with the 'property rights' of corporations, inasmuch as they derive

---

[30] See below, text accompanying nn. 221 ff. for an in-depth consideration of this trust.
[31] See below, text accompanying nn. 177 ff.
[32] See e.g. *Hutchinson* v. *Ross*, 262 NY 381, 187 NE 65 (1933).
[33] See below, text accompanying nn. 150–1.

their legal being from a particular jurisdiction, and do not have internationally observed or 'fundamental human rights', as do individuals.

2.7. The Settlor's Specification of the Law Governing the Trust

The foregoing discussion has assumed that no specification of governing law has been made by the settlor with regard to matters of validity. If such a designation is made, it will usually be given effect by a court.[34] This ability to prescribe the law governing a trust is central to the success of any asset protection trust. By specifying the governing law, many of the uncertainties of choice of law described above can largely be eliminated.

The reason offered in the multistate American context for deference to the settlor's choice of law is that the settlor could have transferred the moveables in order to assure that the trust would be administered in a particular jurisdiction. The fact that he has not done so should not affect the outcome. As in the typical contract law case, no important policy is contravened by permitting his exercise of free choice. The international and corporate context may, however, generate a far more restrictive attitude towards governing law clauses. The Commerce Clause of the United States Constitution, the existence of a single currency, and the unlimited rights of corporations from one state to operate in any other do not exist in the international milieu. It is not necessarily true that a corporation can freely transact business or transfer capital across national lines. With the premises underlying free choice of governing law not nearly as compelling in the international setting, a court may not be as inclined to give the same leeway to a corporation that it gives to an individual settlor in the choice of governing law. Furthermore, to the extent that the law of a civil law jurisdiction is controlling, the freedom to choose a governing law may be extremely limited.[35]

In the United States, the freedom to choose the law governing the validity of a trust of moveables is not entirely unrestricted, even in the case of an individual settlor. The choice will not be respected if the state whose law is invoked has no substantial relation with the trust. What constitutes a sufficiently substantial relation is open to some speculation.[36] Probably, any

---

[34] See e.g. *In re Pratt's Trust*, 5 AD 2d 501, 172 NYS 2d 965 (1958), *aff'd mem.*, 8 NY 2d 855, 168 NE 2d 709, 203 NYS 2d 906 (1960); *Peterzell Trust*, 7 D & C 2d 400 (Montgomery Co. Ord. Ct. Pa. 1956). See generally Scott, above, n. 12, s. 598. See also Restatement s. 270(a), which provides that an *inter vivos* trust of movables is valid if valid 'under the local law of the state designated by the settlor to govern the validity of the trust, provided that this state has a substantial relation to the trust and that the application of its law does not violate a strong public policy of the state with which, as to the matter at issue, the trust has its most significant relationship.'

[35] See e.g. Schoenblum, above, n. 8, at 485. See also Dölle, Die Rechtswahl in internationalen Erbrechts (1966) 30 *Zeitschrift für ausländisches und internationales Privatrecht* 205; U. Drobnig, *American–German Private International Law*, 2d 1972, 168.

[36] In the Restatement (Second), for example, the term 'substantial relation' is not precisely

of the factors taken into account in validating a trust without a governing law clause would suffice—the place of administration, the domicile of the trustee or settlor, the place of execution of the instrument (though this is a fairly slender reed to lean on), or the location of the trust assets at the time of the trust's creation.[37]

When the designated state has no contacts with the trust, the results can be dire.[38] On the other hand, courts are likely to be quite deferential toward the settlor's choice of governing law if *some* contact can be demonstrated between the trust and the jurisdiction whose law is designated.[39] The cases also establish that depeçage is permissible.[40] The law of one state may be designated for one issue and the law of another state for another issue. Within the United States, this could prove quite beneficial. A menu of options in the form of different states' laws will be available, while the trust will still be assured of the overall stability and protection afforded by the United States government.

Of course, there may be circumstances in which the law of a jurisdiction other than one of the American states may be chosen. This may be done in an effort to maximize efficiency by using an American trustee to take advantage of the superior facilities and political stability necessary for proper trust administration, while obtaining the benefit of a more favourable law. Yet, this superficially appealing approach may result in the trust's increased exposure to hostile governmental acts. In addition to the acts of the corporate domicile and the jurisdiction of trust administration, it may now have to contend as well with the country the law of which has been designated as governing. This suggests that the theoretically safest structure for the asset protection trust is one in which the assets, the trustee, and the designated governing law are all in a single, stable jurisdiction. However, this may not be practical in the case of an enterprise that engages in business transactions inevitably having numerous international points of contact.

A further nuance in the field of governing law clauses is reflected in state statutues that address the subject in quite specific terms. For example, New York has a statute that provides that a non-domiciliary's choice-of-law clause invoking New York law will be given effect with respect to (1) trust property situated in New York at the creation of the trust, and (2) trust property consisting of personalty, whether situated in New York or elsewhere, if the trustee is 'residing, incorporated, or authorized to do business in this state or

---

defined and can be based on any number of contacts. However, certain ties are singled out as especially important: the state designated by the settlor for administration, the place of business or domicile of the trustee at the time of the trust's creation, the domicile of the settlor at that time, or the domicile of the beneficiaries. See Restatement (Second) s. 269, Comment f and s. 270, Comment b.

[37] See Scott, above, n. 12, s. 598, at 306.

[38] See e.g. *City Bank Farmers Trust Co.* v. *Cheek*, 202 Misc. 303, 110 NYS 2d 434 (1952).

[39] *Shannon* v. *Irving Trust Co.*, 275 NY 95, 9 NE 2d 792 (1937).

[40] See below, text accompanying n. 119 for the English approach to depeçage.

a national bank having an office in this state'.[41] The New York statute is an important enactment. It does not, on its face, apply only to individual settlors. It condones legislatively the avoidance of foreign laws. It permits New York law to be asserted even with respect to foreign-situated assets if there is a New York trustee. While this last benefit may not, as a practical matter, be enforceable if trust assets are outside the United States, the benefits will almost certainly be assured if the assets are anywhere within the United States.

Of course, the great danger in designating a specific jurisdiction's law as controlling is that no escape will be available if that jurisdiction's law changes. The most desirable solution would seem to be the drafting of the trust instrument to permit a change of governing law upon directions of a protector after the occurrence of certain threatening events. It is far from clear, however, that all jurisdictions will give recognition to such a provision. In light of this, the recently enacted Turks and Caicos ordinace on trusts is especially noteworthy.[42] By statute, it expressly recognizes the right of a trustee, in its discretion to change governing law, and also recognizes that the trust instrument can provide for the automatic change of such law to a designated substitute law on the occurrence of certain, specified events. There has been little in American trust law to compare favourably with this sort of legislation.

2.8. CONSTRUCTION OF TRUST PROVISIONS

When the construction of the terms of a trust involves an issue of administration, the law of the situs of administration generally controls.[43] A different rule will typically apply when the identities and relative rights of beneficiaries are at issue. Most courts will then apply the law of the settlor's domicile.[44] The reasoning here is that the answer to the question 'who is to get what' depends on the settlor's intent and is not so intimately tied to administration that it should be controlled by the same law that governs the latter. This is an exceptionally troubling outcome for the multinational corporate settlor. If the trust is being used to protect American assets from adverse conditions that may arise at the domicile, the very law that is being avoided will be regarded by the American court as controlling. That law may require, for example, the transfer of equity ownership to certain designated beneficiaries, thereby accomplishing *de facto* the very consequence the trust was designed to avoid.

---

[41] NY Est., Powers & Trust Law s. 7–1.10 (McKinney 1992). Rhode Island has a comparable statute. R.I. Gen. Laws ss. 18–1–1 to 18–1–3 (1989) (also applies when settlor was a resident at the time of the creation of the trust).

[42] See below, text accompanying n. 129.

[43] See Scott, above, n. 12, s. 576, at 204.

[44] See e.g. *Santoli* v. *Louisville Trust Co.*, 550 SW 2d 182 (Ky. 1977); *Boston Safe Deposit & Trust Co.* v. *Fleming.* 361 Mass. 172, 279 NE 2d 342 (1972); *Second Bank-State Street Trust Co.* v. *Weston*, 342 Mass. 630, 174 NE 2d 763 (1961); *Bank of New York* v. *Shillito*, 14 NYS 2d 458 (Sup. Ct. 1939).

An attempt is ordinarily made to identify the actual law the settlor probably intended to be controlling, and to construe the instrument according to that law. The main problem is of course that of determining which jurisdiction the settlor had in mind. When a corporation is involved, there is no single mind and reliance must be placed on corporate resolutions or other written records. However, because of the sensitive matters involved, there may be no such records. The inclination, under the circumstances, may be to look to the law of the domicile, the jurisdiction that defines the corporation's very existence. There is certainly a basis in the case of trusts established by individuals to look in the direction of the domicile.[45]

Even if a court has resolved to follow the rule of construction applied by the situs of administration rather than domicile, difficulties may arise. For example, the settlor may have failed to designate a place of administration for the trust and it may not be readily discernible from the surrounding facts. A statement of governing law is not the same as the designation of the place of administration.[46]

There may be other omissions or gaps in the trust instrument, such as what is to be done with principal of which no disposition to beneficiaries can be made?[47] Likewise, an issue may arise concerning the disposition of income during a period of time with regard to which no express directions have been given or circumstances anticipated.[48] Is the income added to corpus? Is it distributed currently? How is a holder of bearer shares to establish entitlement to a distribution as a permissible trust beneficiary?[49] Different jurisdictions have quite different answers to the problems. When dealing with former corporate assets now held in trust and administered for the benefit of corporate shareholders, unanticipated allocative and distributional issues are likely to be legion.

Furthermore, jurisdictions with little or no exposure to trusts are likely to have no law. Yet, especially when the trust will hold various assets, including corporate securities, and possibly have millions of beneficiaries, the choice of law issues raised will be of immense practical significance. One can foresee endless choice of law questions having to be confronted by the forum, seriously undercutting the efficiency of operations and generating unending conflict. Furthermore, the applicable law it adopts may offer no or few clues about how the issues are to be resolved.

One way to avoid the many pitfalls examined above is to incorporate a governing law clause in the trust instrument. As previously noted, the jurisdiction designated in a choice-of-law clause governing validity must have some connection with the trust. In contrast, in the United States, there need

---

[45] See e.g. *Staley* v. *Safe Deposit & Tr. Co.*, 189 Md. 447, 56 A. 2d 144 (1947).

[46] See e.g. *In re Waterbury's Trust*, 35 Misc. 2d 723, 231 NYS 2d 208 (Sup. Ct. 1962).

[47] Cf. Scott, above, n. 12, s. 584, at 236.

[48] See ibid., s. 583, at 235.

[49] Cf. Mann, 'The Confiscation of Corporations, Corporate Rights and Corporate Assets and the Conflict of Laws', (1962) 11 *ICLQ* 471, 499–502.

not be any nexus between the trust and the state whose law is designated in matters of construction.[50]

Finally, account will have to be taken of the interaction of choice of law at the trust situs and local rules at the situs of assets. For example, if a beneficiary of the trust lives in country X and is dissatisfied with accounting allocations by the trustee, she might bring suit in country X. If trust assets are situated in that country, a judgment could be rendered based on local law or a choice of some foreign law contrary to the law applied at the trust situs. Assets of the trust situated in country X could be used to satisfy the judgment. This prospect highlights the difficulty associated with attempting to establish a single governing law with respect to a multinational enterprise's assets, even when there is no expropriatory threat. It suggests that the most one can reliably hope for is to control the outcome with respect to assets in the United States which are in an American trust.

2.9. TRUST ADMINISTRATION

Trust administration consists primarily in the implementation of the trust's stated objectives. The central concern of administration relates to the powers and obligations of the trustee, the administrator of the trust.

2.9.1. *In General*

In the case of *inter vivos* trusts of movables, the prevalent principle is as follows: except where public policy in an interested jurisdiction might be offended seriously, the settlor will have broad discretion in designating the law that is to govern administration. In so far as an interested state's public policy is contravened, the settlor's choice of law is likely to be sustained only if the state he designates has a substantial nexus with the trust.[51]

When the settlor has made no designation of the governing law, the law of the state of administration (assuming that the settlor has indicated that state expressly or implicitly) will control administration, in the absence of an expression of contrary intent by him. The premise here is that a settlor would ordinarily intend, in designating a situs of administration, that its law govern administration issues.[52]

When the settlor has not fixed a place of administration, that place will often be determined to be the trustee's domicile or principal place of business, especially if the trustee or a cotrustee is a company.[53] The law of that jurisdiction governs administration.[54]

2.9.2. *Changing the Situs of Administration*

The situs of administration may be changed for any number of reasons. Most notably, in the asset protection context, a trust may wish to depart from the jurisdiction when it is under siege by a government intent on controlling or

---

[50] See Scott, above, n. 12, s. 575 at 202.   [51] See ibid., s. 611, at 349.
[52] See ibid., s. 612, at 350.   [53] Ibid.   [54] Ibid.

expropriating corporate shares or other trust assets. When such a change is contemplated, the question will arise whether the trustee is under the jurisdiction of a court and accountable to it. If not, the trust assets can be moved to another jurisdiction without court approval. Inter vivos trusts are generally not subject to such supervision, but there are noteworthy exceptions.[55] Naturally, the situs of administration can rarely if ever change when the trust is one of immovables.

On the other hand, to the extent the trust is comprised of movables, there should be little difficulty in moving it. In this regard, the trust is likely to prove superior to other entities, such as a corporation. Even when the trust instrument does not explicitly permit a shift of the place of administration, authorization is still likely to be inferred from a clause empowering someone to name a new trustee, if that provision can be read as not limiting the choice to the substitution of another local trustee.[56] The express naming of a successor trustee located or domiciled in another jurisdiction will also normally be read as evincing an intent to change the place of administration.[57]

Indeed, even when there is no evidence of the settlor's intent to permit a change in the place of administration, courts have authorized the change when it would facilitate the trust purposes and improve the protection afforded the beneficiaries.[58] For example, a change in the situs of administration has been upheld, although the motive was the avoidance of taxation. This decision in *In re Whitehead's Will Trusts*[59] is especially encouraging. This is particularly true to the extent that UK precedent is traditionally followed in offshore trust havens and has some influence on American trust law.[60]

While an express provision in the trust instrument authorizing a change of the situs of administration is desirable, problems can arise with such clauses. In particular, once a state has been designated as the place of administration, the settlor may find itself bound by that decision, even when a change of situs provision is incorporated in the trust instrument. Local objectants can stall, obtain executive orders, or have enacted legislation that prevents the change of trust situs. The argument may be made that special concerns override a general policy of permitting change or a strained reading of the settlor's intent may be adopted.

This possibility of the subversion of a change of situs clause is of major concern in the international context. If the situs of trust administration

---

[55] See e.g. Uniform Probate Code s. 7–101.

[56] See e.g. *Application of New York Trust Co.*, 195 Misc. 598, 87 NYS 2d 787 (Sup. Ct. 1949). See also *Wilmington Trust Co.* v. *Wilmington Trust Co.*, 26 Del. Ch. 397, 24 A. 2d 309 (1942); *Kerr Trust*, 40 Pa. D & C 2d 415 (1966). See Scott, above, n. 12, s. 614, at 356.

[57] See e.g. *Robb* v. *Washington & Jefferson College*, 185 NY 485, 78 NE 359 (1906).

[58] See e.g. *Finch* v. *Reese*, 28 Conn. Supp. 499, 268 A. 2d 409 (1970); *In re Benedito's Estate*, 83 Misc. 2d 740, 370 NYS 2d 478 (Nassau Co. Sur. Ct. 1975). But see *In re Turrentine's Estate*, 83 Misc. 2d 170, 371 NYS 2d 615 (Schnectady Co. Sur. Ct. 1975).

[59] [1971] 2 All ER 1334.

[60] But see below, text accompanying n. 123.

becomes inhospitable, there will be a desire to change situses. Yet, the unfriendly local government may manipulate events to prevent the trustee's and, thus, the trust's departure. Suppose the trust is in an offshore haven, but most assets are scattered about the United States. Many of the courts of the different American states in which the assets are situated may well conclude that the law of the offshore haven is decisive on the question of the validity of the right to transfer the situs. Moreover, the receiving American state may be reluctant or even refuse to accept jurisdiction of a trust that has not been released by its prior situs.[61]

In any event, a shift in the situs of administration does not necessarily trigger an alteration in the governing law. When no express statement exists, the courts have been divided on the question whether a change in governing law automatically follows upon the heels of a change in the place of administration.[62] Clearly, a simple change in the trustee's domicile will not bring about a change in the law governing matters of administration.[63] The one positive side of this is that a provision that was previously valid will not be invalidated simply because the new state of administration would regard the provision as invalid.[64]

From the foregoing, there is no avoiding the conclusion that flight from a jurisdiction of trust administration does not necessarily assure protection of assets. What it does accomplish is the creation of jurisdiction over the trust in the new situs, which may afford a more favourable environment.[65] Still, its courts may choose to enforce the unfavourable laws of the former situs and may refuse jurisdiction altogether or postpone it until the trust is released by its prior situs.[66] This potential divergence between the situs of administration and the relevant law of administration emphasizes the need to abandon finite distinctions with respect to trusts in the international realm. If asset protection trusts are to flourish and successfully adapt to the needs of multinational corporations, a more predictable, simplified set of choice of law rules will have to be instituted. Undoubtedly, they will have to be legislated and will have to give absolute primacy to settlor intent, and where that intent is not clearly decipherable, the law will have to consist of rules that carry out

[61] See e.g. Uniform Probate Code s. 7–101.

[62] Cf. *In re Shipman's Will*, 179 Misc. 303, 40 NYS 2d 373 (Queen's Co. Sur. Ct. 1942) (change in governing law) with *Stetson* v. *Morgan Guaranty Trust Co.*, 22 Conn. Supp. 158, 164 A. 2d 239 (1960) (no change). See Scott, above n. 12, s   615, at 366. Of course, freezing the governing law could prove detrimental, if the law is changed in a way that is adverse to the trust. For example, Massachusetts previously permitted the use of revocable trusts to defeat a spouse's elective share claims. This is no longer the case. See *Sullivan* v. *Burkin*, 390 Mass. 864, 460 NE 2d 572 (1984).

[63] E.g. *Ex parte Moots*, 217 Ill. App. 518 (1920). See Scott, above, n. 12, s. 615, at 369.

[64] See *In re Griswold's Trust*, 99 NYS 2d 420 (Sup. Ct. 1950).

[65] An invalid trust may be considered valid in the new state of administration. See *Wilmington Trust Co.* v. *Wilmington Trust Co.*, 26 Del. Ch. 397, 24 A. 2d 309 (1942); *Robb* v. *Washington & Jefferson College*, 185 NY 485, 78 NE 359 (1906). See Scott, above, n. 12, s. 615, at 369.

[66] See above, n. 61.

the overall protective purposes of the trust. Of course, no such rules are likely to evolve until there is a consensus that the protection of the world-wide assets of multinational corporations is a worthwhile objective of sovereign states.

2.9.3. Investment of Trust Assets

The question of investment power, strategy, and requirements of fiduciary duty involving investments presents yet another aspect of trust administration in which an expression of the settlor's intent will be determinative. It is one of particular significance for a trust administering a continuing business operation. In a properly drawn instrument, the settlor will set forth precisely the scope of the trustee's investment powers.[67] In addition, unaddressed matters should be made subject to a specified governing law. This law may be from a jurisdiction having no connection with the trust.[68]

When no choice of law is indicated, reference is likely to be made to the law of the state of administration.[69] However, for some courts, the law of the domicile still has an allure.[70]

2.9.4. Distributional Powers of Trustees

Some powers and duties pertain to the financial management of the trust—what the trustee can sell, purchase, mortgage, and so forth. The choice-of-law principles applicable in these instances have already been considered.[71] However, in addition to financial management, the trustee's powers encompass the proper distribution of trust assets. This could prove an extremely complex and tremendously important issue in the context of an asset protection trust for a multinational corporation. Generally, the question tends to be viewed by the courts more as one of construction than one of administration. What did the settlor intend various beneficiaries to receive and who were intended as beneficiaries?[72] Actually, this would seem in the first instance a question of interpretation, but if the settlor's intent cannot be ascertained from the instrument and surrounding circumstances, then resort must be had to construction, and the conflicts rules concerning that topic will be applicable.[73] This would include the situation in which there is a

---

[67] See Scott, above, n. 12, s. 618, at 374.

[68] The governing law clause, however, can be so inartfully worded as to give rise to a problem of construction: e.g. *In re Missett's Will*, 136 NYS 2d 923 (1954).

[69] E.g. *In re Carter's Trust*, 13 Misc. 2d 1040, 178 NYS 2d 569 (Sup. Ct. 1958); *In re Lowman's Trust*, 92 NYS 2d 238 (Sup. Ct. 1949); *Irving Trust Co.* v. *Natica, Lady Lister-Kaye*, 157 Misc. 32, 284 NYS 343 (Sup. Cit. 1935). See also Scott, above, n. 12, s. 618, at 375.

[70] See *Stetson* v. *Morgan Guaranty Trust Co.*, 22 Conn. Supp. 158, 164 A. 2d 239 (1960). Of course, the same result should occur if there is a governing law clause specifying the domiciliary state. See *Application of City Bank Farmers Trust Co.*, 9 Misc. 2d 183, 166 NYS 2d 772 (Sup. Ct. 1957). See also Scott, above, n. 12, s. 618, at 378.

[71] See above text accompanying nn. 67–70.

[72] See Scott, above n. 12, s. 619, at 382.

[73] See above text accompanying nn. 43 ff.

governing law clause. Thus, the characterization of the question will be crucial to the outcome. While it might seem that the entire distributional scheme could be addressed in the instrument, this should not be assumed. There may be a multitude of shareholders all over the world. They may have different classes of shares and some may simply hold bearer certificates.[74] There is a great likelihood that the trust instrument will not address all the issues that may arise, especially in times of emergency.

2.9.5. Termination of the Trust by Beneficiaries

The power to terminate the trust is of critical importance. One popular technique for shifting situs is to decant one trust by pouring over the corpus into another trust.[75] A prohibition at the original situs of administration against termination without the consent of all interested parties could stall or even prevent the use of this strategy, especially if this required the consent of all beneficiaries, that is, corporate shareholders. Furthermore, a jurisdiction may take an extremely expansive view of what constitutes a termination and when it commences, thus requiring beneficiary approval. If the choice of law issue at the new situs is resolved by applying the law of the former situs, and that former situs has a restrictive approach, termination will not be a viable option.

An additional question that remains unsettled is when the beneficiaries can compel a termination. Most states of the United States permit termination only when all beneficiaries are adults, all consent, and the termination would not defeat a material purpose of the trust.[76] Some jurisdictions permit a termination even if it would defeat the purposes of the trust.[77] In this situation, the law governing the administration of the trust will generally be determinative.[78]

From the foregoing, it is clear that the right to terminate may be limited even when an express provision in the trust instrument specifies the circumstances for termination and these have been fulfilled. Moreover, the right of termination is a two-edged sword. A flexible termination power in the trust instrument or in the governing statute could permit a hostile jurisdiction in which a majority of beneficiaries are concentrated to exercise their right to terminate and thereby compel a distribution of trust corpus to them.[79]

2.9.6. Share Registration

One topic of particular import concerns the controlling law governing registration of corporate securities.[80] Since the choice of law rules are

---

[74] For a consideration of various choice of law problems involving bearer shares, see Mann, above n. 49.

[75] See Klein, 'Repatriating the Foreign Trust', in *Foreign Trusts and Foreign Estates: Planning for United States and Foreign Persons* (PLI 1977). The strategy is considered in Ch. 10.

[76] See Scott, above n. 12, s. 621, at 385.

[77] This is generally regarded as the English position. See ibid.

[78] See e.g. *Franklin Foundation* v. *Attorney General*, 340 Mass. 197, 163 NE 2d 662 (1960).

[79] The precedents do not appear to consider this prospect.

[80] Under English practice, there may be more than one share registry. In the US, shares are registered in the state of incorporation.

unsettled, this uncertainty may stimulate challenges by disgruntled share-holders and claimants,[81] as well as by governments intent on freezing, expropriating, or otherwise controlling the ownership of shares.[82] In the United States, the Uniform Act for Simplification of Fiduciary Security Transfers generally designates the law of the jurisdiction of incorporation as controlling.[83] To the extent that its rule is followed and the country of incorporation is deemed by the trust situs to have ultimate regulatory authority over the corporation,[84] restrictions regarding share ownership could be imposed by that country even after the creation of the trust. These restrictions would have to be observed, even if they were not anticipated at the time of trust creation. Put another way, the American trust situs's recognition of the unceasing control of the share registry by the country of incorporation would very likely undermine the effort to protect corporate wealth through use of the asset protection trust, unless the trust and any corporations it controls could be delinked, at least in times of expropriation, from the parent corporation and those jurisdictions with the authority to determine who owns the parent.[85]

2.9.7. *Trust Advisers, Protectors, and Governing Committees*

Especially when trust principal consists of varied investments or a continuing business calling for sophisticated financial decisions, the trust instrument may require the trustee to consult with an investment advisor before taking certain steps. A protector may be authorized to intervene at certain crucial moments and make vital decisions affecting the trust. Alternatively, a governing committee may be granted binding authority with respect to some or all of the corporation's business activities. Are the adviser, protector, and governing committee all trust fiduciaries? Will trust choice of law principles govern them and their activities? Certainly, a veto power over the acts of the named trustee, as well as plenary power to bind the trustee, would suggest such an intimate connection with the trust's administration as to give rise to a fiduciary duty. Nevertheless, different jurisdictions, depending on the facts, may have conflicting views on the level of the duty owed by and authority of the adviser, protector, or governing committee.[86] Here is another important setting in which the choice of governing law could prove important and yet is wholly unsettled.

Even when the adviser, protector, or governing committee[87] is not regarded as a true fiduciary, it may be subject to treatment and state

---

[81] See e.g. below, text accompanying notes 270–1.

[82] If the law of the country of incorporation is deemed to control registration, and that country simply refuses to recognize a transfer of shares, its determination might well be given effect in an American forum.

[83] The Act is reprinted in J. Schoenblum, *Page on the Law of Wills* (Appendix vol., 1991), 695.

[84] This is the traditional American rule. See P. Hay & E. Scoles, above n. 8, at 885.

[85] See, e.g. below, text accompanying nn. 270–1 for a discussion of the prospects in this regard.

[86] See Scott, above n. 12, s. 623, at 394.

[87] The conduct of each member of the committee is likely to be evaluated independently.

regulation as a 'quasi-fiduciary'. Difficult questions will have to be confronted as to which jurisdiction's law decides capacity to serve, duties, and powers. Moreover, this person may be hesitant to assume the financial exposure that might be entailed. For example, the adviser may lend support to alleged 'self-dealing' by the trustee. Which law would then determine whether there had been self-dealing and whether the adviser had breached some duty or was otherwise liable: the law of the situs of trust administration; the law indicated in a governing law clause; no law, but rather the exculpatory provisions of the trust instrument itself; the law of the domicile of the adviser; the law of the place where the acts occurred; or, perhaps, the law of the domicile of the corporate-settlor or shareholder-trust beneficiaries? In this regard, there is only the slightest authority supporting the same choice of law rules as in matters of negligence and other party misconduct.[88] The problem is that the substantive rules, even in these areas, are in a state of flux, assuming that they are indeed the appropriate rules to apply.

2.9.8. *Special Limitations on Non-Resident Trustees*

Various American states impose restrictions on the capacity of a non-resident to serve as trustee.[89] For example, a resident co-trustee may have to be appointed. Even more common is a requirement that a public official be named for purposes of service of process. This, of course, would provide an entrée for governmental regulation and access to confidential information. In some states, the statutes are less precise. They may simply give the court 'jurisdiction' over the trustee or authority not to confirm him. In certain states, foreign banks and trust companies are absolutely prohibited from acting as trustees. In others, they can serve if there is reciprocity with the jurisdiction in which the trustee is organized to do business.[90] As a result of the foregoing restrictions in a large number of states, the objective of having several non-local trustees may not be realistic. Likewise, if a number of co-trustees in different jurisdictions have been appointed as part of the strategy of asset protection, a forum applying restrictive provisions may not recognize the appointment of the other trustees, thereby complicating administration and hampering the trust's ultimate opportunity to flee a jurisdiction. As for other types of out-of-state fiduciaries and quasi-fiduciaries, there is no certainty as to whether they would be subject to the same regulation as non-resident trustees.

3. Conflicts in English and American Trust Law and Choice of Law, and Their Consequences

Prior to the English adoption of the Hague Convention on the Law Applicable to Trusts and on Their Recognition, the English choice of law

[88] Cf. *Warner* v. *First National Bank*, 236 F. 2d 854 (8th Cir. 1956) (Florida executor and Minnesota 'managing adviser'; Minnesota statute of limitations applied to adviser's alleged negligence).

[89] See Schoenblum, above n. 8, Appendix A.

[90] See ibid.

rules with respect to trusts were quite uncertain,[91] apparently, even more so that in the case of the American states.[92] In *Dicey and Morris on the Conflict of Laws*, the rule was stated that

[t]he validity, interpretation, effect and administration of a trust of movables are governed by its proper law, that is, in the absence of an express or implied selection of the proper law by the settlor, the system of law with which the trust has its closest and most real connection.[93]

In the Comment that followed, the authors acknowledged that

[t]here is a remarkable dearth of English and Commonwealth authority on what law governs the validity of a trust; the literature is almost equally sparse. Such authority as there is does, it is submitted, support the proposition expressed in the Rule.[94]

The uncertainty that existed has been ostensibly addressed by the Recognition of Trusts Acts 1987.[95] However, the choice of law principles embodied in that law offer no greater predictability for those creating an asset protection trust.[96] In particular, the governing law is determined by consideration of several factors.[97] These are: the place of administration designated by the settlor,[98] the situs of the assets,[99] the place of residence or business of the trustee,[100] and the objects of the trust and the places where they are to be fulfilled.[101] Other factors, such as the domicile of the settlor, the legal style of the trust instrument, the domicile of the beneficiaries, and the place of execution of the instrument may also be considered in certain circumstances.[102]

The weight to be accorded these various factors is unspecified.[103] Furthermore, the relevance of certain factors, such as situs of assets, when they are in more than one jurisdiction, is also uncertain. Thus, whatever uncertainties there are in American choice of law[104] are considerably amplified in these English developments. To the extent that this represents a

[91] See generally R. Hendrickson and N. Silverman, *Changing the Situs of a Trust* s. 11.09[4][b].

[92] See above, text accompanying nn. 6–90.

[93] See L. Collins, *Dicey and Morris on the Conflict of Laws*, 10th edn. 1987, Rule 157, at 1072. See generally Mann, 'The Proper Law in the Conflict of Laws' (1987)336b *ICLQ* 437.

[94] Ibid.

[95] Recognition of Trusts Act 1987 (c. 14).

[96] Note also that the law is extended, with certain modifications, to such other jurisdictions as Bermuda and the Virgin Islands by the Recognition of Trusts Act 1987 (Overseas Territories) Order 1989, SI 1989, No. 673, Art. 2(1), Sch. 2.

[97] Schedule 1, Ch. ii, Art. 7.

[98] Ibid., Art. 7(a).

[99] Ibid., Art. 7(b).

[100] Ibid., Art. 7(c).

[101] Ibid., Art. 7(d).

[102] See L. Collins, Dicey and Morris *on the Conflict of Laws* 254 (4th Cum. Supp. to 11th edn. 1991). See also Wallace, 'Choice of Law for Trusts in Australia and the United Kingdom' (1987) 36 *ICLQ* 454, 468–9.

[103] See Dicey and Morris, above n. 102, at 254.

[104] See above, text accompanying nn. 6–90.

general movement towards a gravity of contacts approach[105] in trust law, it spells real trouble for the asset protection trust.

In the discussion of American choice of law principles, the point was made that the settlor could designate the governing law and, thus, eliminate any uncertainty that might otherwise exist.[106] One concern, however, was whether any governing law could be chosen. With respect to certain topics, such as the construction of the terms of the instrument, this *laissez-faire* approach was noted as being widely accepted.[107] Note was also taken of developments permitting relatively unfettered discretion to designate governing law on a variety of issues, such as matters of trust administration.[108]

The English situation prior to the enactment of the Recognition of Trusts Act was less oriented towards settlor discretion. While the settlor could technically designate governing law, the widespread assumption was that a 'substantial connection' between the trust and chosen law was required.[109] In Dicey and Morris, the point is made, however, that 'there is no express English decision to this effect'.[110] Moreover, no clear-cut guidance existed as to what 'substantial connection' meant.[111]

A further aspect of prior English law that was especially troubling was the possibility of a non-observance of the governing law designated if it offended 'public policy'. Since the public policy exception is a rather amorphous concept, subject to much result-oriented manipulation,[112] it was hardly reassuring in terms of the use of asset protection trusts. An even more troubling question was, which jurisdiction's public policy? For example, in the most recent edition of Dicey and Morris, the issue is framed in terms of a choice of governing law that offends English public policy.[113] In the prior edition of the treatise, however, the statment is made that

if there is a strong public policy in the system of law with which the trust has its closest and most real connection, it seems doubtful whether the settlor would be allowed to evade it by selecting some other law.[114]

---

[105] An example of a somewhat similar development in American jurisprudence is *First National Bank* v. *Shawmut Bank*, 378 Mass. 137, 389 NE 2d 1002 (1979) and *Ford* v. *Newman*, 77 Ill. 2d 335, 396 NE 2d 539 (1979). See also *Rudow* v. *Fogel*, 12 Mass. App. 430, 426 NE 2d 155 (1981). However, this is not a widespread phenomenon and is not imposed nationally by statute. Furthermore, the gravity of contacts approach has been the subject of much academic criticism. The Restatement s. 6 has been criticized to the extent that it endorses this approach. See e.g. P. Hay and E. Scoles, above n. 8, ss. 2.15–2.15. See also above n. 20.

[106] See above text accompanying n. 34 ff.
[107] See above text accompanying n. 50.
[108] See above text accompanying n. 51.
[109] See R. Hendrickson and N. Silverman, above n. 91, at 11–28.17.
[110] See Dicey and Morris, above n. 102, at 1074.
[111] See R. Hendrickson and N. Silverman, above n. 91, at 11–28.17.
[112] See e.g. above text accompanying n. 32.
[113] See Dicey and Morris, above n. 102, at 1074.
[114] See the discussion in R. Hendrickson and N. Silverman, above n. 91, at 11–28.17.

This left open the possibility that the designated law could be successfully challenged in a common law forum on the ground that the public policy of the home country, not the forum, had been offended.[115]

The Recognition of Trusts Act fails to overcome these concerns because it, too, incorporates a public policy exception.[116] To the extent that the choice of governing law will not be observed due to the public policy exception, the unpredictable gravity of contacts approach embodied in the Act as previously described will be given effect. In short, the current English approach needs considerably greater evolution before its principles can form the basis for widespread adaptation of the asset protection trust for multinational corporate purposes.

Another issue of crucial importance is whether the governing law can be changed, as, for example, by naming a trustee in another jurisdiction. English law was quite unsettled on this point, far more so than American trust law. While methods for changing the law existed, such as approval by all beneficiaries or court approval, the unsupervised authority to do so by a person designated in the trust instrument or as a result of certain triggering events was undecided.[117] Under the Act, the issue is resolved, but in an entirely unsatisfactory way. The law applicable to the validity of the trust also determines whether the law of the trust of a particular aspect can be changed.[118] Since the law of trust validity is itself likely to be uncertain or unreliable, the same will be true of the right to change the governing law.

In one respect, the new law has advanced the cause of sophisticated designation of governing law. Depeçage will now be recognized.[119] Previously, the assumption in some quarters was that there had to be a single governing law for all trust issues. This will no longer be the case.

The prior English law was also in a state of some uncertainty on the question of capacity to create a trust.[120] The prevaling view was that the 'proper law' controlled. The 'proper law', as noted, was unsettled, but was deemed by some to be the law of the jurisdiction with which the trust has its 'closest and most real connection'. The new Act does not address this topic. 'Preliminary' issues are very clearly not part of its subject matter. Thus, it would appear that the initial creation of the trust, as well as transfers to it,[121] most vital issues in the asset protection context, remain unsettled under English law. Most likely, with regard to intangibles, the laws of the country

[115] See also the discussion of the Hague Convention on the Law Applicable to Trusts and on Their Recognition, below, text accompanying n. 145.

[116] Sch. Ch. IV, Art. 18 states: 'The provisions of the Convention may be disregarded when their application would be manifestly incompatible with public policy.'

[117] See R. Hendrickson and N. Silverman, above n. 91, at 11–28.18 to 11–28.19.

[118] Sch. Ch. II, Art. 10.

[119] Sch. Ch. II, Art. 9.

[120] See R. Hendrickson and N. Silverman, above n. 91, at 11–28.19.

[121] Sch. Ch. I, Art. 4 states that: 'The Convention does not apply to preliminary issues relating to the validity of wills or other acts by virtue of which assets are transferred to the trustee.'

in which the corporation is domiciled or registered would be given effect.[122] Concerns associated with the successful establishment and enforcement of the asset protection trust vehicle for corporations with foreign operations were clearly not factors in the framing of this legislation.

4. Choice of Law and Offshore Trust Situses: the Developing Hybrid International Trust Law

Intense dissatisfaction with English trust law has existed in Caribbean and other English-law-oriented offshore jurisdictions. As noted, there had been little English legislation adapting the law to changing circumstances of international commerce. Furthermore, there had been few decisions fleshing out the law. The circumstances surrounding the 'choice of law question' had been particularly troubling, with English courts relying on the vague, 'proper law' concept that affords little guidance and predictability for settlors.[123]

As has been discussed, the enactment in the United Kingdom of the Recognition of Trusts Act 1987 has not eliminated unpredictability. Moreover, the offshore centres lack much precedent in their own law as well.[124] Accordingly, there has been a veritable explosion of legislation in offshore jurisdictions involving 'international' trusts and matters of choice of law, jurisdiction, and enforcement of foreign judgments.[125] Offshore jurisdictions have tended to look to the more dynamic, and perhaps responsive, American trust law in shaping their own laws. As a result something of a hybrid trust law is developing, derived primarily from English common law and older English trust statutes, with a substantial overlay of American concepts as well as responses tailored to the needs of those individuals utilizing the offshore trust.

Many of the choice of law issues raised by the use of offshore trusts were first tackled in a comprehensive manner by the Cayman Islands Trust (Foreign Elements) Law 1987. The concepts embodied in that legislation have since been refined in a number of jurisdictions, with the most current manifestation being the Trusts Ordinance 1990 (No. 25 of 1990) of the Turks and Caicos Islands (hereinafter referred to as the Ordinance). This law came into force on 1 February 1991. Provisions of this legislative enactment will be considered below to ascertain whether offshore jurisdictions such as Turks and Caicos offer the sort of legal structure needed by an asset protection trust

[122] For a discussion of the law governing multinational corporations and, in particular, the divergence between the common law and civil law concepts of domicile, see Hadari, above n. 27. See also Beveridge, 'The Internal Affairs Doctrine: The Proper Law of a Corporation' (1989) 44 Bus. L. 693 (recognizing a nascent move away from the law of the state of incorporation to a gravity of contacts approach).

[123] See generally Mann, above n. 93.

[124] See generally Duckworth, 'The Offshore Trust in Transition', in D. Kozusko and J. Schoenblum, eds., *International Estate Planning: Principles and Strategies* (1991), 129.

[125] Offshore jurisdictions would also include the Cook Islands (Pacific) and the Channel Islands (English Channel).

for a company operating world-wide. In this regard, offshore statutes might be viewed as transitional in nature, precursors of similar developments in American and English trust law, that seek to convert the trust into an internationally oriented asset protection and management vehicle.

Although not explicitly stated, the Ordinance (1990) clearly implies that a corporation can be the settlor of a trust. While an explicit provision would be more reasuring, this provision represents an important advance with respect to a crucial issue that remains unresolved in various jurisdictions, including the United States.[126]

As for choice of governing law, the Ordinance permits the trust instrument to designate the law of the Turks and Caicos as controlling. Furthermore, the principle of depeçage is explicitly endorsed, so that a designation of Turks and Caicos law can be made with respect to certain matters, such as administration or construction, while leaving other matters to be governed by a different law.[127] In choosing Turks and Caicos law, no actual connection with Turks and Caicos appears to be required. Of course, this represents something of a trap, since without some connection, the likelihood of recognition and application of Turks and Caicos law by another jurisdiction is highly questionable, notwithstanding the Hague Convention to the contrary.[128] Thus, to the extent that administration, trustees, and assets are all at a different situs, the option afforded by the Ordinance of having Turks and Caicos law may prove an empty gesture. There can be no assurance that courts outside Turks and Caicos would apply Turks and Caicos law. Less certain is what other jurisdictions would do when the trust has some, but not a predominate, nexus with the Turks and Caicos, such as if a trustee were domiciled there. However, while the Ordinance cannot control the amount of deference a foreign court will give to a choice of law under the Ordinance, it does, at least, establish the legal basis for a foreign court that is willing to defer to a Turks and Caicos judgment.

The authority to change the governing law is also acknowledged by the Ordinance.[129] That authority may be exercised in the discretion of the trustee or may be automatic on the occurrence of certain events specified in the trust instrument. Still, this provision is not all that it first seems. Specifically, no change of law will be permitted if the terms of the trust do not explicitly provide that a change of governing law cannot invalidate other terms of the trust, any of the trust's purposes, and any interest of a beneficiary. Furthermore, the trust must state that any change of law, to be effective, must be consistent with the intention of the settlor.

There are several problems with this provision. It imposes unnecessary technical requirements as to the language essential for a viable change of governing law clause. Aside from the foregoing technical criticism, the provision implies that the purpose of the trust and intent of the settlor must

---

[126] See below text accompanying n. 264.
[128] See below text accompanying nn. 144–5.

[127] s. 4(3).
[129] s. 40.

be specified. To the extent that the domicile country of the settlor-corporation or a country in which corporate assets are situated prohibits trusts for the purpose of avoiding expropriatory and similar deleterious state action, the Ordinance creates a not insignificant barrier to its own use. Significant political difficulties would be generated by explicit statements suggesting a lack of confidence in the stability of the country.

The Ordinance is not simply a conflicts of law statute. It also sets forth certain key elements of substantive trust law. At the same time, the Ordinance is not comprehensive or exclusive. Matters not addressed in the Ordinance would still be governed by English common law, as interpreted by Turks and Caicos courts and by English statutes, as amended locally. The Ordinance explicitly abolishes the rule against perpetuities.[130] The ability of the trust to function in perpetuity is of particular importance when the settlor is a corporation with perpetual life. By eliminating the rule, the Ordinance obviates the need to draft clauses that assure trust survival for a sufficiently lengthy period of time. More importantly, in contrast to jurisdictions that permit a lengthy term for the trust, but still adhere to a complex system of rules against perpetuities, mastery of and planning around those arcane rules would no longer be necessary. At the same time, the Ordinance permits the trust instrument to specify the circumstances under which the trust shall terminate or a specific term for the trust, if that is preferred.[131]

Other provisions of the Ordinance permit additions to the trust and additions of beneficiaries.[132] These are obviously of critical significance when a corporation is involved. Changes in corporate organization and in the identities of those with equity and other interests are likely to be commonplace. As these changes occur, so, too, will the corpus of the trust and, possibly, its beneficiaries.

The Ordinance requires beneficiaries to be identifiable by name or as members of a class.[133] Thus, whether the principal beneficiary of the trust is a corporation or, for example, 'shareholders' of the parent corporation, there should be little doubt that the Ordinance's requirements can be met.

The Ordinance is worded quite broadly with regard to the powers trustees may exercise and the ability to provide in the trust instrument for powers not otherwise recognized by statute.[134] This provision is essential in the case of a trust, which may be required to make business decisions on a day-to-day basis and will require great leeway and flexibility. The provisions regarding the trustee are also quite liberal. However, there are several provisions that do present problems. First, the beneficiaries are empowered to apply to Turks and Caicos courts to have a resident trustee appointed.[135] Second, if the trust does not address the issue of voting, unanimity of the trustees is

---

[130] s. 14(2).
[131] s. 14(1). See also below text accompanying nn. 299–300.
[132] ss. 8(b) and 9(2).
[133] s. 9(1)(b)(ii).
[134] s. 23.
[135] s. 44.

required.[136] The combination of these provisions indicates that a Turks and Caicos resident trustee could readily be appointed and used in troubled times to stymie efforts of the named trustee or trustees to flee that jurisdiction or otherwise function in a manner most salutary to the interests of the settlor.

Another provision that presents a problem concerns trustee exposure to liability. The instrument may provide for the number and replacement of trustees.[137] However, there appears to be no discretion to relieve a trustee of liability for his negligence.[138] This could have negative implications for the willingness of professional trustees to serve, since they often seek exculpation or indemnification for negligent as well as grossly negligent or fraudulent conduct. Also, the tendency on the part of the parent multinational corporation to regard the trustee or members of a governing committee as mere appendages of the parent[139] would have to be carefully monitored. The very purpose of naming affiliated parties so as to keep control indirectly over trust administration, and, thus, business operations, could clash with traditional standards of fiduciary conduct. In particularly, rules regarding good faith, prudence, and the duty to segregate assets would seriously complicate choices for a trustee, who may have a close affinity for the multinational corporate parent.

There are two other aspects of the Ordinance that are even more troubling. The first of these relates to the validity of the creation of the trust itself. Section 13 specifically does not 'affect the recognition of foreign laws' in determining the settlor's ownership of property transferred into trust and whether the settlor has the power to transfer such property to the trust. Paragraph (1)(b) indicates that the terms of the trust cannot override Section 13.

Subsection 2 of section 13 does cut back this deference to foreign law to a substantial degree. The provision, however, refers only to rights arising out of "personal relationships".[140] That term is defined by the ordinance in a way which would not include corporations.[141] Thus, the consequences of these provisions is that corporations and their property rights will be subject to the very foreign laws the corporation is seeking to avoid.

This conclusion is further reinforced by section 13(1)(c) of the Ordinance. It states that "as regards the capacity of a corporation", the recognition of the laws of the place of incorporation are not affected. The provision is imprecise as to what is encompassed by the term "capacity", but the term probably includes such matters as the corporation's "capacity" to create a trust in the first place and its "capacity" to transfer assets at the trust's creation, as well as subsequently, to the trust. The effect of this provision is to create

---

[136] s. 21.
[137] ss. 15 and 16.
[138] s. 29(10). However, under certain circumstances beneficiaries or a court may do so.
[139] See, e.g. below text accompanying nn. 239 and 256.
[140] S. 13(2)(b).   [141] S. 2(1).

considerable uncertainty as to the use of a Turks and Caicos trust for protection of corporate assets.

Section 13(1)(c) of the statute emphasizes that the substantial effort to accommodate the international asset protection needs of individuals in offshore jurisdictions has not advanced to the same degree with corporations. Indeed, this author has discussed the matter with individuals involved in the drafting of the ground-breaking Caymanian legislation. Very little consideration was given to asset protection for corporations. In large part, this is attributable to the perceived lack of demand. However, these jurisdictions now have it within their power to offer a situs of administration with a thoroughly modern trust law that caters to the needs of international corporate, as well as individual, property owners.

Of course, even if such developments took place, there would still be certain drawbacks to the utilization of these offshore centers. Political insecurity is one. The long history of questionable, and, sometimes, criminal conduct of local leadership in certain offshore havens does raise obvious concerns. In addition, the offshore haven might impose its own restrictions on the trust or trustee at some point. The United States could freeze US-situated assets of trusts in hostile offshore centers, as has been done in the case of Cuba and Panama. Finally, the offshore center's favorable choice of law and trust recognition laws would not necessarily be applied by other jurisdictions in which assets are actually located.

Perhaps, then, the key significance of these offshore trust havens is that they serve as a laboratory for a developing trust law that is evolving in a more responsive way to international asset protection needs. The legislative developments in these offshore jurisdictions, if focused on multinational corporations, might stimulate similar interest in some, if not all, American states as well.

5. The Impact of The Hague Convention on the Law Applicable to Trusts and on Their Recognition

As previously discussed, much of English choice of law has been altered in light of that country's adoption of the Hague Convention on the Law Applicable to Trusts and on Their Recognition (hereinafter referred to as The Hague Convention).[142] This Convention was drafted primarily to aid civil law countries facing trust law issues and to eliminate uncertainties created by the absence of a trust law in many of these jurisdictions.

In fact, The Hague Convention is not so limited. Since it incorporates choice of law, as well as substantive rules, it also modifies the principles of trust law previously observed in common law jurisdictions. To the extent that the Convention rules introduce greater flexibility and effectuate the settlor's intent, they are helpful. To the extent that they introduce greater uncertainty

---

[142] Recognition of Trusts Act 1982 (c.14). See also supra text accompanying nn 91–122.

and unpredictability, the Convention ought not to receive broad acceptance.

While the United Kingdom has enacted the Convention, with certain modifications, as its law, the same is not yet true of the United States. To the extent that the Convention is not adopted throughout the United States, the potential will exist for markedly different choices of law in those American jurisdictions that have adopted the Convention and those that have not. If some states adopt the Convention and other do not, and if some offshore havens do and others do not, the patchwork will become more confusing and make the use of trusts for asset protection all the more complicated.

Indeed, one further complication with the Convention is that it may or may not apply to trusts that do not have a multinational dimension. The intent of the drafters was to limit the Convention's application to "international" trusts. Yet, there is no attempt to indicate what that concept encompasses or what the relevant criteria are for classifying a trust. On its face, the Convention's language is not so limited. It indicates that all trusts are covered by its provisions.[143]

However, assuming that the convention applies only to international trusts, what makes a trust international? Indeed, the possibility exists that an asset protection trust for a multinational corporation may not be on "international" trust and not be covered by the Convention, even in a jurisdiction that has ratified or acceded to it. For example, a trust like the US Philips Trust[144] might not be deemed an international trust in that its trustees and assets all claim an exclusive US situs.

A detailed analysis of all of the provisions of the Convention is well beyond the scope of this chapter. Several provisions have already been analyzed in the context of the United Kingdom's Recognition of Trusts Act. However, there are additional, important aspects of the Convention that are likely to have a dramatic impact on choice of law and the viability of the asset protection trust.

Perhaps the most important drawback from the standpoint of a corporation establishing a trust is that the Convention does not address the issue of the capacity of a corporation to create the trust by way of a transfer of assets. While Article 2 of the Convention does not define settlors so as to limit the term to human beings, Article 4 makes clear that the Convention does not apply to the validity "of acts by virtue of which assets are transferred to the trustee". Thus, a country that does not recognize trusts as part of its internal law could refuse to credit a transfer to a foreign trust. If the forum applied that country's law, the trust would fail. Furthermore, even if trusts were generally recognized by the home country, restrictions that it enforced with regard to corporate transfers to trusts would not be subject to the Convention's rules. If the forum's choice of law rules incorporated the internal law of this home jurisdiction, the trust or transfer of assets to it would be invalid. This would be the the the case if the forum had adopted the convention.

[143] Ibid. [144] See infra text accompanying n 223.

A second fundamental pitfall of the Convention is that it has a most ambivalent attitude towards choice of law and trust recognition. Despite the fact that Article 6 permits the settlor to designate the governing law and Article 7 specifies the governing law when no designation has been made, Articles 13, 15, 16, 18, 19, and 21 afford escape devices that make the Convention's application in a particular situation entirely unpredictable.

First with respect to Article 13, it permits a signatory state not to recognize a trust when "the significant elements . . . are more closely connected with states which do not have the institution of the trust or the category of trust involved". The "significant elements" of a trust are not enumerated in Article 13, but certain factors are expressly excluded from the calculation. These include the governing law chosen by the settlor, the place of administration, and the habitual residence ('domicile?') of the trustee. If none of the situses that have connections by way of these elements can be considered, the "significant elements" may well not be based in a common law trust jurisdiction and may result in non-recognition. This Article and Article 4 would, therefore, suggest a strategy, to the extent possible, of first transferring assets to a corporate subsidiary in a common law situs and then having that subsidiary transfer assets to a common law situs trust.

Article 15 makes the application of the Convention even more unpredictable. It permits a signatory to bypass the Convention and apply its own conflicts rules when certain matters are involved, such as "the transfer of title to property and security interests in property". As a result of the foregoing, if a jurisdiction had a rule that property cannot be transferred by a corporation to a trust, it would not be bound by a Convention rule that would otherwise require application of the law of a country that did permit such a transfer.

Article 18 reinforces the discretion afforded to a state by Article 15. Article 18 permits a signatory state to disregard the provisions of the Convention "when their application would be manifestly incompatible with public policy (*ordre public*)". The vast leeway afforded courts by the public policy doctrine in order to opt out of choice of law rules is well-recognized. The possibility that this may involve the public policy of a country other than the forum has already been considered in the context of English law.[145] The Convention imposes no limits on the use of the public policy doctrine to evade Convention rules. A government taking highly politicized actions against corporate entitites or protective trusts might well invoke Article 18 and defend its actions in terms of public policy. Thus, the recognition of trusts purportedly assured by the Convention seems a nebulous, if not empty gesture, in the very cases when trust recognition would be crucial—the use by corporations of the trust to protect foreign assets from hostile action at the domicile.

Yet another provision, Article 19, explicitly prohibits the Convention from prejudicing "the powers of States in fiscal matters". One means for a country to take control of trust assets within its territory would be by confiscatory

[145] See supra note 115.

taxation. Article19 simply does not address the choice of law issue here nor the obligation of the taxing country to recognize the trust as a distinct entity. Moreover, Article 19's reference to "fiscal matters" could be construed as including within its scope not only taxation, but also exchange controls and even outright takings.

One final provision requiring analysis is Article 21. The focus of that Article is on the absence of an obligation of a signatory country to apply the Convention and recognize a trust when the country that is having its law applied is not a signatory itself. For example, a civil law country which is a party to the Convention might be required, under Convention choice of law rules, to apply the law of American state X. If the United States had not ratified the Convention or the Convention did not apply in state X, then the civil law country being discussed could refuse to recognize the trust. It could do this, even though the local law of state X clearly recognizes trusts. The basic premise of the provision is reciprocity. Its key consequence is that there is no requirement that a jurisdicition recognize a trust worldwide, but rather only in those countries that have adopted the Convention. Indeed, the only limitation of this nonrecognition right is that a country must make a reservation in order to take this approach.

In sum, The Hague Convention, while well-meaning in purpose, advances the cause of trust recognition and asset protection very little. Indeed, by adding yet another source of law to the mix, it may actually complicate matters and certainly make the reliability of the asset protection device all the more questionable. The action of the Cayman Islands, a principal trust haven, in enacting the Trusts (Foreign element) Law (1987) was an explicit and direct repudiation of The Hague Convention.[146] It was a response by knowledgeable practitioners with years of skill in dealing with international trusts, who realized the disutility of the largely academic and unrealistic compromises reached by the delegates to The Hague Conference that formulated the Convention. With the Cayman Islands in the lead, other leading offshore havens, notably Turks and Caicos, Bahamas, Bermuda, and the Cook Islands have followed suit. Thus, a variety of models of trust choice of law presently exist: the traditional approaches of the relevant common law and civil law jurisdictions, the Hague Convention, which certain jurisdictions such as the United Kingdom have adopted, at least in part, and the recently enacted statutes of the offshore havens. None comprehensively address the concerns associated with the asset protection trust for the multinational corporation.

6. Recognition and Enforcement in the United States of Foreign Expropriatory Acts

A fundamental assumption underlying reliance upon a US or offshore trust for the protection of American or third country assets is that the situs

---

[146] See Duckworth, *supra* note 124, at 138–9.

jurisdictions, especially the United States, will not give effect to illegal or inequitable foreign takings. As the preceding discussion has shown,[147] the trust choice of law rules of the American states in many instances will apply the law of the corporate or shareholder domicile. Nevertheless, there appears to be an assumption that what would qualify as illegal behaviour under American or international legal norms will lead the American forum to refuse, on public policy grounds, to recognize expropriatory acts of a foreign country. In fact, this is only partially the case. The situation is considerably murkier than this generalization might suggest.

The typical situation being discussed is one in which a foreign government seeks to take control of US-situated assets owned by a foreign corporation. The corporation has either had its property expropriated, there has been a nationalization, or the foreign government has through one form or another gained control of the management of the enterprise or restricted its profitable operation as a private entity. Control over US-based assets is sought by way of litigation in American courts or by enforcement of a foreign judgment in those courts.

A second setting in which litigation ensues would be one in which a corporation's assets have been taken at home and aggrieved shareholders, creditors, or trustees seek a set-off out of the foreign government's assets in the United States. Since various countries and their controlled entitites are likely to have substantial investments and credit balances reachable in the United States, an offset against this pool represents a strategy for indirectly protecting assets back home or in some third country.

As a general matter, American courts have been vehemently opposed to foreign expropriatory acts without just compensation or imposed without due process of law.[148] This stance has been taken most aggressively by state courts. New York, for example, has steadfastly enforced a statutory provision which reflects this anti-expropriatory attitude.[149] Since international law recognizes that each country has full authority to control the property within its borders, the fact that another country has reached a different judgment with respect to the status of or rights in the property is not consequential.

In spite of this general proposition, protection from foreign expropriation is far from predictable. The federal judiciary has consistently deferred to the executive branch on the theory that these sensitive political and diplomatic issues are best left to that branch of government. Indeed, pursuant to the act of state doctrine, the judiciary refused until recently to judge the actions of a foreign state with respect to property under its control, unless the State

---

[147] See, e.g., supra text accompanying note 43.

[148] See generally R. Lawrence, *International Tax and Estate Planning* , 2d (1989), 392–3. The presumption is that a foreign decree of expropriation or confiscation is contrary to public policy. See, e.g., *Republic of Iraq* v. *First Natl. City Bank*, 353 F.2d 47 (2d Cir. 1965), *cert. denied*, 382 US 1027 (1966).

[149] 1936 NY Laws c. 917, §877(b), *repealed and superseded* by NY Civ. Prac. Law c. 308 (McKinney 1962). The current statute is N.Y. Bus. Corp. Law §1202(a)(4) (McKinney 1990).

Department indicated explicitly that it was not opposed to court intervention.

The historical experience has been that the Executive may recognize by treaty or otherwise, for political reasons, the expropriatory acts of a foreign sovereign, and the courts, accordingly, feel compelled to validate takings by the foreign government of assets *within* the United States, with or without compensation or due process. The most notorious example of this occurred in 1933, when the United States entered into the Litvinov Agreement with the Soviet Union. As part of this Agreement, the Soviet Union assigned to the United States the claims of nationalized Russian companies against US nationals, in exchange for US agreement not to pursue claims against the newly recognized Soviet government. As a consequence, certain foreign nationals claiming compensation for nationalized assets were denied such compensation. This result was upheld by the Supreme Court in two famous cases, *United States* v. *Pink*[150] and *United States* v. *Belmont*.[151] A similar occurrence involving claims of American nationals was approved more recently with respect to Iran.[152]

Treaties and bilateral agreements need not be between feuding countries. The United States has routinely recognized nationalizations by friendly, foreign governments, such as Mexico. Indeed, a precedent for this was established prior to the Second World War, when American courts recognized the transfer of Dutch corporate seats and jurisdiction over them to the Dutch government in exile in the Netherlands Antilles.[153]

A supposed benefit of the trust is that it interposes an independent level of ownership. Thus, it may be mistakenly assumed that, even if the United States were to recognize foreign expropriatory acts against nationals of the foreign country, it would not have an impact on an American national, such as a trust established and administered in the United States.

This supposition overlooks the fact that the agreement reached between the United States and the other country might be broadly worded to reach entities created from property originally owned by foreign nationals or created with the purpose of defeating the foreign country's laws. Furthermore, choice of law principles already discussed may well require a reference to the foreign country's laws in order to ascertain validity of transfers to the trust and the validity of the trust itself. If foreign law is determinative under choice of law principles, the law of the foreign corporation's place of incorporation or seat will most likely decide the rights in the "trust" property. Moreover, under the Federal Rules of Civil Procedure, the law of

[150] 315 US 203 (1942).

[151] 301 US 324 (1937)

[152] See *Dames and Moore* v. *Regan*, 453 US 654 (1981).

[153] See, e.g., *Anderson* v. *NV Transandine Handelmaatschnappij*, 28 N.Y.S. 2d 547 (Sup. Ct. 1941), *aff'd*, 289 NY 9, 43 NE 2d 502 (1942), *approved*, *State of Netherlands* v. *Federal Reserve Bank*, 201 F.2d 455 (2d Cir. 1953). But see *Bank voor Handel en Scheepvaart* v. *Slatford*, [1951] 2 All ER 779 (KB). See generally W. Knight and R. Doernberg, *Structuring Foreign Investment in US Real Estate*, 2d §18.02[e] n. 3.

the jurisdiction of incorporation determines whether the corporation can sue or be sued.[154] The result may thus be that no effective challenge to the expropriatory actions may be readily mounted in United States courts, if the trust is not recognized and the corporation cannot sue or be sued due to restrictions imposed in the country of its organization.

A treaty or agreement between the United States and another country may come long after the expropriatory act has occured. Moreover, the expropriatory act itself may have occurred years before the United States actually recognizes the insurgent or invading force that was responsible for the expropriatory act. Still, the agreement may well be given retroactive effect by American courts.[155]

Of course, a treaty or other agreement may actually be protective of private property rights. In this sense, the long-standing network of bilateral trade treaties that the United States has entered into with other countries may actually prove of considerable benefit. However, to the extent that these treaties countenance expropriations in the event of "adequate compensation", they may pose a serious problem. In particular, American courts have tended to defer to the expropriating country in deciding what is "appropriate". Thus, a treaty provision designed to guard against *un*compensated takings may justify *under*compensated takings.

It is entirely unsettled whether these treaties would protect trusts with an American nationality or whether the validity of the trust would first have to be ascertained under the law of the person creating the trust and making the transfer to it. Moreover, unlike a corporation, a trust's nationality and residence under American law are extremely difficult to ascertain. For example, some recognition has been given to a weighing of several factors, including the domicile of the settlor and beneficiaries, in determining trust nationality and residence.[156] To the extent that these factors outweigh others, the trust could be deemed to be governed by the same law as the corporation and, thus, subject to the foreign expropriating authority.

Perhaps the most insidious weapon that the foreign expropriating authority has is the propensity of American courts to pinpoint the situs of various intangible assets.[157] In recent times, this judicial preoccupation has had the effect on several, though perhaps not the majority of occasions, of subverting the general American hostility to uncompensated foreign takings. Since most wealth is intangible in form and, thus, has no readily apparent situs, this development ought to be the cause for concern.

---

[154] See Fed. Rules Civ. Proc. 17(b), which provides that the "capacity of a corporation to sue or be sued shall be determined by the law under which it was organized".

[155] E. *Oetjen* v. *Central Leather Co.*, 246 US 297 (1918); *Ricaud* v. *American Metal Co.*, 246 US 304 (1918). See generally 'Extraterritorial Effects of Confiscations and Expropriations' Seidel-Hohenvelden, (1951) 49 Mich. L. Rev. 851, 854.

[156] See e.g. Lawrence, supra, note 148, at 620–1.

[157] See also Smedresman and Lowenfeld, 'Eurodollars, Multinational Banks, and National Laws' (1989) 64 N.Y.U. L. Rev. 733; Comment, 'A Conflict of Laws Model for Foreign Branch Deposit Cases' (1991) 58 U. Chi. L. Rev. 671, 686–91.

For example, in certain recent instances involving Mexican exchange controls and devaluations, federal courts have held that the assets were situated in the debtor country.[158] Emphasis has been placed on the terms of the contract itself, which may have identified the situs of the debt, or which may have required payment in one of these countries, or specified payment in the foreign country's currency. There is a similar development with respect to continuing business operations that have not reached the point of being a mature account receivable. In this case, the country with the closest nexus to the contractual relationship may be deemed the situs as concerns rights of the parties.[159]

To the extent that indebtedness, obligations, and operations associated with a protective trust can be fixed within the United States, the situs inquiry just discussed will represent no problem. On the other hand, to the extent that operations transcend national boundaries, as would be the case with most multinational enterprises, the American trust affords no more substantial protection in dealings with assets in third countries than does the unprotected corporation. Thus, the trust offers, at best, only protection against home-country actions and does not address in a comprehensible way the asset protection needs of an enterprise operating worldwide.

Apart from the intangible assets of the trust itself, the intangible equity ownership of shareholder-beneficiaries cannot be ignored. In the typical asset protection trust, the US assets would be owned by the trust for the benefit of the multinational corporation's shareholders. A foreign government may take over the shares or control their beneficial use, rather than the company itself. At least one federal descision indicates that the United States will not credit such indirect takings.[160] On the other hand, there is very limited authority to this effect.[161] Certainly, in the context of American domestic law, there is considerable uncertainty as to the sort of municipal regulation that rises to the level of a taking justifying compensation.[162]

If a standby trust in the United States is involved, one to which assets are to be poured over upon an emergency, the triggering events would have to be carefully described so as to encompass acts beyond the obvious, blatant, uncompensated expropriation of the company.[163] Alternatively, responsible persons would have to be authorized to act promptly when corporate assets were deemed to be in jeopardy. Even if American courts were prepared to

---

[158] See e.g. *West* v. *Multibianco Comermex, S.A.*, 807 F.2d 820 (9th Cir. 1987); *Braka* v. *Bancomer, SA*, 589 F. Supp. 1465 (SD NY 1984). But see *Bandes* v. *Harlow & Jones, Inc.*, 852 F.2d 661 (2d Cir. 1988). Cf. *Citibank, NA* v. *Wells Fargo Asia Ltd.*, 110 S. Ct. 2034 (1990).

[159] See e.g. *F & H. R. Farman-Farmaian Consulting Engineers Firm* v. *Harza Engineering Co.*, 882 F.2d 281 (7th Cir. 1989), *cert. denied*, 110 S.Ct. 3301 (1991).

[160] *Zwack* v. *Kraus Bros. & Co.*, 237 F.2nd 255 (2d Cir. 1955).

[161] See generally Mann, supra, note 49, at 488–90.

[162] See e.g. *Hodel* v. *Irving*, 481 US 704 (1987) (involving right of American Indians to dispose freely of property by will, rather than have it escheat to the tribe).

[163] See generally Lawrence, supra, note 148, at 606–14. Schoenblum, supra, note 8, at §18.18:11; Note, 'Creation, Administration, and Effectiveness of the "Failsafe" Trust for Nonresident Aliens' (1987) 17 Ga. J. Int. Law 121, 140–46.

hold that *certain* governmental actions represent indirect expropriation of shares, the contrivances available to a foreign government are seemingly endless and include such measures for control as licensing requirements, taxation, and appointment of board members or managers.

In the event that the expropriation of company shares or other indirect expropriatory acts are not validated in the United States, the question still remains for whose benefit the American-situs assets are to be administered. In the case of a corporation, a few American courts have adopted what amounts to the split corporation theory.[164] However, they have not satifactorily indicated the law to which the "American" corporation is subject.[165]

In the case of a truly impregnable asset protection trust, the same issue would have to be addressed. That is, for whose benefit is the trust ultimately being administered, if distributions cannot safely be made to the trust beneficiaries? While the problem may not prove too troubling in the case of a temporary trust during a short-lived crisis, it is a very serious question in the case of a trust whose beneficiaries are subject to the hostile foreign authority over an extended period of time. Indeed, if shareholders cannot escape the control of the foreign country, the trust in its own way will work an uncompensated expropriation. These shareholders may simply be deprived of all beneficial enjoyment. At a minimum, this would seem to place a great deal of importance on preliminary shareholder approval after full and comprehensive disclosure regarding the costs involved and the risks to their property ownership.

American states have a long history of restricting payments from American trusts and estates to nationals of Communist countries. Attempts by the states to escheat the property in question have been rejected,[166] especially if the action is motivated by political considerations. However, the instrument may be construed simply as requiring that the beneficiaries be able to enjoy the property in order for assets to be distributed. This may lead to a denial of benefits. On the other hand, it may lead to a finding that equitable interests can be relatively freely enjoyed, despite a system of state control. In this case assets, such as shares, could be released to individuals, though subject to ultimate foreign governmental dominance.

There is one final aspect of the U. S. attitude to foreign takings to be considered and that is the possibility of reaching foreign government assets in the United States to indemnify shareholders for the taking of corporate assets at home or in third countries. In other words, the trust might be able to

---

[164] See e.g. *Maltina* v. *Cawy Bottling*, 462 F.2d 1021 (5th Cir. 1972); *Ron Barcardi* v. *Bank of Nova Scotia*, 193 F. Supp. 814 (SD NY 1961).

[165] See generally Mann, supra, Note 49, at 493–4; Note, 'Corporations in exile' (1943) 43 Colum. L. Rev. 364, 371–2.

[166] See e.g. *Zschernig* v. *Miller*, 389 US 429 (1968). Contrast *In re Estate of Kosek*, 31 NY 2d 475, 294 NE 2d 188, 341 NYS 2d 593 (1973) with *Daniunas* v. *Simutis*, 481F. Supp. 132 (SD NY 1978).

recover assets if the trust instrument empowered it to do so for the benefit of corporate shareholders.

The starting point for the analysis would have to be the act of state doctrine. Just as the United States is not bound to honour a foreign expropriatory order with respect to property within the United States, it will typically not question the propriety of expropriatory acts in the foreign country. Accordingly, there would be no basis for a suit seeking set-off or damages from local assets for acts done in the home country with respect to assets situated there.

Despite the foregoing, a number of exceptions to the act of state doctrine have been recognized. They offer the possibility for some recovery. The pre-eminent one is the commercial activities exception. In *Alfred Dunhill of London, Inc.* v. *The Republic of Cuba*,[167] a plurality of the Supreme Court maintained that the act of state doctrine does not apply when a foreign government or one of its instrumentalities acts in furtherance of commercial activities.

Major difficulties with the exception exist, in addition to the fact that only a plurality of the Supreme Court has endorsed the theory and that the lower federal courts are sharply divided on the issue. First, courts may be hesitant to recognize foreign entities as governmental instrumentalities, despite the foreign government's obvious control over such entities.[168] Recognition as an instrumentality is a prerequisite to reaching the foreign government's assets. Additionally, some courts have only allowed counterclaims when a foreign entity has intiated a suit in an American court. Others have been even more restrictive and held that the act of state doctrine rigidly applies even though the foreign government initiated the action if the person making the counterclaim is an assignee of the claim.[169] A distinction has been drawn between submission to American jurisdiction by a foreign government and

---

[167] 425 US 682 (1976). Of course, the question of what is a commercial activity can prove highly controversial. Moreover, formal ratification by the foreign government may convert a commercial activity into an official government act. See e.g. *D'Angelo* v. *Petroleos Mexicanos*, 422 F. Supp. 1280 (D. Del. 1976), *aff'd*, 564 F.2d 89 (3d Cir. 1977). Furthermore, in light of the more plurality in *Dunhill*, not all courts have been persuaded to recognize a commercial activity exception. See e.g. *Callejo* v. *Bancomer, SA*, 764 F.2d 1101 (5th Cir. 1985).

In the related area of sovereign immunity, the Foreign Sovereign Immunities Act explicitly recognizes a commercial activity exception that would permit a suit against a foreign government in the US. See 28 USC §§1330 (creating original jurisdiction in federal courts in suits against foreign sovereigns) and 1602–11 (setting forth circumstances when the foreign sovereign is not entitled to immunity); §1605 (specifically setting forth the commercial activity exception). There has been much controversy as to what is a commercial activity under this Act as well. See e.g. *Callejo* v. *Bancomer, SA*, 764 F.2d 1101 (5th Cir. 1985); *McDonnell Douglas Corp.* v. *Islamic Rep. of Iran*, 758 F.2nd 341 (8th Cir. 1985). See also supra, note 11.

[168] See e.g. *Banco Para el Commerci Exterior de Cuba* v. *First National City Bank*, 658 F.2d 913 (2d Cir. 1981). The Supreme Court reversed, 462 US 611 (1983). However, it recognized no mechanical formula and endorsed the general principle of international law that the separate judicial status of a government instrumentality will ordinarily be respected.

[169] See e.g. *Empresa Cubanan Exportadora de Azucar y Sus Derivados* v. *Lamborn & Co., Inc.*, 652 F.2d 231 (2d Cir. 1981).

the authority of these courts to question the foreign government's conduct at home. Certainly, there is little authority supporting suits initiated by American nationals. Such suits are typically regarded as a direct assault on the foreign country's authority over property within its jurisdiction and in violation of the Foreign Sovereign Immunities Act.[170]

A second purported exception to the act of state doctrine is the *Bernstein* exception.[171] In the United States, the act of state doctrine has traditionally been grounded on deference by the judiciary to the executive branch.[172] Thus, in the *Bernstein* decision, the court indicated that it need not refrain from exercising jurisdiction over the matter when the State Department or other relevant executive agency has indicated no political or foreign policy concern.[173] Under these circumstances, a court is free to adjudicate the propriety of the foreign taking. Yet, even if there are no political or foreign policy concerns, the question remains whether an expropriation should be judged by American constitutional standards or standards of the expropriating country. One other complicating factor is that the role of the *Bernstein* letter itself is unsettled. For some courts, a less formal manifestation of the executive's attitude will suffice.[174] For other courts, an explicit letter in hand from the executive branch is sought.[175]

The current status of the act of state doctrine and its major exceptions is entirely unsettled. As a result of the recent decision of the Supreme Court in *W. S. Kirkpatrick & Co.* v. *Environmental Tectonics Corp., Intl.*,[176] its very theoretical underpinnings are in doubt. In this case, the Court permitted an action to proceed that raised embarrassing questions about the bribe-taking of Nigerian officials. The Court did not deem this to be foreign governmental action. On the other hand, the Court stated that had *official* acts of a foreign

---

[170] 28 USC §§1602–11. See generally Lawrence, supra, note 148, at 478–87. See also supra, notes 11 and 167.

[171] See generally Lawrence, supra, note 148, at 464–7 for a discussion of this much-noted exception.

[172] As a result of the Supreme Court's decision in W. S. Kirkpatrick & Co. v. *Environmental Tectonics Corp., Intl.*, 493 US 400, 417 (1990), this has now been cast in doubt. The Court seems to have limited the application of the doctrine to cases in which a foreign country acts against property in that country.

[173] See *First National City Bank* v. *Banco Nacional de Cuba*, 406 US 759 (1972). See also, *Bernstein* v. *Van Heyghen Freres, SA*, 163 F.2d 246 (2d Cir.), *cert. denied*, 322 U. S. 772 (1947); *Bernstein* v. *N.V. Nederlandsche–Amerikaansche Stoomvart v Maatschappij*, 173 F.2d 71 (2d Cir. 1949), *amended*, 210 F.2d 375 (2d Cir. 1954). In *Banco Nacional*, while the Supreme Court recognized the exception, six of the nine justices actually refused to apply it.

[174] See e.g. *Banco Nacional de Cuba* v. *Chemical Bank New York Trust Co.*, 594 F. Supp. 1553 (SD NY 1984).

[175] See e.g. *Nacional de Cuba* v. *Chemical Bank NY Trust*, 822 F.2d 230 (2d Cir. 1987). There is also a bilateral treaty exception to the act of state doctrine. See e.g. *Kalamazoo Spice Extraction Co.* v. *Provisional Military Govt. of Socialist Etheopia*, 729 F.2d 422 (6th Cir. 1984). The Hickenlooper Amendment, 22 USCC §2370(e)(2), provides another exception. However, it applies only where the foreign act is violative of international law, does not involve contract claims, and where the executive has not determined that foreign policy concerns require application of the act. Thus, instances of its application are quite limited. See generally Lawrence, supra, note 148, at 467–8.

[176] Supra, note 172.

government with regard to property on its own territory been involved, American courts could not have questioned the action. It regarded the Act of State Doctrine as an absolute rule of decision rather than a self-imposed theory of judicial abstention. To the extent that this approach is followed, there would seem to be no persuasive basis for invoking the commercial activities or *Bernstein* exceptions; nor would there be a basis for the assertion of a counterclaim in a suit brought by a foreign government or one of its instrumentalities.

7. The Security of Assets from United States Vesting and Freezing

7.1. INTRODUCTION

A prevailing assumption underlying reliance on an American asset protection trust is that the assets will be secure in the United States. In fact, the United States has the authority to freeze or confiscate assets and has exercised that authority on numerous occasions, especially in the recent past. While there are obvious benefits from situating assets in the United States, there are also risks. The very fact of its pre-eminence and worldwide interests often puts the United States into conflict with other countries. Many nationals of these countries or the countries themselves are likely to have assets in the United States. While conflicts are from time to time resolved through a declared war, the United States has been far more inclined to use economic warfare. In recent years, restrictive property measures have been imposed in varying degrees on China, Cuba, East Germany, Haiti, Iran (twice), Libya, Nicaragua, North Korea, Panama, South Africa, and Vietnam, and nationals of these countries, and those trading with these countries.

At the core of American confiscatory authority is the Trading with the Enemy Act (hereinafter also referred to as the TWEA), first enacted during the First World War.[177] Section 5(b)(1) of the Act gives authority to the executive to prohibit assertion of rights in or dealing with property under the jurisdiction of the United States in which specified foreign governments or nationals of those countries have any interest. A 1933 amendment to the Act gave the president the authority to seize foreign assets in the United States and regulate financial and commercial transactions with other sovereigns whenever there is a "period of national emergency" even if a state of war does not exist.[178]

The great uncertainty over the meaning of "period of national emergency" and fears of excessive executive authority in domestic crises led to the enactment of two statutes dealing with the concept of "national emergency". In addition, the Trading with the Enemy Act was amended, so that it only applies "during war". As for the new statutes, the first of these, the International Emergency Economic Powers Act (hereinafter also referred to

[177] 50 USCA App. §§1 *et seq.*
[178] See generally Lawrence, supra note 148, at 405 and n. 68

as IEEPA),[179] restricts the president's discretion in regulating economic transactions, exchange controls, trade, investment, or ownership of property over which the United States has jurisdiction. While it generally permits the president to do what he is permitted to do under the Trading with the Enemy Act, his authority can only be exercised with respect to 'any unusual and extraordinary threat, which has its source in whole or substantial part outside the United States, to the national security, foreign policy or economy of the United States' and "if the president declares a national emergency with respect to such threat".[180]

The point has been made that this limitation affords significant protection for foreign investors concerned about American expropriatory acts. In fact, this author finds very little comfort in this language, since in times of great political conflict, the likelihood is slight that a threat will not be found to be "unusual and extraordinary".

Indeed, the most important constraint imposed by the International Emergency Economic Powers Act is that it technically does not permit outright seizure of property without compensation, as does TWEA. However, the new law empowers the president to prohibit transactions in foreign exchange, transfers of credit or payments to a bank if it involves the specified foreign country or its nationals, or the importing or exporting of currency or securities. Additionally, while property cannot be expropriated, it need not be returned until the emergency is declared over and claims against the country and its nationals are settled. The Supreme Court has construed this provision as giving the president authority tantamount to confiscation without any compensation.[181]

A third Act purportedly restricting presidential authority is the National Emergencies Act.[182] This statute affords Congress oversight authority and, essentially, makes it a participant in any assertion of governmental authority over foreign assets. Again, this promises some protection against undue assertion of expropriatory powers, but is not likely to insulate foreign assets in the event of any major crisis or perceived threat to the United States. Moreover, there is a controversial body of constitutional authority that indicates that the president has inherent authority to act in an emergency and does not require statutory authorization.[183]

7.2. THE BROAD RANGE OF AMERICAN EXPROPRIATORY POWERS

If either TWEA or IEEPA are invoked,[184] the US-situs assets of corporations organized in the foreign country or owned by it or its nationals

---

[179] 50 USC §§1701–6

[180] 50 USC §§1701.

[181] See *Dames and Moore* v. *Regan*, 453 US 654 (1981) (relating to Iranian assets).

[182] USC §§1601, 1621–2.

[183] See L. Tribe, *American Constitutional Law* 2d ed. 1988) §§4–8 (the theory is sometimes interpreted as requiring Congressional assent, although such assent may be found in Congress' inaction).

[184] See e.g. Foreign Assets Control Regulations, 31 C. F. R. §§500.101 *et seq.*; Libyan

will be subject to vesting or freezing. In determining whether a corporation is owned by a national or a foreign country, the search for a "taint" under the TWEA has been exceptionally far-reaching and the norm has been to pierce the corporate veil in search of who truly controls the entity.[185] Thus, foreign enemy shareholders of a domestic American corporation have had their shares vested in the Alien Property Custodian.[186] Courts have also been concerned with when shares have been transferred, since attempts to transfer shares to non-enemy aliens after war has been declared do not avoid vesting by the Custodian.[187]

The Supreme Court has directed its attention in part to the treatment of neutral or even friendly country corporations and shareholders.[188] The first, very crucial point here is that the TWEA permits the government to seize assets of any domestic or foreign entity, whether enemy or not. However, non-enemies can sue to recover their property or interests, and will succeed if they can show they are not controlled.[189] As a result of the foregoing, it is obvious that assets held even by an American entity could be taken, with control over its operations at least during the war passing into governmental hands.

The second point is that the "taint" can be of the most marginal degree.[190] A single share owned by an enemy alien could lead to seizure. The same would be true if any enemy alien is serving as an officer or director. Likewise, the alien's affiliation need not necessarily be with an enemy country. It would suffice if it were with an ally of an enemy alien country. Even when the formal structure of ownership legally precludes the enemy alien from exercising control, the *de facto* exercise of such control will justify the vesting of property.[191]

The third point is that, when an entity has a mix of enemy and non-enemy equity ownership, the non-enemies will be entitled to have their proportionate interest in the entity returned. They will also have a right to pursue their rights independent of efforts by the corporation or other entity to recover property. Still, as a preliminary matter, the burden will be on them to

Sanction Regulations, 31 C. F. R. §550.210 (part of Libyan sanction regulations).

[185] See e.g. *Standard Oil Co.* v. *Clark*, 163 F.2d 917 (2d Cir. 1947), *cert. denied*, 333 US 873 (1948).

[186] E.g. *Miller* v. *Kaliwerke Aschersleben Aktien-Gesellschaft*, 283 F. 746 (2d Cir. 1922).

[187] See e.g. *Magg* v. *Miller*, 296 F. 973 (DC Cir. 1924) (however, the pre-war transfer of the equitable interest in shares, rather than the shares themselves, probably does suffice to avoid the reach of the statute).

[188] E.g. *Kaufman* v. *Société Internationale pour Participations Industrielles et Commerciales, SA*, 343 US 156 (1952); *Clark* v. *Uebersee Finanz-Korp, AG*, 332 US 480 (1947). See also *U. S.* v. *Algemene Kunstzijde Unie, NV*, 226 F.2d 115 (4th Cir. 1955), *cert. denied*, 350 US 969 (1956).

[189] See 50 USCA App. §§7(c), 9; *Brownell* v. *Nakashima*, 243 F.2d 787 (9th Cir.), *cert. denied*, 355 US 872 (1957).

[190] See *Kaufman* v. *Société Internationale pour Participations Industrielles et Commerciales, S.A.*, 343 US 156 (1952).

[191] *Ueberse Finanz-Korp., A.G.* v. *Clark*, 82 F. Supp. 602 (D.D.C. 1949), *aff'd*, 191 F.2d 327 (D.C. Cir. 1951), *aff'd in part and remanded in part*, 343 US 205 (1952).

establish the absence of a taint. This could be catastrophic with respect to preserving control over a multinational enterprise.[192]

Based on the foregoing, as well as numerous trust cases involving the TWEA, certain broad generalizations can be made regarding the viability of an asset protection trust. To the extent that the trust continues any business dealings directly or indirectly with the parent corporation, the trust risks vesting or freezing of assets. Furthermore, to the extent that any principal officers or directors of the corporation play a role in the adminstration of the trust, as either trustees, advisors, or custodians, the trust and its assets will be placed in jeopardy. If the trust is entirely pure of such taint, but assets are not transferred to it until after the declaration of war or national emergency, the assets are not likely to be deemed free from the government's vesting or freezing power. In determining whether there is a trust, if the trust is subject to any revocatory authority or demand right[193] by the corporation or is being administered by an agent or party holding a power of attorney given by the corporation, then vesting or freezing is not likely to be avoided.[194] Indeed, a pattern of communication and consultation with the corporation and its officers would probably suffice to support a vesting or freezing order.[195] The fact that corporate officers have fled to the United States is irrelevant if the corporation is a citizen of the enemy country.[196] The same would be true of a corporation and its officers subject to an occupying force.[197] Finally, the existence of even a *de minimis* beneficial interest of a person linked to an enemy or other designated country may well result in vesting or freezing, subject to recoupment of the portion owned by untainted persons.[198]

This last aspect obviously makes the insulation of the trust highly problematical. While a number of trust cases, decided during World War II, raise the possibility of avoiding the TWEA, the trust would have to be extremely fine-tuned in a way that might hamper its ultimate objective of protection for corporate assets. For example, the decided cases indicate that a provision denying any benefits or rights to a tainted person until the war or

[192] Ibid. See also *Kaufman v. Societe Internationale pour Participations Industrielles et Commerciales, SA*, 343 US 156 (1952); *Commercial Trust Co. v. Miller*, 281 F. 804 (3d Cir. 1922), *aff'd*, 262 US 51 (1923) (where securities held in trust for the joint account of a neutral person and alien enemy were subject to vesting).

[193] *Garvan v. Commercial Trust Co.*, 275 F. 841 (D. N.J. 1921), *aff'd*, 281 F. 804 (3d Cir. 1922), *aff'd*, 262 US 51 (1923).

[194] See e.g. *Second Russian Ins. Co. v. Miller*, 268 US 552 (1925). See also *Fujino v. Clark*, 71 F. supp. 1 (D. Haw.), *aff'd*, 172 F.2d 384 (9th Cir.), *cert. denied*, 337 US 037 (1949).

[195] See e.g. *Von Hennig v. Rogers*, 187 F. Supp. 914 (D.D.C. 1960), *aff'd*, 296 F.2d 420 (D.C. Cir. 1961), *cert. denied*, 369 US 859 (1962).

[196] *H. P. Drewry, S.A.R.L. v. Onassis*, 266 App. Div. 292, 42 N.Y.S. 2d 474 (1st Dept. 1943). However, if the government is in exile and recognized by the United States, this will probably remove the trust from exposure. See, e.g., *Chemacid, S.A. v. Rothschild*, 180 Misc. 929, 44 N.Y.S. 2d 356 (S.Ct. 1943).

[197] See generally *Agajan v. Clark*, 381 F.2d 937 (D.C. Cir.), *cert. denied*, 389 US 976 (1967).

[198] See *Kaufman v. Société Internationale pour Participations Industrielles et Commerciales, S.A.*, 343 US 156 (1952).

emergency ends would not forstall governmental action.[199] Consistently with the theory that the TWEA must be interpreted flexibly in order to deal with enemy subterfuges, the very retention of an interest in the trust, whether or not postponed in enjoyment, and no matter how contingent in nature, could still result in vesting.[200]

State laws, or trust provisions, which prevent alienation or other assignments of interest, would also not bar seizure or freezing by the government. Thus, for example, attempts to invoke spendthrift clauses have failed in the face of overriding federal interests, as reflected in the TWEA.[201]

One area in which trusts have succeeded in defeating the government's seizure attempts has been in connection with beneficial interests that only spring into existence upon the termination of the government's power to confiscate or freeze. The difficulty, however, is in determining whether a designated beneficiary has a contingent interest or no interest prior to that time. The outcome will turn on the relevant American state's, not federal, property and future interests law—thus making any planning extremely uncertain as to outcome.[202] These decisions indicate that the safest way to insulate the trust protecting corporate assets would be to provide for the creation of beneficial interests in shareholders of designated countries only upon the end of enforcement of the TWEA or the IEEPA. An alternative beneficiary would have to be named, who could not be regarded as an agent or functionary for the corporation or its shareholders.[203] Still, there is no guarantee that this approach would not be regarded as *de facto* a contingent interest subject to defeasance that could be vested or frozen by the United States.

Note that the termination of hostilities does not necessarily free up interests in property.[204] Indeed, the executive, in conjunction with Congress, would retain supervision over assets and could even confiscate them long after the war or

[199] See, e.g. *Kammholz* v. *Allen*, 256 F.2d 437 (2d Cir. 1958); *In re Bendheim's Estate*, 124 Misc. 424, 209 N.Y.S. 141 (Sur. Ct. 1924), *aff'd*, 214 App. Div. 716, 209 N.Y.S. 794 (1925); *In re Neumeister's Estate*, 146 Cal. App. 2d 290, 304 P.2d 67 (1956).

[200] See e.g. *In re Zuber's Estate*, 146 Cal. App. 2d 584, 304 P.2d 247 (1956).

[201] *Id.*; *Brownell* v. *Leutz*, 149 F. Supp. 78 (D.N.D. 1957); *Central Hanover Bank & Tr. Co.* v. *Markham*, 68 F. Supp. 829 (S.D.N.Y. 1946).

[202] See e.g. *Brownell* v. *Mercantile Trust Co.*, 139 F. Supp. 834 (E.D. Mo. 1956); *Security First Natl. Bank* v. *Rogers*, 51 Cal. App. 2d 24, 330 P.2d 811 (1958); *In re Paszotta*, 172 N.E. 2d 904 (ind. App. 1961); *In re Schmidt's Will*, 97 N.W. 2d 441 (Minn. 1959); *In re Reuss' Est.*, 196 Misc. 94, 91 N.Y.S. 2d 479 (Sur. Ct. 1949); *Clark* v. *Edmunds*, 73 F. Supp. 390 (196 Misc. 94, D. Va. 1947); *In re Schneider's Estate*, 140 Cal. App. 2d 710, 296 P2d 45, *app. dismissed*, 352 US 938 (1956). See generally Knight and Doernberg, supra, note 153, §19.02, at 19–9 and n. 1. See also Greenapple, 'Control of Alien Property in Time of War or National Emergency: Avoidance of Vesting Under the Trading with the Enemy Act' (1951) 37 Corn. L.Q. 110.

[203] See e.g. *Keppleman* v. *Palmer*, 91 N.J. Eq. 67, 108 A. 432 (Err. & App. 1919), *cert. denied*, 252 US 581 (1920) (power of attorney). See also *In re Ronkendorf's Estate*, 160 Cal. App. 2d 145, 324 P.2d 941 (1958); *Fujino* v. *Clark*, 172 F.2d 385 (9th Cir. 1949).

[204] See e.g. *Swiss Natl. Ins. Co.* v. *Miller*, 267 US 42 (1925) (the termination of dealings with an enemy also does not free up the property); *Farmers' Loan & Tr. Co.* v. *Hicks*, 9 F.2d 848 (2d Cir.), *cert. denied*, 269 US 583 (1925) (certain interests were actually seized after the First World War in 1921).

emergency has ended.[205] Thus, the trust provisions would have to take this possibility into account as well. Of course, a treaty between the warring countries could entirely alter the rights of private parties.

To this point, the discussion has been in terms of vesting and freezing of trust assets or the beneficial interests in the trust. However, the possibility exists that a license can be obtained from the government to permit the release of assets or the continuance of operations in private hands.[206] In order for the trustee to recover property or continue adminstration of the trust, it will have the burden of establishing that there is no taint on the part of those with the beneficial interests in the trust.[207] Arguably, the trustee has a fiduciary duty to undertake all efforts to recover assets of the trust and assure their continued profitability.[208] If they are all tainted, however, the trustee will have no standing to sue to recover trust corpus.[209]

The duty to seek to preserve and protect trust property may come into conflict with the well-recognized duty of maintaining grantor and beneficiary confidentiality.[210] This principle is especially recognized by statute in a number of offshore jurisdictions.[211] Thus, to the extent that there is a foreign trustee from one of these jurisdictions, that trustee would be on the horns of a very serious dilemma. Any disclosure could subject the trustee to criminal prosecution in the offshore jurisdiction. Nevertheless, the state might impose a non-waivable duty requiring the preservation and recovery of trust property.

One very important aspect of any asset protection trust is the situs of trust assets. Notably, in the context of the TWEA and IEEPA, the United States has acted quite aggressively, and has not been especially concerned whether or not the situs is deemed to be in the United States. For example, the government has moved against a paying agent who happened to be in the United States, even though the situs of the underlying intangible asset was technically abroad.[212] Courts have also held that stock certificates of a corporation organized under a foreign law can be seized if physically present in the United States.[213] On the other hand, even if the shares are not in the

---

[205] See *Woodson* v. *Deutsche Gold und Silber Scheideanstalt Vormals Roessler*, 292 US 449 (1934); *In re Bendit's Will*, 214 App. Div. 446, 212 N.Y.S. 526 (1925). See also *Gmo. Neihaus & Co.* v. *US*, 153 F. Supp. 428 (C. Cl. 1957); supra, note 204.

[206] 50 USC App. s5(b) (1). Under this licensing procedure, the US retains substantial oversight and can require substantial disclosure.

[207] See e.g. *Manufacturers Trust Co.* v. *Kennedy*, 291 F.2d 460 (2d Cir. 1961). See generally Lawrence, supra, note 148, at 422.

[208] See Lawrence, supra, note 148, at 422. See also *Isenberg* v. *Trent Trust Co.*, 26 F.2d 609 (9th Cir. 1928), *cert. denied*, 279 US 862 (1929); *Craig* v. *Bohack*, 19 App. Div. 2d 891, 244 N.Y.S. 2d 737 (1963) (duty of holder of power of attorney).

[209] See e.g. *Kober* v. *Brownell*, 149 F. supp. 510 (N.D. Cal. 1957).

[210] See Lawrence, supra, note 148, at 424–5.

[211] E.g. the Cayman Islands' Bank and Trust Companies Regulation Law, Law 8, s10 (1966).

[212] *McGrath* v. *Agency of Chartered Bank*, 104 F. Supp. 964 (S.D.N.Y. 1952), *aff'd*, 201 F.2d 368 (2d Cir. 1953) (power over the debtor suffices).

[213] In other contexts, the situs of shares is much disputed. See, e.g., *Direction Der Disconto-Gesellschaft* v. *United States Steel Corp.*, 267 US 22 (1925). See also Schoenblum, supra, note 8, s16.07.4.

United States, a shareholder's interest in a domestic corporation can be seized.[214]

The foregoing is not intended to suggest that there are no constraints on the federal government in periods of war or national emergency. For example, certain courts have emphasized that trust assets that are deemed outside the territory of the United States are not subject to TWEA. Thus, the Alien Property Custodian was not permitted to reach interest income of an enemy national where the bond certificate was in London and the interest was therefore payable there. On the other hand, the beneficial interests in the trust of the same enemy nationals could be reached, since the trustee was in the United States, the instrument stated that the trust was to be a New York trust, and New York law was to govern its construction and administration.[215]

Several other facets of these cases are worthy of note. To the extent that there are beneficiaries, even unborn, who may not be enemy aliens, the trust itself and its property cannot be vested by the government.[216] This is to be contrasted with the beneficial interests of the tainted aliens.[217] The second point relates to the trustee. Even when none of the beneficiaries are enemy aliens, if the trustee is, the government has prevailed in its contention that the trustee should not be allowed to manage the trust corpus. Although the trustee's interest is not beneficial in nature, its legal authority is regarded as a form of control that the TWEA permits the government to prevent.

A related third point derived from these cases is that the powers of the settlor or other powerholder are exercisable by the Alien Property Custodian under the TWEA, but only if the powerholder is an enemy alien or similar designated person. If not, then the fact that the government can replace the trustee or seize beneficial interests does not mean it can revoke the trust and recover the assets.[218] On the other hand, if the settlor is an enemy alien, then the power to terminate the trust does exist. Moreover, based on the corporate cases, the trust itself could be undone altogether if it was deemed to be a cover for the operations of a controlling enemy alien corporation.

A fourth point derived from these cases is that the American TWEA cannot be considered in isolation. That is, other friendly nations or allies may have similar legilsation. Although the trustee and trust may be American, the

[214] See e.g. *Kaliwerke Aschersleben Aktien-Gesellschaft*, 283 F. 746 (2d Cir. 1922) (this despite the fact that certificates were in the possession of the British Public Trustee, an officer of an ally). As for bearer bonds of a US entity where the bonds are physically situated outside the US, see *Cities Service Co.* v. *McGrath*, 342 US 330 (1952) (obligations deemed within the US); *Rogers* v. *Smith*, 185 F. Supp. 401 (D. Ill. 1960).

[215] *In re Masayo Huga's Estate*, 155 N.Y.S. 2d 987 (Sup.Ct. 1956).

[216] See e.g. *In re Toshizo Huga's Trust*, 155 N.Y.S. 2d 1001 (Sup.Ct. 1956).

[217] Where the government seizes all beneficial interests and the corpus, it may act as absolute owner and is not required to do more than preserve the property. See *Central Hanover Bank & Trust Co.* v. *Markham*, 68 F. Supp. 829 (S.D.N.Y. 1946); *In re Sandhagen's Estate*, 200 Misc. 847, 107 N.Y.S. 2d 73 (Sur. Ct. 1951). There is a different result where some of the beneficiaries are American. See *Isenberg* v. *Trent Tr. Co.*, 26 F.2d 609 (9th Cir. 1928).

[218] See e.g. *In re Rihei Huga's Trust*, 155 N.Y.S. 2d 998 (Sup. Ct. 1956) (New York law required consent of settlor as well for termination of trust).

location of assets outside the United States may lead to conflicting claims by the USA and other countries.[219] This prospect reinforces the fundamental principle that the asset protection trust situated in the United States can offer no real protection with respect to assets and operations in third countries. Indeed, as noted, it may simply enhance the risk of expropriation that already exists in the home country and at the situs of a particular asset.

Finally, once the Alien Property Custodian steps in by vesting a beneficial interest in a trust, the government takes the rights that the enemy beneficiary had.[220] Under these circumstances, an untainted trustee who continues to administer the trust can be surcharged in a suit by the government if the trustee fails to transfer to the government the income or corpus to which the tainted beneficial owner is entitled. The fiduciary duties previously owed to the private beneficiary would now be owed to the government. On the other hand, this would presumably not be the case to the extent that trust property is beyond the jurisdiction of the United States.

8. Practical Considerations of Implementation and Drafting

Any serious evaluation of the adaptability of the asset protection trust for use by multinational corporations ought to move beyond abstract legal theory as well as case analysis and give consideration to the experience of trusts that have actually been implemented. In this regard, the model most often referred to is the United States Philips Trust, which was initially established prior to World War II by N. V. Philips Gloeilampenfabriken, the giant Dutch electronics manufacturer.

While reference is often made to the United States Philips Trust as the paradigm for multinational corporate asset protection trusts, there has been, to this author's knowledge, no serious analysis of the U. S. Philips Trust (hereinafter also referred to as the Philips Trust) experience and what it presages for similar efforts in the future. Indeed, there even appears to be an assumption that the Trust is still in existence,[221] when, in fact, this is not the case. The circumstances of the termination of the Philips Trust are highly instructive as to the deficiencies inherent in the adaptation of the asset protection trust for multinational corporate use.

The specific experience of the Philips Trust suggests a wide assortment of issues regarding drafting and implementation of the asset protection trust for corporations that simply cannot be avoided. Against the background of the Philips Trust experience, the remainder of this chapter considers these issues. The purpose is to illustrate that, while the trust is often offered as an alternative for asset protection, and may be the best alternative available,[222]

---

[219] See *In re Masayo Huga's Estate*, 155 N.Y.S. 2d 987 (Sup. Ct. 1956).
[220] See e.g. *In re Weingartner's Will*, 185 Misc. 481, 55 N.Y.S. 2d 823 (Sup. Ct. 1945).
[221] See infra, text accompanying note 232.
[222] See Ch. 10 for a consideration of other possibilities.

closer analysis indicates that its adaptability for corporate use is far more problematic than what might appear, superficially, to be the case.

8.1. THE UNITED STATES PHILIPS TRUST

Before analysing the Philips Trust in operation, some background is in order. The trust was established on 25 August 1939,[223] shortly before the Germans invaded the Netherlands. The stated purpose of the trust was to assure the continued operation of the company, despite the German invasion. Thus, the significant operations centered in the United States were transferred to a free-standing trust, the American Trust. The trust was designed as an entirely independent entity, so that it would be an American national and would not be treated as an enemy national subject to having its assets seized.[224]

After World War II the trust continued in operation, this time maintained in the event of a Soviet invasion of Western Europe.[225] On 19 December 1956, the trust was altered in certain respects. Specifically, the original trustee, the Hartford National Bank and Trust Company, transferred trust assets to be administered by a wholly owned subsidiary, the Hartford American General Corporation. This was part of a reorganization to eliminate certain Latin American assets that were to be administered separately.[226] By the 1956 trust indenture, the Hartford American General Corporation transferred certain assets back to the Hartford National Bank and Trust Company to hold for a newly created trust. Initially, this United States Philips Trust was funded with minimal cash, as well as shares of Philips Industries, Incorporated and shares and debentures of North American Philips Company (hereinafter referred to as NAP). NAP was and has been the chief operating and profitmaking Philips-entity in the United States. thus, the structure of Philips operations in the United States was as shown in Fig.1.

Of course, the United States operations were an extension of the activities of the Dutch electronics multinational firm. Indeed, as noted earlier, N. V. Philips Gloeilampenfabriken, the operating company, had settled the intitial trust in 1939, along with its holding company, N. V. Gemeenschappelijk

[223] See Indenture of Trust, as amended, between the Harteford American General Corporation and Hartford National Bank and Trust Co. 2 19 Dec. 1956) (hereinafter referred to as the Trust Indenture).

[224] See e.g. Reuters, 'Talking Point, North American Phillips Corp., New York', 17 Aug. 1987 (by P. Domm); *Financial Times*, 'Going Dutch', s I, p. 10, 24 Dec. 1986; *Communications Daily*, 'Impact Unclear; N.V. Philips Takes Over N. American Philips', 6: 246, at 323 (Dec. 1986). See also W. Kolvenbach, *Protection of Foreign Investments* (1989) 271. A second trust was established in 1939 in the United Kingdom, with the Midland Bank Executor & Trustee Co., Ltd., London, serving as trustee of the British Trust. See Moody's International 2811 (1986).

[225] See e.g. Kolvenbach, supra, note 224, at 271 n. 2, reporting on comments by Dr Fritz Philips in the Dutch newspaper *De Telegraaf* on 9 Aug. 1976, that the company had prepared a complete scenario in the event of an invasion of Europe.

[226] See *Moody's*, supra, note 224.

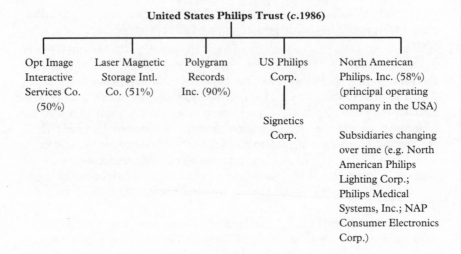

FIG. 1

Bezit Van Aandeelen Philips' Gloeilampenfabriken.[227] In effect, then, two theoretically independent operating entities existed (Fig. 2).

Both amalgams of companies were charged with conducting the electronics and related business worldwide. For example, the preamble of the Trust Indenture states that:

The said Trust is carrying on and engaged in, either directly or through subsidiary and affiliated companies, world-wide business of manufacturing, selling, exporting, importing, and contracting in the fields of electrical devices and other fields, in accordance with the provisions of said Indenture providing thereby the maintenance of activities formerly carried on by [N. V.] Philips and the employment of a considerable number of employees and many others who were dependent on said business' being carried on even under such disastrous circumstances as did occur as specified in said Indenture . . .[228]

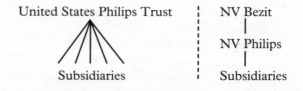

FIG. 2

---

[227] Trust Indenture at 2. During 1982, the coroporate structure was reorganized with N.V. Philips' Gloeilampenfabriken becoming a holding company. See *Moody's International* (1991) 3048–9.

[228] Trust Indenture at 2–3.

To assure that the Philips Trust was not subjected to the United States TWEA or similar legislation the Trust Indenture explicitly imposes a number of restrictions. The trustee is required to be an American citizen and resident and any successor, pursuant to article twenty-ninth, would have to be a bank or trust company organized under the laws of the United States or one of the states. In addition, a governing committee charged with directing the trustee in the administration of the trust was to consist of six, and beginning in 1983, of seven members, all but one of whom had to be American citizens and residents and qualify for security clearance.[229] The non-American was to have no access to sensitive information requiring security clearance and was to have his membership on the governing committee terminated during any "period of Emergency (as herinafter defined in clause Twenty-Seventh)".

To address the problem of trust beneficiaries under the TWEA, the Trust Indenture specifically limited their rights. The beneficiaries of the Philips Trust are not specifically identified. However, three possible distributional patterns are set forth. First, if there is no emergency, the governing committee can decide to terminate the trust and distribute the assets to N. V. Philips. The trust cannot be terminated during its term if there is an emergency. If at the end of the permissible term of the trust there is no emergency, the assets of the trust must again be distributed to N. V. Philips. However, if at that time there is an emergency, the assets must be distributed for the benefit of the shareholders of N. V. Philips and N. V. Bezit.[230]

While distribution must be made for the benefit of the shareholders, it need not be direct and can be in such manner "as may be approved by the Governing Committee and approved by Hartford or as may be orderd by a court in Connecticut which has assumed jurisdiction thereof at the petition of Hartford [the trustee]". Most significantly, distributions may only be made to "Admissible Shareholders" and not all shareholders. Admissible shareholders are those shareholders owning shares of N. V. Philips or N. V. Bezit, who are not persons, firms, companies, or bodies of a country at war with or occupying any portion of the United Kingdom of the Netherlands or the United States. Ownership can be in the form of direct or indirect control. Moreover, the same would apply if the party is adhering to or taking instructions in any manner from the enemy country or is even temporarily resident there. If shares cease to be so controlled, it must be proved to the satisfaction of the governing committee that no valuable consideration has passed or been promised to the firm in connection with the cessation of direct or indirect control and disposition. Special provision is also made for the possibility of a U. S. court allowing a shareholder to participate, notwithstanding the foregoing exclusion.[231]

Despite the care that went into the design of the United States Philips Trust, its effectiveness had come into serious question by the 1980s.

[229] Clause Fifth; Tenth Supplemental Indenture, 18 Nov. 1982.
[230] Clause Twenty-Third.
[231] Clause Twenty-Seventh(g).

Although a number of commentators have referred to the trust as a model and assumed that it is still in existence,[232] it was terminated on 17 December 1986. The reasons for its termination and the surrounding circumstances are quite instructive in terms of the less tangible, but very real costs associated with the use of a free standing and fully funded asset protection trust.

The first consideration relates to the risk itself. After World War II, the Philips Trust was maintained in light of the looming Soviet threat. That threat, by the mid-1980s, simply did not seem credible any longer. While some unanticipated threat could unexpectedly arise,[233] a Europe character-ized by a crumbling Eastern bloc and an increasingly unified Western Europe did not justify the caution reflected by the maintenance of the trust.

Of course, if no cost were involved in the maintenance of the trust, it might still have been retained. By the mid-180s, however, a far greater risk to the corporation, in the form of international competition, compelled stream-lining the company. As Pieter C. Vink, then chairman of the governing committee of the United States Philips Trust, stated: "In the face of this challenge, and particularly the intense competition from the Far East, relationships among Philips companies can no longer be governed by a legal instrument formulated almost 50 years ago."[234] The chairman of N. V. Philips, C. J. van der Klugt, said that restructuring "will hasten the realization of Philips' vision of the future as a unified company and one well able to compete effectively on a global basis."[235] The chairman and president of NAP, Cees Bruynes, emphasized that NAP and one of its subsidiaries, Signetics, would increasingly participate in Philips' top-level product policies and strategies".[236] Vink agreed and added that integration "will clearly establish a unified Philips strategy and product policy worldwide under unified co-ordination".[237]

As these comments indicate, the recent concern has been less with political forces than with other multinational entities. When an asset protection trust of the kind utilized by N. V. Philips is employed, the multinational's operations are duplicated. To protect against seizure in the United States and to assure recognition of the independent status of the entity, the trust's operations must be kept as separate as possible from the corporation's own operations. But this produces a duplication of research and overhead costs, as well as of scientific effort. To the extent that an attempt is made to divide up responsibilities and avoid duplication, or share technology, the charge can be made that the trust is not an independent entity.[238] Moreover, the trust's

[232] See e.g. Kolvenbach, supra, note 224, at 271.

[233] For example, on 19 August 1991 a sudden change in the government of the Soviet Union caused substantial concern in the financial community. The dollar rose sharply.

[234] PR Newswire, 'U.S. Philips Trust Terminated', 17 Dec. 1986.

[235] *Communications Daily*, supra, note 224, at 3.

[236] Ibid.

[237] Ibid.

[238] See ibid. for a description of the strong response to any public charges that the trust and N.V. Philips were not independent.

assets in the United States really need to be fairly representative of all of the corporate assets. Otherwise, a takeover of the corporation could result in the confiscation of vital operations without the real potential of carrying on the enterprise from friendly territory via the trust vehicle. As with assets, a full management structure would have to be in place. Otherwise, the capture of or control over home-country managers would impede the successful operation of the business from abroad.[239]

An associated problem that has not received a great deal of public attention is the natural competitiveness of the controlling boards. N. V. Philips and its board members considered themselves to be the parent and to be in *de facto*, if not *de jure*, control of the trust. The United States Philips Trust governing committee had a quite different attitude. After a history of fifty years of decision-making in the United States, including a number of war years, when the governing committee was the only functioning managerial board, there was no particular allegiance to N. V. Philips. It should be recalled that virtually all of the members of the governing committee of the Philips Trust, as well as the trustee, had to be American citizens and residents. Their view was that they were more cosmopolitan than their counterparts in Eindhoven, the Netherlands, and certainly understood better the American market and Philips's competitors in that market.[240]

The competitiveness of these managerial groups eventually deteriorated to the point where a lawsuit was commenced by N. V. Philips to regain control of the trust after the refusal of the governing committee to surrender voluntarily its autonomy and terminate the trust. That committee, of course, had enjoyed a great deal of independence and essentially hoped to split off the U. S. operations. Two of the most prominent American law firms, Sullivan & Cromwell (for N. V. Philips) and Paul Weiss, Rifkind, Wharton & Garrison (for the trust) confronted one another in the battle.

Eventually, the members of the governing committee gave way to various pressures. In the process, however, one especially potent concern arose. There was a recognition that the trustee and, almost certainly the governing committee, had a fiduciary duty to the trust beneficiaries. That meant a duty to N. V. Philips itself or N. V. Bezit shareholders, depending on the construction of the trust instrument.[241] They also owed a duty to the shareholders of NAP and the various other corporate operating entities and their subsidiaries ultimately controlled by the trust. Especially since the American branch had often outperformed its Dutch relative, and had certainly drawn more positive reaction from American investors on Wall

---

[239] Again, with respect to the termination of the trust, chairman Vink noted that "[w]ithin the new structure, plans also provide for the intergration of U.S. and N.V. Philips' management on operational, managerial and board levels". Ibid.

[240] The description of events here is based on discussions with persons who witnessed these developments, but were not members of either the governing committee of the Trust or of the N.V. Philips board.

[241] Depending on the circumstances, either the corporation or the individual shareholders of Bezit were entitled to the trust assets. See supra text accompanying note 230.

Street, where both stocks were traded, the decision to terminate risked breaches of fiduciary duty and even securities violations.[242]

The actual termination was therefore handled rather gingerly. But after the trust was terminated, further problems arose because the most significant asset of the trust, NAP, was owned only 58 per cent by the trust and 42 percent by public investors. As with such companies as British Petroleum Co. plc and Royal Dutch Shell Group, the bid price for shares in U. S. operating units had to be raised to avert minority shareholder suits.[243] On the other hand, continued minority ownership by the public would have involved inefficiencies of accountability, reporting, and potential fiduciary duty that could stymie the corporation's efforts at worldwide operational integration and competitiveness. Thus, the existence of a complex, dual structure of enterprise ownership presented serious costs not only in operational terms, but also in terms of the process of corporate reorganization and reintegration.[244]

One further cost of termination became apparent from the missteps following enterprise reintegration. N. V. Philips entered the American market with a personal computer business development plan that was a disaster costing approximately $150 million. The failure has been ascribed by some insiders to a lack of appreciation of the market by the leaders of the newly integrated N. V. Philips, which had so long kept its distance from that market. It has also been explained as attributable to personal competition of managerial classes, in which the Dutch felt that they needed to and could show that they would successfully manage the American operations.[245] This example demonstrates the internecine competition and the costs that may surface during the reintegration process after a dual-entity structure has been utilized over an extensive period of time.

The dual-entity structure also involved significant issues of antitrust and autonomy of decisionmaking while it was in effect. The appearance, if not the reality of absolute independence, offered the best chance to avoid the reach of any home-country takeover of N. V. Philips. It also offered the most promise for avoiding vesting or freezing of assets in the United States on the basis of the trust's being directly or indirectly controlled by an enemy alien.[246] Thus, in an effort to establish its autonomy, NAP and its controlling trust had a history of instituting lawsuits against those failing to treat them as independent from N. V. Philips.[247]

---

[242] See e.g. Domm, supra, note 224.

[243] See *id*. See also 'Philips Under the Spotlight', *Euromoney*, Oct. 1987, 105, 107.

[244] There were very good reasons for N.V. Philips to buy out the remaining 42%, apart from the concern over minority disruptions. The dollar was down and the NAP stake alone contributed as much as 20% of N.V. Philips' total worldwide earnings. Further, the need to streamline was imperative in the light of intense, worldwide competition. Ibid.

[245] The American market was the most important and promising market, and may have been an additional motivation for the termination of the trust and takeover by N.V. Philips. See Euromoney, supra, n 243.

[246] See supra, text accompanying n 193.

[247] See infra, text accompanying n 255.

The emphasis on independence, however, meant that any collaborative efforts between the trust and N. V. Philips could be regarded as the concerted effort of separate entities in restraint of trade, despite the historical links between the entities. In short, the legal principles for maximizing asset protection were directly contrary to those for avoiding antitrust violations.

The very real potential existed for the Philips-type structure to be regarded as a possible violation of section 1 of the Sherman Act.[248] That provision prohibits contracts, combinations, or conspiracies in restraint of trade. A persistent issue confronted by American courts has been whether an intra-enterprise effort in restraint of trade constituted a violation of section 1. For example, an unsettled question was whether two affiliated entities, wholly controlled by the same parent, could ever be in violation given the requirement of a plurality of actors for a violation.

The United States Supreme Court in *Copperweld Corp* v. *Independence Tube Corp.*[249] addressed the "intra-enterprise" conspiracy theory that had been gaining ground in American courts. It rejected this theory, specifically holding that a corporation and its *wholly owned* subsidiary cannot enter into a contract, combination, or conspiracy within the meaning of section 1 of the Sherman Act. The Court also expressed in an *obiter dictum* the view that a corporation and its employees or agents could not engage in concerted action violative of section 1 of the Sherman Act.

While the *Copperweld* case is regarded as having resolved the intra-enterprise issue in a way favourable to internal corporate collaboration, it has left unsettled the outcome when 100 per cent control of an agency relationship is not involved. For example, a number of lower court decisions have since found the necessary plurality of independent actors when the parent, owns only a portion of the related entity, even if it is a majority and controlling interest equal to as much as 75 per cent.[250] Indeed, the Supreme Court in *Copperweld* indicated that some sort of multi-factor analysis would be required in such cases. Based on this multi-factor analysis, one federal court has held that a rural electric co-operative formed by a number of corporations is a single enterprise with a common goal. Since the corporations had never been competitive, had divergent interests, and never worked for other than a common goal, they were a single entity for antitrust purposes.[251]

The precise point at which a Philips-type trust would be situated on this developing spectrum is difficult to predict. However, it very much concerned the Philips management. Based on *Copperweld*, there would definitely seem to be a plurality of actors in this dual-entity structure. On the other hand, the decision in the cooperative case, *City of Mr. Pleasant* v. *Associated Electric*

---

[248] 15 U.S.C. s1.
[249] 467 U.S. 752 (1984). See also J. von Kalinowski, *Antitrust Laws and Trade Regulation* (1991), s6.01[2][c].
[250] See e.g. *Aspen Title & Escrow inc.* v. *Jeld-Wen, Inc.*, 677 F. Supp. 1477 (D. Or. 1987).
[251] *City of Mt. Pleasant* v. *Associated Electric Coop., Inc.*, 838 F.2d 268 (8th Cir. 1988).

Cooperative, Inc., [252] indicates that *Copperweld* may be applied to exempt certain horizontal arrangements in which the entities have historically acted in concert and for a singular purpose.

Of course, before there can be a section 1 violation, there must be some attempt at a restraint of trade. The Sherman Act evaluates different activities by different standards. Certain concerted actions are per se violations of the Act, while others are only violations if they tend to be anti-competitive for the market involved. This distinction between per se violations and those determined pursuant to a "rule of reason" is significant in the case of the Philips Trust and similar arrangements. In particular, a horizontal market division, in which territories, customers, or product markets are divided by "competitors" is regarded as a per se violation of section 1 of the Sherman Act, as well as other provisions of the antitrust laws.[253] Yet even here there are a number of decisions that suggest a rule of reason will apply if the effects of an agreement are pro-competitive in nature or at least unclear.[254]

To the extent that there is absolutely no collaboration between the trust, its corporate subsidiaries, and the parent corporation, there should be little concern about antitrust violations. However, the Philips experience would suggest that this is not a realistic or even desirable expectation. A great deal of evidence suggests that N. V. Philips and the United States Philips Trust divided up the worldwide light-bulb market. There are also indications that joint pricing decisions were made. A report indicates that '[f]or many years, NAP was operated as [a] company completely independent from N. V. Philips, and suggestion of any relationship or affiliation between the 2 drew stinging letters from NAP lawyers and dark threats of legal action.' However, the report goes on to state that '[t]his pretense ended in 1975 with the NAP acquisition of Magnavox, and since then [the] companies have drawn closer together, to [the] point where it generally has been conceded that NAP is a Philips subsidiary.'[255]

It should be recalled in this regard that until the Philips Trust's termination in 1986, it generally controlled between 55 and 60 per cent of NAP stock, not the 100 per cent of the *Copperweld* decision. Moreover, N. V. Philips owned no interest in NAP. Thus, the quoted evidence of collaboration might well have been found to be a conspiracy involving horizontal restraints between independent enterprises.

The intimate relationship of the companies is further established by comments of Pieter Vink, chairman of the governing committee of the Philips Trust. Explaining the trust's termination, he stated that its continued existence "would not be consistent with its purpose and objective—advancing the businesses in the United States in which [N. V.] Philips has an

---

[252] Ibid.

[253] E.g. the Federal Trade Commission Act, s5, 15 U.S.C. s45.

[254] See e.g. *National Collegiate Athletic Assn.* v. *Board of Regents*, 468 U.S. 85 (1984); *Northwest Wholesale Stationers, Inc.* v. *Pacific Stationery and Printing Co.*, 472 U.S. 284 (1985).

[255] See *Communications Daily*, supra, n 224.

interest".[256] In sum, the Philips experience indicates that the dual structure is threatened from two directions. On the one hand, there is the risk of antitrust violation from too close collaboration. While an impenetrable wall between the trust and the corporation could be constructed, this would be antithetical to the very purpose of the trust—to preserve the enterprise and not to create a new and entirely independent competitive entity. The other side, however, is that the more the trust is depicted and conceived as an affiliate of the corporation, the more it risks sacrificing asset protection at the corporate domicile and in the United States. Thus, while antitrust dangers are averted and the enterprise functions in a more competitive and efficient manner through autonomy, the very protection sought by the creation of the trust may be placed in jeopardy through the loss of managerial control over formerly corporate assets.

One of the greatest fears of N. V. Philips's management was that Philips Trust management would use the antitrust laws as a lever to force a formal and irreconcilable rupture between the corporation and the trust. Specifically, the concern was that disaffected and independence-minded members of the governing committee of the Philips Trust would release information to the American government establishing the requisite antitrust violations. With sufficient evidence to support its position, the government would press for a divestment of all interest in the Philips Trust and its controlled entities by N. V. Philips and its shareholders.

Ironically, these very shareholders confronted Philips with another, different sort of problem. The root of the problem was the Philips Trust's practice with respect to reinvestment of earnings. Historically, the trust did not remit its share of NAP's sizeable dividend to the shareholders of N. V. Philips. Through 1981, it had made only one cash distribution. Instead, the dividends were accumulated and reinvested in NAP. For example, in 1974, the Trust provided $142 million of the $170 million paid by NAP to purchase Magnavox. In 1975, it purchased not only its portion of a rights offering by NAP, but also many shares not acquired by other NAP shareholders.[257]

The Philips Trust's practices in this regard led to at least one formal legal challenge. Undoubtedly, the Trust Indenture, by its very terms, could have stimulated many such challenges. The Indenture is quite ambiguous on the duty to distribute trust income to N. V. Philips shareholders. Clause First of the Indenture provides simply for the distribution to the beneficiaries of trust income after deduction of expenses of administration. Subsequent pro-

---

[256] See PR Newswire, 'United States Trust Terminated' (by J. Briggs), 17 Dec. 1986. See also *Forbes*, 'Uncle Philips' American Nephew', 14 Apr. 1980, stating: 'In practice, whatever the legal separation, the relationship between the two companies [N.V. Philips and NAP] is as close as one might assume from the stock ownership, the exchange of technology, and the fact that NAP's top two men are old N.V. Philips employees' and quoting Cees Bruynes, then president of NAP, referring to N.V. Philips as NAP's "Dutch uncle". *Financial World*, 13 Sept. 1983, reported that "[m]ost of [NAP's] products are based on the parent company's developments".

[257] See Briggs, 'Uncle Philips' American Nephew', above, n. 256. See also *Financial World*, supra, n 256.

visions, such as Clause Sixth, seem to give the governing committee absolute discretion in determining when and in what amounts income should be distributed. Yet, even if the governing committee were assumed to have this authority, and that Clause Sixth overrides Clause First, this might well not excuse the members under American trust law of abuse of discretion if acting for their self-interest or without properly informing the beneficiaries.[258]

Furthermore, the fact that a trustee does not have to distribute income in any one year does not mean that he can choose never or hardly ever to distribute it. If, as Clause Sixth indicates, certain operational considerations must be factored in, this only emphasizes the need for the Governing Committee to make the most deliberate evaluation and to do so consistently with exacting fiduciary standards of due diligence.[259] In short, the dividend policy of the trust proved to be the source of conflict, with the Governing Committee torn between the dictates of trust duty to beneficiaries and their own interest to use the trust as a pocketbook for the financial needs of NAP and other controlled corporations.

In addition to the fiduciary side of the distribution issue, there was also a tax side, which engendered a number of problems. Though this chapter is not concerned with tax aspects of asset protection trusts, it is important to note that the failure to distribute income and its undue accumulation threatened additional taxation of the Trust as an association taxable like a corporation.

Indeed, one of the problems of the Trust for taxation, as well as for other purposes, was that it could be subjected to several levels of regulation and taxation, because of its difficulty of classification. For example, it risked being treated as a trust in terms of the imposition of the most rigorous fiduciary standards on the trustee and governing committee, but as an association for tax and other purposes.

Another area of concern was corporate law. Suppose the Philips Trust's governing committee had NAP make or maintain an investment in an unprofitable activity in order to establish an N. V. Philips foothold in the American market. To the extent that NAP's minority, public shareholders were disadvantaged by these actions, they could contend that the Philips Trust, the majority shareholder, had violated a duty of fairness. While ill-defined, this duty has been recognized by a number of courts.[260] A similar duty of directors was reflected in the 1984 version of the Model Business

---

[258] Scott, supra, note 12, §§182 and 183. See also §173.

[259] Ibid., §170. Among the potential fiduciary violations would be use of trust property for the fiduciaries' own purposes, §170.17, competition with the beneficiaries, §170.23, and lack of impartiality among beneficiaries, §183.

[260] See e.g. *South* v. *Tele-Communication, Inc.*, 134 Cal. App. 3d 338, 184 Cal. Rptr. 571 (1982). See, generally, 3 Model Business Corporation Act Annotated §8.61, at 1142.42 to 11.42. 42.1, 1142.85 (1991 Supp.). Some courts have reached a similar conclusion with respect to directors, e.g. *Neponsit Investment Co.* v. *Abramson*, 405 A.2d 97 (Del. 1979) (the rule is "clearly established" that when directors are on both sides of the transaction they have the burden of showing that it is "intrinsically fair").

Corporation Act (MBCA), §8.31, which was adopted in many states.[261] The same would probably be true of any arrangement by which N. V. Philips sold products to NAP or some other entity controlled by the Trust at a higher than market price. In effect, a disproportionate transfer of corporate wealth would be received by the N. V. Philips shareholders. Another example, with a wealth transfer effect in the other direction, involves intellectual property. As has been noted, NAP benefited from the laboratory discoveries and technological innovations of N. V. Philips. If inadequate or no payment was received for this know-how, the NAP minority shareholders arguably would benefit materially at the expense of the N. V. Philips shareholders.

Case law suggests that when unusual or unique organizational arrange-ments are involved, courts may be prepared to scrutinize transactions for conflicts that may adversely affect certain shareholders of one affiliate to the benefit of shareholders of another affiliate.[262] While there may not be clear evidence of self dealing, an adverse determination may simply be founded on suspicions and explained on the basis of some contrived, alternative theory of relief. A court may also rely on a vague doctrine, such as a duty of fairness, to reach the same result.[263] In either event, evolving fiduciary corporate law principles augur poorly for the dual Philips structure of operations. They exert considerable pressure on the entities to act entirely independently, even though this results in significant inefficiencies and decreased competitive-ness, and undercuts the very purpose of the trust—which is to preserve the company during times of emergency, and not to split the enterprise on a permanent basis into two wholly competitive organizations.

Despite the foregoing, the dual trust-corporate structure did afford certain tangential benefits to Philips that could prove of primary importance in certain cases. For example, a number of banks imposed absolute ceilings on the amount that would be loaned to any one corporation and its controlled subsidiaries. Since the Philips Trust and the companies it controlled were deemed entirely independent of N. V. Philips for borrowing purposes, the total amount of funds available to Philips worldwide was considerably more than might otherwise have been the case.

A second benefit from the dual structure experienced by Philips was in the area of embargoes and boycotts. As a result of New York law and a special tax by that state, the Philips Trust and affiliated entities doing business in New York could not, apparently trade with and do business in South Africa. On the other hand, N. V. Philips had no such constraints placed on it at certain times by the Dutch government. Accordingly, the dual-structure permitted markets around the world to be allocated so as to avoid legal restrictions and not offend political or social norms in certain jurisdictions.

---

[261] The new version of the MBCA s8.60, which is based on the concept of "conflicting interest", provides more of an emphasis on disclosure.

[262] See e.g. *Litwin* v. *Allen*, 25 N.Y.S. 2d 667 (Sup. Ct. 1940).

[263] See *id*. See also R. Clark, *Corporate Law* (1988), s3.4, at 127–8.

Yet another benefit related to import–export and customs duties. There were innumerable transfers of products between N. V. Philips and its subsidiaries and the Philips Trust and its controlled entities. Apparently, the pricing that was used was assumed by government officials to be fairly stated, rather than understated, on the theory that the entities were really independent and unaffiliated. Thus, a dual structure may substantially eliminate world trade costs. Nevertheless, in the Philips case, there was so much concern about eventual governmental challenges, resulting in the imposition, retroactively, of huge tariffs and penalties, that customs officials were regularly kept appraised of dealings between the Philips entities. This above-board strategy was successful in forestalling later allegations of concealment or fraud in the handling of transfers between the entities for customs purposes. Similar pricing concerns and disclosures were involved in tax reporting as well, and, apparently, did not develop into a serious challenge by the Internal Revenue Service. Of course, in other cases, governmental entities might choose to ignore the dual structure, and deny the benefits derived from a less than arm's-length relationship.

8.2. GENERIC PROBLEMS IN PROTECTIVE TRUST IMPLEMENTATION AND DRAFTING

A study of the United States Philips Trust reveals many of the actual problems as well as exposures to risk resulting from the dual structure or organization. There are additional difficulties as well that were not issues in the Philips experience, but that could be encountered in the adaptation of the trust for use as an asset protection vehicle for other multinational corporations.

8.2.1. Authority to Create the Trust

Earlier discussion focused on the possibility that a civil law country's law would be applied, and that that law would not recognize the institution of the trust. Consideration was also given to the possiibility that the law governing the foreign corporation would not permit the transfer of its property to the trust. One aspect of the problem that has not been given consideration is the American attitude towards the creation of trusts by corporations. In this regard, the assumption should not be made uncritically that corporations can create such trusts.

There is very little authority on this point. The Restatement (Second) of the Law of Trusts recognizes the issue and then shunts it aside as a matter of corporate law.[264] The fact that there is virtually no authority on the question makes the creation of a protective trust a risky proposition—even if the local American common law of trusts would ultimately be applied by the forum.

Assuming any legal owner of property, even if not a natural person, can create a trust, certain corporations may, nonetheless, be prohibited from

[264] See Restatement s18, Comment b.

doing so. A number of cases, for example, have held that a bank could not transfer assets to a trust it had settled. In large part, this was due to the fact that state banking regulations were construed as preventing the bank from taking such steps.[265] Thus, local American law or federal regulatory provisions may restrict the creation of a trust and the transfer of corporate assets to that trust. This may be the case even for a foreign corporation, to the extent that it owns assets or is doing business in one particular state.

Another basis for the restriction is the corporate governing instruments themselves. They must permit the creation of a trust by the corporation and the transfer of corporate assets to it. The fact that the domiciliary jurisdiction permits such steps to be taken may not suffice if the instrument itself can be construed as barring such conveyances. In this last regard, the assumption that articles of association may be retroactively amended to permit the establishment of a trust and transfers to it may be misplaced. By the time an amendment is contemplated, the company, its directors, and principal shareholders may all find themselves in a difficult situation in the home country, unable to exercise authority or no longer having legal authority to act.

8.2.2. Authority of the Trust to Create Controlled Corporations

An even more troubling issue is the authority of the protective trust to operate through controlled corporations and the severe consequences, on the other hand, that could flow from its failure to do so. The transfer of trust assets to a newly created corporation in exchange for its shares may be assumed by trustees to be a permitted activity. Under American trust law, however, there is considerable doubt as to whether this is, in fact, permissible conduct on the part of the trustees.[266]

Suppose the trust instrument authorizes the trustee to sell or otherwise dispose of trust property. Any number of courts have held that this directive would not suffice to empower the trustees to create a corporation and transfer property to it.[267] In an effort to rectify the situation, various states have enacted statutes permitting courts to approve the creation of corporations by trusts. Also, the Uniform Trustees' Powers Act §3(c)(3) explicitly empowers the trustee "to continue or participate in the operation of any business or other enterprise, and to effect incorporation, dissolution, or other change in the form of the organization of the business or enterprise".[268] However, this provision has not been adopted in all of the states.

---

[265] See e.g. *Ulmer* v. *Fulton*, 129 Ohio St. 323, 195 N.E. 557 (1935); *Gallagher* v. *Squire*, 57 Ohio App. 222, 13 N.E. 2d 373 (1938). See generally G. Bogert and G. Bogert, *The Law of Trusts and Trustees* 2d ed. rev. 1984, §44, at 450 and n. 12.

[266] See Scott, supra, note 12, §190.9A for a discussion of the cases and statutes, Another possibility would be for the parent to create the subsidiary corporation and then transfer the stock to the trust. This approach has its own problems. See e.g. below, text accompanying notes 274–5.

[267] See *ibid*. See also *In re Franks*, 154 Misc. 472, 277 N.Y.S. 573 (1935).

[268] Reprinted in Schoenblum, above, n. 83, 739.

Failure to incorporate business operations has its own obvious problems. From a tax standpoint, the trust could be regarded as just another association operating a business and be taxed as is a corporation. Perhaps, more significantly, the limits on legal liability available through corporate operation would be unavailable. The liability incurred in any one venture could result in all of the trusts's assets being reachable by creditors or other claimants.

8.2.3. Statement of Trust Purposes

The recommendation has been made by some commentators that the trust purposes should be clearly spelled out in the trust instrument.[269] The instrument should acknowledge the concerns resulting in the creation of the trust, including the fear of disruptions at home affecting the settlor and the interest in preserving and developing further the American operations of the company. It is also recommended that the trustee ought to be excused from traditional standards of investment and freed to act in accord with the traditional management and investment policies of the corporate settlor.

The foregoing recommendations may be highly desirable objectives, but they run the risk of foundering on the uncharted territory of trust and private international law in this area. As has already been pointed out, too explicit a statement in a trust instrument as to concerns about political upheaval in the home country could prove extremely embarrassing to that government. It might precipitate hostile action by the government even before a crisis has arisen and many assets have been transferred. Moreover, political instability and threat of invasion may not be a permissible basis for conveying corporate assets for less than full value under the corporate laws of various countries. It is unlikely that American courts will recognize the validity of the transfer, if the corporation had no authority to do so under the laws of the jurisdiction of incorporation.

The likelihood that the trust instrument could remain private is uncertain. Disgruntled shareholders of the corporation, less concerned with hypothetical political risks than current profits, might be able to compel disclosure in their effort to stall or prevent the arrangement. In any event, the exchanges of information between the United States and other countries under various treaties, as well as required securities disclosures in the United States, would suggest that the trust terms would become public back home.

Furthermore, a statement of purpose and intent in the trust instrument alone would not suffice. The corporate charter would have to authorize this conduct as well. The domiciliary country might not find this an acceptable purpose in connection with its authorization of corporate existence. The amendment of the formative documents might be costly, time-consuming, and difficult to accomplish.

[269] See e.g. Christensen and Goldsmith, *A New Challenge: Drafting Fail/Safe Trusts for U.S. Investments by Nonresident Aliens and Foreign Corporations* (American Collegle of Probate Counsel, 17 and 18 Mar. 1986) A–47).

The alternative approach is equally troubling. Failure to state concerns about the security of assets in the relevant corporate and trust instruments could be relied upon to challenge the corporation's capacity to establish the trust. Failure to make reference to the concerns in the trust instrument could result in American courts refusing to recognize the trust, as intended, as a free-standing and wholly independent entity not subject to the jurisdiction of the country in which the corporation is organized.

In this author's opinion, the foregoing conflicting pressures associated with the purposes clauses emphasize the need to have co-operative governments both at the domicile of the corporation and in the United States. The home jurisdiction ought to regard the asset protection trust as a mechanism for preserving national wealth in times of turmoil. Along these lines, the Netherlands has enacted explicit legislation permitting the transfer of a corporate domicile to any other part of the realm.[270] Few other countries, however, have gone even this far. Certainly, there is a dearth of legislation addressing the fate of assets transferred to an asset protection trust in another jurisdiction.

If a purposes clause is included, it must be carefully drafted. A statement in the purposes clause of the Philips Trust indicates that the trust is to continue developing the American business of the corporation. This sort of statement could prove highly controversial. On the one hand, it will justify the trustee acting more like a business manager than a trustee; on the other hand it links the trust to the parent corporation. If the trust is charged with developing the American interests of the corporation, it would, presumably, have to be in close contact with the parent to ascertain how the United States interests ought to be developed. Since the direction of corporate interests could change over time, an expectation of continuing co-ordination could be read into the trust instrument. Yet this could severely undercut the asset protection afforded by the trust through its autonomous existence. At bottom, the fundamental contradiction in the dual-entity structure, between autonomy and ultimate corporate control in the service of its corporate objectives, is difficult to reconcile.

8.2.4. Trust Assets

The initial creation of the trust involves the transfer of corporate assets to the trust. A serious question arises regarding the initial funding of the trust. Strong pressures will exist to fund the trust minimally, so as to preserve the integrity of the corporate enterprise as long as possible.

As admirable as this objective may be, there are substantial concerns associated with utilization of this standby trust approach. As regards corporate assets the basic problem is that once the emergency occurs, it may prove too late to transfer the assets successfully to the trust.[271] An American

---

[270] See State Act of 9 March 1967, Off. Gaz. Kingdom of the Netherlands 1967, No. 161.
[271] See e.g. Schoenblum, supra, note 8, §18.81.11.

court would not be looking at a fully operational American trust, but rather a receptacle designed to receive assets being claimed contemperaneously by the country of incorporation of the transferor corporation. The likelihood that the transferred assets will be protected in these circumstances would seem considerably less than in the Philips-type situation, where the assets are transferred before the actual emergency to an American trust, remain in trust, and are reorganized by allocation to a variety of operational entities controlled by the trust.

Of course, as desirable as a free-standing trust may appear, the problems discussed above with respect to this structure cannot be brushed aside. An enterprise must be artificially split. Many assets, especially if intangible in nature, cannot simply be allocated to either the corporation or the trust. Unlike the standby trust where, essentially, the entire enterprise or a segment thereof flees and assumes a new trust form of organization, the dual structure requires a division of the enterprise that is almost certainly inefficient and difficult to accomplish.

For example, suppose certain American subsidiaries of the parent corporation have assets and operations in the home country of the parent. A simple conveyance of the shares of the American subsidiary to a newly formed American trust is a very superficial and unsatisfactory solution to the objective of asset protection. The home country could succeeed in expropriating physical assets situated on its territory, as well as taking over business operations and intellectual property to which it has direct access or which is present there in some form.

Likewise, the parent, or one of its subsidiaries incorporated at its domicile, may own assets or operate businesses in the United States. The retention of these shares by the parent will possibly result in deference by American courts to the home country with respect to its expropriation of these assets. Alternatively, the United States could vest or freeze these assets in the event of a war or national emergency. Thus, at least a partial realignment of assets and operations within the corporation on a geographic basis is a required preliminary to the actual division into the dual corporate–trust structure. This restructuring could prove costly, inefficient, and difficult to justify on the basis of some speculative threat. As noted, the Philips Trust was terminated in 1986 when it became clear that the costs of this form of enterprise organization were unjustified, as the threat of catastrophic political instability or invasion at home had become virtually nonexistent.

One other facet of the asset problem relates to assets and operations in third countries. Again, no simple solutions exist with regard to how these properties or the local companies that control them should be allocated between the parent and the trust. If the concern is with home-country instability or security from outside threat, leaving corporate assets under the control of the parent would be entirely unsatisfactory. The assets would remain exposed. Thus, a strong argument can be made for the transfer of control of these assets to the American trust. At the same time, a significant risk exists with this strategy. If any of the beneficiaries of the trust are shareholders or the parent corporation itself, or there are other ties with the home country, the worldwide assets of the enterprise may be vested or frozen in the event of a conflict between the United States and the home country. Still, confronting this risk seems preferable to permitting the potentially hostile home country to take control.

Another possibility in this last situation is the creation of a trust offshore the United States. The trust used would then avoid the risk of instability at home as well as the possibility of freezing or vesting by the United States. While this approach has much superficial appeal, it fails to address the risk of instability at the situs of trust administration and the fact that any trust assets reachable in the United States could still be frozen or vested.

When a Third-World corporation, or perhaps one domiciled in an Eastern European country or South Africa, is involved, the risk of offshore trust jurisdiction instability and United States vesting or freezing pales next to the prospect of eventual home-country expropriation. Yet, while a trust might appear to have a role to play in asset protection in this context, closer analysis reveals substantial obstacles to its successful use. This is not to say that efforts at asset protection should not be pursued in this situation, but only that they should be pursued with considerable caution and with a recognition of the difficulties that may be encountered along the way.

The first concern is again that the offshore trust situs may itself prove unstable. Several such jurisdictions have quite abruptly become unreliable and risky centres for trust adminstration. A second concern is that the effort will be for naught if the principal assets are fixed in the home country. While the offshore asset protection trust may prove helpful for a company that manufactures in the home country, but keeps low inventories and relatively minimal capital investment there, this would not be the case in many instances. Moreover, an alternative base of operations would have to exist so that manufacturing could proceed with minimal delay.

In addition to the foregoing, any effort to transfer intangible wealth of the corporation to an independent offshore vehicle could raise serious questions in the home country about the legality of the transfer. Disabling laws might well be given effect in the United States, which would have effective control over such intangibles as American investment securities and bank accounts. Possibly, the home country would have no proscriptions at the time of transfer. However, this would not insulate the transfer from later challenge in the American courts based on a retroactive change of foreign law. In their own laws, the American states have recognized the validity of retroactive regulation of corporate activity.[272] While the jurisprudence is murky, American and English forums have been prepared to apply retroactive

---

[272] See generally McNulty, 'Corporations and the Intertemporal Conflict of Laws' (1967) 55 Calif. L. Rev. 12.

foreign laws as a matter of choice of law.[273] Numerous distinguished commentators have approved of this conflicts of law position.[274]

A further practical consideration relates to credit. Securities that are pledged or otherwise reachable by corporate creditors could not readily be transferred to an independent entity. Moreover, the initial transfer could well bring corporate captial below permissible limits allowed by the home country, even if it otherwise permitted transfers to trusts. The reduction in capital might also violate the corporate charter or other controlling agreements.

The actual transaction might be one in which intangible assets were transferred to an offshore corporation, such as in the British Virgin Islands. The assets might then be dropped down further to a second BVI subsidiary, while the shares of the BVI holding company would be transferred to the parent corporation in exchange for the intangibles. The parent might then be prepared to transfer its shares in the BVI holding company to an offshore trust, perhaps situated in yet another jurisdiction. The trust would be a standby trust. To avoid undue triggering events, some sort of protective committee, situated in other safe jurisdictions, would order the transfer of BVI corporate shares to the trust in an emergency.

Even assuming this structure would move the shares to the trust in a timely fashion, there is no certainty that American courts would recognize the independence of the trust if the foreign government sought to reach the assets or reverse prior corporate action through a subsequently imposed board of directors. Certainly continued control of the trust's administration or that of the BVI corporations during the emergency by officers or related parties of the parent corporation would undercut the argument that the trust is an independent entity. While this problem could be solved by putting control of the offshore assets in the hands of untested managers, their loyalty to the parent corporation and its shareholders, as well as their expertise in managing the enterprise, would be open to serious question. This would be especially true in the case of a prolonged emergency.

The transaction just described might also face challenges under the securities laws, especially if there had been inadequate disclosure to public shareholders. Recent developments in American law make clear that the fact that

---

[273] Perhaps the most pertinent case in this regard is *Re Helbert Wagg & Co. Ltd.* [1956] Ch. 323. The court applied a 1933 German Moratorium Law requiring repayment of debt in German currency, even though the private contract, executed nine years earlier, required payment in London in English currency. The proper law of the contract was considered to be German law and, accordingly, the terms of the contract were overridden. See also *R. v. International Trustee for the Protection of Bondholders A.G.* [1937] A.C. 500. This case involved the US invalidation of gold coin and gold value clauses. The court held that the law of New York was the proper law and that the law could override a gold coin clause in previously issued bonds by the British government. The decision, of course, benefited the forum's government.

[274] See e.g. Dicey & Morris, supra, note 93, at 63–4 (describing the approach as "certainly the prevailing practice of courts on the continent of Europe" and with certain exceptions "is probably the prevailing practice of the English courts . . ." See also Mann, 'The Time Element in the Conflict of Laws' (1954) 31 *Brit. Yearbook Int. Law* 217.

transactions take place offshore will not insulate them from U. S. law, particularly if shares are traded on American markets, there are any American shareholders, or corporate assets are reachable in the United States.[275] As a result of these developments, disclosure may be required early on that will draw the attention of potentially hostile governments and shareholders who may then take steps to impede the implementation of the asset protection plan or, at least, make it too costly to implement.

None of the foregoing take account of tax considerations. These considerations, though beyond the scope of this chapter, would involve several jurisdictions and would prove quite complex. The proposed transaction might well have to be reshaped due to these tax considerations in a way that would make it less attractive from the standpoint of asset protection.

Undoubtedly, the instability of developing countries makes planning for expropriatory actions especially urgent. The trust may have a role to play in the protection of corporate assets in this context. However, analysis suggests that this may not truly be the case in many instances. In this author's opinion greater emphasis, perhaps, ought to be placed on express investment guarantees with the foreign country, insurance mechanisms, and encourage-ment of bilateral conventions assuring truly adequate compensation in the event of expropriations or similar acts. Even a revolutionary successor government is likely to be susceptible to considerable pressure to honor contractual or treaty commitments, especially if it is desirous of attracting foreign investment in the future.

In any event, an American court is likely to repudiate efforts of a foreign government to reach assets in violation of its explicit promises and may well permit aggrieved parties to reach American situs assets of the offending government. Thus a somewhat more promising approach would seem to be the creation of a trust vehicle in the United States or offshore, coupled with the obtaining of enforceable guarantees, either on a particularized basis or pursuant to a more generalized treaty. However, even then, many of the problems identified would remain to be addressed.

8.2.5. The Trustees

The asset protection trust requires the appointment of an American or third country trustee. The designation of a trustee from the home country will create the very real possibility of fixing the situs of the trust there. This would have the consequence of affording home-country control and, in case of conflict, American classification of the trust as an enemy alien.

---

[275] See e.g. Mann and Mari, 'Current Issues in International Securities Enforcement', and Grundfest, 'International Cooperation in Securities Enforcement: A new United States Initiative', in *Internationalization of the Securities Markets: Business Trends and Regulatory Policy* (1988), 99, 61. See also Goelzer, Gonson, Riesenberg, and Sullivan, 'Judicial and Other Developments in the Securities Laws Under the Restatements of Foreign Relations Law and the Hague Evidence and Service Conventions' (1989), ibid. 41, 65–82.

Suppose an American trust company is selected as trustee. This sort of appointment will not assure accomplishment of the purpose underlying the establishment of the trust. Rather than preserve assets for the benefit of the overall enterprise, the trustee may well feel compelled to pursue an entirely independent course, that might even put the trust and its controlled subsidiaries over time in direct competition with the parent.[276] Alternatively, if the trust instrument requires pursuit of corporate policies, the trustee may not be sufficiently informed about those policies and may need to consult regularly with the parent. Yet this would suggest the very sort of control sought to be avoided.

Some commentators have emphasized the need for trustees who have a connection with the parent.[277] For example, the suggestion has been made that there be two tiers of trustees—local and controlling. During non-emergency periods, the controlling trustees administer the trust. These trustees are closely affiliated with the corporation and may even be nationals and residents of the home country. With the onset of an emergency, control over the trust automatically shifts to the local trustee or trustees. These persons are ideally American residents and will administer the assets during the pendency of the emergency.

The suggestion set forth above is satisfactory as far as it goes, but it does not really come to grips with various dimensions of American law. To begin with, if only one or a few of the local trustees are American residents during an emergency, the presence of other trustees who are resident in the enemy country or an ally of an enemy country could result in vesting or freezing.[278] Furthermore, even if the trustees are all residents of the United States, their foreign nationality could also serve as a basis for United States action against American-situated assets.

As for the sudden shift of control from home country to American trustees, this move is only likely to reinforce the perception that the assets have been subject to the control of and really still belong to the parent corporation. This will be especially true if the grantor corporation or controlled affiliate retains the power to substitute trustees. An analogy to the United States estate tax suggests that such a power could result in the grantor corporation still being deemed the owner of the assets.[279]

In contrast to the above-described approach, there is the Philips Trust model. This very carefully crafted instrument also provides for two tiers of fiduciaries. The trustee is to be an American trust company. This assures continuity of administration and a more certain situs of the trust in the United States. Presumably, the trustee is to be chosen from a state that affords a favorable law for the objectives sought to be accomplished.

---

[276] See e.g. supra text accompanying notes 240–2.

[277] See generally Christensen and Goldsmith, supra, note 269.

[278] See also supra, text accompanying notes 217–18 and infra, text accompanying note 280.

[279] See Rev. Rul. 79–353, 1979–2, C.B. 325, as modified by Rev. Rul. 81–51, 1981–1 C.B. 458.

Additionally, the trust company may be permitted to establish a subsidiary entity to serve as trustee, thereby insulating the parent company's operations from any liabilities or conflicts that may arise, especially since the substantial assets and operations of a multinational corporation are involved.

The trustee, however, does not have plenary authority with respect to the administration of the trust. It must work with a "governing committee". The committee members of the Philips Trust, for example, were actually designated by name in the trust indenture. As noted, five of the six were citizens and residents of the United States.[280] All were required to be eligible for security clearance from the Department of Defense, to obtain such clearance, and to retain it for continued membership on the committee. The sixth member would not be required to have clearance, but in the event of an emergency would lose his seat on the committee. The sixth seat would not be reinstated until the end of the emergency. It would be filled by a person approved in writing by the N. V. Philips board of management. New members, in the event of other slots becoming vacant, could only be elected by a majority of the American members.

The governing committee of the Philips Trust is permitted to specify its own rules and procedures for conducting business. It is entitled to employ agents and counsel, and the members may be paid for their reasonable expenses and compensation.[281] The trustee is not liable for the acts of the committee's agents and counsel, and the committee is specifically excused from liability in its selection if reasonable care has been exercised.[282]

The relationship of a governing committee to a trustee is of central significance. If not carefully spelled out, a great deal of uncertainty could prevail as to who has proper authority and responsibility. Moreover, even if the instrument is detailed, the exact status of the committee members from a legal standpoint is uncertain.

In the case of the Philips Trust, the governing committee, rather than the trustee, has principal authority with respect to all administrative matters, since, under Clause Twenty-fifth, the trustee's powers are subject to rules imposed and advice given by the governing committee. Moreover, on certain matters, such as trustee compensation, replacement of the trustee, allocations between income and principal, and distributions the governing committee has primary authority. The last of these items is of particular import and indicates the nature of the interaction of the trustee and governing committee. Under Clause Third, a directory trust is clearly contemplated, with the trustee required to administer the trust "as directed by the Governing Committee". Under Clause Sixth, the governing committee has the power to "decide exclusively" what income shall be distributed,

---

[280] Clause Fifth. Later, the governing committee was expanded to seven members by the Tenth Supplemental Indenture, dated 18 Nov. 1983. Six of the seven had to be American citizens and residents.

[281] Clauses Third-Sixth.

[282] E.g. Clause Twenty-Fifth.

consistent with the policy of protecting trust assets and maintaining the operating efficiency of the trust's affiliated or subsidiary companies.

Despite these provisions, the trustee is empowered to seek a court order authorizing distributions and the terms on which they shall be made.[283] Thus, a rather complex relationship exists and, while the governing committee and trustee are likely to co-operate, the division of authority and veto power seem designed to deter distributions, except when there is complete agreement as to their desirability.

As for other administistative powers, these are assigned to the trustee, subject to direction from the governing committee.[284] To the extent that the trustee carries out the directions of the governing committtee, it is to be protected from liability. Thus, day-to-day management rests with the unaffiliated professional trustee, with policy and distributional decisions primarily placed in a governing committee consisting of top-level American executives of N. V. Philips, which in non-emergency periods has its own representative on the governing committee. This highly sophisticated governance model seems well designed to assure proper administration, pursuit of corporate policies, and avoidance of classification as a foreign entity.

Still, even this shrewdly crafted model raises some troubling questions. Perhaps, most significantly, the legal status of the governing committee members remains uncertain. Under American trust law,[285] these trust "advisors" are almost certainly regarded as fiduciaries, subject to the same duties as is the trustee, but without the trustee's legal title to the property. While Clause Twenty-sixth of the Indenture exonerates the governing committee members from liability as "partners", it fails to state that they are free from liability for their conduct as "trustees" or "fiduciaries". The same clause specifies that the trustee can be held personally liable to the extent of the trust assets the trustee holds. The provision, presumably, does not apply to the governing committee members, since they have no title to property.

Interestingly, the Philips Trust has no provision for removal of the trustee or the members of the governing committee. Again, this reflects a deep understanding of the dangers posed by such a provision. For example, any power in the parent corporation or one of its controlled entities could well be regarded as manifesting retained control. Certainly, no such power could be allowable during emergency periods. Even during non-emergency periods, a power of this sort would seem to undercut the character of the trust as an independent American entity.

Although the Philips Trust utilized American citizens and residents as members of the governing committee, the former, close association of these members with the corporation[286] could have raised problems in terms of the classification of the trust as an enemy alien, even if the committee members themselves were not technically capable of being so classified.

---

[283] Clause Sixth.
[285] See Scott, supra, note 12, s185, at 566.

[284] Clause Tenth.
[286] See e.g. supra, note 234.

There is an additional problem to the extent that the governing committee members are officers or directors of the parent, in this case, N. V. Philips. In this situation, the committee members will find themselves owing conflicting duties. As trustees, they owe a duty to accomplish the purposes of the trust for the benefit of the beneficiaries, who happen also to be shareholders of the parent corporation. However, their duty is to maximize the assets and profits of the autonomous trust. For example, if the parent corporation were expropriated or the shareholders' rights confiscated, the new owners of the corporation and the beneficiaries of the trust would be quite different persons. The fact that the equity owners may ultimately be different persons emphasizes the need for the governing committee members to maximize the profit of the trust, even though this may mean harsh competition with the former parent during non-emergency periods. If the governing committee members are also directors or officers of the parent, they are faced with an obvious conflict as to which entity's interests to pursue.

Another problem encountered in this situation relates to the different standards of conduct required of trustees and corporate directors or officers. In the case of corporate law, the business judgment rule prevails and it is rare for a director or officer to have his decision questioned successfully, at least in the absence of fraud, self-dealing, or the like.[287] On the other hand, the trustee is likely to be held to a considerably higher standard. For example, the Uniform Probate Code requires him to "observe the standard in dealing with the trust assets that would be observed by a prudent man dealing with the property of another".[288] The trustee is required to be more proactive in conduct; good faith is no defence and unintentional violations are not likely to be excused.

Even in cases of self-dealing, the standards seem to be quite different. Under the Model Business Corporation Act, sections 8.60–8.62, disclosure by a director need be made only to the board and typically not to shareholders. By way of contrast, American trust cases emphasize the duty of the trustee to keep beneficiaries (possibly the shareholders mentioned above) informed of all major risks and conflicts that could impact upon their equitable interests.[289]

8.2.6. The Beneficiaries

Few areas are likely to prove as complicated in the adaptation of the trust to corporate needs as are matters pertaining to beneficiaries. An immediate problem is the one of defining who are the beneficiaries. This, in turn, would depend on the sort of protective trust being employed. If a "fail-safe" type of trust is being employed, the grantor is likely to be the beneficiary during

---

[287] See generally Clark, supra, note 264, s3.4.
[288] Section 7–302.
[289] See e.g. *Allard* v. *Pacific National Bank*, 99 Wash. 2d 394, 663 P.2d 104 (1983). See also *Mayfield* v. *First National Bank of Chattanooga*, 137 F.2d 1013 (6th Cir. 1943).

nonemergency periods. Once an emergency occurs, the beneficiaries will typically be the shareholders of the grantor rather than the grantor itself.

This approach strikes the author as inadequate. The real possibility exists that many of the shareholders will be citizens of, or have links with, the domicile country. As a result, the assets are still likely to be threatened by this foreign country. Moreover, the shareholders' interests will be subject to American vesting or freezing, possibly also placing the burden on non-enemy shareholders to establish that they are free of taint.

Another possibility that has been suggested is to have a subsidiary create the trust and then make a corporate parent the beneficiary. Again, this will almost certainly not solve the problem. For example, if the grantor of the trust is an American corporation organized to hold United States operations, nothing will be accomplished by having as beneficiary the foreign corporation subject to expropriation or similar risks.

An alternative might be to withhold benefits from those whom the trustee believes would not be able to retain control of their equitable interests. The problem with this approach is that it is not likely to insulate the property from American freezing and confiscatory action. Those laws will apply even though the trustee can withhold beneficial enjoyment. The beneficial interest would have to be subject to divestment or the trustee would have to have total discretion as to distributions. Yet, this strategy overlooks one vital factor— shareholders are not likely to wish to have their shares go by default to other beneficiaries any more than to a hostile government.

Apart from the foregoing, there are immense difficulties in knowing who the beneficiaries are. One very real problem relates to the foreign practice of relying upon bearer shares. There are three facets to this problem. First, the trustee must be able to ascertain who is genuinely in control of the shares. This flexibility is desirable, but places an enormous burden on the trustee. Presumably, there must also be some avenue of recourse for a shareholder who wishes to question the trustee's determination. Yet, even if there is, this avenue may require the abandonment of the confidentiality that was a prime reason fo the nominee or bearer share ownership in the first place. The second problem is that in vesting or freezing situations, the United States may well presume enemy status, in the absence of a clear demonstration by the shareholder to the contrary. Finally, during nonemergency periods the law governing such shares will be uncertain. Some American states are likely to look to the same law which governs registered corporate shares, which, as the first part of this chapter indicates, is itself an unsettled question. Other states are likely to apply the law of the place where the shares are physically situated at the relevant moment. Of course, there would be much controversy in identifying the "relevant moment" and in pinpointing the physical location of the paper at that time. Moreover, there seems little to justify the determination of property rights on this basis, especially since the situs jurisdiction may have little to do with the underlying corporation or the real shareholder. This would especially be the case if the share certificates were in the possession of a nominee or other agent.

8.2.7. Flee Provisions

A staple of asset protection trusts for individuals is the flee clause, which triggers the transfer of the trust situs upon the occurrence of some undesirable event, such as political instability. Another, and preferable, approach empowers an individual or entity to determine when the requisite event has occurred and to order the transfer of trust assets and the appointment of a new trustee, or to take other steps to salvage the trust.[290]

In the case of the asset protection trust for multinational corporations, these provisions appear to this author to be of little utility. Unlike individuals, corporations often own substantial tangible, operational assets. These cannot be readily removed from a jurisdiction.

In the case of an individual, the situating of a trust offshore is largely ascribable to tax considerations. In these cases, there is a risk of political instability in the offshore jurisdiction, with the possibility of the government taking control of the trust or the trustee. By way of contrast, the asset protection trust for the multinational corporation typically obtains no special tax benefit by being offshore. Moreover, to the extent it has assets reachable in the United States, the offshore situs will not avoid American freezing or vesting.[291]

Of course, a standby asset protection trust might be funded with United States situs assets only upon the occurrence of some triggering event in the home country. Such an approach is quite risky. Continuing operations and assets in the United States could be frozen while the issues of whether there had been an effective and timely transfer were endlessly litigated.

The foregoing is not to be confused with a provision, as in Clause Second(b) of the United States Philips Trust that defines the emergency circumstances under which the trust may *not* be terminated and distributions may *not* be made to certain trust beneficiaries.[292]

8.2.8. Trustee Compensation and Other Costs

A real consideration with the use of any worldwide asset protection strategy is the cost of its creation and its administration, when weighed against the risks and the comparable costs and effectiveness of other asset protection devices or no action at all. One aspect of this is the question of compensation. Especially when an affiliate of the parent corporation is being employed as

---

[290] For a discussion of these mechanisms, see Schoenblum, supra, note 8, ss18.18.6–18.18–21.

[291] The tax consequences associated with the asset protection trust are not within the scope of this chapter. See generally Christensen & Goldsmith, supra, note 269, at A–37.

[292] See also Clauses Twenty-Seventh (e) and (g), the former of which provisions defines "emergency".

trustee or in some other fiduciary role, allocation, accounting, and tax problems could make this a very delicate and important issue.[293]

In the corporate context, the possibility exists that shareholders will not accept substantial diversions of funds to administrators based on some vague expropriatory threat that may occur at some distant point in the future. There may be substantial pressure, especially if the corporation is experiencing losses, to streamline the corporate structure and eliminate the trust administration costs, particularly in light of the hypothetical nature of the risk. Moreover, the expense associated with this arrangement may have to be disclosed in financial statements and other required reports, thereby destroying confidentiality. This would be especially troubling in the standby trust context, since it would give the home country and possibly the trust situs jurisdiction the opportunity to take steps to subvert the protective arrangement before it became fully operational. In the case of a standby trust,[294] to which few assets had been transferred, it might also result in a shareholder or governmental challenge to the payment of excessive compensation or some other challenge based on the diversion of corporate assets, especially if these funds are going to affiliated entities, employees, or shareholders of the parent corporation.

8.2.9. *Trustee Liability*

Great care must be taken in evaluating the trust laws of the relevant jurisdictions. Even some that have taken the lead in developing clear-cut statutues to facilitate asset protection trusts for individuals impose stringent requirements with respect to the trustee's standard of care and liability. An example of this would be the recent Turks & Caicos Ordinance (1991) on Trusts.[295] These rules do not appear to be waivable by instrument.

In the case of international asset protection trusts, the trust is being used to protect the corporation from government acts. The trustees, or, more likely, certain quasi-fiduciaries, may well be affiliated or related parties, if not subsidiaries or other persons directly controlled by the parent corporation.[296] They are likely to act for the benefit of the business enterprise in ways not entirely consistent with traditional fiduciary norms. However, trust law may require a higher standard of conduct than anticipated. If the trust is employed, the trustees may be persistently exposed to challenges regarding their conduct, at least if it is active and not just a standby vehicle.[297]

Even if the trust instrument exculpates the trustees or indemnifies them, there are likely to be problems. One problem with this, as noted, is that

---

[293] The discussion in this portion of the chapter regarding trustee compensation is intended to apply as well to persons acting in fiduciary and quasi-fiduciary capacities, such as members of a governing committee.

[294] See e.g. supra, text accompanying n 272.

[295] See supra, text accompanying n 126.

[296] See e.g. supra, n 256.

[297] Corporate officers and directors who approved the arrangement may also face this problem.

almost all American jurisdictions require the trustee to satisfy a minimal level of conduct that cannot be waived.[298] Another problem is that the corporation itself, from the standpoint of a sensible organizational structure, should be concerned about giving free-wheeling authority to autonomous managers in the United States.[299] Third, it is unlikely that the parent corporation's shareholders, if fully informed, are likely to approve this sort of exculpation or indemnification. Finally, terms, such as "negligence" and "bad faith", may have quite different meanings in different jurisdictions. Thus, any attempt to exonerate fiduciaries may fail as a result of different conceptions of fiduciary duty in different legal systems, unless a statement of the law to govern such constructional matters has been clearly indicated.

8.2.10. Future Interests

No drafting of an asset protection trust can succeed without careful consideration being given to future interests. In particular, if not properly drafted, the trust may violate a rule against perpetuities, a rule against accumulations, or a rule against the suspension of the power of alienation. Moreover, serious choice of law questions are likely to be confronted, since future interests have been subject to much idiosyncratic reform in various common law jurisdictions. If the law of a civil law jurisdiction is regarded as controlling, matters will be even more complex, since the common law rules mentioned above have not developed in a corresponding fashion under the civil law.

The experience with pension trusts is of particular relevance. Concerns about the pertinence of the various future interests rules mentioned led to the enactment of statutory exemptions in the various American states.[300] No similar development has occurred with regard to asset protection trusts, thus emphasizing the importance of the most careful drafting.

9. Conclusions

From the American legal perspective, the prospect of adaptation of the asset protection trust for use by multinational corporations may have more superficial appeal than real substance. The assumption behind the use of the trust, of course, is that certain risks in the home country can potentially be averted. As has been demonstrated, this assumption is far from certain. Moreover, there is a real danger of American governmental intrusion in the

---

[298] See e.g. G. Bogert, *Trusts and Trustees* 2d rev. (1984), s94.

[299] See supra, text accompanying n 240.

[300] See Scott, supra, note 12, s112, at 158–61. See also Lauritzen, 'Perpetuities and Pension Trusts' (1946) 24 *Taxes* 591; Note, 'The Rule Against Perpetuities and Pension Trusts: An Obstacle in Tax Planning' (1958) 10 Ohio St. L.J. 336. In the United Kingdom, similar issues have arisen. See e.g. *In re Dodwell & Co. Ltd's Trust Deed* [1978] 3 All E.R. 738 (statute pertaining to accumulations held not applicable to trust for employees created by corporation). But see *Oesterlin v. Sands* (1969) 120 C.L.R. 346 (trust of shares for company employees violated rule against perpetuities, since it was not the kind of employees' trust exempted from the rule).

form of a vesting or freezing of assets of the trust or the beneficial interests of shareholders.

The likelihood of and severity of home-country versus United States interference can be weighed and might well indicate utilization of the trust. However, there are other factors that must also be taken into account. Specifically, the long-term competitive and regulatory costs associated with a dual-structure operation cannot be underestimated, as the N. V. Philips experience so graphically demonstrates. Furthermore, trust, corporate, and antitrust constraints further complicate the calculation and make the utilization of the trust far less appealing.

Finally, the current status of choice of law and the directions in which it is evolving in various crucial common law trust jurisdictions are entirely unsatisfactory from the standpoint of the multinational corporate asset protection trust. There is especially no guarantee that the trust could sustain a challenge to its creation or to its funding, even in the case of litigation in an American forum. The law governing the day-to-day actions of fiduciaries in administering the trust's interests as well as the trust's construction would also, potentially, present very difficult problems. In this regard, there is a considerable need to address the unique choice of law concerns associated with this sort of trust and to achieve a meaningful international agreement. That does not seem possible in the near future.

Index